KT-387-610

UNIVERSITY OF
WINCHESTER

KA 0267712 1

*Lay theology in
the Reformation*

1 'Who knows, by what judgment of God the laypeople have begun to preach, especially since our greatest and most learned prelates have for so long regarded preaching with scorn'

Matthew Zell, 1523. *Christliche//veratwortug M. Matt//hes Zell von Keysersberg Pfar// = her vnd predigers im Münster zu//Strasburg*...MD xxiij. in Adolf Laube et al., eds., *Flugschriften der frühen Reformationsbewegung* (Berlin, 1983), I, 285.

Lay theology in the Reformation

Popular pamphleteers in Southwest Germany 1521–1525

PAUL A. RUSSELL

Lecturer in History, Boston College

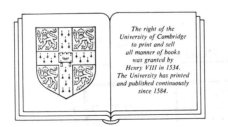

The right of the
University of Cambridge
to print and sell
all manner of books
was granted by
Henry VIII in 1534.
The University has printed
and published continuously
since 1584.

CAMBRIDGE UNIVERSITY PRESS

Cambridge

London   New York   New Rochelle
Melbourne   Sydney

Published by the Press Syndicate of the University of Cambridge
The Pitt Building, Trumpington Street, Cambridge CB2 1RP
32 East 57th Street, New York, NY 10022, USA
10 Stamford Road, Oakleigh, Melbourne 3166, Australia

© Cambridge University Press 1986

First published 1986

Printed in Great Britain by the
University Press, Cambridge

British Library cataloguing in publication data
Russell, Paul Albert
Lay theology in the Reformation: popular
pamphleteers in Southwest Germany, 1521–1525.
1. Reformation–Germany (West)–Pamphlets
I. Title
274.3'06   BR303

Library of Congress cataloguing in publication data
Russell, Paul Albert.
Lay theology in the Reformation.
Bibliography: p.
Includes index.
1. Reformation–Germany–Pamphlets. 2. Theology.
Doctrinal–Germany–History–16th century. I. Title.
BR355.P36R87   1985   274.3'306   85–11353

ISBN 0 521 30727 9

KING ALFRED'S COLLEGE
WINCHESTER

274.3
RUS   0267712 1

UP

Marie Haug, geb. Stauch (†1976)
Zwanzig Jahre Treue, Liebe und Fürsorge

Contents

List of illustrations	*page* viii
List of figures	xi
Preface	xiii
Acknowledgements	xv
Introduction	1
CHAPTER I	
The call to prophesy: piety and discontent in the urban community of late-medieval Germany	21
CHAPTER II	
Reformers and laypeople	56
CHAPTER III	
Memmingen: a furrier, a preacher, and a peasants' war	80
CHAPTER IV	
Augsburg: a weaver, a soldier, and a radical Franciscan	112
CHAPTER V	
Nuremberg: a shoemaker, a painter, and an inquisition	148
CHAPTER VI	
Female pamphleteers: the housewives strike back	185
Conclusions	212
Notes and abbreviations	228
Bibliography	266
Index	283

Illustrations

1   Title woodcut from Diepold Peringer's, *Ein Sermon von der Abgotterey*, 1524.   *frontispiece*
2   Augsburg. Oldest woodcut showing the city of Augsburg, 1483. 22
3   A *Bürgermeister* and two councillors. From Rodericus Zamorensis *Speculum Vitae Humanae*, 1488.   24
4   Life and Martyrdom of St. Sebastian. St. Cyprian's Church, in Sarnthein, 1492.   27
5   The Pilgrimage to 'Our Lovely Lady' in Regensburg. Engraving by Michael Ostendorfer, 1520.   29
6   A sign used to advertise a schoolteacher's lessons, by Hans Holbein, the younger. Basel, 1516.   32
7   Detail from a broadside with text by Hans Sachs, showing poor artisans and wealthy burghers. Augsburg, c. 1524?   34
8   The martyrdom of John Huss (c. 1524).   36
9   Detail from the Herrenberg High Altar, by Jörg Ratgeb (+1526), 1515.   38
10 St. Dominic preaches to common people, unknown master, 1432.   40
11 Woodcut from Ulrich Tengler's *Laienspiegel*, 1508.   43
12 The six works of holy mercy. From Hugo von Trimberg's *Der Renner*, MS, c. 1490.   46
13 Title woodcut from Joseph Grünpeck's *Eine newe Ausslegung*, 1507.   47
14 *Karsthans* – a familiar symbol for the common man.   49
15 The Persistence of Evil in the World. Joseph Grünpeck's *Spiegel*, 1522.   50
16 The Sermons of the Drummer of Niklashausen. From Hartmann Schedel's *Weltchronik*, 1493.   51
17 A pious peasant at prayer. Title woodcut from Diepold Peringer's *Ain schone Ausslegug*, 1523.   53
18 Martin Luther, 1520. Title woodcut from the German edition of his pamphlet, *On the Babylonian Captivity of the Church*.   57

19 *A Sermon on the Blessed Sacrament*, 1520.   59
20 *A Report on the Two False Tongues of Luther*, 1525.   65
21 Huldrych Zwingli, by an anonymous artist, 1539.   66
22 *Answer by a Swiss Farmer*, with an introduction by Huldrych
    Zwingli, 1523?   69
23 Erasmus of Rotterdam by Albrecht Dürer, 1526.   74
24 *On Pilgrimage*, by Erasmus of Rotterdam, 1522.   75
25 Memmingen. Detail from *Topographia Sueviae*, 1643; St. Martin's
    Church.   81
26 Interior of St. Martin's Church, Memmingen.   84
27a Memmingen. Detail from *Topographia Sueviae*, 1643; Our Lady's
    Church.   85
27b Interior of St Mary's Church, Memmingen.   87
28a *A Christian Missive*, by Sebastian Lotzer, 1523.   89
28b The house where Sebastian Lotzer lived, Herrenstrasse 3, in
    Memmingen.   95
29 Collecting the Easter tithe. From Rodericus Zamorensis, *Speculum
    Vitae Humanae*, 1488.   97
30 Christoph Schappeler, by an anonymous artist, 1551.   108
31 Augsburg. Detail from Hartmann Schedel's *Weltchronik*, 1493,
    showing the city hall and St. Moritz parish.   113
32 Johann von Freiburg, O.P.   116
33 Drs. Urbanus Rhegius and Johannes Frosch, from an unpublished
    MS, *Chronica ecclesiastica Augustana*, 1749.   119
34 The Franciscan Church in Augsburg, scene of several disturbances
    in 1524. Engraving, 1648.   120
35 Weavers at work. From Rodericus Zamorensis, *Speculum vitae
    humanae*, 1488.   122
36 *A Nice Dialogue between a Priest and a Weaver*, by Utz Rychssner,
    1524.   124
37 *His Imperial Roman Majesty's Entry into Bologna*, 1529.   128
38 *A Mirror for the Blind*, by Haug Marschalck, 1524.   131
39 Woodcut from Joseph Grünpeck's *Spiegel*, 1522.   134
40 The world turned upside-down. Woodcut from Joseph Grünpeck's
    Spiegel, 1522.   139
41 Imprisonment in a Tower (*Turmstrafe*). Woodcut from Ulrich
    Tengler's *Laienspiegel*, 1508.   142
42 The Red Gate in Augsburg and settlements outside the city wall.
    Detail from the 1521 city plan by Andreas Seld.   144
43 View of Nuremberg, showing the two parish churches, St.
    Lawrence's and St. Sebald's. From Hartmann Schedel's *Weltchronik*,
    1493.   149
44 St. Sebald, patron saint of Nuremberg.   151

45   Andreas Osiander by Georg Pencz, 1544.   154
46   *A warning to beware of the Devil*, by Hans Greiffenberger, 1524. 163
47   Hans Sachs, woodcut by Michael Ostendorfer, 1545.   166
48   A Shoemaker's workshop in the early sixteenth century.   168
49   Two versions of the prophet to appear to herald the return of
     Christ: (a) from Grünpeck's *Spiegel*, 1522; (b) from Eberlin von
     Günzburg's pamphlet, *A Friendly Warning*, 1524.   170
50   *A Dialogue between an Evangelical and a Lutheran Christian*, by Hans
     Sachs, 1524.   178
51   Women attack the clergy, by Lucas Cranach, 1526.   186
52   St. Verena, Anchoress; from the parish church in Ditzingen, near
     Leonberg, 1524.   188
53   *A Little Book for Women*, c. 1522.   190
54   *A Christian Noblewoman from Bavaria's Missive to the Faculty in
     Ingolstadt*, 1523.   193
55   A medal with a likeness of Argula von Stauffen (+1564?). 199
56   Strasbourg. From Hartmann Schedel's *Weltchronik*, 1493. 204
57   Customary instruments of torture in the sixteenth century. 206
58   A woman performs works of holy mercy. From *Bruder Claus
     Nuremberg*, 1488).   209

Figures

1 A Mystical Economy of Salvation   *page* 44
2 A Theology of Conscience Liberation in Sebastian Lotzer's
  Pamphlets   93
3 The Economy of Salvation in Sebastian Lotzer's Pamphlets   105
4 The Economy of Salvation in Haug Marschalck's Pamphlets   140
5 The Economy of Salvation in Hans Greiffenberger's Pamphlets   162
6 Revelation, History, and Salvation in Hans Sachs' Pamphlets   176
7 The Economy of Salvation in Argula von Grumbach's
  Pamphlets   200

In order to facilitate comparisons in the theology of individual pamphleteers, graphic figures have been designed with a general uniformity. Triangles have been used as symbols for man and God. For God the triangle has broken lines, to symbolize an ideal, less perceptible, state of existence. The triangle used to symbolize man is solid, readily perceptible. Man created in the image of God has a tripartite soul, divided into memory, reason, and will, a mirror of the Godly soul. The spiritual soul is the reverse side of the physical soul, divided into conscience (the top of the soul), heart (where man can feel love), and *Gemüthe* (or loosely translated, 'might').

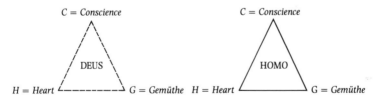

In each figure, God and man are juxtaposed in similar form; letters symbolize the parts of the spiritual soul: C = Conscience, H = Heart, G = *Gemüthe*. Just as man physically returns to God from dust to dust, birth to death, so man's life is a spiritual return to God. The figures in this work try to explain that return or economy of salvation, using these symbols. In the general medieval system, *Opera Pietatis* or pious works brought man back to God on the road to salvation. In the works of many of the pamphleteers in this study, *Opera Caritatis*, a narrow definition of pious works, is substituted for the medieval pious works. In the medieval economy of salvation, the sources of inspiration were varied. In the works in this study, the bible or word of God, written and read, or heard in sermons is the key to transforming man from a sinful state into a state of grace. The bible replaces the penitential system of the medieval church.

Preface

In 1521, Martin Luther wrote to his friend George Spalatin, that he hoped a pamphlet entitled *The Passion of Christ and the Anti-Christ* might help win over common people to his side in his struggle with the papacy. Luther was eager to use anti-papal propaganda to enlist the support of common people in a debate of considerable theological depth. Luther's concern for the simple layperson was both personal and pastoral. When a laywoman, Argula von Grumbach, published a letter written to the university faculty at Ingolstadt in 1523, Luther cheered her on, calling her a 'special instrument of Christ.' Many Protestant reformers eagerly enlisted the support of common laypeople. A few years later, reformers' enthusiasm for publishing laypeople had waned: Luther condemned common people who misused their Christian freedom. City authorities, tolerant of publishing citizens until 1525, began to prosecute them. When a prolific pamphleteer in Augsburg, Haug Marschalck, tried to publish a pamphlet on the importance of receiving the eucharist, he earned a prison sentence. Many others were silenced or exiled.

The four years between 1521 and 1525 provided common people with a previously unparalleled opportunity. Active laypeople had often been persecuted for heretical ideas by inquisitors and city authorities, but with clerical protection, they were free to explore a lay apostolate and take a stand on the issues of the Reformation. They crossed the boundaries of accepted social classes to write to scholars, princes, and city councils. The printing press brought their ideas to an even broader public: for the first time in history, common people had a means to influence public opinion beyond the local marketplace and tavern, independent of established authority. This book takes a close look at these pamphleteers and their contribution to the history of the Reformation, a study long overdue – especially in an age when scholars like to speculate about the ideas of the 'common man.'

This research is the result of several years of study and preparation. The idea for a work on lay theology developed in a seminar with Professor Heiko Oberman at the university in Tübingen, West Germany in 1973.

Subsequent research encouraged by Professor Oberman led to a dissertation under Professor Samuel Miller's direction at Boston College in 1978. Since that dissertation, new issues, ideas, and methods have helped to reshape the study and expand the sample to eight pamphleteers. This work could not have been brought to fruition without the aid and encouragement of my colleagues and friends, from my seminar *Kommilitionen*, who helped to edit the German text of my seminar paper, to Ms Heather Grady, who checked the typescript for me. Outstanding was the help and encouragement given me by the staff of the Tübingen pamphlet-project, especially the director of the project, Dr. Hans-Joachim Köhler and his associates Drs. Christoph Weismann and Hildegard Hebenstreit. Special thanks must also go to Ingo Carl, Axel Lins and the residents of Leibnizhaus III in Tübingen. The American University in Cairo provided funds for continuing research during my five-year stay in Egypt. Dr. Josef Bellot, director of the Stadt- und Staatsbibliothek in Augsburg, never failed to provide useful information in my search for lay pamphleteers as well as valuable help in locating illustrations. Dr. Stefan Krenn of the Kunsthistorisches Museum in Vienna offered important advice on illustrations. Dieter Böcksteiner and the residents of Paradisgasse 27 helped to dispel those mid-winter blues, while I carried out my research in Vienna.

Back home in America, invaluable encouragement was provided by Drs. Mark O'Connor, Clarissa Atkinson, and James Weiss, and Boston College bibliographer, John Atteberry. Without the efforts of my aunt Harriet Wilson Dodge, who was always willing to type and retype successive drafts, this work would never have been completed. Finally, a very special note of gratitude must go to Mr Gottlob Ruck and family in the village of Plattenhardt/Filderstadt near Stuttgart, West Germany, who taught me so much about the lives and work of farmers and artisans in Southwest Germany. Had it not been for the care and attention of Mr. Ruck's Godmother, Marie Stauch Haug, who served my family for over twenty years, who taught me the Swabian dialect and to whom this work is dedicated, this study would never have been possible. To all of them, a resounding note of thanks.

Brookline, Massachusetts
1 February 1985

Acknowledgements

Illustrations were graciously provided by:
Biblioteca Apostolica Vaticana, Vatican City, Il. 45; The Pierpont-Morgan Library, New York, Il. 12; Bildarchiv der österreichischen Nationalbibliothek, Vienna, Ills. 4, 26, 32; Stadtbibliothek, Memmingen, Ills. 27b, 28a, 28b; Kantonsbibliothek-Vadiana, St. Gall, Il. 30; Württembergische Landesgalerie, Stuttgart, Ills. 9, 10; Württembergisches Landesmuseum, Stuttgart, Il. 52; Stadt- und Staatsbibliothek, Augsburg, Ills. 1, 2, 3, 8, 11, 17, 25, 27a, 31, 33, 34, 35, 36, 41, 42, 43, 50, 57; Sonderforschungsbereich 8, Spätmittelalter und Reformation: Flugschriftenprojekt, Tübingen, Ills. 13, 14, 19, 20, 37, 38, 49b, 53, 54; Germanisches Nationalmuseum, Nuremberg, Ills. 5, 18, 21, 23, 44, 47, 51; Kunstmuseum, Öffentliche Sammlung, Basel, Il. 6; Staatliche Münzsammlung, Munich, Il. 55.

All other illustrations were taken from the author's private collection. Graphic illustrations for the text were produced by J. R. Moselsky, Boston, Massachusetts.

Introduction

This book is a study of lay theology in the pamphlets of a sample of eight lay pamphleteers with common education. That theology contains evidence of personal piety and political propaganda for the Protestant Reformation. The ideas and suggestions for reform in this theology are scarcely very original, but the interesting combinations of ideas and variations in the works of these pamphleteers demonstrate both consensus and individuality. Their theology is testimony to a spiritual depth and mystical orientation in some, political consciousness and a vision of a world about to end in others. The vigor of this theology consists in its independence of either Lutheran or Catholic dogma. Although inspired by Martin Luther, few of these pamphleteers are dependent on the reformer for their theological ideas. To unravel the complicated threads of their piety and theology, expressed in harsh, German polemic and copious biblical citation, it is necessary to use methods and principles of investigation from several areas of Reformation studies. Social history offers analytical lines of investigation that can help to focus on the 'common man' and his role in the Reformation.[1] Intellectual history can help us trace the roots of their ideas. Literary historians, who use mass communication methods for content analysis can offer a means to isolate and reconstruct important arguments and attitudes. Historians of medieval heresy and historians of the Anabaptist movement can provide important conclusions to help integrate the theology of these pamphleteers into a greater church-historical framework.

An understanding of the intellectual importance of this theology requires an examination of historiographical development. Pamphlet literature has only recently served as an important source for the study of Reformation history. The study of lay theology is scarcely ten years old. Few historians have been content with generalizations about the history of the Reformation, based on the higher theology of magisterial reformers, the activities of princes, or the decisions of city councils. Certainly the close relationship of the Reformation to the social upheavals in the Peasant Wars suggests that Protestantism had dimensions of peculiar social

1

importance that led to direct and defiant action.[2] The Marxist description
of the Peasant Wars as a form of early capitalist revolution suggests that
religious ideas were a less important motivation to direct action than
economic discontent.[3] Social historians have inherited the task of unlocking
the mystery of collective behavior among social groups in sixteenth-century
society, a society that seldom fits modern assumptions about social
organization. Our inability to view this complex society as a whole forces
us to focus our studies on smaller groups in a rapidly changing social
milieu. What one tries to define as collective culture or even urban–rural
distinctions in such research must be carefully qualified. Peter Burke's
solution to this problem is to speak of cultures and subcultures, creating
an even more complex picture of early modern society.[4]

Among the more important challenges for social historians of the
sixteenth century is the understanding of the nature of change. The
frequent use of 1517 as the dividing point in history, marking the end of
the Middle Ages and the beginning of the modern world, still burdens
historians with an intellectual problem unique to historians of this
century. Social historians must understand the nature of demarcation
between the age of 'childlike faith' and an age of political consciousness,
of a world where the church was first in the mind of the 'common man,'
but soon after the state replaced the church. The sheepish follower became
the politically motivated citizen. Although the problem just described is
over simplified, the necessity to denote change in the lives of common
people forces social historians to study religion as pious practice (both
public and private) in hope of documenting historical change.

The nature of this historical change lies in the acceptance of Protestantism by different social groups. Since it is difficult to speak of Protestant
'dogma' before 1530, the historian tends to rely on artificial general
formulas in the place of codified theology to study the early Reformation.
Jean Delumeau in his *Naissance et Affirmation de la Réforme* (Paris, 1965)
reduces Protestantism to three dogmatic principles: salvation *sola fide*,
revelation *sola scriptura*, and a universal priesthood of all believers. He tries
to link these principles to actual pious practice. Delumeau notes that in
the fifteenth century the faults of the Roman church were not enough
to provoke a split in the church. By the beginning of the sixteenth century,
a 'mauvaise conscience dans la mentalité collective' characterized late
medieval religion. For this 'mauvaise conscience' Protestantism had the
ideal antidote, salvation by faith alone. Universal priesthood, Delumeau
discovered, was the result of a great surge of individualism and lay activity,
that resulted in the intervention of a powerful bourgeoisie in the life of
the church. The Catholic priesthood was devalued as the result of a
subsequent confusion of the sacred and the profane in religious practice
of both clergy and common people. Revelation *sola scriptura* in Protes-

tantism was caused by Humanist preaching and the new importance of the printed book in the sixteenth century.[5] In a later work, Delumeau outlines a sociological method for further investigation of popular piety. He separates religious systems, conceptualizations, organizations, and practices calling for new studies in all four areas.[6] Social historians of popular culture have eagerly followed his lead.

The 'mauvaise conscience' of pre-reformed people has provided a theme for several studies, most important of which is Steven Ozment's *The Reformation in the Cities* (Yale, 1975), where Ozment elaborates on the new freedom of Protestants from a religion that was anxiety-causing to a new religion that compensated for the failure of the penitential system of the Catholic church.[7] More recently Ozment remarked 'that the Reformation relieved perceived religious burdens of a psychological and financial nature for thousands of people from every identifiable social group.'[8] Thomas Tentler's *Sin and Confession on the Eve of the Reformation* (Princeton, 1977) examined the importance of confession manuals for confessors and for common people to show how anxiety was created by the old confessional system and how it was supposed to be resolved.[9] Both Ozment and Tentler examine one aspect of pious practice as carrying the key to understanding the decision made by large numbers of common people to become Protestants. For both historians, Protestantism became popular in Northern Europe because it provided needed psychological compensation the old church could no longer provide.

Researching 'la mentalité collective' has been an important theme in French scholarship since Braudel. More recent interest in popular culture reflects this search for the foundations of a collective mentality, certainly presupposed by the ideology of revolution. If the Reformation is to be considered among the more important revolutions in history, then the collective mentality of common people can provide clues to the reasons for its acceptance. Robert Muchembled's *Culture Populaire et Culture des Elites dans la France Moderne* (Paris, 1978) searches for 'la vision du monde populaire.' Muchembled argues convincingly for cultural distinctions between rural and civic communities in Europe, suggesting that cities, more dynamically and economically oriented than rural areas, demanded a different kind of piety, a more personal form of religion, certainly more suited to the exigencies of urban life. A world full of magic, demons, and witches fits a rural economy more appropriately. Muchembled sees the Reformation as an urban phenomenon. He highlights the urban processes of rejection and integration, the restriction of pagan beliefs (formerly tolerated) and integration of all classes of people into the urban order, including priests, beggars, and vagrants, who once stood outside the urban corporation. He notes that before 1520, there were no boundaries between the sacred and the profane. After 1520, both Protestant and Catholic

reformations redefined the sacred apart from the secular, influenced by
the new morality of Europe's bourgeoisie. City authorities could no longer
tolerate the pagan extravagances of *les fêtes populaires*. The number of feast
days was reduced, carnival celebration controlled, begging defined as
criminal. Priests and ministers needed to be above moral reproach. For
Muchembled, the acceptance of the Reformation was the result of a
triumph of a 'mentalité urbaine' as the new capitalist economy of cities
rechanneled energies to production and a new morality. Historians of this
school of thought even suggest that the majority of the population of
Europe was never really very Christian. Pagan rituals survived the
missionary efforts of the church and the real Christianization of Europe
took place at the Reformation.[10]

Some historians who followed Delumeau and Muchembled study
popular religion in specific social organizations and practices in order to
understand the nature of religious behavioral change. Natalie Davis
investigated journeyman printers in Lyons to discover that the attraction
of these lower-level artisans to Protestantism was not based on convictions
that the Protestants offered a superior form of religious solution to human
problems, but that Protestantism was a convenient means to express
general social discontent. When the Protestant Consistory of Lyons
objected to artisans' strikes and protests, they found their way back to
a more tolerant Roman church.[11] Lionel Rothkrug studied pilgrimage
patterns in the North and South of the German speaking part of the empire
to discover that the pilgrimage tradition was more firmly rooted in rural
areas of Bavaria, where the power of the *ministeriales* had been solidly
established. Northern cities displayed a more sober, 'feminine' piety, that
even before the Reformation was more mystical in inspiration. Christians
in Northern cities rejected the cult of saints and endorsed a more personal,
private piety, according to Rothkrug.[12] William Christian examined the
swearing of vows to saints in early modern Spain, to note that the Catholic
Reformation succeeded to some extent in cities, but not at all in the
countryside, where local religious traditions were more tenacious, due to
the nature of the rural economy.[13] All of these historians point to a
vigorous and thriving lay piety, institutionally creative and potentially
defiant. Yet each of these attempts falls somewhat short of effective
generalizations about the acceptance of Protestantism because neither
pilgrimage, nor vows, nor *fêtes*, can be entirely representative of popular
piety. One wonders whether people were ever moved by hope or charity!
Certainly the differences between city and countryside are important, but
these were so often obscured by geographic mobility in the sixteenth
century. Closer to an effective study of religious motivation is the recent
work of Donald Weinstein and Rudolf Bell. In their important and
convincing *Saints and Society* (Chicago, 1982), the basic premise 'is that

pursuit as well as the perception of holiness mirrored social values and concerns.'[14] This focus on the pursuit and perception of holiness rather than social organization or individual practices may more appropriately explain changes in popular piety. It is important that the social values and concerns are reflected by, but do not dominate religious expression, or determine the nature of piety.

Steven Ozment in a recent essay on the importance of pamphlets for the study of the Reformation, indicates the dangers of historical reductionism, either for ideological reasons (Marxists and *Annalistes*) or for sociological reasons by historians of popular culture. He notes that these historians fail to mediate the gap between intellectual historians of the Reformation who study the ideas and aspirations of magisterial reformers, and the historians of popular culture who 'run the risk of romanticizing the lives of ordinary people.'[15] He suggests that a 'preoccupation with material structures...limited their penetration of the intellectual and religious dimension of historical reality.'[16] Ozment calls for a look at pamphlets as a new source that can offer particular advantages in hope of closing the gap created by diversion of study from the framework of popular piety. In order to close or at least bridge this gap between the new ideas produced by magisterial reformers and the recent interest in the popular reception of the Reformation, one needs a particular kind of source, namely pamphlets.

A pamphlet is defined as 'a printed work consisting of more than one page [to distinguish them from broadsheets], not produced as a periodical and unbound, which was designed to influence readers as propaganda, addressed to the general population.'[17] According to Richard Cole, 'the brief, blunt, vulgar Reformation tract (pamphlet) intended for a wide, but often unsophisticated and sometimes confused audience, became a major tool of those who sought change in the religious loyalties of large numbers of people.'[18] Thus the pamphlet literature of the Reformation period provides an ideal source for understanding why people made the decision to join the Protestant cause. But why have these pamphlets, common in many libraries since the sixteenth century, so long been overlooked? The problem is one of collection and perspective.

Since the end of the eighteenth century, historians of the Reformation have been interested in the corpus of pamphlet literature published during the Reformation. Hans-Joachim Köhler estimated that about four hundred works have been written about pamphlets, mostly related to the early Reformation and the Peasant Wars, based on pamphlet literary sources.[19] Until very recently, a scholar's ability to collect individual pamphlets or to travel to libraries to read selected pamphlets determined the scope of conclusions. Widely scattered in private and public collections, often bound together with unrelated materials (sometimes protected from dust but not from worms by a folded jacket of illuminated medieval manuscript!) these tiny treatises presented scholars with an enigmatic puzzle. Pamphlet collecting was neither systematic nor in any way representative of the great variety of published pamphlets. Even the variety of these pamphlets defied attempts to generalize from them as sources.

Now thanks to more modern methods of pamphlets collecting and cataloguing, a more complete picture of the corpus of pamphlet literature, authors, and publishers is beginning to emerge. In our own time, by using computers, photocopiers, and cameras, the catalogue of pamphlets editions is growing. A project in the special research division at the university of Tübingen, West Germany has been funded by the German Research Foundation to collect editions of all the published pamphlets in Central Europe in German and Latin between the years 1500 and 1530.[20] One presently estimates that about 4,000 different pamphlets were published in several editions.[21] The subjects addressed in this early and affordable form of printed propaganda vary from prophetic prognostica to imperial reform proposals. The circulation of such works was as broad as their varied contents. Because pamphlets were brief (usually under twenty quarto-pages) they could be quickly published and sold at an easy profit. Princes and paupers alike read them or had pamphlets read to them. Kings wrote them, scholars studied them, even shoemakers dabbled in pamphlet publishing. Pamphlets were the first broadly based form of popular literature after the invention of printing: the woodcuts that illustrated them can be considered, according to one scholar, as the 'primitive comic strip'![22] Pamphlets are particularly important as a source for social history. At a recent symposium on pamphlet literature research sponsored by the Tübingen project, the director of that project noted: 'The pamphlets of the early Reformation period are an historical source, which unlike any other allows for a detailed examination of opinions, convictions, and values of an epoch. Because of their propagandistic intentions and their agitating effect on a broadly distributed readership in particular political situations, these pamphlets provide insights into the social dynamics of sixteenth-century society.'[23] Although past historians were aware of the importance of pamphlets, they were seldom able to use pamphlets very effectively as historical sources, beyond the limited objectives of illustrating local history. They did not have representative collections of pamphlets beyond local archives and personal collections. The more recent availability of systematic catalogues and national surveys has already produced interesting and intriguing works that approach the social history of the Reformation with new vigor. This rich corpus of pamphlet literature now provides an important source for national and soon international Reformation history in Europe.

Now that Michael Pegg's *Catalogue of German Reformation Pamphlets*,

1516–1546 in the Libraries of Great Britain and Ireland (Baden-Baden, 1973) and the important publications of the Tübingen project available on microfiche as *Sixteenth Century Pamphlets in German and Latin, 1501–1530* (Zug, Switzerland, 1978f.) have eclipsed many earlier catalogues and collections, new and important works on printing in the Reformation have appeared. These works are directly concerned with the effect of printed pamphlets on the social history of the Reformation.

Bernd Balzer's *Bürgerliche Reformationspropaganda* (Stuttgart, 1973), examines the printed works of Hans Sachs, written between 1523 and 1525. Balzer rejects methods used by social scientists, who study contemporary propaganda, because sixteenth-century people reacted to an entirely different systematic code of symbols.[24] By means of literary analysis, Balzer sought to uncover important signals that were linked to a system of stereotypes in order to rediscover the images that motivated Hans Sachs. He noted that Sachs presented nothing original in his arguments, but relied on familiar themes, echoed in countless other pamphlets. As a propagandist, Sachs articulated the moral failure and corruption of the church in antithetical forms, easily understood by less-educated common people. Sachs did this consciously, according to Balzer, in hope of exploiting the fears of his readers to drive them into the Lutheran camp. By late 1524, Sachs changed the direction of his works to criticize the left wing of the Reformation who misused their newly gained Christian freedom. In doing so Sachs proved himself to be a devout subject of the Nuremberg city council and a devotee of his major mentor, Martin Luther, who began preaching against left-wing enthusiasts in 1524.[25]

In 1977, Joseph Schmidt pioneered a work of major importance; *Lestern, lesen, und lesen hören* (Bern, 1977) using Harold D. Lasswell's 1948 formula for communications analysis – Who says what, in which channel, to whom, with what effect? – to interpret a group of satirical pamphlets written by Humanists for consumption by the common man. By employing terminology from Marshall McLuhan's works, Schmidt supplements the Lasswell formula with a sequence for the transfer for the information, streamlined to fit the kind of mass communication represented by sixteenth-century pamphlets: Information Source – Coder – Communication Channel – Decoder – Recipient.[26] Schmidt is practically the first to recognize the importance of the listener as recipient, acknowledging the role of the reader of pamphlets to illiterate friends. This methodology helps to understand the transfer of coded information in the pamphlets. Schmidt presents the German sermon of the late Middle Ages as a model for the pamphlets so often described as 'formless, colloquial, and rude' in character. He traces frequent repetition and biblical quotes to methods commonly used by preachers to convince an audience. He noted that

Humanist pamphleteers in the Reformation directed their works toward common people, a group not interested in new and original ideas, but tradition-bound and relatively stable. Common people understood things painted in colors of opposition and blasphemous in tone. They could generalize but seldom differentiate. Thus, pamphlets appear monotonous, gossipy, and formless because they were aimed at a half-educated audience and emphasized already accepted opinions. He suggests that a sub-culture existed in the sixteenth century among common people, which was out of tune with the language of official publications, hence pamphlets written for them are composed in rude, primitive, German.[27] Schmidt's work is important because it aims at a contemporary understanding of the language of pamphlets, something Monika Rössing-Hager would take further in her essay on the illiterate recipients of information from pamphlet literature. She discovered that more learned 'people conscious' preachers, like the Franciscan Eberlin von Günzburg considered and used syntactic structures common people would more easily understand.[28]

Robert Scribner's most recent work, *For the Sake of Simple Folk: Popular Propaganda for the German Reformation* (Cambridge, 1982) breaks through the frontiers of pamphlet research to consider the effect of pamphlets as visual propaganda. Using both illustrated broadsheets and pamphlet illustrations, Scribner notes that one cannot assume that the Reformation took hold by the printed word. The audio-visual aspects of pamphlet communication – listening and looking – were equally important, if not more so than the written word. Like Schmidt, he describes the importance of ideas in opposition and particular 'root paradigms,' understood by most common people: anti-clericalism, socio-economic grievances, biblical images, and common proverbs, as the channel through which most reformed ideas had to be communicated.[29] Scribner finds this audio-visual communication part of an older spiritual and cultural tradition. He sees the most important effect of pamphlets in their motivation to action, particularly acts of defiance. He concludes that printing was not a very effective means of spreading reformed ideas, because most people could not read. The 'side-effects' of the pamphlets sparked people to support the Protestant cause more than the written message.

Berndt Hamm's recognition of the uniqueness of the theology of the layman Jörg Vögeli, secretary to the city council in Constance, is an important milestone in the study of Reformation pamphlets. In his essay 'Laientheologie zwischen Luther und Zwingli...,' Hamm dissected three pamphlets and two unpublished works by Vögeli in 1523–24 to discover what he calls a 'theology of the alternative,' explained in a list of juxtaposed and contrasting alternatives: 'the prison of human teaching vs. true Christian freedom..., trust in the efficaciousness of good works vs. trust in Christ's infallible promise..., the sacrificial mass vs. the true mass, the true Christian veneration of the saints,' etc.[30] These alternatives can be equated with Balzer's discovery of antithetical forms used by Sachs to communicate with the less educated, the root paradigms understood by common people, described by Scribner, and the colors of opposition noted by Schmidt. Hamm observes these contrasts being woven into something new, a lay theology that was distinct, because it used both Lutheran and Zwinglian theology to produce an individualistic, if not original theology. Hamm recognized, too, the importance of the old communal vision of the city in determining Vögeli's emphasis on practical Christian life.[31] Hamm's investigation was the first to recognize the contributions of a layman, whose theology was distinct and not simply propaganda taken from magisterial reformers. He was also among the first to note the importance of the city and its influence on the theology of the Reformation. He helped to dispel the old theory that Zwingli's theology dominated everything in the areas of Southwest Germany nearest to Zürich.

Each of these works indulges in what communications researchers call content analysis, 'a research technique for the objective, systematic and quantitative description of the manifest content of communication,' and further, 'any research technique for making inferences by systematically and objectively identifying specified characteristics within text.'[32] Balzer indicates the changes in Hans Sachs' attitudes as the Reformation progressed. Joseph Schmidt and Monika Rössing-Hager use language analysis to clarify meanings of words and expressions transformed since the sixteenth century.[33] Robert Scribner suggests the importance of 'hearing, looking, reading, discussion and action,' motivated by pamphlet propaganda.[34] Few of the above works are particularly concerned with the sort of analysis Steven Ozment has called for, to address those 'ideological forces that moved the Age of Reformation, (that) were also the work of intellectuals and reformers...who spoke to an informed laity unusually sensitive to the societal consequences of religious issues.'[35] Ozment cites Thomas Tentler's *Sin and Confession on the Eve of the Reformation* as a good example of the use of literary sources to demonstrate the way in which the church used the creation and absolution of guilt as a means of social control. Tentler has shown how the higher culture of intellectuals had a direct effect on the lives of common people.[36]

My own study uses Tentler's general methodology to examine literary sources for the patterns Scribner identifies as 'root paradigms,' or the genre of propagandistic expression in pamphlets. I am interested in reconstructing the content of pamphlets written by common people for common people (or an even wider audience) to note the form of piety expressed and recommended, the nature of the propaganda, and to what extent these authors were influenced directly by the theology of magisterial reformers. Ozment presupposes that the higher theology of Humanists and reformers was communicated to the 'common man,' that the decision to accept the Reformation was not made for economic reasons. If this is so, then it must be clearly reflected in pamphlets written by common people. To do so, I have chosen a sample of eight pamphleteers and their thirty-nine pamphlets written from different parts of Southwest Germany between 1521 and 1525.

This study has been prefaced by nearly ten years of searching for authors who would qualify as common people. Obviously the resources of the Tübingen project have been critically important for this research. Thanks to their greater catalogue, it has been possible to locate works by different authors in scattered collections from Zürich to Yale University Library. The sample of eight authors has grown from three in 1976. It comprises:

Haug Marschalck	Imperial army paymaster	Augsburg
Utz Rychssner	Weaver	Augsburg
Sebastian Lotzer	Furrier (Journeyman)	Memmingen
Hans Sachs	Shoemaker	Nuremberg
Hans Greiffenberger	Painter (Journeyman)	Nuremberg
Argula v. Grumbach	Housewife	Lenting
Ursula Weyda	Housewife	Eisenberg
Catherine Zell	Pastor's wife	Strasbourg

These authors were from different towns and cities. All of them had German, but no Latin education. There is no knowledge of Latin evident in their pamphlets or other writings. Their social and economic status varied. Peter Burke would consider the males in the sample as participants in artisan and soldier subcultures.[37] One woman in the sample, Catherine Zell, was the daughter of an artisan. Argula von Grumbach was from an impoverished noble family, ruined by the prince–bishops of Würzburg, who was married to a caretaker of ducal estates in Bavaria. Marschalck was the son of a fairly prosperous Memmingen merchant. Some of my sample, like Hans Sachs, were financially successful; others like Marschalck, Rychssner, and Lotzer were apparently less successful. All of them responded to particular dangers they saw coming as secular authorities began to restrict free expression, to imprison wandering lay preachers, and to intervene in theological affairs.[38] Concurrent with their writing is the flood of pamphlet literature about the nearing end of the world, expected by many in 1524, that probably hastened their sense of immediacy and encouraged them to write.[39]

This sample cannot claim to be representative of any particular social class or group. The fact that five of the group had their origins in the artisan classes probably accounts for their literacy and interest in church affairs. Although only an estimated 5 per cent of the German-speaking part of the Holy Roman Empire was literate in 1500, the percentage of people in cities who could read may be as high as 30 per cent.[40] Southern cities in particular produced greater numbers of literate artisans. These artisans needed some German education for commercial reasons. Even women and girls were taught by private teachers.[41] The activism of these people from the artisan classes can also be accounted for as part of a long tradition of theological interest. Shoemakers and weavers in particular have a long history as literate advocates in heretical movements.[42] Although this sample cannot be considered representative of a particular social group, this fact does not lessen the value of their pamphlets as sources. These pamphlets provide us with a unique source, early documentary evidence of lay theology and certainly a useful test for the generalizations of social historians who seek to analyze collective behavior and mentalities from other kinds of sources. Very significant is the fact that these pamphlets were written by common people themselves. In some cases we have as many as eight pamphlets written by the same author. These writers do not seem to have had contact with each other. There is only one reference to another pamphleteer in one single pamphlet written by a member of this sample.[43] Geographically, these authors were distributed throughout the Southwestern part of the German states. Six of them wrote from cities and it is certainly significant that the urban environment provided the setting and audience for their printed works. Yet, whether or not we can call them 'urban' people is open to question. Lotzer grew up in the village of Horb-am-Necker. Argula von Grumbach spent much of her later life in the countryside, though she grew up in Munich. Ursula Weyda was from a mining town in Saxony. Marschalck and Sachs both grew up in and lived in cities. Many of these people were not living in the same cities and villages where they were born. It is important too, that even as lay pamphleteers these people are only eight out of thousands who must have been interested in the ideas of the Reformation. Yet, given the generally low assessments for literacy in villages and cities in the sixteenth century, perhaps these eight people are a significant number as publishing common people. My purpose is not to suggest that this group represented any kind of collective mentality. Their works should serve as a useful test for the conclusions of social historians using different kinds of sources and even more important, for an examination of the vision of the Reformation in the minds of these particular pamphleteers. This vision should reveal the effect of magisterial reformers on the ideas of these activist common people.

Although these pamphleteers were only marginally educated, they were familiar with the ideas of Humanists who sought to reform the church. Paul Oskar Kristeller noted in an essay entitled 'The Scholar and His Public in the Late Middle Ages and Renaissance' that Humanists chose orations (sermons), treatises, dialogues, and letters most commonly as vehicles to express their ideas. They addressed a more varied public than traditional scholastic academicians, directing their works to a new literate laity, dedicating their works to powerful princes, and even to 'women, businessmen, artists and artisans.'[44] After 1470 Humanists addressed spiritual letters and devotional tracts to confraternities in the vernacular, seeking the edification of even the most common man. Rolf Engelsing listed such tracts among books common in artisan households.[45] Sermons and devotional tracts probably served as models for our pamphleteers. The titles of their pamphlets suggest Humanist inspiration. Of our thirty-nine pamphlets, there are eight letters addressed either to individuals or to the general public, nine expository treatises, seven examples of dialogue literature which all indicate some familiarity with Humanist literary form. In addition, they used several other forms of debate common to Humanists and scholastics alike: answers, apologies, and admonitions. Among them one finds only one *Speculum* and one chronicle. However Humanist-inspired the form of these works might be, addressed to the general public and in one case even dedicated to an important military figure, their content is peculiarly disorganized. In these pamphlets, religious ideas, economic grievances, biblical citations, and proposals for reform are interspersed in no logical order. Several scholars have shown how learned people may have profited from Latin rhetorical tradition to present works for common people with logical organization and coherent presentation, but these works by common people indicate no familiarity with any organized method of presentation.[46] Their works tend to present thoughts and arguments as they occurred. Popular sermons are a possible source of inspiration but not organization; only one of the pamphleteers in this study mentions how often he sought out good preachers. Only one of our authors actually wrote a sermon. Our writers were familiar with satire. Joseph Schmidt notes four characteristics of satirical literature that are applicable to the pamphlets in this study: in our pamphlets there are marked tendencies to generalize, but not to differentiate; to overemphasize the new against the old; to be very critical of the present situation; and to assume that their opinion represents a majority viewpoint.[47] Perhaps even the greater Humanists themselves could be found guilty of similar logical flaws, in their reforming enthusiasm! Yet most Humanists were careful to separate fact and opinion; these common people tended to present their opinions as empirical fact.[48] Few of their works could be called genuinely satirical in spirit. Most of them are very serious attempts to create a unified consensus of opinion among those people who called themselves common. But can our writers rightfully call themselves common?

Siegfried Wernicke, a scholar writing his dissertation on Hans Sachs in 1913 noted that: 'If we seek a yardstick, against which the progress of the Reformation can be measured, then we must look to the "common man", who, as a group apart from more learned people, formed a solid class, raised above the mob by healthy instinct and practical sobriety.'[49] But who was this 'common man'? Even in Wernicke's time, social definitions for class structure in the sixteenth century had scarcely been formulated. The only work on the subject available to Wernicke was Kurt Kasser's *Politische und soziale Bewegungen im deutschen Bürgertum des 16. Jahrhunderts* (Berlin, 1899).[50] From this early attempt at social analysis, we learn that the term 'common man' was a reference to the citizenry in general, to members of the third estate, differentiated in cities between the chosen few or 'patricians,' deemed worthy of governing and those not so worthy 'common men.' Wernicke suggests another definition in his work on Hans Sachs: the 'common man' was a member of the middle class, located somewhere between the street mob and the patricians.

The problem of definition for the term 'common man,' stems mostly from its use during the period before the Reformation. Common people had more often been the subject of ridicule in the Middle Ages. Then, the 'common man' seemed at best an illiterate bumpkin, a fool, whose naive comments in medieval dialogues and plays, could reinforce the intellectual superiority of the listener/reader.[51] During the Renaissance, however, this image changed. At the hands of Humanists, the simple common sense of the 'common man' became a useful tool to oppose the vain, self-seeking, socially useless wisdom of scholars who sat in universities. The 'common man' was transformed into the wise citizen.[52] This transformation of space and character makes an accurate social definition problematic.

Theologians – well-educated in the Humanist tradition or who at least preferred Humanistic studies to the vain wisdom of the scholastic tradition – were eager to point out the innate wisdom of the 'simple layman' and to prepare works in the vernacular for his edification. Jean Gerson (+ 1429) spent much of his energy writing works which the simple layman could read. His *Ars Moriendi* was translated into French, German, Spanish, and Italian. This work was not written out of any morbid fascination with death, but out of genuine concern for the spiritual welfare of simple laypeople.[53] Other expositions of the Lord's Prayer, confession manuals using the Ten Commandments rather than the seven deadly sins, were intended to raise the 'common man' to new spiritual levels.[54] Martin Luther himself once stated that, if his entire productivity served to enlighten one common layman, he would gladly see all his books destroyed.[55] In scholastic debate the simple layman with his common sense could be a useful means to embarrass more learned opponents. Luther states definitively, that he would prefer condemnation by a simple pious layman, than by all the distinguished masters of Louvain and Cologne.[56] Reform-minded clergy, influenced by the Humanist tradition in the fifteenth and sixteenth centuries could hardly say enough about the importance of the simple truths of the bible, the plainer, clearer word of God, uncomplicated by scholastic speculation. In their attempts to circumvent the speculative web of developing theological tradition and to reduce teaching to its simplest form, they introduced a biblical conservatism, a primacy of scripture and its plain truths, that began to characterize reform proposals long before 1517. Their 'simple layman,' bible in hand, was prepared to meet the challenges of a growing secular society. Simple layman and 'common man' were defined by a lack of Latin education. In order to understand the simple truths of the bible, translations were needed, as were schools to instruct people in the vernacular. Educated in new schools, usually founded for commercial purposes in cities, common people would provide an important new market for vernacular literature.[57]

The literary use of the term 'common man' makes a clear social definition next to impossible. New approaches were needed to find a more accurate means to indentify common people. Founded in 1960, the Study Group for Southwest German Urban Historical Research has begun to unravel the social structure of the late-medieval city, using economic criteria to sort out the various levels or classes, in order to reconstruct late-medieval urban social structure.[58] This sort of population research, instead of helping to define the 'common man,' whose opinions are critical for understanding the acceptance of the Reformation, presents a vision of the city which is even more complex than previously assumed. Such research also indicates how difficult it is to identify the 'middle class,' suggested by Wernicke. Yet, some historians continue to discuss the 'middle class' in the late medieval city, conveniently averaging estate values to isolate those at the top of society from those at the bottom.

During the Peasant Wars, the appelation 'common man' is used in a different way, to denote the contrast between those who had and exercised political power and those who had none. To celebrate the 450th anniversary of the Peasant Wars in 1975, several scholars turned their attention to definitions of the common man, often as a means to clarify Marxist interpretations of the Peasant Wars as the great revolution of the common man. Peter Blickle, foremost among those historians, defined the common man as 'peasant or a citizen of cities under princely control, people of imperial cities unable to sit on city councils or minors.'[59] This definition is linked to common participation by a broad spectrum of powerless groups in the countryside and in cities during the Peasant Wars. These groups shared a common desire for a 'righteous, Christian world,' that obscured the customary differences in interest between rural and city people.[60] Robert Lutz's 1979 study *Wer war der gemeine Mann?* (Munich and Vienna, 1979) does much to improve on the Blickle thesis by examining contemporary literary documents, using both urban and rural (village) models. As a result of his broader survey of the use of the term 'common man,' Lutz concludes that the 'common man' was not the pitiful, powerless, immobile, propertyless rebel or peasant. Certainly in cities and villages by 1525, common people owned some property, and probably had some recourse to political power through guilds or the village assemblies. Common people were not powerless. Lutz notes that the 'common man' tried to restore his legitimate political rights in the revolution of 1525 from usurping clergy and nobility or greedy patricians. Some common people did rise through the guild ranks to considerable power before the Peasant Wars, but after the failure of their revolution, were forced to submit to new restrictions and even the abolition of the guild system of representation in some cases.[61] In fact, Lutz's study presents a definition closer to Wernicke's early conclusion, that the common man represented the middle class, and further from assumptions made by many social historians, that the common man was entirely propertyless and without political power.

Social historians like Erich Maschke working within the Study Group for Southwest German Urban Historical Research emphasize how difficult it is to generalize about the social structure of late medieval cities. Maschke uses the order of guilds, different in each city, as a means to indicate actual rank. He uses the classifications 'middle class' and 'lower class' to describe the 'haves and have nots' in cities. The term 'poor,' Maschke discovered is no indication of whether people actually paid taxes or not.[62] Even people who owned some property and paid taxes were described as poor or considered themselves poor. The term 'common' is therefore every bit as ambiguous as the term 'poor.'

At least in 1985, we are closer to a social classification for the term 'common man,' in a category that is less narrowly defined than it was ten years ago. All of the people in this survey addressed themselves to the common people of their time in their pamphlets. They cannot be classified as entirely powerless or propertyless, although certain economic and political developments in their own time reduced their political power. Argula von Grumbach was bold enough to write to a university faculty and initiate a debate with learned scholars, insisting that they knew German, even though she knew no Latin, to emphasize her educational link with common people. She considered herself common. Her letters to powerful relatives and her failure to move them reflect the political power her family once wielded, before being reduced to relative poverty. Although technically of noble rank, she felt herself to be common in both education and actual political power. Hans Greiffenberger, the Nuremberg artist, complained that 'So many people say that a common man should not speak about the gospel, since it is not appropriate to his station. A shoemaker should carry on with leather and shoepolish, not with pen and ink!'[63] Some of this sample of pamphleteers were propertied: Hans Sachs owned property. Haug Marschalck, as a paymaster in the imperial army, had funds at his disposal, even though he complained shortly before his death that he scarcely had money enough to pay his soldiers. Sebastian Lotzer owned no property, but paid taxes. Hans Greiffenberger was probably propertyless, but unfortunately proper tax records for the period are lost and consequently we cannot establish his tax status. Utz Rychssner lived outside the city walls of Augsburg, but he paid taxes between 1503 and 1525. The women in this sample enjoyed whatever property their husbands might lay claim to. Ursula Weyda as wife of a tax collector certainly enjoyed some property, as did both von Grumbach and Catherine Zell, but their actual political power as women was certainly circumscribed.

By virtue of their education, social status, and political power, therefore, we can safely classify these pamphleteers as common people considering our definition of 'common man' as more a statement of actual political power than social status. They appealed to a solid class of common people that hardly existed. Certainly their writings were designed to create a consensus among readers and listeners. When called to classify themselves, the members of our sample use ambiguous terminology, which reflects both the less-defined social structure of their time and contemporary literary usage of the term 'common man.' Our pamphleteers more often call themselves 'simple laypeople of poor understanding,' though this poor understanding did not prevent them from claiming the right to preach and teach. To emphasize their lack of 'appropriate' political power, they denote the contrast in political groups: they juxtapose noble and commoner, cleric and layman, the simple and the learned. They insisted that they were common, simple, laypeople. Further attempts to socially classify this nebulous group would be futile. Their use of expressions like 'common,' 'simple,' and 'poor' reflects more their own personal dissatisfaction than their actual status. These pamphleteers constitute a small minority of participants in the active debate on the Reformation, something that makes them very uncommon. Despite their obvious lack of sophistication, their understanding of the church and the world is anything but 'simple.' Compared with beggars and other marginal people in the sixteenth century, their poverty too was indeed relative.

An analysis of these pamphlets implies and demands an examination that combines both intellectual and social history. This is certainly implicit in Steven Ozment's call for a study of pamphlets as a means to clarify the actual influence of the ideas of Humanists and reformers, to close the gap between traditional historians of the Reformation and the social historians of the sixteenth century. In any case, a purely intellectual history of people who were by admission and education not intellectuals, would present a contradiction in terms. It would be misleading too, to cite only the economic grievances in these pamphlets, without mentioning the theological ideas central to the early Reformation piety indicated in them. In a recent essay, Adolf Laube uses some of the pamphlets written by four of the people in this sample to cite only socio-economic complaints.[64] One needs to use all of their extant pamphlets to examine them effectively, before concluding that such pamphlets presented mainly economic grievances. The actual social and political situation in their different cities, where most of these pamphleteers lived and wrote is important as well to the understanding of their perceptions of themselves and their role in a changing society. Their protest is a combination of visions and grievances.

Evidence presented in this pamphlet literature written by common people can provide a useful test situation for historical theories based on other kinds of source material. The traditional historians of the magisterial Reformation, some of whom were familiar with pamphlets, have usually assumed that these writers were intellectually dependent on the greater reformers.[65] Some historians suggest greater dependence on Luther in the great geographic circle around Nuremberg, a center of Lutheran publishing activity, or dependence on Zwingli in areas of Southwest Germany nearer Zürich, particularly Württemberg. Other historians link these pamphleteers with Thomas Müntzer and the Anabaptists. Are these people Anabaptists? Are they perhaps more dependent on Luther and Zwingli? Do they conform to a geographic distribution of Reformation theological dissemination?

Historians of popular culture insist on division and subdivision in urban society where a tenacious lay subculture exemplified 'the values of generosity and spontaneity and a greater tolerance of disorder.'[66] Peter Burke contrasts this cultural vigor with the more sober, decent, reasonable attitudes of Protestant and Catholic reformers. If this is true, then the former ethic ought to be reflected clearly in the pamphlets of our writers, whose belonging to such a tenacious lay culture and its various subcultures would have determined the direction of their thought. Robert Muchembled suggests that village people in rural culture are more willing to tolerate whoring priests in their vision of the world than urban people. Do we note an appropriate lack of tolerance in the works of these common people? Lionel Rothkrug suggests that there is a marked difference in the piety of cities and rural areas, a difference determined by governmental structure of cities and towns. In the South particularly, the area controlled by the *ministeriales*, pilgrimage, crusades, the cult of our lady queen of

heaven were encouraged in opposition to the pretensions of papal power
and the threats of imperial power. Rothkrug makes an exception for free
imperial cities, which rejected aristocratic influence in religious life. For
this reason, he notes strong support for Zwingli in the South among urban
Franciscans who had anti-aristocratic and anti-imperial tendencies. In the
North, Rothkrug refers to 'feminine religious piety,' which he calls more
personal, mystical, sober, and individualistic than the collectivist mentality
of the South, with its aristocratic notions and crusading fervor.[67] Are
female pamphleteers proponents of the feminine piety described by
Rothkrug or perhaps its masculine counterpart, common to Southwest
Germany? Rothkrug thinks that these basic pre-Reformation differences
in piety underscore the differences between Protestant and Catholic
Reformations, between feminine-inspired Lutheranism and more vigorous,
hierarchical Counter-Reformation Catholicism.

The mythology of the early capitalist revolution endorsed by the
Marxists which creates a great revolution led by the common man has
already been qualified or discredited.[68] It will be interesting to see whether
or not revolutionary motives, either in theology (Anabaptism and
enthusiasm) or in society, can be detected in these pamphlets. Do these
writers seek a destruction of the hierarchical order for the restoration of
a great Christian commune of equality? Whom do these writers see as their
greatest enemies? Patricians? The pope? City authorities? To what extent
are the motives for the Peasant Wars, or the spirit of the Peasant Articles
evident in these works by common people?

There is also a tendency in Reformation studies to emphasize the
newness of the ideas of magisterial reformers and the change to Protestant
piety.[69] Is the piety we note in this study more medieval in character or
more reformed? Other historians consider popular religious movements
as part of a continuing development, whereby laypeople sought to recover
their rightful role in government of the church. The Waldensians of the
twelfth, Hussites of the fifteenth, and Anabaptists of the sixteenth
centuries all sought reform in the church as a means to re-integration in
a religious institution that had become a clerical monopoly.[70] Do these
common people resemble their predecessors in earlier religious movements? Is their criticism of the church different in character from their
predecessors and followers? Steven Ozment in his work *Mysticism and
Dissent* (New Haven, 1973) suggests that a tradition of mystical theology
inspired protestors on the radical left wing of the Reformation. He
indicates Luther's 1518 edition of the *Theologia Deutsch* as the probable
source of motivation for the enthusiasts of 1524–25. He highlights aspects
of the work that attracted radicals: a quest for deification and union, an
elevating anthropology, ascetic exhortation to suffering and denial.[71] Was
the *Theologia Deutsch* a source of inspiration for our pamphleteers? Can

these common people be described as mystics from the theology contained in their printed pamphlets?

Piety is theology in action. Popular piety is the piety of laypeople. It may or may not imitate clerical recommendations for practice. In form, piety consists both of preparation for activity and active works. Weinstein and Bell's description or rather definition of popular piety comes close to an appropriate definition of the sort of piety found in these documents: 'When we speak of popular piety, we refer to the more or less spontaneous, at least partly autonomous religious ideas of men and women who were neither sophisticated doctrinalists, nor members of the...clerical hierarchy.'[72] In our documents, we can note both personal pious practice and recommendations to readers and listeners. We have the ability to compare their piety to practice in Southwest Germany before and after the Reformation. Do we find a revolutionary change in the pious practices of these lay pamphleteers? Are they more Catholic or Protestant in their recommendations?

To what extent these ideas were shared with a reading public is a matter for debate. Scholars who study Reformation satire note that people spoke in accepted codes that were stereotyped and not very original, suggesting that pamphlets were not necessarily vehicles for new ideas. Other historians, like Steven Ozment, are more certain that pamphlets helped to convey new ideas. Robert Scribner doubts whether or not the printed word had very much effect, since the actual medium of communication was the woodcut/illustration, not the printed word itself. In a less literate society oral communication and visual communication is more important than printed words.[73] Are there copious illustrations in the works of these pamphleteers to help communicate their ideas? Bernd Balzer in his study of Hans Sachs feels that Sachs addressed a particular audience in his pamphlets, but not the radical left wing of the Reformation. Sachs, according to Balzer, wrote as a mouthpiece for more conservative attitudes towards reform, specifically Luther and the Nuremberg city council.[74] Do our pamphleteers appeal to a particular audience? Do they represent the ideas of official authorities, magisterial and civic? Do they try to manipulate their audience? It is also important to examine the relative importance of theology and socio-economic grievances. Heiko Oberman and others have suggested that the real motives behind the Peasant Wars were religious, not political or social-revolutionary in nature.[75] Since these pamphlets were written on the eve of the Peasant Wars, it will be important to note and define the actual motives of these lay theologians as propagandists.

To answer these questions appropriately, we need to look at the latest research on the role of the 'common man' in both city and church in the late Middle Ages. The first chapter will describe common people as citizens, active laypeople, and prophets in an age of economic decline. The second chapter examines magisterial reformers as patrons of a new lay apostolate and source for theological ideas. The chapters to follow focus on the pamphleteers by city and their particular role in their civic reformations.

CHAPTER I

The call to prophesy: piety and discontent in the urban community of late-medieval Germany

Until 1525, the pamphleteers in this study enjoyed an environment of benevolent tolerance in their cities. As often as bishops might complain about their publishing activities, city councils did not proceed against them. Why? To find the answer we need to look at both the historical and the immediate situation. Historically, city council and church struggled for power in cities. The position of the church as a privileged institution beyond the control of city government led to a series of successful attempts by city councils to assert their authority over the church. City councils gradually gained control of appointments to parishes and rights to tax incomes on land and inheritances given to the church. City councillors saw it in their interest to protect common people from unfair and unjust treatment by greedy churchmen. This did not mean that councillors were irreligious. The great surge of interest in church affairs among the laity since the twelfth century was shared by councillor and common man alike. City councillors encouraged their sons and daughters to join institutions in the church that served the poor, like the Beguines or Franciscan tertiaries. Cities even protected the rights of Beguines and tertiaries against complaints of secular clergy that such houses were hotbeds of heresy. City fathers condoned such lay activity, so long as it served the municipal commune and did not seek to create disorder or challenge the power of city government. Urban pamphleteers in this study declared their loyalty to their city councils, something that assured them tolerance. City councils used the Reformation as an opportunity to finally incorporate the church and its clergy into the urban corporation, without the usual lengthy and complicated negotiations with Rome. Common people who supported this reform in their publications could aid the cause of city fathers in extending their control over the church.

Most of the pamphleteers in this study lived in imperial cities, making the history of cities in the late Middle Ages important in understanding their role in the Reformation. The historian A. G. Dickens noted in his book *The German Nation and Martin Luther* (New York, 1974) that 'the Reformation arose in its greatest strength within the cities.'[1] Very recently

2 Augsburg. Oldest woodcut showing the city of Augsburg, from *Ursprung und Anfang Augsburgs*, 1483.

the French historian Robert Muchembled suggested that the urban world was always more dynamic and economically oriented than the countryside. This dynamism provided the genesis for innovative change. The traditional division of society into three estates in the Middle Ages did not fit the urban environment. Cities maintained an independent social structure, where a patrician hierarchy ruled and set the tone for urban life. City fathers tolerated raucous festivities and lay activity so long as these did not interfere with commerce or keeping the peace. In the late Middle Ages urban society presented civic authorities with new challenges. Repressive legislation was required to counteract growing urban crime and violence, and to reinforce class divisions as ruling authorities became more and more insecure. Clothing regulations, private drinking clubs, private bathhouses were all designed to maintain social distinctions within the city. Change and problems in the city were effected by changes in the economy. Strategic planning to meet crisis situations was impossible in the late Middle Ages because crises – plague, famine, wars, invasion – were so unpredictable.[2] The councils of cities tried to force other religious and social institutions to conform to the exigencies of a new economic system, while maintaining and reinforcing their own privileges.

The late medieval economy was markedly different from the traditional medieval economic system. The usual exchange between town and countryside in an economy based on agrarian staples was interrupted, as towns became centers for the production of luxury goods, precious metals, textiles, beer and wine.[3] In an economy increasingly based on specie instead of barter, traditional social relationships changed: serfs could contract their obligations in specie payments; the nobility turned its eyes from the codes of chivalry to the means of production.[4] This fundamental change in the economy and social relationships had a direct effect on the status of cities. The nobility could no longer afford to wage wars against rivals in contests based on privilege and honor. Wars might be waged for economic advantages or the political interests of dynasty. The town as the center of wealth and production took on new significance. It was in the interest of both territorial princes and emperors to see cities prosper. Cities were granted charters in exchange for regular payments to noble treasuries. Charters granted towns municipal autonomy.

Cities themselves were hardly passive recipients of change. Social changes that resulted from a re-distribution of wealth after the Black Death and a new noble interest in cities increased tension within city walls. Ideally, the town of the Middle Ages was a commune, where groups within the town worked toward prosperity and salvation. Subjects paid taxes to support the army of a prince to defend them against invasion; the clergy of the town prayed for the souls of their noble patron and distributed alms to the poor of the town. Church courts might help preserve liberties of

3 A *Bürgermeister* and two councillors decide a case that has been brought before
them by two citizens. From Rodericus Zamorensis, *Speculum vitae humanae*,
1488.

individuals against the abuse of noble power. Things had changed by the
fourteenth century. The church with its tax freedom and large tracts of
land shared in economic growth. Soon city councils would have to protect
common people against unfair competition from the church. Townspeople
had to rely more on their own arms and fortifications than fickle,
belligerent nobles to protect them. Chartered towns took on increasing
responsibility for protecting the citizenry in law courts and in the streets.
In the process, they adapted the medieval patriarchal system and vertical
hierarchy to their own needs. Traditionally, a small governing council was
chosen from worthy families chosen by a prince, who governed a city with
the prince's personal representative or *Schultheiss*. The elite council of
patricians took responsibility for maintaining and expanding fortifications
and establishing the prince's justice through his judicial representative or
Vogt. In chartered cities, the right to choose a mayor was granted to the
patricians. In cities with a healthy economy, the city was divided into
twelve guilds whose guildmasters served as advisors to the council of
worthy patricians. As guilds became more powerful, they demanded a
share of power in city government. In the late Middle Ages, important
guilds took control of city government, electing their own mayors or
Bürgermeister.

Most of the pamphleteers in our sample lived in imperial free cities. Cities that were raised to imperial free city status had to pay direct taxes to the emperor, had obligations to raise and pay armies, as well as maintaining their own fortifications. Imperial free cities enjoyed a particular advantage: the emperor's personal protection, benefit of the imperial courts, and international representation at imperial diets. Augsburg became an imperial free city with the right to appoint its own mayors in 1316, Frankfurt in 1372, Nuremberg in 1385, Memmingen in 1438. There were also greater risks in becoming an imperial free city: the city might find itself pawned to another noble or monastery to pay imperial debts or to fund an imperial campaign. Such dangers required a new international awareness among councillors, an awareness that was politically and economically critical for survival.[5]

In most cities, tension grew between old noble-appointed worthy families, who wanted to maintain political power in municipal government, and guilds of artisans, whose growing economic importance necessitated a greater political role. Merchant guilds, weavers, furriers, and brewers assumed special status in cities as 'greater' guilds; in the fifteenth century they were joined by goldsmiths, silversmiths, and printers. As greater guild members became richer, they were raised to patrician rank, making them eligible to serve on the powerful smaller city council with patricians. Greater council meetings where all guilds were represented became confined to ceremonial occasions. The guildsmen who could sit with patricians on the smaller city council, *novi homines* as they were called, soon distanced themselves from their brother craftsmen, emulating patricians and sending their sons to Italy for education. As older worthy families died out, *novi homines* assumed the entire responsibility for city government. Augsburg, which boasted some 51 worthy families in 1368, counted only ten of those old families on its city council in 1538.[6] Lesser guilds, shoemakers, bakers, fishermen, etc., and a growing number of day-laborers, had little hope of gaining political power in the late Middle Ages.

The creation of *novi homines* or nouveaux riches often resulted in the parallel development of nouveaux pauvres, a problem which continued to disturb city fathers in the fifteenth century. The traditional medieval attitude toward the poor was positive: aiding the poor was a means to gain entrance to heaven. Yet, the new economic system which evolved had little room for poor people, who seemed more an economic burden than a spiritual advantage. To be poor in the fifteenth century was no longer a particular honor, but a peculiar shame. A citizen, a full-fledged member of the urban corporation, had to pay taxes. Have-nots could neither pay taxes nor enjoy full rights as citizens. They were forced to live outside the protecting walls of the city. City fathers were intent on preserving their own status. The poor were shut out from public feasts and private drinking houses. The maintenance of order by such regulations was less an issue in more prosperous times than in times of economic decline. In most cities, wealthy citizens attempted to alleviate their guilt by providing housing for poor people and levying taxes for their relief. By the time of the Reformation, the medieval vision of the poor as a gateway to heaven was lost. Progressive Protestant clergymen wrote treatises on why the poor ought to be driven to work.[7]

Less prosperous times created problems for cities. Wars, plagues, international events all affected city life. Revolts by disgruntled peasants and lower classes in cities put fear in the hearts of city fathers. A *coup d'état* by guildsmen excluded from the smaller governing council was a real possibility. Artisan revolts in Flanders, France, and Great Britain were very serious in the late fourteenth century. Southwest Germany was spared these bloody revolts, partly because it was less prosperous and wealth was more evenly distributed. Political tension in imperial cities occasioned the emperor's interference. Emperors used their rights in imperial free cities to their own political advantage.[8] Charles IV (+1378) supported the guilds' demand for a role in city government in Reutlingen because they had been loyal to him in a conflict with a local prince. In Nuremberg, the same emperor supported the patricians against artisans from lesser guilds who had tried to gain an advantage by supporting the rival Duke of Bavaria.[9] Most German cities were economically behind those in Flanders and Italy. Tax and property distribution tended to be more even in small cities (population of five to six thousand). In larger cities with important textile or metal industries, the tax burden was borne by the majority of the people, but property was in the hands of very few. In medium-sized cities (population approximately ten thousand) the rich and poor seemed to grow in number at the expense of citizens in the middle.[10] The tax freedom of some institutions, notably those associated with the church and the inability of others to raise enough tax money to pay their share were a constant problem. Many poor weavers could not pay their taxes. When greater guilds limited the number of guildmasters, poor journeymen were reduced to day laborers. While patricians and wealthy guildmasters isolated themselves in private drinking clubs, poorer journeymen and lesser guildsmen organized brotherhoods, church-affiliated corporations to aid each other in times of need and to sponsor masses for the deceased. Brotherhoods provided a place for guildsmen to serve the poor and to take up an active role in the redemption of society, one of the few places in the church where common laypeople might actually gain some political power.[11]

When revolts did take place in Southwest Germany, they were less serious than those in Flanders or Britain. For example in Augsburg in 1476, the wealthy guildmaster of the salt producers overthrew the old city council and replaced it with a committee of guildmasters. Since salt

4 Life and Martyrdom of St. Sebastian. Fresco in the nave vaulting of St. Cyprian's Church, in Sarnthein, South Tyrol. The work was sponsored by the Brotherhood of Tailors in 1492 to decorate their parish church with the story of the life and martyrdom of their patron saint.

producers were not among the greater guilds, the new city council destroyed the old divisions which had separated guildsmen. To preserve their own recently won status, ousted greater guildsmen conspired with old patricians to overthrow the usurper. The old order was restored. When lesser guildsmen rose up in rebellion against the city council in Nuremberg in 1349, the guilds were dissolved and the city council assumed control of production.[12]

   Although Germany remained far behind Italy and Flanders in production, international events could bring brief periods of prosperity. At the end of the fourteenth century, the Mongol invasion of Russia began to interrupt the geographically horizontal exchange between Eastern and Western Europe, shifting the trade axis to the North–South routes. Imperial cities enjoyed a brief flourish. After 1450, things began to decline. Many former imperial free cities lost their free city status. In 1462, Mainz lost free city status and the city government was once again subjected to the archbishop. When the guilds in Mainz supported the peasants in 1525, the archbishop disolved them.[13] Erfurt was subjected to the old Saxon feudal nobility in 1483, losing its free city status. In Northern Germany the Hanseatic League of free cities was practically destroyed.[14] In the hundred years between 1450 and 1550, few cities grew in population, except those cities near mines or important manufacturing centers. Both Freiburg and Heilbronn, once medium-sized cities, declined in population as thousands of laborers abandoned them to work in more important mining areas, like Saxony or banking centers like Augsburg. Nuremberg and Augsburg grew tremendously, boasting over thirty thousand inhabitants respectively. Nevertheless, a general decline affected everyone's social status. Increasing taxes and increasing poverty prompted a series of uprisings in the Rhineland, Ulm, and several other cities between 1509 and 1513.[15] Anti-Jewish riots in imperial cities focused the blame for economic calamity on privileged groups in municipalities, outside the urban corporation.[16] Where guilds did exercise some power in city government, they sought to eliminate competition from the countryside. The weavers of Memmingen refused to let village weavers participate in the yearly trade fair in that city.[17] Guilds generally tried to maintain the status quo, to preserve the privileges they had won, to resist takeover by a local noble or to prevent change that resulted in a lower social status. Guilds also refused technical advances and tried to prevent any competition in their production by either monasteries or princes.[18]
   The church became an object of discontent in this economic decline, too. A decadent, ignorant clergy was even less tolerable to people at all levels of society in times of economic decline. City councils did their best to encourage reformed monastic orders. Patricians advised their sons and daughters to join reformed monasteries. Because papal politics was so complicated and church councils so infrequent, local control seemed the only logical method to bring the church and clergy into the urban corporation. Resistance to reform from within the church was a constant obstacle to change. Much of that resistance came from cathedral chapters and universities. Only in a few areas could the municipal government effect some change: the right of monasteries to inherit without paying taxes could be abridged; parish appointments could be assumed; some clerics guilty of

5 The Pilgrimage to 'Our Lovely Lady' in Regensburg. Engraving by Michael
Ostendorfer, 1520. The woodcut was used to describe the pilgrimage to a figure
of the Virgin Mary set on a column, which was alleged to have caused many
miracles: 'In 1516, a learned doctor, Balthasar Hubmeier, preached so vigorously
against the Jews, that with permission of the Emperor, the city council drove them
out. Some of the Jews' houses were confiscated by Christians. Others were destroyed
like their synagogue. On the place of their synagogue a church dedicated to the
Virgin Mary was built. A spontaneous pilgrimage began. All sorts of people came,
some with musical instruments, some with pitchforks and rakes; women came with
their milk cans, spindles, and cooking pots. Artisans came with their tools: a weaver
with his shuttle, a carpenter with his square, a cooper with his measuring tape.
They walked many miles, but did not tire from the long journey. They all walked
in silence. If asked, why they were going, they answered, "My spirit drives me
there.''...Thousands came each day to see the miracle...The pilgrimage continued
for six or seven years, until Dr. Martin Luther preached against it.' (From a
contemporary description.)

civil crimes might be tried in municipal courts. Yet, the economic advantages of the church remained more or less intact. Individuals and cities could only gain concessions from bishops or the curia in Rome when traditional privileges stood in direct opposition to a progressive vision of the church and if appropriate compensation were promised by city fathers. Nuremberg kept a permanent representative to this end at the papal court in Rome.

There was another path to reform: endowed, privately funded preacherships. Bad Windsheim had a funded preachership as early as 1421, Memmingen in 1479, and Augsburg in 1517.[19] These new preacherships were founded by private citizens. Preachers had to be university trained in theology and be above moral reproach. Such preachers were to be secular priests, not monks. They were expressly forbidden to keep a prostitute.[20] Every preacher was instructed to preach 'the louder, plainer word of God,' not fables from lives of the saints. When the founders died, their families retained the rights of appointment or the appointment was put directly in the hands of the city council. These newly appointed preachers provided keen competition for mendicant houses, whose preachers had special papal commissions, granting them special status. Competition for listeners was likewise keen. Although little new church building was begun after 1450, many churches had to expand their naves to accommodate large numbers of listeners. Secular preachers encouraged bible reading. Mendicants extolled the value of more emotional forms of religious experience, using mystical affective sermons to motivate their hearers. Some encouraged pilgrimages and described miraculous events. Clerical competition could result in some confusion among listeners. One preacher might advocate attendance at mass, sermons, and bible study in private. Another appealed to emotional ecstasy. The church as an institution had no effective means to coordinate such diverse pious recommendations. Episcopal leadership was crippled by political and administrative work with the curia. In the midst of economic decline, historians note an increase in 'popular piety': hearing sermons, reading the bible, devotion to relics, the pilgrimage.[21]

The particular popularity of bible reading is linked to advances in literacy among common people as well as the theology of the *Devotio Moderna*. This increase in literacy was fostered within church circles and without. Most mendicant convents had reading masters to teach tertiaries how to read. Women in convents were encouraged to read, discuss, and sometimes even write their own devotional literature.[22] Cities, too, founded their own schools. In 1330, the city of Hagenau founded its own school because, 'when children attend the monks' schools, they must assist the monks in singing their office, spending most of their time at that to the disadvantage of the other arts and conversational speech.'[23] The influence of Renaissance education in Italy affected the attitudes of citizens who wanted education to have a practical emphasis. Schools had to serve society in the fifteenth century. Guilds sponsored their own schools. Artisans needed to read in order to keep their books. Literate artisans even dabbled in history. Chronicles written by artisans like the brewer Heinrich Deichsler in Nuremberg and the baker Hans Brülinger (+1457) in Basel took their place alongside bibles and devotional tracts in the private houses of artisans. To prevent competition between schools, city councils often intervened in private schools to appoint instructors, to set fees and to make rules.[24]

The curriculum in all schools was influenced by the church: religious works were usually the basis for instruction. City fathers were as eager to see that their children learned their prayers, as they were hopeful to see them calculate profit percentages. Vernacular translations of the bible gave both substance and direction to the curriculum. In schools children learned the articles of faith. Progressive churchmen reinforced this: in 1493, Berthold von Henneberg, reforming archbishop of Mainz offered forty days indulgence to every priest who would rehearse the articles of faith from the pulpit in German with the people.[25] The goals of the new preaching and concurrently developing secular attitudes were often at odds. Members of the movement called the *Devotio Moderna*, who sought to use the bible and basic articles of faith to encourage a Renaissance of Christian virtue, confronted newly literate artisans with suspicion. Thomas von Haselbach (+1460) gave up a professorship in Vienna to accept a parish appointment in Bavaria. He told his listeners: 'Many of you have mechanical professions, weavers, smiths, shipbuilders, that serve the call of function and necessity. Others serve conceit and materialism: painters, goldsmiths, and stonemasons create works for vain people, spending more time on precious objects than useful things. They are more interested in useless new inventions designed to swindle people or add to human pride...fancy buttoned shoes and brocade cloth... They cheat people by selling burned leather for good, old cloth for new.'[26] Growing materialism went hand in hand with the new literacy.

After 1450, more and more lists of grievances (*gravamina*) were submitted by common people to city councils for action. People protested new taxes; villages outside cities complained of attempts by lesser nobles to monopolize hunting and fishing rights. They protested new monastic foundations and the expansion of present monasteries, that used their tax freedom to sell their wares for less, creating unfair competition. When cities developed more modern bureaucracies, farmers protested new regulations that forced them to sell in towns at weekly markets for fixed prices.[27] The young were attracted to Italian fashions and the rich paraded in luxury. The old values seemed more and more remote. A world turned upside-down

Wer jemand hie der gern welt lernen dutſch ſchriben vnd laſen vß dem aller
kúrtziſten grundt den jeman erdncken kan do durch ein jedez der vor nit ein
buchſtaben kan der mag kúntzlich vnd bald begriffen ein grundt Do durch er
mag von jm ſelber lernen ſin ſchuld vff ſchriben vnd laſen vnd wer es
nit gelernnen kan So vngeſchickt werr Den will ich vm nut vnd ver
geben gelert haben vnd gantz nut von jm zů lon nemen er ſyg
wer er well burger Ouch handtwerckß geſellen frowen vnd ju
nckfrouwen wer ſin bedarff Der kum har jn der wirt drúwlich
gelert vm ein zimlichen lon. Aber die jungen knaben vnd meit
lin noch den fronuaſten wie gewonheyt iſt. Anno. m rrrr xvi

6 A sign used to advertise a schoolteacher's lessons, by Hans Holbein, the younger.
Basel, 1516. It reads: 'For whoever wants to learn to read and write German in
the shortest possible time, even those who cannot even read a letter, who want
to be able to write down and be able to read their debts. Satisfaction guaranteed.
Will take on burghers, journeymen, women, and maidens, whoever needs to learn.
Reasonable prices for instruction. Young boys and girls only accepted after the
ember day fast.'

meant that the individual lost traditional bonds in a society where a feeling
of political impotence among the lower classes encouraged a radicalization
of ideology as protest moved toward rebellion. If city councils delayed or
rejected grievances, they became *civium oppressores*. The great crisis
occurred in 1525, when the lists of grievances highlighted differences
between rich and poor, privileged and under-privileged. These grievances
point to the growing inflation, higher taxes, unfair tithes, uncontrolled
competition in production and the growing distance between 'haves' and
'have-nots' in society. Artisans in the cities were willing to join the
peasants of the countryside to redress their own grievances with direct
action.[28]

Such protest usually sought a more conservative solution, a restoration of the *status quo ante*, not radical change. Guilds insisted on maintaining their rights and privileges. Instead of demanding an abolition of class differences, they wanted distinctions maintained. They articulated this program of restoration for the benefit of the commune, clinging to an essentially medieval concept in hope of rescuing some political power that had been gradually drifting from their hands to patricians and the church. The preservation of the *bonum communis* against new abuses of power by the upper classes suggests reactionary not revolutionary behavior. The protest against the church did not seek to abolish the hierarchy, but abuses, that excluded monasteries and clergy from taxes. In smaller cities where the city council took grievances seriously in 1525, an escalation of violence did not ensue. In large cities, when municipal councils refused to acknowledge the righteousness of such protests, rebellion was more serious.[29] When territorial princes intervened, both city councils and guilds lost their independence and much of their political power. The Swabian League severely punished guildsmen who had joined forces with the peasants. By mid sixteenth century, guilds, seeking the preservation of hierarchy, lost their status when a horizontal work situation subject to the dictates of princes erased any hope of restoring either privileges or political power.[30]

It is not surprising that the articles of protest in the *gravamina* are laden with religious rhetoric, appeals to the moral demands of the gospel and demands for conformity to the word of God for the benefit of the entire community. Grievances reflect the message of sermons, which sought moral reform in a society ravaged by rapidly growing economic differences and frustration by church reform that failed to articulate a unified, coherent message. The general demand for the restoration of a *status quo ante* almost suggests that desire for reform was more medieval than modern in expression. Political impotence in cities is mirrored by similar inability to obtain redress for grievances in the church. At least some city councils could accept lists of grievances. The church had no institution within its bureaucracy for such a process: brotherhoods had no place in the official hierarchy of the church. Grievances submitted to city councils often demanded the right to choose a parish priest, to give common people some control over parish life, if not a direct means to redress their grievances. This would have been impossible for city councils to accomplish. Gaining control over parish appointments for city councils was no easy matter. Only after long deliberations and considerable payments were councils able to obtain rights of appointment to parishes. Negotiation with Rome was expensive and could take years.[31]

Laypeople had been shut out from effective government in the church for centuries: by 1200, they had lost any role in liturgy or government in the church. In Southern France about 1170, the poor of Lyons, armed

7 Detail from a broadside with text by Hans Sachs, showing poor artisans and
wealthy burghers. Augsburg, c. 1524?

with a translation of the gospel, began their own reform. Measuring their
contemporary church against the demands of the gosepl, they tried to bring
the church back to apostolic virtue. These simple, often illiterate men and
women took the biblical call to *vita apostolica* seriously. They sold their land
and possessions to begin a preaching mission, in churches, houses, taverns,
and market-places. They demanded absolute conformity to the writ of the
bible, admonishing their companions to abandon the cult of saints,
non-scriptural sacraments, swearing of oaths (on which medieval society
was based) and military service. Their open defiance of the medieval order
earned them a condemnation by their bishop and a papal declaration of
heresy. These poor of Lyons or Waldensians (after their leader Peter Valdes
[+1217]) inspired a series of similar movements in Northern Italy,

Germany, Bohemia, and Austria.[32] Waldensians were particularly active in artisan groups. Their critique of the church identified the authority of the church with the authority of the bible: 'Quidquid praedicatur quod per textum bibliae non probatus, pro fabulis habent.'[33] They rejected the teachings of the church on purgatory, prayers to the saints, prayers for the dead, and indulgences. They made the Lord's prayer the center of their liturgy, abandoning the historic creeds. They demanded conformity to the teachings of Christ without human additions. They denied the authority of tradition in the church. They rejected the church hierarchy. Waldensians appeared in Germany about 1230. The first papal inquisitor in Germany, Conrad of Marburg (+1233) was assassinated when he accused a local noble in the Rhineland of heresy. Neither emperor nor bishops seemed particularly concerned about Waldensians in Germany. A few Waldensians were tried and executed, but no crusade against them took place like the great Albigensian crusade in Southern France.[34]

The failure to rout effectively, or at least systematically, the Waldensian heresy, insured the sect's survival. In cities, where artisans were willing to renounce their worldly goods and preach reform of society, they did so in secret.[35] Several groups of heretics were inspired by the Waldensians. In the Netherlands, lay men and women organized communities to serve the poor. These Beghards and Beguines lived in communities without vows. Such communities were a threat to medieval society; because they were lay and functioned without vows, they were often accused of diverse heresies. Beghards became synonymous with wandering preachers. They were often confused with contemporary Free Spirit Brethren, who having reached a perfect state of union with God were no longer subject to Godly or human laws.[36] To avoid such accusations, many Beguines became Franciscan tertiaries. Yet, even tertiaries were subject to the same suspicions. Emperor Charles IV encouraged papal inquisitors in Germany. He asked them to rid Germany of those vernacular devotional tracts, which were 'vicious, erroneous, and infected with the leprosy of heresy.'[37]

Enthusiasm for crusades against heretics was always short lived. Germany had no institution comparable to the later Spanish Inquisition. Usually, investigation of heretics was local in character. Sometimes civic authorities established their own inquisitions, especially after Charles IV declared that cities could confiscate and sell property belonging to heretics. There is indication, however, that city councillors were tolerant of alleged heretics, so long as they did not cause trouble. Often cities defended Beguine houses because they housed the daughters of powerful families. Cities seldom burned heretics. They usually drove them out or exiled them for a fixed number of years. Attention paid to Beghards and Beguines distracted inquisitors from Waldensians, who continued to practice. Weavers seemed to be particularly attracted by Waldensian preachers.

8 The martyrdom of John Huss from *Processvs//Consistorialis//Martyrii Io. Hvss, cum corre =//spondentia Legis//Gratiae, ad ius//Papisticum,//in Simoniacos & fornicatores Papistas.//* (c. 1524). The woodcut shows the soul of Huss being carried into heaven as two common people recognize his sainthood.

Many of those apprehended in Germany were weavers. In most cases, if they confessed their heresy, they were released with penance, usually the wearing of a penitential cross on their clothing.[38]

Municipal governments were less tolerant of Hussites. The Hussites were more radical and political in their protest. Hussites adopted millenarian ideas, identified the pope as the Anti-Christ, and advocated armed rebellion in some cases. By 1430, some Hussite followers demonstrated a well-developed chiliasm and armed themselves to destroy all organized authority. They took on a body of ideas entirely opposed to the existing order, a vision of perfect life on earth based on a Christian commune without class distinctions. They were convinced of their own ability to effect the end of the world by violent means. The Taborites, who withdrew from Prague to a mountain outside the city, sent manifestos to imperial cities in Germany to enlist their support against Emperor Sigismund (+1437).[39] The Emperor's crusade against the Hussites was a failure. Their schism was ended by negotiation. Cities became more and more suspect of heretics as a result of the Hussite rebellion. Millenarian ideas made Hussites much more dangerous than the Waldensians, who were less conspicuous, meeting in private homes and cellars for prayer.

What could heresy offer people that the church could not? Three important characteristics were shared by all heretical movements: a *lex evangelica*, which demanded conformity to the ideals of the gospel that assured a community of equals; a *vita apostolica* of absolute poverty, that went hand-in-hand with predictions of a nearing End; the opportunity to aspire to a level of *perfecti*, who by mystical meditation were able to achieve oneness with the Godhead. Conversion was central to the mystical piety of these heretical movements. It was in this conversion that the vision of a suffering Christ and a Christ the vindicator at the last judgment were reconciled. The *perfecti* would certainly be saved. Each individual heresy emphasized one of these characteristics over others. A Beghard experienced states of election: the initiate left his former life for the freedom of the saved community.[40] A Waldensian carried out his apostolic mission in complete poverty. Hussites tried to create the community of the *perfecti* on Mt Tabor. Free Spirit brethren sought perfection to take them beyond the limits of earthly law.

When Jean Gerson (+ 1429) the influential rector of the university in Paris and father of the *Devotio Moderna* demanded the condemnation of the Hussites at the Council of Constance in 1415, he recognized the fact that not all of their teaching was based on fanatic chiliasm and that the popularity of the movement was a sign of the crying need for reform. Laypeople attracted to heresy were not just ignorant barbarians, nor illiterate countryfolk, who sought only destruction of the established order.[41] Nor was the church entirely blind to the need of common people. Lateran IV recommended that cathedral churches hire confessors and preachers to instruct people in their native language.[42] The council authorized the Dominicans as a preaching order to convert the heretics and bring them back into the fold of the church. Franciscans took to the countryside too, in hopes of bringing common people back to the church. To prevent heresy, many of these mendicants preached conversion by using a formula for mystical affective piety they hoped would guide souls back to the true fold. The tradition of affective piety was shared by many groups in the church, mendicants, devotees of the *Devotio Moderna*, cloistered monks and heretics. Affective piety was not an attempt to teach doctrine or formal worship, but 'to move the heart of the believer...through a personal, passionate attachment to the human Jesus, and particularly to the aspects of Christ's life which belong to universal experience: birth and death, nativity and passion.'[43] The object of meditation on the life and passion of Christ and Mary was a mystical reunion between the human and Godly soul, which seems on the surface intended to bring people to a special level of perfection. Affective piety assumes that after the individual by contemplation or mediation had ascended to God in spirit, he/she would be converted, transformed in the heart. The reunion created a special affection in the human soul (hence the term 'affective') which

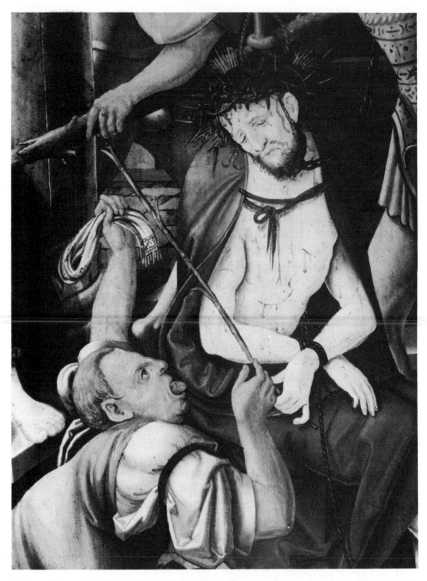

9 Detail from the Herrenberg High Altar, showing the passion, crucifixion, and resurrection of Christ, by Jörg Ratgeb (+1526) 1515. Depictions of scenes from the passion became more and more realistic in the early sixteenth century, as devotion to the passion and wounds of Christ took on increased significance.

could grow in love. The contemplation of biblical mysteries provided the path of ascent. Certainly within the monastic tradition, reunion often demonstrated a state of perfection where natural law could be broken: monks and nuns might see visions, receive the sigmata, or levitate. This pious tradition has its origins in Bernardine theology, where conversion of the heart as the necessary preparation for Christian life began a climb up the ladder of perfection. Conversion could even occur outside the walls of the cloister. For preachers against heretics this affective tradition had tremendous potential: it could capture the heart of the listener, who through proper union could be moved to do works of Christian virtue, hoped for by the *Devotio Moderna*. If the goals of mendicants and the *Devotio Moderna* were not always in harmony, the means to those goals was identical. They differed in their recommendations for appropriate devotions. Since vernacular translations of the bible and devotional tracts had often been blamed for heretical developments, many preachers were sceptical of their value in the hands of the less learned. Franciscans David of Augsburg (+1272) and Berthold of Regensburg (+1272), the Dominican Conrad von Marburg, and the Augustinian Brother Eberhard (+1285) brought the affective tradition in their sermons to Germany.[44] The use of mystical monastic piety as a new standard for personal piety is the key to understanding the growing interest of laypeople in sermons. When the Franciscan St John Capistran (+1456) came to Germany on a papal preaching mission, he drew crowds of 20,000. His conversion sermons were so successful, that people carried out their gaming boards and sleds, cut their hair, throwing all into a great bonfire at the end of the day to symbolize their contrition.[45]

The same people who began preaching affective piety were also the fathers of devotional literature in the vernacular. David of Augsburg's *Seven Stages of Prayer* and *Mirror of Wisdom* remained standards for future works of religious devotion.[46] Based on the warm, homely, transcendent theology of SS. Bernard and Bonaventure, they focus on humility and obedience as the object of meditation. A classic among such works was Otto von Passau's *Twenty Four Elders*, written about 1386. The work is a comprehensive manual for laypeople, using the twenty-four elders at the last judgment to move people to good works. The fifth elder tells his listeners that a 'clear conscience from which all good works flow' is the key to contrition. Doctors of the church (including Seneca!) assert that the conscience can only be purged by prayerful contemplation, resulting in a soul ascended to and united with God, who imputes to it the grace necessary to do good works: 'Grace is the first choir by which man is called and pulled toward God. Grace seeks a cleaner, purer heart, free in its innocence, with a strong firm *Gemüthe*, patient in all suffering, a strong

10 St. Dominic preaches to common people. Detail from the high altar in the church of the Cistercian abbey at Maulbronn. Painted by an unknown master. 1432. The altar shows scenes from the lives of SS. Bernard, Francis, and Dominic.

fortress against all folly.'[47] The *Elders* went through at least seven editions before the Reformation and several subsequent publications.

Fathers of the *Devotio Moderna* provided their own pious works for the newly literate. Jean Gerson used mystical, affective piety in his important *Little Work in Three Parts: On the Decalogue, On Confession, and on the Art of Dying*. Composed in 1408, it was published in most European languages and served as a model for later works. German synods meeting in 1452 recommended Gerson's work to laypeople.[48] Such works had a pragmatic function: to prevent heresy and encourage Christian virtue by redirecting the theology that had produced the heresy. Authors relied on a new literacy and a trust that Christian virtue would result from the grace of mystical union. Laypeople would become humble, obedient, and charitable. Why did this pious literature fail? As the individual was brought back to God by prayer and penance, the sacramental life of the church was subverted to devotional practice, beyond the liturgy and mediating priesthood. Laypeople had no mediating means or direct link to the institutional church as they did to their cities, where grievances might be heard. Devotional practice and *bonum communis* were first in the hearts of most laypeople.

By the late fifteenth century, the printing press, publishing in Augsburg since 1468, was able to flood the available market with bibles and devotional tracts. Most of the research and collection of pious printed tracts was done by Catholic apologists of the last century. Vincent Hasak, one of the chief apologists, thought the church would have reformed itself, had people been left to their pious literature. He re-published nearly seventy devotional tracts in 1868. Of the seventy, nearly half are gospels and passions.[49] These works were aimed at conversion of the heart, by meditation on Jesus' life. By meditation, the heart received faith and the ability to recognize true good works. Meditation on sermons lifted the soul to God. Faith proceeded from scripture, through sermons or the printed word to the heart to good works. There is no 'balance' between faith and works as a means to salvation in these tracts, but a continuum of faith active in works. Geiler von Keisersberg (+1510), the reforming preacher in Strasbourg wrote in his tract *The Pomegranate* in 1510: 'Listen diligently to the holy word of God and preserve it in your heart, considering how it might be applied to your life. When you hear a sermon, but don't preserve it in your heart, your soul is lacking in Godly grace; just as food is necessary for your body, so grace is necessary for your soul.'[50]

Meditation on Christ and his mother Mary was a special means to make the heart fertile for divine grace. St Bernard's sermons on the Virgin remained an important source of inspiration for devotional writers. The humanity of Christ, long a model of monastic humility, symbolized the particular kinship God showed for man. Mary as a model for the church and humanity personified the best monastic virtues. To extend monastic virtue to the secular world, it was the humanity of Christ that provided that pathway, in sermons, pious literature, and for that matter, in late-medieval painting and sculpture as well. The stern medieval Christ in judgment becomes the tender child and loving master in the pious press. The homeliness of devotional tracts presented saints and sinners in the familiar garb of the city and its institutions. Saints were no longer the stern sentinels on the portals of churches, but familiar friends and neighbors. An interesting portrayal of this new homeliness is Ulrich Tengler's *Mirror for Laypeople* (Augsburg, 1509), where a tug-of-war between angels and devils for people's hearts takes place in a courtroom. At the judge's bench, the trinity sits to hear a case, brought by the advocates of the devil, who demand the full harvest of souls due the devil in the coming judgment. At first, the trinity finds it difficult to defend mankind, since so few people demonstrate redeeming features in their character. As the trinity is about to decide in the devil's favor, the cries of the saints in heaven reach the Virgin Mary, at work spinning wool for altarcloths in her home. Mary leaves her work, enters the courtroom and pleads for a mistrial. Immediately, the devil tries to have her removed from the courtroom: she is a woman and women could not bring suit in court; since she was the mother of the trinity, she could prejudice a fair decision. Not one to be upstaged by the devil, Mary produces a twenty-five page defense of mankind, which she proceeds to read. The judge, impressed by her defense, reverses the previous decision. St John the Evangelist, the heavenly notary, prepares the writ of damnation. SS. John the Baptist, Francis, and Dominic sign the writ. The twelve apostles add their signatures. The devil is cast into hell and Mary is invited by the trinity to wear a crown and reign with them, as special attorney for the defense.[51] Here one notes how things sacred and secular blend into a harmonious whole, the sort of unity people expected from their communities and institutions in those communities. If heavenly things were not so far removed from earthly things, spiritual reunion, even the path to salvation might seem more available to the average person, who otherwise might be led from the path by the temptations of the secular world or the false teachings of heresy. Monastic values and piety were no longer confined to the cloister, but could be extended to the secular world: this was the substance of the *Devotio Moderna*. The road to heaven was no longer blocked by seven raging sins, but was opened by ten columns (ten commandments) to warn man of his obligations. It is interesting that in Spain in the sixteenth century, villagers acted out mock trials, where insects were accused of destroying crops; the clergy played the role of the apostles and the common people the saints in condemning the work of the devil.[52]

Confessional books account for much of the pious literature from German presses in the late Middle Ages. These works follow Gerson's model,

11 Woodcut from Ulrich Tengler's *Laienspiegel*, 1508. The woodcut shows the victory of the Virgin Mary over the devil. Mary protects cardinals, bishops, and common people under her cloak, while the writ for the devils' damnation is being prepared by the four evangelists. Christ seated in Judgment looks on with angels on his right hand and holy monks, bishops, and popes on his left.

ordering sins under the ten commandments. Actual satisfaction in the penitential process is realized in contrition, not absolution from the priest. The cleansing of the conscience is the efficient cause of true contrition. A conscience free of sin is able to ascend to God, when the heart is fired with contrition, a sign that the conscience is free is the ability to do meritorious works. Meritorious works could be pilgrimages and long fasts or even attendance at mass. Works of mercy from the commandment to love one's neighbor were at the top of the list. For laypeople any confusion that might arise from diverse pious recommendations could be mediated through the consensus presented by the joint efforts of mendicants and secular reformers. The economy of salvation was marked by a clearing of the conscience, realized in contrition, where infused grace allowed man to do meritorious works. The means to this grace was faith, received from meditation on the word, heard, read, and painted. The formula of salvation follows this pattern:

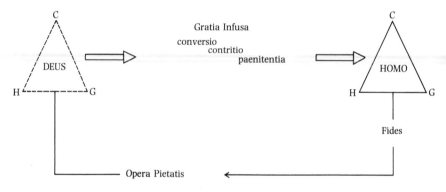

Figure 1. A Mystical Economy of Salvation

Man, though created in God's image, is naturally estranged from the creator. Yet, at creation, a natural grace or *gratia prima* was implanted in his soul that allows man to turn toward God. Through acts of contrition and penance man grows in grace: the heart is converted; the conscience, where sin rests, is cleared. As a result of this process, the faith of the believer grows. As faith grows, the *gemüthe* is released to allow man to spiritually return to God. As the spiritual soul unites with God, pious works, pilgrimages, prayers, indulgences and works of charity bring the physical soul closer to God. In the process, man begins to do God's works on earth and continually grows in grace, becoming more and more Godlike. For a selected few, enough grace can be gained to even break through the boundaries of natural law, allowing physical man to levitate or fly or perform miracles, as the apostles did. Such extraordinary states of grace are sure signs of sainthood and probable eternal election.

The Bernardine supposition that all meritorious works depended on affective personal preparation was an accepted principle in the late Middle Ages. Meditation as a means to true contrition was enhanced by the availability of printed devotional literature. Active works, be they the veneration of saints, a pilgrimage, purchase of an indulgence, or even the more laudable six works of holy mercy could only be effective with proper preparation. Popes also recognized the importance of the written word for the newly literate. Pope Leo X (+1521) was not opposed to vernacular translations of the gospel, as long as they were properly licensed.[53]

When one considers 'popular piety' in the late Middle Ages, one must accept that piety as reflecting a change both in religious values and the clergy's response to the challenge of heresy. When historians examine this piety, they are often more concerned with the increase in interest in pilgrimage or veneration of relics, outward manifestations of piety, than with the preparation for such works. Too often, the sermons of the late Middle Ages are discredited as simply 'moralistic.' In doing so, historians ignore the deeply mystical, affective pious tradition which is at least of equal importance. Marxist historians in particular try to see Humanism paving the way for early capitalism, changing the content of the church's message to address a more materialistic, secular, urban society.[54] An examination of piety *in parte* results in misleading conclusions, both about the nature of piety and the original protestant message. Catholic apologists Johannes Jansen and Vincent Hasak saw the Protestant Reformation as a negative force which destroyed the great flourish of devotional piety in the late Middle Ages.[55] A contemporary, Johannes Geffken, suggested that a medieval preoccupation with legalism translated a new emphasis on old testament law into a rigoristic, oppressive penitential system. Therefore Protestants preferred the new freedom from the confessional in reformed religion.[56] Twentieth-century scholars point to an insubstantial and formal religion, lacking in depth, that emphasized works as the way to heaven. Common people sought a personal identification with God, lacking in the old religion, which they found in the new Protestantism. Bernd Moeller calls the pious literature of the period 'lacking in originality and frequently in depth.'[57] Steven Ozment described late medieval piety as 'flawed, unsatisfying.' Despite the publication of pious literature, external religiosity 'failed to quiet inner anguish.' Ozment saw Protestantism as providing just the right antidote to such inner anguish, a religion based on faith and freedom from the oppressive confessional.[58] Peter Baumgart described the publication of *Ars moriendi* as indicative of a morbid fascination with death after the period of catastrophic plague in the fourteenth century.[59] The piety of the period was neither flawed, nor particularly morbid. An absence of central authority and spiritual leadership as well as a direction of religious practice away from the sacramental life of the church doomed

12 The six works of holy mercy. From Hugo von Trimberg's *Der Renner*, MS c. 1490. Here all six works are indicated: giving shelter to a pilgrim, clothing the naked, feeding the hungry, ministering to the sick and imprisoned, burying the dead.

late medieval piety to failure. Competition between mendicants and secular clergy for hearers confused people. Neither pope nor episcopate could provide effective spiritual leadership. The extension of monastic values to secular society by the *Devotio Moderna* was a reactionary move to save a system that had become obsolete. Although Gerson's idealism is laudable, the level of education required to comprehend his works had not been achieved. Such works could appeal to an urban, partly educated population, but probably not to the large number of illiterate folk. Scribner's work on the effect of Reformation woodcuts indicates the level of popular thinking. In attempts to combat heresy, preachers directed attention away from the institutional church and the sacraments by their mystical theology. They substituted extra-sacramental contrition for the sacrament of penance. There are good historical reasons for this and the Catholic Reformation, which arrived on the scene fifty years too late for reconciliation, did much to correct this situation. Despite attempts of individual, reform-minded clergy in the late Middle Ages, the church had no institution to hear popular complaints or redress grievances. Preachers were often alienated from their bishops bureaucratically and intellectually. The church also refused to take the demands of laypeople for a more active role in the

13 Title woodcut from Joseph Grünpeck's *Eine newe Ausslegung*, 1507, showing signs recently seen in the heavens: instruments of Christ's passion, monstrances, lances, rings around the sun, armies charging into battle. Also, unnatural events on earth are depicted, a mother kills her baby, a man hangs his brother, etc. all to prove the end of the world was nearing.

redemption of society seriously. Instead of accepting the challenge, the clergy retreated behind a wall of canon law. The 'inner anguish' which Ozment emphasizes may be more the result of increasing political and economic frustration vented against the privileged in society, than of inadequate preaching or unsatisfying penitential practices. There is no indication that the church was any more the object of discontent in the sixteenth century than were the privileges of the patricians.

Predictions of a nearing End helped to shape much of the rhetoric and demands for reform at all levels of the society in the late Middle Ages. The coming of the Anti-Christ was as real as the growing tension and frustration, created by the inability of the politically impotent in church and state to redress grievances. Late medieval Humanists were concerned with the historical fate of Christendom as well as reforming society. Since most believed that natural disasters came as punishment for human sins, then if people ended their sinful ways, the plagues, famines, and wars ought to end. Free will – to reform or not to reform – became a critical and decisive factor in determining not only the salvation of the individual, but also the historical fate of Christendom. Medieval people had to rely on the stargazers of their time for information about important changes and signs in the heavens, much in the same way we rely on natural scientists for information about the future. Falling stars, heavenly visions, and meteorites were frequently documented signs of historical change. Common people were particularly interested in these things. They are often noted in diaries and chronicles. *Prognostica* in German were popular publications, as people anticipating the End sought explanations from astrologers.[60] It was not unusual for curious people to take to the streets to preach the gospel of doom or the nearing end of the world, begging their fellow citizens to reform to prepare for that End. This *typus foedus*, who so frightened many in authority, usually came from poor artisans or peasants, was semi-educated, and took to the streets as prophet. Often called Beghards, these wandering prophets were occasionally, but never very systematically persecuted. Unlike wandering Franciscans, these preaching laypeople had no license from proper authorities, even though the content of their 'preaching' might be similar to that of the Franciscans. Why were these curious individuals not systematically persecuted? There are several reasons. Certainly biblical accounts of prophesying sons and daughters led people to expect that the poor and simple would proclaim the End. 'Preaching' was also difficult to define. Common people could discuss in public. The subject of their discussions might be theological and could not easily be forbidden, especially in a largely illiterate society where oral communication provided the most important means for the transmission of news and ideas.[61] Shut out from private taverns and drinking houses, common people might meet in homes and cellars for discussions, as the Waldensians did.[62] City authorities were watchful, lest millenarian ideas be used to encourage a rebellion against authority. City council records are full of complaints that common people read from books and commented on their readings. In the midst of one of the greatest millenarian scares in 1523–24, the city council of Ulm forbade discussions by common people in private houses, where they were reported to read the bible and comment on it.[63] The Karsthans, or man with a hoe, who took to the roads to share his ideas with passers-by is a common figure in late medieval literature.[64] Although these preaching common people were considered dangerous, there are too few records to say with any certainty how often they were apprehended. Clearly, in times of general millenarian scares and social

14 The *Karsthans* became a familiar symbol for the common man in the iconography of woodcut illustration in the early sixteenth century. Sometimes depicted with a hoe (*Karst*), sometimes with a flail (*Dreschflegel*), or occasionally with a scythe (*Sense*) he was used by Humanists as a model of common sense and wisdom, despite his peasant origins. Particularly after the *Bundschuh* rebellion, 1502 in the Diocese of Speyer, he served to warn those in power of the dangers of oppressing the lower classes in society.

15 The Persistence of Evil in the World. This illustration from Joseph Grünpeck's *Spiegel der naturliche himlischen//vnd prophetischen sehnungen aller trublsalen/*, 1522, presents examples to show the crying need for reform on a personal level, before society could be reformed: A man takes a bribe; a priest steals money from a pilgrim; a monk takes money from a cripple; a woman pours a bucket of water on a scholar's head, while he is mocked by two students.

unrest, such people were especially dangerous. Forbidding discussion was difficult to enforce.

Researching such spirited evangelists is difficult, partly because so few of their ideas were ever written down and because heresy trials focused on traditional heterodoxy, so that inquisition records remain singularly unreliable. We do know that wandering preachers often exhorted their listeners to repentance, appealed to an ideal medieval community of fixed values and duties, decried a world turned upside-down by countless innovations and declared that the End was near.[65] A time of particular disaster was not necessary to arouse such sentiments, nor were leaders of millenarian movements always from the uprooted poor, inspired by renegade members of the lower clergy as Norman Cohn suggested in his *Pursuit of the Millennium* (Oxford, 1957). The appeal of wandering preachers was very broad. Sociologist A. N. Wilder described their activity

16 The Sermons of the Drummer of Niklashausen. From Hartmann Schedel's *Weltchronik*, 1493. Hans Beheim preaches to a group of common people, encouraged by a Dominican, who whispers what to say into the simple man's ear. Next to the crowd is the Church of Our Lady, long a place of pilgrimage after Beheim's execution by the Bishop of Würzburg in 1476. Eventually the church had to be torn down to stop the pilgrimage.

as 'peculiar, in that they dramatize group hierophany in a situation of broken communities.'[66] Wander preachers longed for lost unity in society.

An early example of such a prophet is the preaching shepherd or drummer of Niklashausen. In the spring of 1476, a very simple layman called Hans Beheim began to preach in the village of Niklashausen in Franconia. Several chroniclers recorded the event and thanks to historian Klaus Arnold, we have a more accurate picture of this preaching shepherd.[67] The drummer exhorted his listeners to penance and confession. He told people to abandon luxurious fashion. Men cut off the pointed toes of their shoes and women cut their hair to be burned. The drummer himself threw his instrument into the fire.[68] The actual substance of his sermons is difficult to verify. From the inquisition, we know that his theological knowledge was weak. He hardly knew his Lord's prayer or credo. He criticized the hunting and fishing monopolies of nobles and monasteries. He opposed taxes that oppressed the 'common man.' He looked forward to a time of blissful equality. 'when the pope, emperor, princes, barons, knights, squires, citizens, farmers and the common man will be the same, equal, one not owning more than the other and all will work.'[69] The drummer was encouraged by a Dominican monk. Arnold thinks that the drummer was not a Waldensian or a Hussite, because he admonished his listeners to make pilgrimages, buy indulgences, and to venerate saints, but recent research has shown that there were some Waldensians who encouraged these works.[70] The drummer was apprehended by the Bishop of Würzburg; his listeners did not abandon him. 12,000 strong they marched on the fortress where the drummer was being held to demand his release. When the Bishop called out his army, the people retreated. The drummer was burned for his heresy, but the pilgrimage to Niklashausen did not end. Even though cities like Nuremberg forbade their citizens to make the pilgrimage, the church where the drummer preached had to be torn down. No investigation of the drummer's Marian vision ever took place. The inquisition did its best to make him into a Taborite heretic to obtain a judgment against him. Despite his lack of theological knowledge the drummer seems to have known the bible, which he often quoted. Beheim thought of himself as a martyr and declared that he was willing to die like the apostles.[71] He was perhaps a Waldensian; he was certainly popular. One account of the drummer noted that the women of Würzburg called the bishop evil for burning the drummer and interrupting the pilgrimage of Our Lady of Niklashausen.[72]

Unfortunately, few such lay evangelists have been well-documented. Many years later in Ulm, the shoemaker Sebastian Fischer described another wandering prophet, who was not apprehended:

In 1550, a man went to the imperial diet at Augsburg, dressed only in a loincloth, without a hat and barefoot. He worked for people who would hire him. He worked for a blacksmith, helped to cut wood and dig ditches, wherever he could find work. He was a diligent worker, but would not take money from anyone, only bread and food, but nothing more than necessary to nourish his body. The same naked man came to Ulm on the Sunday before St. Catherine's day [23 January 1550]. I saw him barefoot, bare-headed, with only a loincloth around his waist, yet the weather was very cold. Many wondered that he did not freeze to death and when people asked him why he was dressed like that, he replied that God had called him to castigate his body. People often spoke to him about this and that and he always gave an answer. When he thought something sinful, he scolded people and admonished them to improve. He said that God did not want such things left unsaid, that one must fear God and always have him before one's eyes. Many people liked him a lot, others less. He even went naked into the church to a sermon. He had long black hair like a gypsy, stayed around here for fourteen days, and then left for who knows where. I would say that he was about thirty or a little older.[73]

There are other mentions of such wandering prophets, but we know very little about their message. A farmer who preached at Wöhrd near Nuremberg during the imperial diet in 1524 drew even the emperor's attention.[74]

17 A pious peasant at prayer. Title woodcut from *Ain schone Ausslegug//*, 1523, *Meditations on the Our Father*, written by a peasant, who could neither read, nor write, but did preach. Attributed to Diepold Peringer, who began preaching in the village of Wöhrd near Nuremberg, until he was banned by the city council, then moved on to Kitzingen, then Rothenburg o.d. Tauber, then Jena, and back to Nuremberg, where he was again driven out and subsequently disappeared.

There is an interesting pattern in the message of lay prophets, who declared that in the last days even the stones would cry out for the truth of the gospel. Their protest calls for reform of society, not just the church or state, and a reform based on the gospel. The gospel is the *lex evangelica* of the *bonum communis*: one society, one people under evangelical law. Their social demands range from the restoration of lost privileges to establishing class equality in preparation for the coming judgment. Social and economic grievances must be seen in light of this ideal vision. They encourage their listeners to do penance and take up an active life of service. They appeal to the common man, who earns his bread by the sweat of his brow. They complain of unjust taxes, providing a basis for unity between urban and rural people. Common religious convictions, too, brought peasant and city protestor together in 1525. The period of economic decline and fear of the End hastened their demands for reform. Their rhetoric is occasionally revolutionary, but not universally so.[75]

Who might help the people who supported these wandering prophets? Certainly the church and state failed them. Many could only hope for a nearing End and a holy vindication.[76] An age of martyred apostles, when Christ gathered a following of poor and simple shepherds and fishermen, provided a romantic assurance of their own righteousness. People looked for prophets as a sign of the last days. For this reason, Luther was greeted by throngs of people on his way to Worms, even in Würzburg, where great crowds gathered to cheer him on. Other reforming preachers were prophets, too. Independence of episcopal jurisdiction protected both secular preachers in stipendiary posts and mendicants. The drummer was neither so sophisticated, nor so lucky. As soon as his Dominican preacher was gone, he made his progress to the flames. People sought out great preachers and prophets. Utz Rychssner, the weaver in this sample of lay pamphleteers, travelled long distances to hear popular preachers.[77] Preachers often befriended common people and worked with them, like the Dominican and the drummer. In Memmingen, Dr. Christoph Schappeler was a close friend to Sebastian Lotzer, the furrier, and godfather of his children. In Nuremberg, Hans Sachs and Andreas Osiander worked together on a pamphlet, like Zwingli and the potter, Hans Füssli in Zürich, or Johannes Wanner and Jörg Vögeli, who may have worked together on a pamphlet in Constance.[78] Prophets, preachers, and pious laypeople worked together in marking time to the End. The mere calling of simple laypeople to the gospel, to prophesy better than great men in the church, was a sign that Christ's return was imminent.

The Reformation was not popular simply because it provided a more psychologically suitable piety. The work begun by mendicant preachers in the fourteenth century was carried on by Humanists and members of the *Devotio Moderna* in the fifteenth and sixteenth centuries. A strong link between preacher and parish provided a common bond of interest in the Reformation. The vision of society that evolved from that bond was more sacred than secular, more medieval-communal than modern.[79] The destiny of the urban corporation in this world was a mirror of the same corporation as heavenly city. Reform in person and in the world was the formula for personal and societal salvation. If preaching common people had been a threat to the established order, publishing common people might present an even greater threat. Yet, well into the sixteenth century city councils were tolerant of active, even publishing laypeople, so long as they did not challenge established authority. Even when pamphleteers, like heretics before them, were charged with disturbing the peace, they were not burned, but exiled or warned. If they enjoyed the patronage of a parish preacher favored by their city council, warnings were more common than exile. By 1525, new prophecies of a nearing End, particularly the conjunction of Saturn and Mars in Pisces in February, 1524, brought common people to the defense of a reformation needed to prepare the bride of Christ. This same enthusiasm may have produced the peasant rebellion, joined by artisans in cities, that not only ended tolerance for publishing common people, but also ultimately ended municipal independence from territorial lords.

How did the leaders of the Protestant Reformation react to this new lay activism? Did they provide a place for a new lay apostolate in the church for the laypeople they so often encouraged? Chapter two explores the works of Luther, Zwingli, and Erasmus for an answer.

CHAPTER II

Reformers and laypeople

According to many historians of the Protestant Reformation, the Reformation was attractive to common people because it gave them a long-denied role in the government of the church, in its active life and work. What Waldensians and Hussites had so long demanded and martyred themselves for was finally achieved in Protestantism. According to one historian, 'the Zwinglian Reformation was primarily a reformation for the layman. The search for true religion was in the hands of the people.'[1] Other historians point to reformers' use of 'universal priesthood' (I Peter 2:4f.) as the reason common people preferred Protestantism. Luther encouraged the laity to take charge of church reform in his address *To the Christian Nobility of the German Nation*: 'everyone who has been baptized may claim that he has already been consecrated priest, bishop, or pope.'[2] Some historians point to mysticism in Erasmus' theology as the cornerstone of Anabaptist freedom.[3] All reformers were shocked by the events of 1525, when peasants and artisans used biblical justification to take up arms against church and state. Despite earlier enthusiasm for popular priesthood, both Luther and Zwingli closed the door to an active lay apostolate in 1525. Did they, in fact, address the demands of the laity effectively before 1525, or did they use common people as pawns in a political game to rally support for their reforms? Where did reformers stand on issues important to laypeople, expressed in their demands for an active life that led to heterodoxy and rebellion? If the continental Reformation did envision a new role for the laity in the church, what was that role?[4] Humanists often commended the piety and wisdom of common people. Did Luther, Zwingli, and Erasmus simply continue the same tradition, unaware of the implications of their rhetoric and its revolutionary potential for church and state? An examination of their attitude toward the simple layman and their vision of universal priesthood may shed some light on what some historians boldly call the 'Protestant revolution.' Was that 'revolution' engineered by reformers from above in a conscious plan to restore the role of the laity in the church, lost since the twelfth century?

Luther's most frequent use of the term 'laity' seems to confirm his own

18 Martin Luther, 1520. Title woodcut from the German edition of his pamphlet, *On the Babylonian Captivity of the Church*.

personal assumptions about the existence of hierarchical order in society and in the church. Even despite some uneasiness about the substance of hierarchical divisions, he always set the laity apart as a separate corporation within the structure of the church to exemplify the contrast between various established orders: clergy and laity, religious and layman, pope and layman, etc. He ranks laypeople below the clergy: 'neither could the inferior judge [his] superior, nor a layman rebuke a cleric, nor might a council reprimand the pope.'[5] Curiously, although he accords the laity an inferior position, he rejects any absolute subjection of the lay to the clerical estate. In the tradition of Northern Humanism, Luther constantly commends the piety of simple laypeople. He would consider one simple recitation of the Lord's Prayer by a layman more effective than all the canonical hours prayed by a priest.[6] To prove his point Luther went even further: 'for in order of succession, I would more easily accept condemnation or recommendation from a simple pious layman, than from our distinguished masters of Louvain and Cologne or all the universities gathered together into one body!'[7] In defending himself and his excommunicated colleagues (among them laypeople) in 1520, Luther states definitively that one ought to believe a member of the laity well-trained in scripture, who demonstrates superior capacity to reason, before any pope or council.[8]

Luther shows considerable respect for learned laymen who were competent to question the authority of the church. Thesis 81 makes specific reference to 'certe argutis questionibus laicorum.'[9] He insisted, too, that the church had an obligation to demonstrate in clear, understandable terms the actual value of indulgences, lest it risk ridicule of the pope and the church by the laity.[10] He recognized that an educated laity armed with scriptural knowledge presented a special challenge to the late-medieval church, an important impetus for his own reform. Should the church fail to take the questions of the laity seriously, it might risk the destruction of its unity. Luther respected learned laypeople and encouraged their criticism of the church.

In protest against the derogatory use of the term 'layman' in the sixteenth century, Luther assails his fellow clergy, accusing them of practically placing the laity outside the ecclesiastical body: 'here is the root of the terrible domination of the clergy over the laity. By virtue of a physical anointing, when their hands are consecrated, and by virtue of their tonsure and vestments, the clergy claim to be superior to the Christian laity, who have nevertheless been baptized with the Holy Spirit. The clergy can almost be said to regard the laity as lower animals.'[11] He also objected to the clergy's exclusive use of the term 'spiritual' to define their estate in the church and the world. Since all Christians might possess the spirit, he argued, it would be wrong to call the clergy 'of the spirit' and lay people 'of the world.' Like many before him, he insisted that the laity often possessed more spiritual gifts than the clergy. According to Luther, all members of the church militant were 'of the spirit,' especially since in scripture, laypeople had been the most important witnesses to Christ's mission.[12] Like Huss, with whom his enemies compared him, Luther

Ain Sermon von dem boch/
wirdigen Sacrament/des hailigen waren leich/
nams Christi. Vnd von den Bruderschafften
Doctor Martini Luthers Augustiner
zu Wittenberg. Für die Layen.

19 *A Sermon on the Blessed Sacrament, the holy and true Body of Christ. And about Brotherhoods.* By Dr. Martin Luther, Augustinian at Wittenberg. For Laypeople. 1520.

protested contemporary practices which reinforced divisions between the clergy and the laity. The eucharist ought to be given to the laity in both kinds. He rejected all superstitions that resulted from a conviction that laypeople were somehow unclean: 'formerly laymen used to administer sacraments as often as the priests do now. Yet the superstitions of our day regard it as a great offence if a layman touch the bare chalice, or even the corporal.'[13] Luther's plans to change the language of the mass from Latin, despite protests from many colleagues, were aimed at decreasing the tremendous division between laity and clergy within the church. He vigorously attacked the assumption that clerical status gave some special passport to salvation; especially the religious – monks and nuns – came under attack for insisting that monasticism offered a sure means to salvation: 'monks are no better than laypeople, since in the eye of God, there is no difference.'[14]

In early works, Luther saw his own mission direction toward the *vulgus laicorum*.[15] Like Gerson, Erasmus and other reform-minded theologians of the late Middle Ages, Luther was eager to communicate the plain truths of the gospel to common people in terms they might understand. In 1519 he prepared his own explanation of the Lord's Prayer for the 'simple laypeople... who seldom understand the arguments of sophisticated theology, certainly not the subtle arguments of scholastic theologians.'[16] He also prepared a prayer book, since 'one could not demonstrate the word and words of God to the common man either too much or too often.'[17] He considered his influence among common people as a yardstick for the effectiveness of his own personal mission: 'God willing, if I have served to improve the lot of one layman with my capacities throughout my entire life, I would be satisfied, give thanks to God, and allow all my books to be destroyed.'[18]

Education of the laity is a prerequisite in Luther's theology for re-integrating the layman into the church. His translation of scripture into German (he felt earlier translations inadequate) is closely linked with plans for the education of common people. 'Laymen must understand holy scripture in order to recognize their own sinfulness, repent and turn to God.'[19] The image of a layman armed with scriptural knowledge parallels his commendation of lay piety: 'for a simple layman who knows scripture is to be believed more than a pope or council which does not know scripture. Why? The holy scripture is the word of God: even if an ass should speak it, it must be heard above all the angels, who might not have the word of God, still less a pope or council without the word of God.'[20] To support and encourage laypeople, he presents copious scriptural evidence that Christ's early mission was directed toward saving common people. Luther states that Christ himself was a common man, 'a poor carpenter's son, then the son of a poor widow, who was not from the learned classes or a member of the clergy, but a layman and common apprentice.'[21] Indeed, the priests wondered that Christ, 'a simple common man, educated as a layman, could preach better than all the high priests and learned men.'[22] When Christ was born, angels did not announce his birth to the learned, but to poor shepherds who 'had such tremendous grace in heaven, yet on earth were nothing.'[23] In his own time, Luther saw the prophecy of Jeremiah (Jer. 5:4f.) fulfilled: 'that among the great men one would find less understanding and justice than among the laity and common people. Thus so is it now, when the poor peasants and children understand Christ better than the pope, the bishops, and doctors; everything is turned upside-down.'[24]

Luther seems less able to define a role for laypeople in his reform than to speculate on the potential of an educated laity. One notes in Luther's early theology an apparent contradiction when he discusses the nature of priesthood and the church. He states that the church ought to be governed by the clergy, i.e., those people in priests' and bishops' orders, yet he continues to insist that all men are priests; all share the same power to loose and bind according to the Petrine commission.[25] It would seem that all laypeople might act as priests and share in the government of the church, in preaching the gospel, and in celebrating and distributing the sacraments. Yet, when confronted by enthusiasts and Anabaptists, Luther clearly rejected this kind of ministry for the laity. His former enthusiasm waned. Why? Luther's theology separates priesthood from office to maintain order. He discusses the difference between priest and layman in his treatise *On the Freedom of the Christian Man*:

Injustice is done those words 'priest', 'cleric,' 'spiritual,' 'ecclesiastic' when they are transferred from all Christians to those who are now by a mischievous usage called 'ecclesiastics.' Holy scripture makes no distinction between them, although it gives the name 'ministers,' 'servants,' 'stewards' to those who are now proudly called popes, bishops, and lords and who should, according to the ministry of the word serve others and teach them the faith of Christ and the freedom of all believers. Although we are all equally priests, we cannot all publicly minister and teach. We ought not to do so even if we could.[26]

Therefore, the essence of the difference between cleric and layman is a special ministry, manifest in preaching and teaching. It is an office with a special teaching mission that seems to define priesthood: 'hence we deduce that there is... really no other difference between laymen, priests, princes, bishops, or in Romanist terminology, between religious and secular, than that of office or occupation, and not that of Christian status. All have spiritual status, and all are truly priests, bishops, and popes. But Christians do not all follow the same occupation. Similarly, priests and monks do not all work at the same task.'[27] He sees *raison d'être* for hierarchical order in a division of labor. Yet the power to make a priest, he insists, derives from the consent of the people: 'to put it more plainly, suppose a small group of earnest Christian laymen were taken prisoner and settled in the middle of the desert without any episcopally ordained priest among them; and they then agreed to choose one of themselves, whether married or not, and endow him with the office of baptizing, administering the sacrament, pronouncing absolution, and preaching; that man would be as truly a priest as if he had been ordained by all the bishops and popes.'[28] Obedience to clerical government, however, precludes any use of the liberties belonging to common people.

Confusion arises when Luther defined priesthood as simply an 'elected' office, rejecting any concept of sacrificing priesthood which would effectively set the priesthood apart from the laity. Although he claimed that he used the word 'priest' only for convenience to denote preachers, he states: 'if we were to call them regents of the church, no one would understand the term "regent".'[29] Luther, however, understood. By 'regents' he meant governors! He linked election and vocation closely: if a pastor should cease or refuse to preach, he automatically would relinquish his office and return to lay status. A layman might be called to preach, but couldn't do so for the preservation of good order, and because he was not elected.[30]

When discussing biblical references to universal priesthood, he stated that the priesthood to which Peter refers is Christ's. All Christians share this royal priesthood: 'this is the only right priestly office and can belong to no one else; thus all Christians are priests, all women are priests, be they young or old, lords or servants, married or single, learned or lay.'[31] Even despite his concern for order in the church, Luther develops potential priesthood for the laity: 'should anyone suggest to you that you cannot absolve, answer thus: "do you agree that I am a Christian? Yes. Would you agree that I can absolve? Yes. If I can absolve, then I can also preach!" Thus you will succeed, and he must admit that we all can absolve.'[32] Luther divorces potential possibility from the order presupposed by a necessary division of labor. He does not mean that everyone *may* exercise their actual power in the church. Yet, when discussing the role of lay pamphleteers, Luther did all he could to encourage them. He called the pamphleteer, Argula von Grumbach, 'discipula Christi,' and asked Spalatin to give her his kindest regards.[33] However, in his theological works he clearly gave two theoretical reasons why a layman might not exercise his or her priestly power. Under attack by his enemy Jerome Emser, Luther answered: 'to that extent you are in error, when you say that I have made all laymen into priests, bishops, and members of the spiritual estate, as if without a true vocation they might exercise this office at will; despite your piety, you omit what I also write, that no one should ever venture to do these things unless called, even in the direst need.'[34]

Another reason why laymen should not exercise their priestly power is the preservation of right order: 'every Christian has the same power as the pope, a bishop or a priest. Should you therefore hear confessions, baptize, preach, administer the sacrament? No. St. Paul says: "everything according to order." If everyone wanted to hear confession, what would it be like? Similarly, if everyone wanted to preach, who would listen? If they all preached at the same time, can you imagine the noise? Just like the frogs: Kar, ker, ker!'[35] Luther demonstrates quite clearly the consequences should this necessary order in the church be lost: 'what a wonderful example it would be if, when the pastor is preaching, someone interrupts him, and then another. Then they are in turn interrupted and instruct one another to be quiet. Then perhaps a drunk staggers out of a tavern with his mug into the church and wants to preach. Finally, even the women join in, first telling the men to be quiet, then each other... In what pigsty would it be worse than in our churches!'[36]

To reinforce order in the church, Luther integrated priesthood and office into the framework of his 'two churches teaching', a distinction between the church visible and the church invisible: 'thus we must differentiate between Christians here on earth, but not before God.'[37] In the non-tangible invisible church, all people are priests and share the same power to preach, teach, absolve, etc. In the sense that all people are one in Christ, the great high priest, they are all priests. Yet, in the visible church on earth, order is necessary. To preserve that order he rationalizes a strict division of labor that differentiates laypeople from clergy. Priests are called by God to a ministry of the gospel, the mark of their office. The laity may not exercise the power they have in fact, but may share in the choice of a suitable pastor to do so for them. The 'consensu communitatis au vocatione maioris' means a *de facto* surrender of power to the clergy.[38]

Since Luther's theology developed amidst opposition from both Rome and various 'sects,' he spent more time qualifying and explaining his ideas than developing new conceptual frameworks. In general, he rejected any speculative theology and genuine innovation. Despite his often radical statements about the power of the laity, in the final analysis, Luther did not stray far from traditional assumptions: his ministers were still in exactly the same position as the priests had been and the laity were still subject to them, even if Luther seemed to make the situation more acceptable with a pastoral office defined by service, rather than in terms of an exclusive sacrificing priesthood.

What seems peculiar in Luther's theology is that, despite his overwhelming concern for order, he continued to acknowledge a form of apostolic vocation for common people. He warned them: 'be watchful, laypeople, that very learned Romanists do not burn you as heretics, for the pope wants to make a courier or letter carrier out of you. However, you have good reason to call yourselves "*Apostolos*" in Greek which means "messenger" in German, to which the entire gospel stands witness.'[39] Luther remains ambiguous about the way in which laypeople might exercise their apostolate. He acknowledged their ability to preach, yet for order's sake, they ought not to preach in churches. Luther presented St. Stephen as a model for Christian laymen. He did not preach in the churches, but in the houses and markets: 'St. Stephen stands firmly here and gives power to preach to everyone by his example, wherever there are people to listen, be it in the houses or in the marketplace; he does not allow God's word to be confined to the stones and long vestments. However, he did not hinder the apostles in their preaching, but exercised his office by watching, preparing, and keeping silent, wherever the apostles themselves

preached.'⁴⁰ Luther chose Stephen as a model because he was a layman
and common man, not a priest. He even assigned common people a
liturgical role and suggested that they had a special mission to the poor:
'such people should be epistolers and gospelers, not the consecrated,
tonsured, people who wear dalmatics... but a common layman who is
pious, who carries a register of the poor, and controls the common purse,
giving to the needy where necessary; that is the real office of St. Stephen.'⁴¹
Yet out of fear of heresy and enthusiasm, he preferred that laymen fulfill
their apostolate in imitation of the virtues of Christ rather than in active
mission: 'believe in Christ and do for your neighbor just as you believe and
as Christ has done for you. This is the only true way to be pious and to be
saved, since there is no other way.'⁴²

Occasionally, he would make very radical statements. He suggested that
laypeople might confess to each other and give absolution. This must be
done privately, according to the Wittenberg theologian, so as not to disturb
the official order of the church: 'we all have the power to absolve, but
no one should take it upon himself to exercise it openly, other than he
who is chosen by the community. Secretely, however, I may use it; for
instance, when my neighbor comes to me saying, "friend, my conscience
is burdened, give me absolution." I would certainly do so, but it must
happen in secret.'⁴³ Luther ascribes the possibility of obtaining absolution
from another layperson to the freedom Christ earned for Christians by his
sacrifice on the cross, yet this freedom must be restrained within the
established order.

Luther presents a rather weak model for a lay apostolate, a model that
seems at odds with his own ecclesiology. He never officially releases
laypeople from the care of pastors whose advice and guidance they must
heed. Despite Luther's own enthusiasm for individual active laypeople, the
experience of Anabaptists and the Peasant Wars ended further theological
development of an active apostolate for the laity. By 1528, Luther decried
any form of street preaching. Luther followed secular authorities on this
issue. By 1525, preaching in the streets was immediately associated with
disobedience to secular authorities, whose responsibility it was to protect
the church as well as to maintain order. Luther himself was dependent
on secular authority for his personal safety. He hoped for some form of
lay apostolate to be realized in the future, but to speculate upon what form
that apostolate might take was too dangerous in his own time. He
applauded the activities of the 'common man' when he sought support
for his own reform. As soon as common, simple, laypeople threatened
established order, he immediately withdrew his support. Like Gerson a
century earlier, he realized that laypeople had a righteous claim to an active
apostolate, but disturbing established order was treachery. Beghards were
no more popular with the later Luther than Turks or Jews.

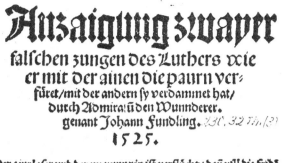

20 *A Report on the Two False Tongues of Luther, how he encourages the peasants with one and damns them with the other.* 1525.

Zwingli's attitude toward society and government was important in shaping his attitude toward the laity. The political leaders of the city of Zürich, among whom Zwingli had influential friends, were instrumental in carrying out the reformation of churches in that city. Even before Zwingli's evangelical reformation in Zürich, the city council exercised considerable control over church affairs. In the Zürich theologian's thought too, the civil magistracy played an important role in the direction of the reformation. Zwingli incorporated the civil magistracy into his ecclesiological theology: 'in the church of Christ both civil authority (*Obrigkeit*) and pastors (*Prophetenamt*) are necessary, even if the latter are indeed superior. Just as a man consists of a body and a soul (although

21 Huldrych Zwingli, by an anonymous artist, 1539.

the body is the inferior and more despicable part), thus the church cannot exist without secular authority, even if that authority commands such things which seem perhaps repulsive and far removed from spiritual things.'[44] Zwingli made nobles and patricians part of the church hierarchy, giving them important responsibilities: 'since, therefore, this church which is visible contains many rebellious and traitorous members who, having no faith, care nothing if they be a hundred times cast out of the church; there is no need of a government, whether of princes or nobles, to restrain shameless sinners. For the magistrate carries the sword not in vain.'[45] Zwingli does not specify, however, the exact relationship of these magistrates and urban patricians to pastors in the church. He makes little distinction between them. Instead of continuing the 'civilization' of the clerical order already begun in Zürich, he 'clericises' the magistrates: 'every bishop is an eye, every clergyman, every officer, who are nothing more than overseers; and the Greek word *Episcopos* is in German an overseer... their duty is to oversee the sheep, feeding, not flaying and shearing too closely and loading them with unbearable burdens, which is nothing else than giving offence, pointing out sins that are not present so that weak consciences are troubled and made to despair.'[46]

But do civil magistrates carry out a clerical function or are they just reinforcing the judgments of the clergy? Do city council and clergy perform identical functions in his church? According to Rudolph Staehelin and other Zwingli scholars, 'Zwingli gave up his original conception of the magistrates' role in the affairs of the church, and replaced it with a theocratic ideal parallel in its purpose to Israel of the old testament, when confronted with Anabaptists and enthusiasts.'[47] This old testament model embodies a legalistic system which would make the laity as much subject to the church as they were to civil magistrates. If one examines the real implications of Zwingli's use of the universal priesthood argument, one discovers, at best, an ambivalent, if not a very pessimistic view of laypeople actually assuming priestly function. The hierarchy in Zwingli's church did not evolve as a matter of convenience and general order, but was established on earth as an extension of God's authority:

let us examine first the words of Paul in Ephesians 4:11–14: 'and he [Christ] made some apostles, others prophets, still others evangelists, and some shepherds and teachers... ' Behold O' pious Christians: these offices were established by God in order to prevent many teachers from teaching. For it is impossible for just anyone to simply declare himself a teacher publicly. There are so many leaders, so many willing minds, that a hypocrite might hide himself very nicely.[48]

God's creation of a hierarchy prevented common people from exercising an apostolate in the church without the express permission of the hierarchy. Otherwise they would automatically change their status from the lay to the clerical order. Just as Zwingli assumed hierarchy was God-given, so was the status of laypeople ordained by God. Here Zwingli obviously differs from Luther: hierarchy in Luther's ecclesiology developed as a division of labor within the Christian community. For Zwingli, it was an established part of order in the mind of God.

Yet to support his own reform, Zwingli like Luther was 'optimistic' about the potential of the laity to understand and perhaps eventually even comment on the scriptures. Prophecy or the ability to comment on the scriptures is the central office of his clerical order. Like many contemporary Humanists, the Zürich reformer argued:

the common people, endowed with the harmlessness of the dove, will yield to the gospel alone, and the less vitiated with the dregs of human traditions, the more capable they are of receiving the heavenly teachings to which they flee for refuge in confidence, as to a sacred anchor. When they see the learned at swords' points with each other, they judge more clearly than the little scholars themselves, which side is right according to Christ, 'for the spiritual man judges all things,' (I Cor. 2:15) and they that are the really spiritual depend wholly on the spirit, that is the mind of God.[49]

He encouraged common people to write and publish pamphlets. He prepared an introduction to a pamphlet by the potter Hans Füssli, who answered an apology for the Roman church, published by one of Zwingli's opponents, Jerome Gebwiler, a Strasbourg schoolmaster. Zwingli wrote in his preface to that pamphlet: 'whoever understands Godly truth will have a breakthrough of God's own word in his heart. For this reason such people oppose the powerful in this world who ignore Christ's teaching. Just as Christ was killed, so also was he proclaimed by the fisherman to the world... therefore, when the powerful reject him, he will reveal himself to potters, millers, glasers, weavers, shoemakers, and tailors.'[50]

Although Zwingli states that the necessity for authority in the church applies specifically to the church visible, he also insists that the equality others attributed to the church invisible, is apparent even in the visible church.[51] Unlike Luther, Zwingli has little use for a 'two churches teaching.' Commenting on universal priesthood, he wrote: 'but Peter's real meaning was that the Lord Jesus Christ has called all Christians to kingly honor and to the priesthood, so that they do not need a sacrificing priest to offer on their behalf, for they are all priests, offering spiritual gifts, that is dedicating themselves wholly to God.'[52]

There is evidence to indicate that Zwingli was sure the end of the world was not far off. He tends to view the elect as synonymous with the visible church, and is more willing than Luther to realize some form of priesthood for laypeople within the church visible. When questioned about the rights of spiritual men, hence all people, to judge all things, Zwingli answered: 'whoever in the church hears an explanation of the heavenly word judges what he hears. However, that which he hears is not the word itself, from whose power we believe. For if we believed through the word which we hear read in the church, so all would truly believe. At some point then, we read or hear the word of faith, especially in our time, when every hall, even the forest itself rings with the gospel.'[53] Rather than rationalize the

22 *Answer by a Swiss Farmer, to the poorly supported propositions of Master Jerome Gebwiler, Schoolmaster in Strasbourg, which he published to protect the Roman church and its spurious claims.* With an introduction by Huldrych Zwingli. 1523?

universal priesthood as part of the invisible church which no one can see or have knowledge of except God himself, Zwingli places an important qualification on it: although everyone potentially may judge scripture, many people hear, yet do not believe. Only those who experience some mystical confrontation with the 'word of faith,' that is Christ, may judge or interpret scripture. Always returning to the necessity for order in the community, he excludes some people from exercising the powers implicit in priesthood.

Zwingli does not deny, however, that ideally all Christians have the power to interpret scripture. He refers back to a time in the church when everyone could prophesy:

> we see here clearly that originally the word of God was dealt with in a very different way than in our own day. For not only could prophets one after another speak about the word in the churches, but even the simple people were allowed to do so from their benches. If this custom had not gone into disuse, never would so many errors have been propagated in the Christian church. Eventually, the worst babblers mounted the pulpit which was reserved for the prophets especially; they claimed to speak from the voice of God, yet anyone who might disagree, or actually opposed them, was unmercifully beaten.[54]

An image of the primitive church so common to Humanist reformers in the sixteenth century was clearly present in Zwingli's mind. To recreate that primitive church Zwingli presents an especially interesting Humanist interpretation of the gift of tongues (I Cor. 14:5f.): he sees the gift of tongues as the ability to understand the language in which the scriptures were originally written:

> here Paul wishes that all Christians might know languages in order that they could prophesy. But he does realize that not all Christians have the ability to learn languages. However, he demonstrates what a useful thing it would be if everyone could understand God's word in the language in which it is written, desiring this gift for all men. He desires this in order that one might be able to prophesy, i.e., to interpret scripture and preach.[55]

The essence of 'priesthood' in Zwingli's theology is prophecy. He, like Luther, separates office and priesthood. Priesthood belongs to every Christian. Prophecy is the gift of the few: 'Thus to be specific... no one should be a prophet unless he can interpret the language of scripture.'[56] Zwingli, like Luther, refuses to use the word 'priest' because of its exclusive sacrificial connotation. Besides interpreting scripture, the prophet must tend his sheep, which, according to Zwingli, is preaching the gospel.[57] Externally, Zwingli's concept of priesthood conforms to Luther's, yet clearly the absence of traditional sacramental theology separates him from Lutheran tradition. Zwingli's insistence on 'local presence' and temporal limitations confine his concept of priesthood to a ministry of the word only.

Vocation plays an important role in defining priesthood. One needs a double vocation, an internal and an external calling to become a prophet: 'there is an internal and an external vocation. The Anabaptists have no internal vocation because they are revolutionaries and are opposed to peace. They also lack the external calling, because they have taken the office (of prophecy) for themselves, without either having been chosen by the community or having experienced a miracle of God.'[58] Like many preachers centuries before him, he assumed that meditation on scripture would reveal God-given order. Vocation occurs as a result of action by the spirit, which comes not just from hearing the word preached, but an affective action of Christ on the heart of the believer. Although Zwingli's use of the 'spirit' often brought him dangerously close to Anabaptist teaching, when accused by his enemies, Zwingli distinguished false from genuine inspiration. How does one know that the spirit in a man is indeed genuine? 'For God is not a God of quarrels and division, but one of unity and peace. Therefore wherever true faith is, one recognizes the heavenly Spirit.' The action of the spirit alters the character of a man; the vocation itself raises a man to the prophetic office:

the more unskilled a man is in human devices and at the same time devoted to the divine, the more clearly that spirit informs him as is shown by the apostles and by the foolish things of this world which God has chosen. And as it is a spirit of unity, harmony, and peace, not of strife and dissension, it will inspire even the most ignorant, so be it that they are pious in such a manner that they will understand the scriptures in the plainest way according to God's purposes.[59]

Like Luther, Zwingli distinguishes potential possibility from reality; even the most ignorant can prophesy, providing he can understand scripture; the spirit imputes knowledge to man, which brings him from ignorance to wisdom, from the laity to the prophetic office.

Zwingli denies the sacramental character of the priesthood for the same reasons that Luther does. He calls the indelible character transmitted at ordination simply human invention. The reference to the laying-on of hands in the new testament was simply a sign that these men had the gift of tongues, i.e., the linguistic ability to study and interpret scripture. Preaching the gospel distinguishes a bishop, not the act of consecration.[60]

Despite the possibility that an ignorant man might be inspired to prophesy, Zwingli's attitude toward the street preachers is identical to Luther's: they break the established order given by the apostles. They act in an un-Christian fashion. Zwingli described the consequence of such disorder in the churches, when a common man demanded the right to preach:

A weaver in a certain town where there was a pious and competent evangelist or bishop, had the audacity to assume the pulpit just as the pastor entered. The weaver said, 'I want to preach.' In order to avoid confusion, the pastor agreed. The weaver began to read I Tim. 4, which the honest people had already understood from their true pastor's teaching. They began to grumble over the boldness of the weaver. Soon he came to the place in verse 2: 'They have a seared conscience.' He said, 'I don't understand that.' The pastor interrupted: 'Then stop and I will interpret it for you.' Just then the honest people began to shout, 'Get down from the pulpit.' In response the pastor said: 'Had I commanded him to step

down, it would have aroused some suspicion; so you have told him to step down.'
Thus the weaver left the pulpit.[61]

Although Zwingli disliked street preachers, he never excluded the possibility
that laypeople might preach and interpret the true meaning of the bible.
The Swiss theologian considered the essence of holy scripture to be a series
of plain truths comprehensible to even the simplest people. Although
Zwingli accorded his clerical order the exclusive privilege of preaching,
within the individual Christian community, laypeople might prophesy. He
was critical of street preachers because they left their own parish churches
and intruded in the affairs of other Christian communities. He gives
directions whereby a layman in his own parish church could be allowed
to comment on the scriptures:

> when the prophets have spoken one after the other in correct order, a layman
> sitting in the congregation to whom God has revealed an understanding of
> scripture, may be allowed to speak. Indeed, right order must be observed, so that
> when someone else begins to speak, the former will be silent. Also, while someone
> is speaking, others must wait their turn when he is finished. You see, all men may
> preach in the church, but only after the prophets, and only then when the prophet
> has neither understood the scripture, or perhaps not explained it clearly. For this
> reason those who pretend to be apostles or prophets do not follow the apostolic
> custom as explained in scripture. They do not stay within their communities, but
> run to other churches and speak in the absence of any prophet.[62]

The contradiction between potential and reality, more correctly the risk
of disturbing established order, makes Zwingli's attitude as ambiguous as
Luther's, although he speculates beyond Luther's limits. His lay apostolate
is based on scripture and implements the universal priesthood within the
church visible. At the same time, Zwingli democratized the liturgy, dividing
traditional clerical responses between the clergy and laity.[63]

Even though Zwingli opens the possibility for laypeople to preach in the
church, his plan seems less 'apostolic' since individual laymen are
confined to the parishes, unable to preach everywhere, a privilege granted
only to official clergy. On the surface his ecclesiology is similar to
Anabaptist teaching. When confronted with their enthusiasm, however,
he referred to the hierarchy which policed the church for notorious sinners
and those who rejected clerical authority. Zwingli's plan was dominated
by an optimism that extended Christ's powers to all men, yet limited these
powers in order to preserve what Zwingli considered 'apostolic order.' His
tendency to identify the elect with the visible church forced him to
recognize a lay apostolate, yet the presence of evil in the church prevented
him from practically realizing that apostolate.

Possibly Zwingli's eschatological sense encouraged him not only to
endorse universal priesthood within the visible church, but also to identify
the elect within the church visible. When Christ returned, the visible

church and invisible church would be united. According to Christ's promises, those who accepted his gospel and maintained faith in his resurrection would be saved. Zwingli's church claimed to be the true church of the gospel, since its teachings were based on scripture, not human traditions. Zwingli attempted to prepare Christians for Christ's return, since all around him he saw signs of the end: false prophets, persecution, division and strife. Therefore he admonished Christians to 'live as innocently as possible... in order that after death we may enjoy eternal peace with God.'[64] The kingdom that Christ would establish would see the final realization of universal priesthood, making all hierarchy unnecessary. Only as the elect might be constituted within the church visible could a semblance of the reality to come be perceived. Zwingli's own political situation both within the canton of Zürich and with the magistrates of the city of Zürich was much too precarious to consider a further development of a theology of the spirit in a lay apostolate. He was willing, however, to recognize the positive influence of the spirit on poor simple laypeople. In his introduction to Hans Füssli's pamphlet, Zwingli commented: 'for he will reveal himself to the children... and destroy the wisdom of the wise... in order to shame those who call themselves wise.'[65] In general, Zwingli's reform suffered from the same political problems Luther's did. Any mention of the word 'spirit' was suspect of enthusiasm, synonymous with political and ecclesiastical anarchy. Zwingli might envision a democratization of parish churches, but dared not carry his ideas to their ultimate conclusion.

Erasmus was more interested in educating laypeople than in speculating about a new lay apostolate. He blamed the church for the Anabaptist and peasant uprisings in 1525. The church had failed common people. Erasmus did not encourage laypeople to take the Reformation into their own hands, to preach and teach, only to withdraw such liberties later, insisting that they conform to God-given order and be obedient. Disruptive behavior was the result of a poorly prepared conscience, a soul not united with Christ, a piety that did not produce Christian virtue.[66] It was their lack of proper preparation and misdirected piety that had caused the disturbance of right order. Erasmus did not blame the peasants for breaking established order, since he was convinced that bishops and priests and monks also were guilty of abandoning the proper order of the church. Bishops created new feast days, which encouraged people to sin. Monks insisted on special status which had never in the tradition of the church been granted them. To Erasmus, all Christians were 'religious' and no particular group had a special claim on salvation.[67] It was the unreformed church which was responsible for the bloodshed of 1525.

Erasmus wanted laypeople to be Christian workers more than he wanted them to be active, working Christians. He wrote in 1522: 'I want every

23 Erasmus of Rotterdam by Albrecht Dürer. 1526.

shoemaker, day laborer, weaver and farmer to read the gospel and epistles
of St. Paul... May God grant that the farmer at his plow... can speak
or sing of the gospel, or the artisan in his workshop, or the wool weaver
at his spool, or the shoemaker at his last.'[68] The ability to speak and sing
of the gospel, he insists, depends on the arrangement of reason in the
soul. Erasmus shared the mystical affective tradition of the late Middle
Ages, which is the reason he insisted that proper preparation resulted in

24 *On Pilgrimage. An admonition on where Christ and his kingdom can be found.* By
Erasmus of Rotterdam, 1522.

proper fruits of the spirit. In his own division of man into fleshy and
spiritual nature, he emphasized spiritual preparation of the soul as
necessary to produce positive good works. The arrangement of reason in
the soul determined human behavior. Erasmus calls lust for power and
envy *morbi animi*.[69] It was this sickness of the soul which caused revolt,
but peasants were no more guilty of this illness than many bishops or civic
leaders. Leaders of society were even more to blame for neglecting their
responsibility to common people in their pursuit of luxurious living and
power. It was their responsibility to shepherd the *infirma plebs* who were
incapable of governing because their souls were unskilled. It was for civic
leaders in particular that Erasmus prepared his *Enchirideon militis Christiani*

in 1504, a handbook which would guide them upon the proper path.[70] Erasmus did not deny the basic corruptibility of human nature, but created instead an optimistic vision of aristocracy, who could use properly prepared reason in the soul as a means to worldly wisdom: like many fellow Humanists, he saw the production of virtue as the paramount object of the religion upon which just government could be built. He saw no reason to over-emphasize faith as the virtue-producing medium, as many reforming colleagues did: this emphasis made men lose sight of the causes of spiritual preparation and the effect desired, proper behavior and good works. An over-emphasis of faith led to lack of humility and pride, which were un-Christian. In a treatise against pilgrimage, he told common people: 'if you want to go to Christ, do it within yourselves, for there is nothing deeper in yourself than your own *gemüthe*.'[71] His emphasis on the positive attributes of the human will did not impress Luther, who wrote about Erasmus' piety: 'such shortsighted piety any Jew or heathen might invent, who didn't even know Christ... as if man could know God alone of his own power without Christ.'[72] Erasmus saw no particular reason to over-emphasize man's sinful nature. He, like many adherents of the *Devotio Moderna* before him, assumed positive human potential for laypeople and an important role for them in a reformed church, which in turn would produce a reformed society. From the walls of his university, most of the evil in society seemed created by the church's failures. He even went so far as to say that true Christians did not raise arms against each other and did not go to war. The Turkish advance on Europe and the emperor's call to arms were alarming signs that the church had failed to reform itself.[73] The Turkish advance came to remind Christians of their distance from the only true law, the *lex evangelica*.

Although Erasmus never denied the effectiveness of sacraments in the process of preparing the human soul, he, like many reforming clergy before him, emphasized personal preparation by meditation of scripture. He applies to scripture the same dichotomy he imposes on human nature. Scripture has a literal and spiritual content: the spiritual is superior to the literal and needs interpretation.[74] For this reason the sermon and learned commentary on scripture seemed the safest means to transmit the grace-giving power contained therein. As sacraments are to the next life, so scripture is to this life for Christians, Erasmus insists. *Sola scriptura* was not his means to ultimate salvation for common people, but it is clearly his means to encouraging virtue and good works. Erasmus sees Christ as the substantial gift of meditation on scripture who accomplishes a conversion of the human heart: 'it takes on this [spirit] and is changed so much that it is transformed in Christ, when it imbibes his spirit, as it searches around, thirsting everywhere to be made united at last in the law of the lord.'[75] The works of love which this conversion can produce are those works which could reform society. It is this conversion by meditation of scripture that is the core of Erasmus' reform program, which he directed in particular toward laypeople. The church could only accomplish reform by proper examples set by church leaders, a return to the principles of the gospel, and an educational system which could raise laypeople to the level of the church. The point of departure for Luther and Zwingli's message to common people, was to bring the simple truths of religion to the level of the common people. Erasmus tried to raise common people to the level of the church by using the affective pious tradition which had often been endorsed in the past as a means to reform. Erasmus had little patience with churchmen who refused reform. Despite frequent disagreement with Luther and Zwingli, he insisted that both reformers intended to restore former liberties to the people.[76] This constitutes an interesting parallel to artisans' demands for a restoration of their former economic liberties. Just as civic authorities, patricians in particular, had used their office to distance themselves from the people they governed, so church leaders too fell victim to the materialism of their time. As civic leaders in many cities sought to civilize the clergy and restore order, so Erasmus, reflecting a much older tradition, sought to evangelize the world as a means to a restoration of lost liberties.

Several editions of the *Enchirideon* were published in Erasmus' own time, in Latin and German. This contained his pious program for laypeople, indicating the importance of internal preparation, knowledge of the gospel, and good works. It was supplemented by several pamphlets, mostly sermons and letters for the edification of common people. The theology of St Jerome is Erasmus' constant guide in these pamphlets.[77] Relying on Jerome, and occasionally Augustine and Ambrose, Erasmus took the message of his reform to the people. Although he may not have been in sympathy with Luther and Zwingli's break with Rome, he shared their vocation to edify common people and their impatience with a lazy clergy. He attacked the church hierarchy in his pamphlets, particularly bishops and monks. The main object of this attack was human teaching which had been raised above the gospel. In frustration he noted: 'what could I say about the burden of human teaching that Augustine didn't say hundreds of years ago? What would he say... to all our ceremonies, customs, the government of princes, bishops, and popes?'[78] He disliked many contemporary practices in the church. He asked bishops to exercise their office of love, not to ban Christians who didn't fast on prescribed days and not to set up so many feast days to give common people occasion for sin. He asked them not to make new laws and to return to older practices, not to appoint so many inexperienced stupid priests and to let these priests have one wife, so as to encourage chastity, not promiscuity. He chastised bishops who preached the miraculous nature of relics and encouraged pilgrimage like the Pharisees. Erasmus insisted that the clergy's responsibility was to prophesy and to interpret scripture in sermons.[79] He told his readers to study the gospel instead of going on a pilgrimage: 'I want to admonish all Christian people to go to the louder, purer font of Christ, the holy gospel which brings a purer conscience and clean hearts.'[80] Erasmus was critical of veneration of the saints which seemed to have replaced Christ in the church. He disliked so much emphasis on music in churches at the expense of sermons. Secular music had invaded the churches with bawdy songs more appropriate for boys and whores in theaters.[81] Using St Jerome's theology, he constantly compares the law of the old testament with the freedom of the new. The Jews of the old testament seemed almost better off to him than contemporary Christians: so many laws were made to oppress the poor common people. Old testament Jews could wear any clothes; in the sixteenth century there were so many clothing regulations. Jews had few fasts and if someone did not fast, that person was not threatened with the pain of eternal damnation.[82]

As a true Humanist, Erasmus had much to say in his pamphlets about vain monks and scholasticism. He blames Averroes in particular for introducing Aristotle to the church.[83] He thinks that philosophy is a valid study in its own right, but Christians should not seek Christ among philosophers. St Jerome insisted that pagan philosophy had nothing to do with scripture. If Benedictines, Franciscans and Dominicans followed the rule of their patrons, then all Christians should follow the rule of their patron, the *lex evangelica*. He tells people to read the gospel even if they do not understand it, with assurance that it will produce good works. Without question or qualification, he recommends reading the bible as the best medicine for the soul.

What Erasmus had to say to common people was not very innovative; his contribution lies perhaps in the parity he assigned to the importance of meditation as personal preparation and his criticism of the established church for failure to reform. In many ways his message is not essentially different from Luther or Zwingli. However, because Erasmus did not have to create a new model for a reformed church or gain support for his own particular kind of reform among common people, he was not forced to lead common people down a golden path and then abandon them when they took their freedom to teach and preach seriously. This consistency left a lasting impression in the minds of common people. The shoemaker–chronicler Sebastian Fischer wrote in his diary in Ulm in 1551: 'this Erasmus ordered in his will that all his possessions be given to the poor, the sick, the helpless, poor abandoned women, and young boys in need of money to study. This Erasmus was a very learned man and since Christ's birth, never has such a man come into this world.'[84]

Luther, Zwingli, and Erasmus recognized that the traditional separation between clergy and laity, re-enforced by new regulations which seemed to draw them even further apart, was contrary to the intentions of the apostles. They were aware that the apostles intended at least a division of labor among Christians, which was exclusive to the extent that it recognized the positive attributes of some and the deficiencies of others. Luther and Zwingli commended the piety of simple people as a model; Erasmus, perhaps more effectively, saw the need for proper education based on an already established pious system and linked directly to the gospel as a means to reform. Luther and Zwingli adventurously tread on very thin ice. Both were forced to reconcile Peter's statements about universal priesthood with the obvious divisions intended by the apostles. Luther did so quite successfully with his metaphor of the church visible and invisible. Zwingli was perhaps less successful at rationalizing the divisions. He theoretically maintained a solid hierarchy on one hand, and a democratic parish system on the other. Zwingli made perhaps the most advanced and boldest plans for the participation of the laity in parish government. Erasmus assumed that slow and determined reform in the church underwritten by scriptural piety would eventually raise laypeople to the level where actual participation in church government might be possible. All of these reformers acknowledged the fact that the key ingredient necessary for the realization of an effective lay apostolate was missing: accurate, uniform interpretation and teaching of scripture and sound education. To this end they worked extensively, preparing sermons and pamphlets for common people to read. Yet together they could reach no agreement on uniform teaching, making the unity they anticipated impossible. Luther became more and more conservative. Zwingli's life ended prematurely on the battlefield. Erasmus withdrew into the scholarly world where he was less open to attacks by vicious opponents.

CHAPTER III

Memmingen: a furrier, a preacher, and a peasants' war

Memmingen was a small city compared to the rapidly growing trade centers, Nuremberg and Augsburg. With a population of only about 5,000 in 1500, this imperial city played a greater role in the powerful Swabian League, where it was ranked just behind Ulm and Augsburg, than it did in the general economic activity of the empire.[1] Memmingen was still very rural in character. It never lost its economic ties to surrounding villages. Yet despite its size and rural character, the city's location just beyond the Alpine borders of the Swiss cantons made it a natural transfer point at the junction of the North–South trade axis – Salzburg, Augsburg, Nuremberg, Frankfurt – and the north-west route – Lyons, Basel, Amsterdam – which brought merchants in the town to rapid prosperity. Trade revenues between 1450 and 1490 made Memmingen blossom. Its city squares and churches were improved. A few *novi homines* who made their fortunes from trade gained entry to the ranks of worthy families. Although free to choose its own mayor, free of any imperial or princely interference since 1347, Memmingen's mayor continued to be a member of a traditional worthy family well into the sixteenth century.[2] Compared with other imperial cities, the contest over city government, between new patricians and old families, between city council and guilds was not acute. Since 1400, the city had been divided into twelve corporate guilds. Memmingen's city government followed a blueprint common to other imperial cities: the smaller council consisted of the mayor, twelve councilors, twelve guildmasters and the council secretary. This smaller council actually governed the city. The greater council included committees of eleven from each of the twelve guilds, bringing the total number of participants in the greater council to 158.[3]

Memmingen shared economic decline after 1490 with other smaller imperial cities. Its weavers could hardly compete with the great textile producers of Venice and Lyons. To ensure the prosperity of weavers within the city, the weavers of villages outside the city were usually excluded from the yearly markets in Memmingen. Guilds tried to maintain their economic prerogatives at a time when the changes in politics had direct international

25 Memmingen. Detail from *Topographia Sueviae*, 1643. St. Martin's Church, where
Christoph Schappeler was preacher.

economic implications, often beyond the comprehension of civic leaders.
As in other parts of the empire, economic decline was borne primarily by
the lower classes. Those who had no facility to cope with changes in
international trade suffered most. A comparison of tax lists demonstrates
this: in 1450, one-fourth of the wealth belonged to 43 citizens; 13 people
could be classified as rich. A considerable 'middle class' could claim
approximately half the wealth, leaving about 731 citizens listed as
'have-nots.' By 1521, the number of rich people in Memmingen was
reduced from 13 to 6. The 'have-nots' grew to 1,206. For this reason,
in 1524, the city council was forced to reduce the tax burden on individual
citizens by half.[4]

The church in Memmingen was carefully watched and to some extent
controlled by the city council. The clergy consisted of 52 secular priests,
28 monks and 50 nuns. Several hospital foundations paid taxes and there
were limits to the amount of property monasteries could inherit without
paying taxes. Although the city itself was surrounded by wealthy and very
powerful monasteries (the Benedictine foundations of Ottobeuren and
Kempten, Ochsenhausen and Rot) monastic organizations played a minor
role within the city walls. The only significant order in the city was a

hospital order from St Antoine near Vienne, to whom the right of appointment to the parish church of St Martin had been given by Frederick II in 1215.[5] The Order of St Anthony paid taxes as well. The city's other parish church, dedicated to St Mary, was less prosperous, located in a poorer section of the city. St Martin's parish was patronized by more wealthy citizens. The wealthiest family, Voehlin, well connected with trading houses in the Netherlands, endowed a perpetual mass and preachership at St Martin's in 1479, with the permission of the prefect of the monks of St Antoine. The preacher, to be appointed by the head of the Voehlin family, was to be a doctor of theology or hold a baccalaureate in holy scripture.[6] The clergy of St Mary's constantly complained of the loss of revenue to St Martin's, since sermons there drew so many hearers from the lower classes. In Memmingen, on the eve of the Reformation, there were two practical issues of major public concern before the city council: the tax burden, how to fairly distribute it in the midst of depression and inflation, and how to keep lands within the taxable category to help continue services and maintain fortifications. With the growing number of poor, fear of an uprising, such as the one which occurred in nearby Ulm in 1516, was in the mind of every councillor in Memmingen.

The special plight of weavers seems to be an important key to under-standing the progress of the Reformation.[7] The Memmingen city council, although opposed by the weavers' guild, decided to admit village weavers from outside the city to the yearly market in 1518, a step taken to relieve their poverty. At the same time the city council forbade contact between its weavers' guild and the rebellious weavers of Ulm. City council members tried to be both charitable and wary of potential artisan revolt. Among weavers, reformed theology and radical solutions for social problems seemed to co-exist. The increasing mechanization of the weaving industry as well as the growth of prosperous weaving centers in Flanders, Lyons, and Northern Italy made competition for survival acute in areas which before the sixteenth century could depend on the local market: as cities grew more prosperous and competition became international, demands for finer luxury textiles from Venice or the Netherlands placed weavers, like those in Memmingen, in a precarious position. Protected by their guild, weavers in the city tried to prevent competition from outside. At the same time, since textiles were among the most important trade commodities, the number of weavers to join a competitive market with hopes of financial success increased. In Memmingen, for instance, the number of weavers in the weavers' guild nearly doubled between 1420 and 1530, while most other guilds stayed the same or declined.[8] Depression reaped a particularly bitter harvest among artisans whose expectations were far beyond their ability to achieve.

The growing tension between artisans and city council might have eased, if city council and preacher had cooperated. However, the preachers appointed by the Voehlin family at St Martin's parish were more eager to curtail city council attempts to interfere in church affairs than to take positive steps in the interest of the greater community. The first preacher in Memmingen, Dr Jodokus Gay, tried to prevent the yearly swearing of oaths of loyalty by the greater council in the church. Gay also preached against city marriage laws. He tried to extend the right of asylum for criminals in churches to the period after the criminal had left the church. He declared that city fathers were *de facto* excommunicated if they continued to tax church properties and prevent the clergy from selling properties willed to them for revenue. In Memmingen, the church enjoyed tax freedom on much of its property. At the same time, to pay for internal improvements, the city council tried to increase taxes on the clergy for use of bridges, city water rights, and on goods produced by the clergy and sold for profit. Dr Gay took the taxation problem to the Archbishop in Mainz, who referred it to Pope Julius in 1504. By 1507, the pope had not yet decided; the council took recourse to the Bishop of Augsburg; when Augsburg refused to reply, it appealed to the emperor. The Emperor Maximilian forbade Dr Gay to preach against the city council, on the grounds that it encouraged public disturbances. The disagreement over taxation of the clergy lasted until Gay's death in 1512.[9] The new appointment to the preachership, the choice of the Voehlin family, Dr Christoph Schappeler (+1551), a Basel-trained preacher from the Latin school in St Gall, was equally difficult. Schappeler proved to be an even greater annoyance to the city council. In 1516, Schappeler was accused of preaching against wealthy citizens in Memmingen who exploited the poor. The minutes of the city council contain frequent mention of Schappeler's critique of the rich and his encouragement to common people to take matters into their own hands. The city council sent its secretary and two councillors to persuade Schappeler to end his dangerous sermons in 1521. There is good reason to believe that the city council feared Schappeler because of his popularity among Memmingen's poor.[10] Schappeler did not choose respectable people as his friends. He was known to befriend poor artisans and to encourage them to preach and teach. It is interesting that not until November, 1521 did the preacher declare himself in favor of a Lutheran reformation. It may have been the furrier, Sebastian Lotzer, who convinced him to do so. Lotzer was both alarmed and angry about the imprisonment of a lay preacher (called Karsthans) who was apprehended by the authorities in his native village, Horb-am-Neckar, which lay in Habsburg territory.[11]

Lotzer began his career as a pamphleteer to protest the decision of secular authorities to procede against a wandering evangelical preacher.

26 Interior of St. Martin's Church, showing the choir stalls from 1507, altar from 1867, and frescos from 1588.

Schappeler encouraged him to publish a pamphlet in the spring of 1523. The Bishop of Augsburg, under whose jurisdiction the city of Memmingen fell, wrote to the city council that 'ignorant laypeople were being converted to Luther's teachings and were attracting others.' The priests at St Mary's parish submitted a list of suspect laypeople to the city council, listing several weavers and the furrier, 'Bastian Lotzer.'[12] Aware of the important social and political consequences of whatever action it might take, the city council hesitated, waiting for other cities in the Swabian League to respond. This hesitancy worried more conservative council members. Artisan revolts were dangerous and often led to bloody confrontation. Although under pressure, the city council refused to take any initiative in reforming the church. In 1523 it ordered the usual processions

27a Memmingen. Detail from *Topographia Sueviae*, 1643. Our Lady's Church, where most of the protests against clergy loyal to the old church took place during the Reformation.

and prayers to the saints for favorable weather on the rogation days.[13]

On 30 July 1523, a group of citizens stopped Jacob Megerich, rector of St Mary's parish church, and tried to force him to acknowledge a list of grievances prepared by the Latin school teacher, Paul Hoepp. The city council wrote to the clergy of the city 'so that you and your preachers do all you can to prevent the active organization or divisions among the laypeople, which will lead to great disturbances and terrible dissent.'[14] When the Bishop of Augsburg excommunicated Lutheran preachers, members of the council were, for the most part, behind Schappeler's principles, though still suspicious of his popularity with the lower classes and wary of his radical tendencies. The mayor, secretary, and another councillor subsequently resigned from the council.[15]

In 1524, the city council even tolerated a few conservative changes in church practices. They also forced the clergy to swear an oath of loyalty to the city, to be subject to secular courts and pay more city taxes.[16] In a letter of defense to the emperor, the council noted that 'up till now, we have heard nothing but the plainer, clearer holy gospel preached,' and that the sacrament, given to the parishioners of St Martin's parish in both kinds by Schappeler, was appropriate, 'for we believe that when Christ gave the sacrament at his last supper, he gave the true bread of heaven and the blood of his lively word, and the command to take and enjoy both in faith.'[17]

In protest against such changes, Megerich and his clergy decided to prevent any evangelical infiltration of St Mary's Church. On Christmas afternoon 1524, an evangelically minded chaplain was scheduled to preach the vesper sermon at St Mary's. By mid-afternoon, a large crowd had gathered to hear the chaplain. The clergy decided to extend the vesper rites to prevent the sermon. And as the thurifer attempted to proceed through the nave of the church to cense the people, the assembled crowd blocked the procession and began to heckle them. The terrified clergy were forced to retreat into the choir. Only the merchant guildmaster, Hans Schultheiss, could calm the crowd. Mounting the pulpit, he announced that the city council would sponsor a disputation between the clergy of both churches. Schappeler submitted seven articles for debate.[18] As propaganda for the evangelical party, Sebastian Lotzer published his *Apology*, insisting that the clergy of St Mary's were responsible for the incident, since they did not allow the word of God to be preached.[19] When after five days the debate remained unresolved, the city council sought advice from other imperial cities experiencing similar problems. As 'evangelical' ideas spread to the countryside, rural disturbances became more frequent. The city council had to appoint a special court to hear peasant grievances. Schappeler was asked to mediate disputes; he agreed, insisting that only holy scripture be used as a basis for negotiation. Both city council and peasants agreed.[20] However, when other imperial cities appealed to the Swabian League to solve the disturbances, Memmingen decided to let the League itself assume responsibility for mediation.[21]

Even before the disturbances in the church, the question of a more effective means of forcing change on the old church occupied the minds of the common people in Memmingen. In July 1524, a group of citizens decided not to pay their tithe, since the bible did not expressly order them to do so. The farmers of Steinheim, one of the villages belonging to Memmingen, refused to pay both their pastor and their share of the local hospital tax. The city council then sent a warning that refusal to pay taxes to the church would result in serious punishment. A baker, Hans Heltzlin, refused to pay and was imprisoned in Memmingen. A large group of artisans in Memmingen protested to the city council, demanding the release of Heltzlin and the freedom to refuse the requisite tithe. Added to their protest was a demand that the gospel be preached in all churches, 'without any human additions.' For fear of an uprising, the council capitulated.[22] Many patricians feared this action, a sign of weakness in leadership which could incite the wrath of the emperor. The disunity of the city council freed Schappeler to act. In early February, 1525 the

27b Interior of St. Mary's Church in Memmingen. The choir stalls and altar are later additions; the frescos survive from the fifteenth century. It was here that an angry crowd blocked the passage of the clergy on Christmas afternoon, 1524, when they feared the clergy would extend vesper rites by a procession through the nave of the church to prevent the scheduled sermon of an evangelical chaplain.

preacher received farmers from Steinheim and agreed to help them organize an official protest to the Memmingen city council. On 13 February 1525, farmers from Steinheim and several other villages belonging to Memmingen appeared before the city council. They demanded the appointment of an evangelical preacher in their parishes, communion in both kinds, reduced taxes and abolition of their serfdom. The farmers indicated that they were in contact with other groups of farmers in the South who had already armed themselves, but would exercise restraint, if the council would meet their demands. To gain time, the council suggested they negotiate and choose representatives. The next day, representatives from 27 villages appeared before the council, with the furrier, Sebastian Lotzer, as their secretary.[23] Lotzer had been given the position on Schappeler's recommendation. Lotzer, who was well known to members of the council, reluctantly agreed to become their secretary: 'I am afraid that I am just a simple artisan, who has never done service in any court or chancellery. I haven't even been a substitute notary! Therefore, I feel that the difficulty of your negotiations could hardly be helped by my service.'[24] Schappeler and Lotzer hoped to peacefully negotiate a local solution and avoid any connections with the rebellious peasants from the villages along Lake Constance. The city council provided the negotiators with a place to work and a barrel of wine. The two worked together with a blacksmith, Ulrich Schmid, to produce the *Twelve Articles*, which summarized the grievances of the farmers and city artisans. They all agreed that the gospel would serve as a basis for negotiations.[25] Despite warnings from the Swabian League, which had begun its own negotiations with the peasants of Lake Constance, the city council did its best to meet the demands of the articles: all parishes would receive evangelical preachers; serfdom would be abolished (though the farmers must pay a tax in the future for the protection of the city); hunting and fishing rights to all city land were given to the farmers. They agreed to wait for any changes in the traditional tithe, since it was used to support important public services, provided by the church. Unfortunately, events outside Memmingen interrupted the peaceful solution achieved by the negotiators for the peasants and the city council. The Swabian League demanded that the Memmingen council disperse the peasants camped outside its walls, as rumors of a planned rebellion spread. The farmers in the meantime, rightly sensing the treachery of the Swabian League which pretended to want to negotiate with them, camped outside the walls of the city. The city council was no longer in control. The negotiators, together with other citizens in the city, tried to convince the city council to declare itself on the side of the farmers. The city council could only buy time for deliberation. By 9 June 1525, it was too late. A thousand troops from the Swabian League marched on the city. Hans Schultheiss sent a message to the commander of the League's forces, saying that the schoolmaster, Paul Hoepp, a stonemason, and an innkeeper had already been executed for encouraging revolt.[26] Schappeler and Lotzer fled the city. They went to St Gall, where Zwingli helped Schappeler to find a position as preacher in a nuns' convent. Lotzer disappeared entirely.[27] The angry peasants lay siege to the city until, on 3 July 1525, the forces of the League were able

28a *A Christian Missive*, by Sebastian Lotzer, 1523. 'To strengthen the poor consciences and sent to his dear father, a burgher in Horb.'

to disperse them. The Swabian League would impose its will on the city council in the future. The council was forced to acquiesce to the wishes of the prefect of the monks of St Antoine and the mass was restored in St Martin's parish. The reforms which had been so important to Lotzer and his friends and for which they had so long negotiated were soon replaced by a complete restoration of the old church with all its rights. The clergy would no longer need to swear an oath of loyalty to the city, and the new taxes on the clergy were abolished.

Sebastian Lotzer is probably the most interesting pamphleteer in this study, both because his writings and experience indicate a deep personal commitment to the cause of reform, and because he provides detailed

theological information about his ideas in the pamphlets he published in
Memmingen and Augsburg between 1523 and 1525.[28] Born in the village
of Horb-am-Neckar to the family of a church warden, the furrier seems
to have rejected opportunities for education.[29] There is some indication
that his father intended for him to become a priest. He wrote in his
Christian Apology in Thirty-one Articles about his 'father, a man of flesh
and the senses. Desirous that his son come to great honor and wealth, he
intended to make him a priest, or perhaps a great prelate. The son refused
his father's wishes and fell from his good graces. The father entirely
rejected his son.'[30] Lotzer's younger brother was perhaps more the model
of success his father had wished. He became personal physician to the
Bishop of Strasbourg.[31] Sebastian Lotzer, probably the eldest, became a
furrier. He went to Memmingen as a journeyman and married the
daughter of a shopkeeper, with whom he resided.[32] In the tax list for 1521,
Lotzer was assessed to pay one pound to the city. Because there were not
enough furriers in Memmingen for an independent guild, Lotzer was listed
as a member of the tailors' guild. Rejection by his father frustrated the
furrier. As his publications became more and more controversial, he
begged his father not to abandon him entirely, while he defended the
integrity of the gospel.[33] Both his *Advice to the Inhabitants of Horb* and his
Christian Missive were addressed to the people of his home town. A popular
lay preacher was apprehended by the secular authorities of the region and
imprisoned. The preacher, a physician from Strasbourg, Hans Maurer was
exiled from his city and took his message to the countryside. He was
captured in Balingen on 4 March 1523 and taken to Tübingen, where
he was imprisoned. Lotzer admonished the citizens of Horb not to be
discouraged or 'turn away from God's precious word on pain of the loss
of your souls.'[34]

In 1524, the furrier turned his attention to events in Memmingen,
writing two theological works, his *Christian Apology in Thirty-one Articles*
and his *Exposition on the Gospel for the Twenty-second Sunday after Trinity.*
Both were published in the autumn of 1524. Lotzer continually admonished
his readers to avoid 'any disturbances or general uprising,' to protect
himself.[35] Yet he came to the defense of his fellow citizens who trapped
Pastor Megerich and his clergy inside the choir of St Mary's church in his
Apology for the Pious Christians of Memmingen, published in early
1525.

Documenting Lotzer's theological sources is difficult. He cites only
scripture, making only one brief reference to Luther. He refused to be
classified: 'for there are those who say, "I am a good Lutheran...," but
St Paul forbids this.'[36] He calls himself, 'simply evangelical,' but his
spirituality is not limited to inspiration from reading the bible.[37] His
thought was shaped by a strong prophetic and mystical sensitivity.[38]

Despite his copious citations of both old and new testaments, he displays a markedly medieval preference for Matthew's gospel, the Pauline Epistles, and the prophets Isaiah and Jeremiah.[39] Some scholars suggest that he was influenced by Zwingli; others see Eberlin von Günzburg's influence on the furrier. But it is very difficult to discern the actual origins of his ideas, since Waldensian thought, evangelical reform, and the Humanist critique of the clergy on the eve of the Reformation shared similar theological ideas. Certainly Lotzer knew of Zwingli's ideas through his friend Schappeler, who was personally in touch with Zürich reformers. Lotzer's ideas on fasting in Lent are probably from Zwingli.[40] Only a few of Eberlin von Günzberg's ideas correspond to Lotzer's, most of which might have come from any German preacher in the Southwest.[41] Lotzer probably read Luther's works in German. His attitude toward confession is Lutheran.[42] Once again, it is difficult to trace his ideas because the traditional critique of the old church is close to the proposals of magisterial reformers. Lotzer's most important contribution to the literature of the Reformation lies in his naive adaptation of reformed ideas to his own vision of active ministry among the poor, admonishing his fellow citizens to prepare themselves for the second coming. The furrier preferred to see the events of his day, the persecution of the word and its advocates, as milestones pointing to the judgment soon to follow.[43]

Anticipation of the second coming and the end of the world play a significant role in determining Sebastian Lotzer's thought and govern his choice of scripture to support his various reform proposals. His sense of the immediate need for church reform stems from his deep conviction that he was living in the last days. His own awakening to the gospel was a sure sign of the prophet's prediction: 'and I will pour out my spirit on all flesh; your sons and your daughters shall prophesy.' (Joel 2:28f.)[44] He often refers to his own time as the last days, when God would again reveal himself to his people and instruct them to prepare for Christ's return: 'for God the almighty looks wonderfully down into this vale of tears, and despite the fact that many clerics and worldly men oppose him, nevertheless it is of no avail: the word of God will clear the path, primarily among the common men. For even if we would be silent, the stones would cry out that the word of God should not be oppressed.'[45] The fact that Lotzer and other laymen had begun to preach the word of God fulfilled the predictions of the prophet Joel; even women had begun to preach: 'not only you and people like you have begun so boldly and fearlessly to preach, but even women begin to practice the word of God honestly and in a Christian manner...Notice how the noble and well born woman Argula von Stauffen proves this as she writes to the university scholars.'[46] Despite all attempts at persecution, the word of God would survive and triumph: 'for even if 2, 3, 5, 100, 300 people are defeated, nothing will help. Before

God's word will be silenced, the children will begin to preach from their cradles!'[47]

The new importance of the gospel is a sign in his theology that the return of Christ was imminent. Laymen must actively prepare for his coming. In nearly every work written by Lotzer he advised his readers to do works of mercy, which are meant to hasten the end of the world and eventually save mankind: 'God orders us to do nothing in preparation for the last judgment other than the six works of holy mercy, as Matthew says in the 25th chapter: 'Come here, O' chosen ones of my father, and inherit the kingdom which has been prepared for you since the beginning of the world!'[48] The six works of holy mercy to which Lotzer constantly refers – providing housing for the poor, giving them food and drink, clothing the naked, caring for the sick, ministering to prisoners, and burying the dead – are both another manifestation of late-medieval works-holiness, and a new call to do those works which would save mankind in the last days. Service of the poor in Lotzer's theology opens the gate of heaven. The furrier envisions a great Christian commune of sharing, collecting money in a tin box like the brotherhoods did: 'where there is a company of good people, they should gather money together in a box, collecting wherever they can, and afterward they should divide the money among the poor people, as they see fit.'[49] The artisan's anticipation of the end of the world and his longing for a community of equals reflects both an ongoing medieval tradition, and the economic crisis of the sixteenth century in which artisans were caught in the middle of changing economic patterns.[50] The furrier wanted more than a restoration of the *status quo ante*. He wanted to prepare the elect for Christ's return.

The merit of all works is dependent on personal preparation in Lotzer's theology. He emphasizes the necessity of a personal inner conversion. Here, primarily, one notes the first emphatic intrusion of mystical theology in his thought: the conscience must be cleared by the word of God, 'for we are saved by the word of God.'[51] The word acts directly on the human heart: 'when it [the word] falls on the field of the human heart, in some it brings forth sixty times as much fruit, in some thirty times as much, depending however on how good the field (that is, the human heart) is.'[52] The word as a vehicle of grace brings man to true repentance: 'for from the moment we fall into sin out of stupidity, we should repent and be sorry, asking God for forgiveness.'[53] Lotzer alters the pattern of late-medieval popular theology only slightly, yet nevertheless significantly. The process to salvation is a combination of reformed ideas in a medieval context: one receives faith as a *gratia infusa* from the word.[54] He limits the vehicles of grace to a single source, the word, since Christ's atonement for man's sins had been sufficient.[55] Here the atonement ceases to be a contemplative vehicle of grace, perhaps because of Luther's influence, and becomes an historical event, important not for its continuing effect, but as a means of unburdening the conscience. Scripture and the substantial nature of the atonement replace any other vehicle of grace in an otherwise unchanged medieval economy of salvation. As man moves from the historical atonement toward the final reconciliation of the elect at the end of the world, the focus of salvation evolves from works of charity necessary to hasten Christ's return, to the reception of Christ, the word, himself. Just as Christ atoned for man's sins before, so he would reconcile man again in a real historical manner. Here faith is but the passive agent of enlightening grace, yet the word – especially as perceived in scripture, read, contemplated, and imprinted in the heart – assures the individual of his election. An infusion of such grace brings with it wisdom, which is a sign of sainthood and election.

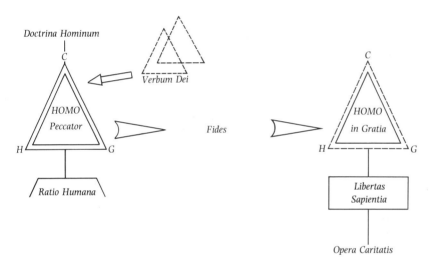

Figure 2. A Theology of Conscience Liberation in Sebastian Lotzer's Pamphlets

A liberation of the conscience, enlightened by exposure to the word of God, brings man to a state of grace, in which he can do the works of charity commanded by Christ in the last days. The word of God reaches the mind, first heard or read, where it travels to the heart. In the heart, love grows and man decides to do the works commanded by Christ, harnassing his wayward *Gemüthe* to enable him to do genuinely meritorious works. At this point man realizes the folly of human teaching and is transformed into a new state of godlike Grace. In grace man receives the freedom to act as a free agent of God to do the works of the gospel, commended by Christ in Matthew 24. Wisdom remains as a sign of God's favor to keep man on the correct path to salvation. The word of God is transformed in the process from the written word or heard word (from sermons) to the active word as Christ works through man toward the last judgment.

Wisdom, imparted to the soul as a gift of grace, allows man to use his freedom wisely: 'I have given these examples from scripture in order that we not use Christian freedom as an excuse to sin; a true Christian uses his freedom wisely, not to excess.'[56] Christian freedom is not a Nominalist *facere quod in se est* license, but the freedom to do works of mercy, both a mark of sainthood and a means to final salvation.[57] Thus the progression of grace from God to man, to works of mercy remains unaltered from traditional medieval piety: 'just as Christ saved us and made us blessed out of sheer grace and mercy, so also we have been made free to serve him, doing his will without ceasing.'[58]

Reform means preparation for the end to the furrier. He often quotes eschatological texts from Timothy (I Tim. 4:1f) where, in the last days, those who had departed from the spirit would forbid marriage and enjoin abstinence from foods created by God. In an historical context he views contemporary hesitancy to accept the Reformation. Just as the apostles had been persecuted for their faith, so evangelical preachers who called people back to the true church would be persecuted: 'oh merciful, good, mild Lord and God: how your precious unchangeable word has been used in these perilous last days, especially by the great men who are supposedly our betters. They allow the righteous pious Christian preachers to be persecuted. They burn them, exile them from their lands, call them heretics, and force them to recant.'[59] Lotzer compares those people who resisted the Reformation with Jews, who persecuted Christ. His *Christian Missive* is critical of Jews' refusal to accept the gospel, reflecting a watershed of medieval anti-Semitism. 'For this and for killing Christ, God has punished them for 1,500 years,' says the furrier.[60] Yet he admires the Jews for their knowledge of scripture.[61] Lotzer wanted to convert the Jews, something he saw as necessary in the last days in order to prepare the final sheepfold for the elect. 'I deplore the fact that until now we have had such lazy shepherds and preachers. ...The scholars have said that laymen ought not to dispute with the Jews because Jews are learned people and would easily win the debate.'[62] It was the responsibility of laymen to convert the Jews and thus hasten the kingdom of Christ. Such conversion, the furrier assumed rather naively, would be quite easy: 'one can easily convince the Jews with the old testament, because they must acknowledge that.'[63] Thus he sees preaching and conversion as an integral part of a lay apostolate in the last days. Early heralds of church reform, prophets like Luther, Erasmus, Zwingli, and laypeople like Argula von Grumbach who called people back to the gospel were all signs of the approaching End. The persecution of lay-preachers fulfilled Christ's promise of persecution to his apostles. Since the hierarchy, secular and religious, refused to recognize the signs of the approaching End, laymen were forced to learn scripture and to preach to the people, preparing them, too, for an active

28b The house where Sebastian Lotzer lived, Herrenstrasse 3, in Memmingen.

apostolate. Thus, by their inner conversion and active apostolate, manifest in works of mercy and preaching, laymen could hasten the approaching kingdom of Christ.

Lotzer's vision of the church is predictably simple and scriptural: 'thus the holy Christian church is nothing other than the congregation of all faithful people, gathered together in the grace of the holy spirit. The holy Christian church is known to God alone.'[64] He makes little distinction between the ministers of the church and laypeople. Although he does not state that the clergy and laypeople have identical power, he does present a formula for an active lay apostolate by presenting examples from church history: 'for the apostles, evangelists, prophets, and St Paul were only men.'[65] When the priest in the temple noted how well Peter and John could preach, they wondered that they were mere laypeople.[66] In the community of the spirit, the laity also shared full membership with priests: 'now what are priests, but mere laymen. St Peter said: "You are a chosen people, a royal priesthood." St Peter does not exclude anyone here. So also ought it to be in the holy Christian church, which the clergy for a long time have limited to the pope, cardinals, and bishops.'[67] Lotzer does not suggest that laypeople and priests have the same mission. He states positively that the official preaching in churches is the duty of bishops: 'preachers who are called to preach the word of God are bishops.'[68] Lotzer refers to Christoph Schappeler as a bishop. He never suggests that laypeople ought to celebrate sacraments or assume other priestly duties. When he insists that the laity ought to be able to preach, he does not mean in the churches, but in the streets, to remind brother and sister Christians that they might be sinning or to convert the Jews. His criticism of the clergy is not simply anti-clericism: it is aimed at the failure of the clergy to preach the gospel in preparation for the second coming. Since the clergy had refused, laypeople would have to assume the responsibility. There is some confusion in Lotzer's theology about actual order in the church. When he speaks of the power of the laity as priests, he envisions a church where absolute equality exists, the church invisible. Still, he had to maintain some respect for clergymen, like Schappeler.

Lotzer's criticism of the Roman church and the pope seems Waldensian. His attack centers on an alleged Roman preference for human teachings as opposed to the *lex evangelica*. Lotzer calls all who prefer human teaching 'disgusting papists!'[69] He attributes three kinds of abuses to the human teaching: first, those things which are contrary to the *lex evangelica*; second, those things which oppress the poor; and third, those things which do not necessarily contradict scripture, but distort the essential nature of the church. Indulgences are at the top of the list in the first category. They are particularly nefarious because 'the pope and all the clergy have sold the forgiveness of sins for money.'[70] Since Christ had commanded his apostles to give freely what they had received, indulgences were obviously contrary to the gospel, because they oppressed the poor: 'if one can buy his way into heaven, where does this leave the poor?'[71] Here Erasmus or Luther might have inspired him. Monasticism, pilgrimage, and confraternities were found to distort the essential nature of the church. Monasticism made an exclusive claim to a special kind of Christian brotherhood, which contemporaries thought afforded a special means of grace: 'monks and nuns seek Christ in their cloisters, assuming that they do enough when they wear habits and are called religious, praying the seven hours in their choirs, yet the nuns are ignorant of what they themselves are praying for they understand as much Latin as any goose!'[72] Pilgrimage suggests that Christ is bound to a particular place more holy than other places: 'for Christ wants to be worshipped in spirit and in truth, and doesn't want to be bound to any particular city. He answers your prayers wherever you pray, in the field, at home, in bed, as long as you praise and honor him.'[73] Brotherhoods and confraternities were particularly exclusive organizations, which betrayed the essential nature of the church: 'we are all brothers and sisters throughout the whole of Christendom and are responsible for and must pray for the salvation of each other.'[74] The humanist critique of the church from the pulpit directly inspired the furrier: feast days also come under particular attack. They drew attention away from Christ: 'for the priests thought up a new feast

29 Collecting the Easter tithe. From Rodericus Zamorensis, *Speculum Vitae Humanae*, 1488.

day each time they had a dream, in order to oppress the body and soul of the poor.' Even worse: 'more sins are committed on a feast day with all its frivolities...for what your people could never do on other days, they may do on a feast day: overeating, drunkenness, gaming, fornicating, dancing, fighting...all kinds of sins and unrighteous acts.'[75]

Echoes of Erasmus can be heard here. By elevating human traditions to Godly commandment, the church had denied individual Christians the exercise of their freedom, and troubled their consciences: 'who would be so blind not to see this as wrong? They have created such things, forbidding men to do this or that, making trouble for Christians who have been given freedom by Christ and ought to use it to do away with such things.'[76] Worst of all, the church set up fast days, obliging people to fast on pain of mortal sin.[77] This tended to encourage observance of church decrees, which had their origin in human teaching, rather than the commandments of Christ. The offering of money was yet another means by which the clergy oppressed the poor: 'for the priests tell you to offer money in order that they can use it for their own enjoyment, deluding the poor sheep of Christ with useless fables and human teaching. Christ wants spiritual offerings, our heart and *gemüthe*.'[78] Lotzer objected to the way in which the tithe was distributed. The *Twelve Articles* insist that part of the tithe be given directly to the poor: 'from now on the tithe will be given to the provost of the church, appointed by the congregation, who will collect it. From that, a portion will be given to the priest, in order that he have proper and sufficient board and lodging; whatever is left must be given to the poor people living in the same village.'[79] In discussing the church's power to excommunicate members, he upheld the right of the church to excommunicate. But the absolute standard for this must be the *lex evangelica*; the clergy ought to use their power to excommunicate as representatives of Christ and his church, 'against those who sin against God's honor and the love of one's neighbor, adulterers, blasphemers, and anyone who opposes the word of God.'[80] The church should still define heresy and excommunicate heretics. The church, however, should never excommunicate debtors. This was a matter which concerned a man's body and possessions, hence a purely secular issue.[81] The church might also appoint fast days; Lotzer even concedes the Friday and Saturday fasting requirements: 'the good old fathers in earlier times advised the people to break the Lenten fast occasionally, also not to eat fleshmeat on Fridays and Saturdays.'[82]

Lotzer's opposition to Rome is expressed in a specific attack on the Petrine commission, traditionally used to support papal authority:

Here they say that God gave the power to St. Peter and entrusted the church to him; Peter and his followers have the power to bind and loose. My answer: Christ said to Peter: 'Flesh and blood have not revealed this to you, but my heavenly father,' and such was a gift from God...The text ought not to be literally understood, that Peter was the rock; the rock to which he referred was Jesus Christ, son of the living God. This is the rock against which the gates of hell will not prevail...Where would the church be if it were founded on someone who denied the Lord?[83]

Christ gave his commission to all the apostles, even to mere laymen; therefore, 'Christ is our head, not the pope.'[84] Here Luther is probably his inspiration. Lotzer accords no authority to the tradition of the church, although he is remarkably silent about many important issues of the Reformation of which he must have been aware. He never mentions purgatory, the sacrifice of the mass, etc. He does not want to wait for a church council to be called to reform the church: 'some say, let us wait for a council and then we will know what to believe. Dear brother: hear the word of God, buy the new testament; let that be council enough... For the councils must act in accordance with holy scripture, otherwise they would not be Christian councils.'[85]

One would hope to be able to detect the influence of a particular reformer in the furrier's sacramental theology. He only mentions three of the traditional seven sacraments: eucharist, penance, and marriage. He frequently discusses the eucharist. Like many reformers, he preferred that the sacrament be delivered to the people in both kinds: 'They [the old-church party] deny the blood of Christ to the laity, because it might be spilled.

Since many men wear beards, this is all the more likely, they say. As if Christ himself could not have anticipated this!'[86] For Lotzer, the blood itself effected the forgiveness of sins.[87] We might assume Lutheran influence, yet the furrier's attitude toward the efficacy of the eucharist seems Zwinglian. Although Christ is truly present in the eucharist, the faith of the individual makes the reception efficacious: 'for more depends on words and faith than on signs. Faith must do it, otherwise the sign is of no use...for Judas received the sign too, yet it was of no use to him because he doubted and did not believe.'[88] Here again, Lotzer seems somewhere between Luther and Zwingli in his interpretation. In tone he is certainly close to Luther: he always refers to the elements as the 'holy body and blood of Christ.' The eucharist is an important channel of God's grace by which sins are forgiven.

The furrier says surprisingly little about baptism. He spends a great deal of time discussing penance. Lotzer does not consider penance to be a sacrament; an historical atonement precluded this: 'many of you are aware how, until now, they have troubled and burdened us with their fictitious auricular confession. Caught in that prison, it has never been possible for anyone to go to the holy sacrament [the eucharist] with a clear conscience, since everyone was aware that he had possibly confessed either too much or too little.'[89] Confession, which was intended to unburden people's consciences, had just the opposite effect. People simply had no means by which to assess their own worthiness in order to receive the sacrament. Since the old church was so polluted with human teaching, how could one be sure too, that absolution were from God, especially if the believer were not quite certain of Christ's promise to forgive sins and his historical atonement for man's sins. Faith from the word helps to clear the conscience; Lotzer condemns the old church for praising the benefits of sacramental penance above 'true faith and trust in Jesus Christ.'[90]

Does Lotzer's emphasis on faith make him more Lutheran? Certainly in penance as in the eucharist, the faith of the believer is critically important. Contrition is the precondition for effective reception of the eucharist: 'one should have a desire for hearty reunion (with God) in grace, and not doubt, in order that one may receive such a sacrament and Godly sign in firm faith and good trust.'[91] Faith seems more the bearer of grace as a means to reunion, than the object of reunion. Our furrier simply combines late-medieval mystical-reunion theology, which demanded contrition as preparation for the reception of grace and faith, with Luther's emphasis on faith. The reunion of the heart cannot occur within the sacramental structure of the church, but must occur between the individual and God, as a sort of extraordinary sacrament. Lotzer consequently rejects the power of the church to forgive sins, which had traditionally been justified by the power of the keys given to Peter to bind and loose: 'now the holy apostles neither bound nor loosed anyone, but through the grace and gift of God. Therefore every pious Christian has the power to bind and unbind through the word of God, though primarily the evangelical preachers have this power.'[92] Here the evangelical preacher's or an individual layperson's knowledge of scripture defines office. In this case our furrier seems completely Zwinglian. Is this statement about the power of preachers to forgive sins a half-hearted acknowledgment of clerical authority? Perhaps. As in most cases, when confronted with the power of established authority, Lotzer thinks in terms of the invisible church, where everyone watches over everyone else for the good of the commune, the *bonum communis*. Christians must warn each when someone has sinned. He insists that despite the fact that many reformers, 'very learned, able, individuals,' felt it necessary to keep penance as a sacrament, Christ's historical atonement precluded this possibility.[93] He says very little about marriage. He only concerns himself with it when discussing clerical celibacy. The furrier considered chastity a gift, 'but whoever cannot be chaste, let him take a wife or a wife a husband, be they monks, nuns, priests, or laypeople.'[94]

By far the most interesting and daring pamphlet in this sample is Lotzer's *Exposition on the Gospel for the Twenty-Second Sunday after Trinity*. The pamphlet is conceived as a sermon. The furrier quotes the text of Matthew 22: 1–14, the parable of the wedding feast. Then he begins his exegesis, in which he reveals his own views on the historical church and its mission. The parable, certainly one of the most difficult biblical texts for exegesis, describes a king who prepares a wedding feast for his son. According to Lotzer, God is the king; the marriage about to be celebrated is that of Jesus with the church. The marriage bond is 'the true and righteous Christian faith, which man has in God and his holy word; by this faith we are one with God and in God.'[95] The first servants whom the king sent to invite guests are the prophets of the old testament who invited the Jews to the feast, but they proved themselves unworthy by killing the servants. Then the king sent other servants, the apostles who announced the slaughter of the fatted calf, Christ. The apostles were killed as Christ had been. Therefore, according to Lotzer, God destroyed the city of the Jews and cursed their race, choosing another people, the Gentiles, in their stead. Thus God gave the Gentiles the commission to proclaim the gospel. For Sebastian Lotzer, the Gentiles signify the common people, betrayed by Pharisees and priests. The secular and church authorities, by forbidding laypeople to read and teach about the scriptures, invited their own destruction. 'Laypeople, the faithful ones and the true kingdom of God will succeed and triumph,' proclaimed Lotzer.[96] Soon God would punish those who prevented the true church from proclaiming the gospel.

The furrier, expecting the End to come soon, always refers to the church invisible, united with Christ at the judgment, 'gathered together in the holy spirit...the holy Christian church, known to God alone.'[97] He avoids the traditional vision of the church as a body made up of both sinners and saints. He exclusively appeals to the saints, cleansed and set apart from the church authorities. He admonishes the potential saints: 'protect yourselves on pain of your soul from the wolves who say that laypeople are not allowed to read holy scripture because they don't understand it. That is a lie. God the almighty has always given his Godly word to the simple, pious lowly people, just as when he was born it was not proclaimed to the scholars and Pharisees, but to the shepherds.'[98] He scolds the old-church clergy, calling them priests, hypocrites and Pharisees, who shut the kingdom of heaven to those who wish to enter.[99] Everyone must personally accept the responsibility to read scripture: 'it will do you no good if someone else knows a lot [about scripture], for you must account for yourself.'[100] Laypeople ought to purchase the new testament and see for themselves how the priests had tried to lead them astray.[101] To prepare the laity for the coming of Christ's kingdom, he hoped to draw the church visible toward his model of the church invisible. By observing Christ's law, to love God and love one's neighbor, one might actively hasten the kingdom. By knowledge of the word, the conscience could be cleared, freeing man to do good works in preparation for the approaching end.

Lotzer accuses the clergy of leading the people of God astray on three counts; first, he calls them false prophets who teach the necessity of human law, rather than the *lex evangelica*, summed up in Christ's two great commandments.[102] Secondly, the clergy tried to hide the gospel from laypeople: 'for a long time they have burdened our consciences, hiding the word of God behind the door, which otherwise stands clearly in front of our eyes.'[103] Lastly, he accuses the clergy of being more worldly than spiritual men, more interested in eating, drinking, and carousing than the cure of souls: 'they [the clergy] threaten the poor working people with excommunication if they don't fast, yet the poor people scarcely have three soups a day to eat, while they [the clergy] are as fat as pigs...We want to see them eat and drink..., but they want to have land and serfs, want to ride great horses, have two cooks, be drunk night and day.'[104]

Apparently many people in Memmingen were reluctant to abandon the faith of their parents for the new evangelical religion. Both Schappeler and Lotzer published pamphlets to tip the scales toward their evangelical preference. Schappeler published his *Answers to Arguments and Reasons for Suppressing the Word of God* to attack the teaching of the old church and to discredit the old works-religion. Lotzer preferred to link the new evangelical teaching directly to the tradition of the church, which would appeal to the people who had not made up their minds: 'had Paul believed like his parents, he would never have achieved sainthood, nor SS.

Katherine or Barbara, or many other dear saints.'[105] What happened to
people who had died before the Reformation? 'I have no doubt that, had
our parents lived in these merciful times, they would have raised their arms
to heaven and thanked God...If they had strong faith in Christ, then they
died well. You must believe for yourself; you need not ask about the faith
of your parents; you never heard their confession.'[106] Repeating
Schappeler's words, Lotzer admonished his readers: 'listen well: before you
would recognize error you would rather stay with the devil. One hundred
years of wrong does not make one hour right. Even Paul recognized that
he had done wrong and was converted.'[107]

Lotzer presents a proposal for church reform in which both clergy and
laity would share the gospel. The church would preach the *lex evangelica*
as Christ taught it. Since the old church had refused the gospel, he shifted
the responsibility to reform the church to the laity, confident that the word
would triumph in the End. He outlined a form of lay apostolate in which
laypeople would read scripture, live and preach the gospel actively. Lotzer
preached a social gospel, a reform of the church from below, but not
necessarily a reform that would alter the structure of the church. Like
many Humanists and reformers, he was much more interested in the kingdom of Christ than in the church visible. By appealing to the security of the
church invisible, Lotzer hoped to refocus the piety and religious practices
of his readers/listeners. His religiosity seems in essence still the same affective piety advocated by late-medieval reformers. Only the medium had
changed; scripture, as the symbolic word, becomes the means of grace.
Lotzer knew that his job would not be easy. He begged his followers to
'strive as knights for the word of God in order to achieve eternal
knighthood!'[108] The furrier's attitude toward the future is determined by
his eschatological expectations, which demand a conformity to the *lex
evangelica* in preparation for Christ's return. Since the clergy refused to
discard the human teaching of the Roman church, Lotzer felt justified in
attacking the principles upon which the church exercised authority.
Convinced that laypeople would have to bear the burden of conversion
in the last days, he necessarily had to justify their apostleship, using the
'universal priesthood' argument. He would not necessarily like to see the
distinction between clergy and laity erased, but he felt that the great
barriers between them ought to be lessened and a lay apostolate officially
recognized. Bishops ought to preach and tend their sheep with care,
instructing them in the scriptures. Priests should collect the tithe
responsibly and divide part of it among the poor.

Throughout Sebastian Lotzer's writings, the enlightenment of the
conscience of the individual serves as the means by which the essential
conversion of the heart can be realized and the soul ultimately saved.
Because the effect of the word on the heart could be sensibly perceived,

at least to some extent proved by life in conformity with the *lex evangelica*, some pre-knowledge of election is assumed. However, only an unburdened conscience was able to attain this knowledge. The greatest stone in the path of that all-important enlightenment was the human teaching which Lotzer continually rails against. Evangelical preaching becomes a ready antidote to humanly devised pollution. A captive conscience, not so much captive by sin, but by humanly contrived laws, could be nurtured by faith derived directly from the word. As the historical Christ atoned for man's sins, so the word in scripture assumes the atoning role in post-scriptural times. Through the senses, by hearing and reading scripture, Godly grace places the human soul in a state to be saved. When the conscience has been cleared and the individual knows directly from the word what he ought to do, then the upper levels of the soul, the heart and *gemüthe* may achieve their natural functioning capacity, the establishment of a mystical union which puts the human soul directly in touch with the heavenly Christ. The result is not so much apostolic power to work miracles, as the obligation to carry out apostolic commandments, to feed the poor and preach the word. Human will, when in conformity with the gospel, is no longer corrupt, but healed to work meritoriously.

Curiously, the furrier still emphasizes a natural antithesis between God the creator and man, the created being. This is not reflected in a discussion of original sin, the fall of Adam, or free will, but in Lotzer's critique of the invocation of saints: 'therefore they put the creature before God, the created before the creator, which does the greatest dishonor to God and the saints.' Sainthood and possible sanctification are particularly important in his anthropology. One might expect the contrasting nature of God and man to give Lotzer a decided prejudice against human nature, but indeed it did not. Since it is of primary importance to prepare the church for the return of Christ, sanctification is not a process by which the dead saints are suddenly recognized in heaven, but an earthly process, by which man, through God's word, can obtain the grace necessary to fulfill Christ's commandments. Lotzer therefore divides saints into two categories: 'the first are those in the flesh, pious believing Christians to whom one ought to show honor by helping the poor and advising them, just as God himself does. The second group are those saints who have died, for they do not need your help; they are blessed and indeed rich. When we desire to honor these saints, we can do them no greater honor than to believe the word of God and ask God to give us the grace to persevere in Godly love and preserve our faith.'[109] He objects not so much to the veneration of saints as to their invocation, since his theology is basically Christocentric: 'oh what kind of idolatry are we guilty of by the invocation of saints, especially with St. Sebastian! How often have we said, "Saint Sebastian protected me from the plague," yet never thought of Christ.'[110] It is a lack of emphasis on Christ as mediator that Lotzer opposes, certainly not the veneration of saints. In the earthly community, Lotzer encourages veneration through an active ministry to the poor. The heavenly community may be best venerated by imitation, remaining faithful to God and performing good works. The saints serve as important models in his theology. Mary, the mother of Jesus, is of particular importance: 'whoever does dishonor to God and his Godly word also does dishonor to the Mother of God and all the saints. It is sinful false pride when we make idols of the mother of Jesus and the dear saints; we ought to seek help by him, our only savior, who has been thrust from the middle, his honor and glory reduced in importance.'[111] One should venerate the Blessed Virgin, as God did 'with the angelic salutation, the Ave Maria, when God gave her boundless grace as the most blessed among all his creation.'[112] Here we note the influence of Luther's *Explanation of the Magnificat* (1521). Lotzer adjusts the mediating role of saints in traditional late-medieval piety, using them as models, indeed worthy of veneration, as long as it be remembered that they received their grace from God, accomplishing nothing by their own merit. The sanctification process is also important, since it presents earthly saints with a means of reconciliation in imitation of saints' obedience or submission to God's word in their works: 'let us ask God to grant us the same wisdom which he gave to the Blessed Virgin Mary and the other dear saints, in order that we too may become blessed.'[113] Here we note an interesting combination of reformed theology and mystical piety. Curiously, the suffering and passion of Christ, indeed the entire human personality of Christ finds no place in his theology. The atonement is not only a frozen historical event, but seems almost the expected mechanical expression of a vengeful Christ, whose ultimate goal is fulfilled only at the last judgment.[114]

Lotzer advocates a piety which is dependent on, not opposed to, a Nominalist conception of human reason. Human reason unaided by Godly grace could not accomplish good, nor could good works alone merit heavenly grace. Yet, aided by Godly grace, the human soul *in fide* acquires two new qualities according to the artisan, wisdom and Christian freedom, which allow men to do good works: 'when we love God and love our neighbor, we hope in Christ that he, by virtue of his suffering and death, will give us more than we even desire...for God judges according to the inner *gemiet*, that is according to the human heart and thoughts. Therefore, whoever has lifted his heart up to God may openly give alms and do other works.'[115] Works, therefore, may be meritorious, since by virtue of Christ's historical atonement for man's sins and his promises in scripture, he will accomplish this. These works, as fruits of faith, do earn the kingdom of heaven, but as humans, one cannot 'hope because of these works to earn that kingdom.'[116] Lotzer, despite his general lack of sophistication, makes a *coram deo/coram homine* distinction. In human terms we may not expect works to be meritorious, yet by virtue of Christ's atonement they indeed may be meritorious. Essentially, the effect of these works is dependent on the inner disposition of the individual, as in the following diagram:

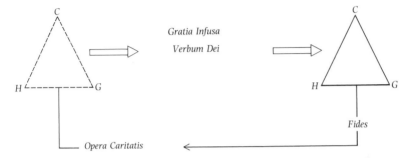

Figure 3. The Economy of Salvation in Sebastian Lotzer's Pamphlets

As the human conscience is liberated by the imputation of faith from the word, the human soul is transformed. To it, Christian freedom and wisdom come, the means by which man can work as Christ commanded and be reasonably assured of his salvation. The necessity of inner conversion as preparation is a clear echo of twelfth-century spirituality on the wings of the *Devotio Moderna*: if indeed the spiritual fathers of this late-medieval reform movement sought to destroy the cloister-wall as a barrier to the profane world, then Sebastian Lotzer's theology is certainly proof of their success.[117] At work here too, is the profound eschatological sensitivity drawn naively from several late-medieval sources and polished with the new scriptural awareness. Since during the Renaissance Christ became more and more an historical figure, the importance of the word increased as the light at the end of a tunnel leading to salvation. Clearly the essential economy of salvation had been altered, but not beyond recognition. Evangelical piety as a piety of the word simply replaces a piety of devotion based on traditional monastic ideals. Reunion of the heart is not a reward for contemplative withdrawal from society, but becomes the means to a new active life in anticipation of the approach of the end of the world.

Lotzer's attitude toward authority, both secular and ecclesiastical, has been much debated by scholars. Since his role in the authorship of the *Twelve Articles* has been reasonably well established, it is easy for Marxists to cast him as a proto-social revolutionary.[118] Yet perhaps the most remarkable aspect of Lotzer's role in the peasant negotiations is his relative pacifism. As long as he was free to preach and teach, he worked desperately to secure a peaceful solution for the peasants, based on principles set forth in the gospel. He encouraged his followers to persevere despite persecution: 'Moses and David accomplished more with their prayers in firm faith than with the sword. If we have strong trust in Christ, he will free us spiritually and physically from the Babylonian captivity.'[119] God himself would take care of the incompetent preachers and those who opposed his gospel.[120] Just as the *lex evangelica* must be obeyed in church affairs, so also must secular authorities be obeyed in other matters: 'we must obey the worldly authorities in all appropriate matters, i.e., in those matters which affect one's body and possessions, and in all other things not expressly opposed to God's commandments.'[121] Church and state could hardly be considered separate entities in Lotzer's time. The key here is the *lex evangelica*; if secular authority accepted the principle of evangelical law in church affairs, it could proceed to reform the church. However, should the authorities reject this principle, supporting the old church party, laypeople ought to stand firmly by the word, willing to martyr themselves: 'therefore, if the authorities, spiritual or secular, want to separate themselves from the word of God, to forbid such understanding as God demands, we should not submit, even if we must lose all that we have.'[122] Still, this protest must be non-violent. Even in the 1525 *Peasant Articles*, Lotzer upholds this principle: 'first of all, the gospel is no justification for rebellion or uprising; Christ especially, the promised messiah, preached nothing in his life and work other than love, peace, patience, and unity. Thus you must be loving, peaceful, patient, and unanimous in Christian faith: for this reason the foundation of these articles is the right to hear his gospel and to live it accordingly.'[123] Only in one instance does Lotzer justify protest which has taken place. In the *Apology for the Pious Christians of Memmingen*, his aim in doing so is to shift the blame for disturbance on the old-church clergy, rather than to justify violence: 'whoever blames the Christian community for not being obedient in all proper civil matters to the authorities spares the truth and speaks thus out of a false, un-Christian heart...the reason for the disturbance was the opposition of the clergy [at St. Mary's] to the holy word of God.'[124]

Despite the fact that the knowledge of God's word gives to Christians a special kind of freedom, that freedom is circumscribed by the limits of the gospel. Lotzer complains about those Christians who only use the Lutheran reform as an excuse to avoid things which they con-sidered inconvenient: 'one often finds people who say they are good Lutherans...When one asks them why, they say: "I can eat cheese and eggs in Lent, and don't bother about confession, fasting, offerings, and such things, (assuming that they do enough)...I hear that Luther doesn't consider them important." They follow the wantonness of the flesh, using Luther as a cloak. They make a lot of trouble for us, since they do not demonstrate true freedom to the poor consciences.'[125] Since his own attitude toward church reform is intimately linked to the gospel, he prefers to call it evangelical, not Lutheran, which is in conformity with St Paul's wishes to avoid the use of sectarian labels.

Lotzer recognizes three kinds of law; the *lex evangelica* is above all other laws. Church and state must serve it. Secondly, the secular state makes civil law, appropriate in all matters of civic concern, where they apply to the physical bodies and possessions of man. Lastly there is a natural law, a rather less specific consensus about the realities of nature.[126] Civil disobedience is in no way justified, unless the state acts contrary to the *lex evangelica*. Then Christians may protest to the point of martyrdom. Clearly, however, Lotzer feels that physical violence is contrary to the spirit of the gospel. God punishes those who act against the word of God; vengeance belongs to God.

The furrier's tact and his care not to stir his readers to violent revolution were of little use. Despite his own commitment to a lay apostleship and non-violence in preparation to meet the End, he was caught in a dangerous political situation. He was banned from his city and family, forced to flee and perhaps was killed on his way to Switzerland. The end of the world, to which he tied the necessity of church reform, was a long way off. Even the reform of churches in Memmingen would have to wait. When the league troops left in October, 1525, the Lutheran George Gugy from a parish near Strasbourg assumed the vacant position as preacher in St Martin's parish. Gugy was admonished by the city council 'not to preach anything against Godly word...or to portray the Roman hierarchy as simple fools and common asses.'[127] At the request of the diet of Speyer in 1526, the city council agreed to leave any effective changes in church order to the decision of a future ecumenical council.

The content of Sebastian Lotzer's pamphlets is overwhelmingly theological, not socio-economic. His inspiration was more deeply rooted in the medieval mystical tradition than any particular economic grievances. Although his reform program has much in common with Luther's early proposals, the letter of his complaints could be found in Waldensian protest or contemporary *gravamina*. His critique of the old church and emphasis on the *vita apostolica* and *lex evangelica* could even be traced to the Franciscan preaching, that inspired a long tradition of protest in Europe. It is this peculiar combination of influences and ideas that makes his solutions for reform sound like those proposed by Erasmus in his German pamphlets. Most important in shaping his convictions was his belief that he was living in the last days.

If Lotzer's ideas are characteristic of a particular subculture in early modern Europe, then that subculture must have been saturated with theological ideas. In Lotzer's case, Christoph Schappeler was probably responsible for the furrier's keen interest in theology. He is the only

D·D·CHRIST·SCHA
PPELERVS· OBŸT·
AN· M·DLI·ÆTATIS
LXXIX·

30 Christoph Schappeler, by an anonymous artist, 1551.

pamphleteer in this group to publish a sermon, from which one can assume that he intended to preach. The sermon is an attempt at biblical exegesis. Lotzer's propaganda relied on several 'root paradigms' in the minds of his readers: the possibility of the nearing End, the reluctance of people to give up the religion of their parents, the dawn of the gospel in the last days, the responsibility of laypeople, the poor and simple to take up the cross in the wake of clergy and nobility who failed to reform society, and the outrages of a clergy who substituted human teaching for the gospel (a theme that dominates his works with marked tenacity). These root paradigms could be used by a learned Humanist or reformer and *were* used by both to rally support for church reform.

Steven Ozment sees auricular confession as the key to understanding the acceptance of the Reformation by common people in German cities. Ozment's thesis is at least partly correct for our furrier: he prefers sure faith to the anxiety caused by uncertainty of absolution, in the case of having confessed too little or too much and in the case of a priest who put human teaching above the gospel and therefore could not give adequate absolution. Yet, although Lotzer is critical of the penitential system of the church, he preferred a more mystical solution to the problem of justification. United heart and mind to God was the only means by which one could reliably receive the eucharist, which effected the forgiveness of sins. But this one aspect of Lotzer's theology is far less important than the overall plan by which laypeople could effect their own salvation, primarily by working their way to the End. Weinstein and Bell in contrasting perceptions of holiness in late medieval and Protestant piety note that Protestants put more emphasis on an individual relationship with God for sainthood.[128] Late-medieval piety 'set forth programs of accommodation between life in the world and the law of the gospel that were not merely copies of clerical guidelines to becoming a saint.'[129] Lotzer would seem to be closer to medieval lay piety than Weinstein and Bell's image of Protestant sainthood, which in itself may deserve revision. The commandments of brotherly love, obedience to secular authority, and the preservation of right order in society are all part of the furrier's reform proposal which he shares completely with the *Reformatio Frederici III*.[130] His admonition to self-sacrifice and hope for brotherly union with all common people exemplifies what Lionel Rothkrug said about a new sense of collective responsibility in imperial cities, 'from performing penance for someone else to taking responsibility for the sins and wrongdoings of one's neighbor.'[131] The preservation of a *bonum communis* on earth directed Lotzer's piety and theology toward practical service of the poor.

How does Sebastian Lotzer's lay theology compare with Jörg Vögeli's theology? Vögeli was a layman writing at the same time in Constance. Although Vögeli as secretary to a city council was more learned than Lotzer, both pamphleteers used similar sources and in some cases came to similar theological conclusions. Markedly different is Vögeli's emphasis on Luther's works as the primary factor that caused his Reformation breakthrough, his decision to join the Protestants. Lotzer mentions no such change in his ideas. Lotzer emphasizes a *lex evangelica*, as a law to which everything must be subject, not a *sola scriptura* formula for salvation. Lotzer, like Vögeli in many respects, organized his theology in Zwinglian colors, contrasting a church based on human teaching and the church of the gospel. Luther's basic sacramental teaching from the *Babylonian Captivity of the Church* influenced both lay theologians. Lotzer's teaching on the eucharist, penance, and marriage are identical to Vögeli's, dependent on both Luther and Zwingli, but certainly more Lutheran in character than Zwinglian. The influence of Luther's *Explanation of the Magnificat* (1521) helped to shape both Lotzer's and Vögeli's attitudes

toward the proper veneration of saints. Major differences between the two
lay theologians can be found in their theology of the spirit, in particular,
in the escatological necessity of holy works of mercy in Lotzer's works.
For Vögeli, man was saved by faith and the gospel. For Lotzer, grace from
scripture, manifest in faith and active in works, saved man. In this case
Lotzer seems still more Lutheran in tone than Zwinglian. It is a bit unfair
to try to divide influences on lay theologians between Luther and Zwingli.
As Berndt Hamm discovered, Vögeli's theology stands on its own
somewhere between Luther and Zwingli, but other influences may have
been of equal importance. Hamm acknowledges the possible influence of
local reformers in Constance, Erasmus, Eberlin von Günzburg, Schappeler,
and several other major theologians published pamphlets that may have
been equally important.[132] The tradition of the *gravamina*, based on the
gospel for the reform of society and the survival of Waldensian ideas, may
have helped as well to shape the theology of lay pamphleteers.[133]

The progress of the Reformation of Memmingen was hindered by the
proximity of the city to a more regional problem: the growing number
of rebellious peasants from villages along Lake Constance camped outside
the city's walls. City fathers found it difficult to negotiate with both citizens
and the Swabian League. Many members of the council, who not long
before had risen from the ranks of the artisan classes, helped Schappeler
and Lotzer to find a solution to the peasants' protest. The support of city
council, negotiators, and peasants for a solution based on the gospel
seemed a sure means to avoid any destructive violence. The obstinacy of
the Swabian League forced city fathers to betray peasants and negotiators.
After the tragedy of 1525, the council was careful to instruct Schappeler's
successor to avoid criticism of the Roman clergy or to encourage laypeople
to preach and teach.

Otherwise the progress of church reform in Memmingen was similar to
other small- or medium-sized cities. Rivalry between parish churches, one
favored by patricians, who equipped their parish with funds for a learned
preacher, and the other serving a poorer district with a less-educated
clergy, is common to the history of the Reformation in Southwest
Germany. Even the direct action taken by parishioners, e.g. stopping a
pastor in the street to force him to sign a list of grievances, or active protest
during church services, was not unusual. The inspiration to take such
defiant action may have come from agitating pamphlets.[134] In Spain,
during the Catholic Reformation, there were similar kinds of protest: In
Burgos in 1575, William Christian notes that local leaders shouted at the
clergy in church. Christian suggested that country people had their own
theology, something they often discussed, paying no attention to church
laws.[135] Christian found in Spain what many French historians perceived
in France; a strong and tenacious lay piety, independent of official

recommendations and teaching. Perhaps such protests might have occurred, even without the flood of agitating pamphlet literature.

In the case of the Southwest German Reformation, the theology of Lotzer and Vögeli suggests a tenacious lay tradition in the context of the development of the city and urban consciousness. This lay tradition was open to the ideas of reformers, more often seen as prophets. For Lotzer, the Reformation was a sign of the End, and one might expect that various prophets would be influential. In Lotzer's theology, we note how the inspiration of Christoph Schappeler and his Zwinglian ideas helped to emphasize the contrast between the Roman church, based on human teaching, and the church at the End, based on the *lex evangelica*. Yet Lutheran or perhaps Erasmian influence still directed much of the furrier's thought on the eucharist, veneration of saints, and importance of grace and faith. The city and the necessity of service to the growing number of poor provided the context for Lotzer's lay apostolate, as laypeople worked their way toward salvation in the heavenly city. The mode of pious expression in preparation for that apostolate is still very medieval, in fact, Bernardine. Steven Ozment hoped that we could see in pamphlets how the ideas of magisterial reformers were received by the populace. In Sebastian Lotzer's case, we can see how the ideas of the various reformers were taken up, used, and adapted to the medieval affective tradition in a new urban context. The vigor of this piety lies in its uncompromising demands and independence of any particular reformer.

CHAPTER IV

Augsburg: a weaver, a soldier, and a radical Franciscan

The clatter of looms and printing presses, of coins on tables and wagons on cobblestone made Augsburg one of the fastest growing cities in the Empire in the sixteenth century. Third in population after Cologne and Nuremburg, the city could boast 20,000 inhabitants in the late fifteenth century, nearly 40,000 in 1540, and over 70,000 by 1570.[1] As an important center for textile production, graced with the largest banking houses in Southwest Germany, the city accepted new immigrants from all other parts of Europe. Bohemians, Poles, and Spaniards all streamed into the city seeking employment, as depression gripped areas still far behind the technological sophistication of Augsburg's workshops and factories. Distribution of wealth was uneven in a city top-heavy with aristocrats. The result of new commercial growth in this city on the axis of north–south trade routes was the rapid rise of merchant families like the Fuggers and Welsers, who soon replaced the old 'worthy families' in Augsburg's city government. The southern connections of these families with Italian banking houses and manufacturing brought to Augsburg a fashion, learning, and style of business that seemed sophisticated and foreign to the average German. The exclusivity of the ruling class made them both the envy and bane of much of the population. A survey of tax lists indicates that in 1475, 66 per cent of the population could be considered 'have-nots.' A mere 2.3 per cent of the population owned 61 per cent of the capital. The families whose wealth could be assessed at more than 3,000 florins number 78 in 1475, 271 in 1526. As the actual number of taxpayers grew at only 36 per cent between 1509 and 1540, the number of rich people (owning more than 3,000 florins) grew at the rate of 128 per cent.[2] The 'haves' intended to keep their wealth; there were only a few attempts by the very wealthy to provide housing and hospitals for the city's poor, whose numbers increased as frequent changes in the economy displaced all but the politically powerful. Merchants, bankers, weavers, and printers with international connections could sense changes coming and adjust; the actual burden of change, of more taxes for fortifications and imperial wars was borne by the upper classes. Many who

112

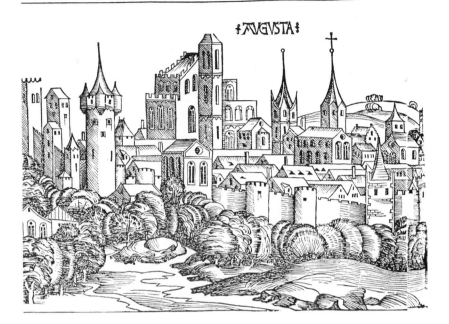

31 Augsburg. Detail from Hartmann Schedel's *Weltchronik*, 1493, showing the city hall and St. Moritz parish.

might be considered in the middle were reduced to poverty. Seventeen monastic foundations in the city claimed tax exemption. Church and patricians were the logical subjects for artisan protest.[3]

Augsburg's civic government consisted of greater and smaller councils, where powerful guilds played an important role. Since 1368 the eighteen guilds had a guaranteed role in city government. Merchant guildsmen had the upper hand in the smaller, more important city council. Councillors, like Artzt, Peutinger, Eber, Rehlinger, Herwart, and Imhof so common in the annals of the city council were all from nouveaux-riches families, who had made their fortunes in the late fifteenth century. Every year the eighteen major guilds chose one or two guildmasters to sit on the smaller council. The number of guildmasters represented on the council increased in the early sixteenth century from 29 to 57, while the number of patricians (chosen from old worthy families by the guildmasters) declined from 15 to 12. The city had two mayors chosen by its smaller council who represented the city in the Swabian League and at imperial diets. Next in importance to the smaller council was the greater council, more representative of all artisans, but an unwieldy organization that usually met only on ceremonial occasions.[4] Governing a society top-heavy with nouveaux-riches was no easy job. The reform initiatives necessary to cope with the great influx of population to Augsburg and displacement due to economic change could hardly bridge the gap between the very rich and relatively poor. The role of the church was among the city council's most important concerns. Religious reform was in the minds of many who sat on the council, as it was important to common people, to whom the traditional prerogatives and economic privileges of the church seemed less and less justifiable.

The church was not only the bank of souls where heavenly interest was credited: it was also an institution with the responsibility for providing social services for an increasingly disgruntled population. Historically, the city council did its best to bring the church under its control. To do so, it had to act independently. The city did little to persecute heretics. Demands from Rome to suppress Beguines and Beghards were sometimes enforced; othertimes, as in 1315, Beguines were protected because among them were daughters of city fathers. When Waldensians were tried and convicted, they were given penance to perform or exiled; if exiled, they could be readmitted to the city. In 1451, Hussites were given a special shelter to worship in. Reforming bishops sometimes cooperated with the city council: swearing was forbidden by council and bishop in 1432. Masked processions at carnival, which not only provided temptations to sin, but also gave the populace an opportunity to ridicule their betters, were discouraged by the bishop and forbidden by the council in 1477. To relieve the burdens of the Lenten fast, the city council had been able to purchase the right for its citizens to eat cheese and butter, freeing them from obligations to buy expensive oil from Spain and Italy. City council and bishops seldom worked well together; only a few progressive bishops shared both an interest in reform of their diocese and an interest in Humanism with city council members. Bishops in Augsburg had to combat the powerful Benedictine convent of SS Ulrich and Afra, the independent mendicant houses, and the cathedral chapter, who usually opposed any curtailment of their privileges or the extension of episcopal jurisdiction. The city council, too, carefully guarded its rights. When in July, 1522, the bishop of Augsburg, Christoph von Stadion (+1543) demanded the recall of two evangelically minded preachers from churches in which the council exercised rights of appointment, the council refused.[5] The tension created by those political divisions in the city allowed printing houses to continue printing controversial literature, much of which was Protestant propaganda. The political situation in Augsburg was difficult: the bishop of Augsburg, despite his personal interest in Humanism and reform, was under pressure from Rome to put an end to Lutheran preaching. The city council was interested in extending its own rights to supervise appointments and visit monasteries. The cathedral chapter opposed both bishop and council. Some of the mendicant houses (Franciscans and Carmelites) applauded Lutheran reforms; other mendicants opposed any kind of reform. Thus reform in Augsburg was slow and uneven, especially with so many competing parties and interests.[6]

In the midst of the competition between the reform-minded and the recalcitrant parties, the needs of the growing *nouveaux pauvres* and the stagnant middle class grew even faster. Humanists favored sound preaching as the most immediate remedy to the social discrepancies in the city. The city council took measures for direct relief of the poor in 1522. The Fuggers had begun a project to provide low-cost housing for the poor in 1512. Conservative churchmen were concerned with other things. The city council fought bitterly with clergymen who wanted more sanctions and privileges from Rome. The cathedral chapter in particular used its lawyers in Rome to oppose both reforming bishops and city council. When Bishop Frederick von Zoller (+1505) attempted to set up a funded preachership in the cathedral, he was bitterly opposed by the chapter, which insisted that there were enough preachers among the mendicants and in other parish churches to serve the needs of the people. The chapter successfully prevented the funding of a cathedral preachership for twenty years. When in 1515, Jacob Fugger tried to fund a preachership in St Moritz parish, the cathedral chapter, retaining the rights of appointment to the parish, refused. Fugger had to organize his influence in Rome, lobby the Emperor Maximilian, and call in the Duke of Bavaria to get permission to hire a preacher. Fugger wanted to call John Eck to the post in 1517, especially since while debating the Bologna, Eck espoused a position on taking interest that suited the attitudes of the Fuggers.[7] (Luther's opinions on the subject were a bit too traditional!)[8] After Eck's refusal to take the appointment, Dr Johann Speiser (+1531) assumed the post.

While the city council worked to gain control of reform and to 'civilize' the clergy, discontented groups from the lower ranks of society sought greater control over city government, which seemed more and more exclusive, and less and less able to meet the rapid pace of economic change with acceptable reform. They were less interested in a preachership in St Moritz's parish which served mostly aristocrats. In 1476, Ulrich Schwarz, guildmaster of the salt-producers, overthrew the powerful smaller council and replaced it with a committee of guildmasters, where all the guilds would be represented equally; the old separation between greater (commercial) guilds and lesser guilds was abolished. Some masters, betraying their fellow guildmasters, used the opportunity to gain entry to the exclusive drinking club of the patricians, throwing their support to ousted aristocrats to help overthrow Schwarz and thus gained entry to patrician rank. The discontent among lower class artisans, particularly poor weavers who often could no longer compete with the greater weaving

32 A preaching mendicant, probably Johann of Freiburg O.P. Preachers often complained that their listeners were inattentive. People were known to gossip, flirt, and fall asleep during sermons.

concerns in Augsburg, led to frequent outbreaks of violence.[9] 1512 saw a particularly vociferous protest against the power and wealth of the city council by poorer day laborers and lesser guildsmen. The revolt was quietly suppressed by the city council. This action did not reduce the influence of guilds as it had in Nuremberg in 1349 when guild organizations were abolished and control of economic production was put entirely into the hands of the city council.[10]

Mendicant monks tried their best to accomplish reform within their own ranks, and were sometimes more successful at reforms than either bishops or city councils; their autonomous status made it possible to appoint competent preachers, to distribute alms to the needy and to expand hospitals and foundations that served the poor. Sermons at Augsburg's Franciscan, Dominican, and Carmelite churches drew large numbers of people. In 1454, St John Capistran preached for a week in the city through a translator, gathering crowds of nearly 20,000 from Augsburg and surrounding villages.[11] Berthold of Regensburg (+1272), the great Franciscan preacher was well remembered in Augsburg. In 1450, when the bishop announced a special papal indulgence, 'there was much complaining among the people who remembered what brother Berthold had preached to them long ago: when someone from Rome comes to your door, make sure you keep your purse closed'[12] Franciscans were immensely popular among the lower classes, somewhat less among the patricians. In August 1524, the reading-master of the Franciscans, Johann Schilling (+1525) preached openly against the exaggerated wealth of many patricians and monastic orders in Augsburg. He met regularly with common laypeople to discuss theology and promote evangelical ideas.[13] In 1518, the prior of the Carmelites in Augsburg, Johann Frosch (+1533) housed the Augustinian hermit Martin Luther during his audience with Cardinal Cajetan. Frosch was also the first to offer the eucharist in both bread and wine at the Carmelite church. The Dominicans and Augustinian canons remained generally loyal to the old church in Augsburg.

Lower-class artisans had long been associated with religious heterodoxy in Augsburg. There were many Waldensians in the city. In 1352, a group of people tried to organize a brotherhood at St James's chapel and were disbanded, since it was rumored that they sought a revolution based on the equality guaranteed in the bible.[14] There are several references in the protocol of the city council to 'cellar-people' who met secretly to listen to sermons preached by common people on indulgences, purgatory, and corruption in the Roman church. In 1393, fifty Waldensians were investigated on order of the city council. Council minutes note: 'there were heretics in Augsburg, all wool weavers and among them other artisans...who complained about the excise taxes, which the weavers in particular were subject to...for there were many poor, ruined weavers in Augsburg.[15] This identification of poor artisans with heresy continued. A preaching weaver in the 1480s attracted a large gathering of people at St Radegund's chapel near Wellenburg. After collecting a large sum of money, the weaver returned to his workshop to invest the money in his business. In 1502, five 'brothers in sackcloth' came to the city preaching conversion and prayed openly in the market.[16] Such wandering penitents and occasional lay preachers were not systematically prosecuted in Augsburg. Prosecution could precipitate an urban revolt in times of acute economic dislocation.

City authorities did their best to check the growth of miraculous cults. They were skeptical of the value of wonder-working relics, despite needed revenue from pilgrims. Yet, it became increasingly difficult to expose frauds when they were sanctioned by Roman privileges. There is the case of Anna Laminit (+1518), a woman who claimed to live from eating only the sacrament; she even drew the attention of the princes and emperor at the Augsburg Diet in 1518.[17] After a long judicial process she was exposed and expelled from the city. The case of the miraculous host at Holy Cross parish became the center of a bitter dispute between church authorities and city council. Bernard Stuntz, vicar of the cathedral chapter who came from one of the more important merchant families, attacked the increasing pilgrimage to the parish in 1497. The battle over the miraculous properties of the host drew the attention of the city council and the bishop. The parish sought special sanctions from Rome, an indulgence for the pilgrims to the miraculous host and even a special feast day. Stuntz was eventually forced to leave the city, only to be readmitted at the mercy of the city council in 1498 if he agreed not to preach against the host.[18] The city council was often forced to compromise its Humanist opinions when in conflict with church authority. Divisions in society and church meant that reform proceeded slowly, unevenly, revealing serious flaws in the ability of church and city to formulate, direct, and institute the reform demands of a changing society.

The tensions between council and lower classes, bishop and cathedral chapter, chapter and mendicants, the reform-minded and the traditional met the coming Reformation with divided opinions and confusion. Johann Geiler von Kaisersberg came to Augsburg to preach at the invitation of the city council, but refused to take the offer of the funded cathedral preachership in 1515.[19] The ascetic theologian, John Oekolampadius (+1531) from Basel, took the difficult post in 1518. When Oekolampadius found it impossible to reconcile growing Lutheran sympathies among the population with his own Humanist vision of the church, he stepped down to enter a monastery in 1519 and was replaced by a protégé of John Eck, Urbanus Rhegius (+1541) in 1520. Rhegius grew more and more sympathetic to Lutheran opinions. Augsburg Bishop Christoph von

D. Urbanum Rhegium
A.C. MDXXIV

Videtur ex imagine Reverendi
D. Regii et legitur, ex suis Scrip-
turis, spiritum et simulationem pæ-
ter veritatem Christi cum anima illi.

D. Johannes Frosch
A.C. MDXXXI

Effigiem connis quondam
venerabilis Rana:
Dum sua pro Christo membra
cremanda dedit. 1522

33 Drs. Urbanus Rhegius and Johannes Frosch, from an unpublished MS, *Chronica ecclesiastica Augustana*, 1749.

Stadion forced him to resign the same year he took up the post. He was replaced by another Humanist, but a more traditional theologian, Dr Matthias Kretz (+1543). Though most members of the city council were not Protestants, they insisted on maintaining their own privileges *vis-à-vis* bishop and cathedral chapter. Rhegius, banned from the city, returned at the mercy of the city council and was eventually appointed preacher at St Anne's.[20]

Representatives of the Bishop of Augsburg carried frequent reports of Lutheran preaching to Rome. On 1 December 1522, Pope Hadrian wrote to the mayors and council of Augsburg, complaining that the Edict of Worms, which forbade further discussion of Lutheran ideas in the press, was not being enforced. The pope noted that printers refused to publish works written by the old-church party. Emperor Charles V protested to the delegations of the city council at Valladolid in July 1523 for the same reason: nothing was being done to stop the progress of the Reformation in Augsburg. Formally, the city council took a neutral position, tolerating preachers from both old-church and evangelical parties.

Artisans constantly created trouble for the old-church party. A baker, George Vischer, interrupted a sermon given by a Dominican on 13 July 1523. The preacher, commenting on the feast of St Margaret, noted that she was the special patroness of pregnant women. The baker shouted at the monk, demanding that he prove this with holy scripture. The monk threatened to have the baker arrested and the baker agreed to go to jail

Templum Minoritanum.   Barfüßer Kirchen.

34 The Franciscan Church in Augsburg, scene of several disturbances in 1524.
From a seventeenth-century engraving.

if the monk could prove that St Margaret prayed for pregnant women by
showing him the place in the bible where this was stated. The city council
warned Vischer, who subsequently tried to interrupt Matthias Kretz's
sermons. He was called before the city council and set free again. On 8
May 1524, in the Franciscan church, the celebrant began the usual
blessing of holy water and salt after mass, before the sermon. Two
weavers, a painter, and about a dozen other artisans were gathered around
the font. When the celebrant raised the salt to bless it, the painter took
it and threw it into the water. When the monk wanted to bless the water,
the painter told him to use German, not Latin. When the monk refused,
the painter threw the Latin missal into the font. A tailor tried to tear the
book apart in the water, but because it was made from parchment, was
forced to take out his knife and cut it apart. Several people were taken
into custody, among them a weaver, Utz Rychssner. When questioned
about the incident, they blamed Johann Schilling, the Franciscan reading-
master. Schilling had met them in the house of a stonemason, where they
discussed theological matters. The Franciscan told them that holy water
was of no use and could not be used to forgive sins. He told them that
he would be happy when someone knocked over the font and got rid of
the salt: all these things were useless human additions to the mass. The
painter received a prison sentence, the tailor was exiled, and the weavers

were warned. The exiled tailor was readmitted nine months later. The city council was in a precarious position. It might tolerate evangelical preachers, but not radical Franciscans, who encouraged artisans to take church matters into their own hands. Through the vicar general of the observant Franciscans, they were able to secure Schilling's recall. On 3 August 1524, Schilling left the city. On 6 August, the smaller council of the city sat to take care of normal business. It was interrupted by a large crowd, estimated at 1,800 people, whose leaders demanded Schilling's return. The angry crowd would not accept the council's excuses, but dispersed, when the spokesman for the council agreed to do what he could to secure the Franciscan's return. In the meantime, councillors prepared a list of 86 rebellious artisans they had seen in the crowd, among them the weaver Utz Rychssner, the baker George Vischer, and the printer Philip Ulhart. On 9 August, the greater council was called together and the insurgents formally accused. The same afternoon Schilling returned. Jacob Fugger and the Benedictine monks of SS Ulrich and Afra could return from Biberach, where they had fled in fear of an artisan rebellion. In case of rebellion, the city council called an extra 600 armed soldiers to protect the city hall. Among these armed soldiers was Haug Marschalck. The council issued a warning to any artisans planning rebellion. To quiet any further unrest, two weavers from among the 86 were charged with plotting to overthrow the city government and were beheaded on 15 September. Many other weavers and other artisans fearing the same fate fled the city.[21] Two Augsburg citizens responded to these events in Augsburg with a battery of pamphlets: the weaver, Utz Rychssner, and Haug Marschalck, soldier and paymaster of the imperial troops in Augsburg.

Between January and November 1524, Utz Rychssner published four pamphlets: two dialogues, a treatise, and a papal chronicle.[22] The weaver is mentioned many times in city council records. He also owned enough property to pay taxes. He came to Augsburg from Strasbourg in 1503. He mentions that he once heard Geiler von Kaisersberg in Strasbourg and an evangelical preacher in Ulm.[23] He was an avid reader and often discussed theological ideas with his colleagues. His brief period of activity probably ended in his flight from the city in 1524. Unique among works in this study is Rychssner's *Selections from the Chronicle of Popes*. He selectively copied and edited an edition of a 1382 Strasbourg chronicle, updated by the Augsburg printer Johann Bämler to include Pope Sixtus IV (+ 1484).[24] The weaver chose his materials from the 1478 printed edition, 'that we might see the true light of godly word and be better able to recognize it among the human inventions which have already burdened mankind for a long time and seem to have no end.'[25] Clearly inspired by Humanist sermons, Rychssner opens his *Selections* with an attack on the tradition

35 Weavers at work. From Rodericus Zamorensis, *Speculum vitae humanae*,
1488.

that St Peter was the first Roman pope and ruled for twenty-five years
before he was martyred under Nero with St Paul. He cites scriptural sources
as lacking any real proof that Peter had been in Rome, claiming that this
is only a fable. The weaver's real purpose in writing is to expose human
inventions of the popes which had nothing to do with scripture. His source
tells him that St Peter commanded the forty-day lenten fast, which he is
eager to disprove with copious scriptural quotations; he claims that Peter
would never have created fasting regulations, citing Paul's reference to
the End, when authorities would try to forbid certain foods and marriage.

What is especially interesting about his *Selections* are the mistakes. Quite
predictably, since he was essentially copying, the chronology generally
follows in order with only two exceptions. Sergius I (+701) is curiously
inserted between Dionysius (+268) and Eutychianus (+283). In his
enthusiasm for telling a story about the only relatively good pope in his
list, he puts Celestine IV (+1198) out of order after Gregory IX (+1241).
Note what he tells us about Celestine IV: 'he was a pious, simple pope
and there was a cardinal who took a pipe, made a hole in the wall of the
papal bedchamber, and for three successive nights spoke this through the
pipe: "O' Celestine, give up the office of pope if you want to be saved."
Then this good, holy pope, who thought this was the voice of the holy
spirit, gave up his office and the same cardinal was elected pope in his

stead.'[26] Here he misquotes his source, from which the story was lifted verbatim. In the source, the story is actually about Pope Celestine V and the future Boniface VIII. Missing from his list of early popes is Clement I. He includes Linus, 'who declared that women must enter churches with their heads covered.' Anacletus is blamed for introducing the ordination of priests. Then Evaristus follows, omitting Clement I entirely. Pope Sylvester I (+335) is also curiously missing. The importance of this pope for the traditional papal claims to secular authority (not to mention his yearly commemoration on 31 December) was something Rychssner certainly must have been aware of. In examining the many gaps in the chronology of the *Selections*, it becomes more and more clear that Rychssner, in copying and editing his text, tried to steer away from the imperial–papal controversies. The difficulties experienced by the Ottonians with Roman popes, in particular John XII (+964) are omitted in the space in the chronology between 896 and 999. The famous investiture controversy is not even mentioned as our author entirely omits the period 1057–1198. The weaver's fifteenth century source points to exaggerated abuses of papal power.

Rychssner consciously chose text to be used as propaganda against Rome, but avoided imperial–papal controversies. Rychssner comments on traditionally 'bad' popes, popes whose use of papal power in the secular world helped them depose emperors. About Innocent III (+1216) he writes only: 'he separated nuns from monks who were accustomed to sing together in the same choir, and forbade laymen to strike a priest. And during this pope's time, the mendicant orders, Franciscans and Dominicans, were established.'[27] There is no mention of the controversy with Frederick II. About Boniface VIII (+1303) he also writes surprisingly little: 'he came to the papacy by trickery and made many additions to canon law and began the first jubilee with a Rome pilgrimage which included indulgences. He was known for his pomposity..., but it wasn't long before he was captured for his misdeeds and died of starvation, so that he ate his own fingers. Today we have this saying about him: he came to the papacy like a fox, ruled like an angry lion, and died like a dog.'[28] The last pope he considers in his chronicle is Innocent VIII (+1492), praised by Rychssner as a reformer because he tried to limit the number of benefices that could be held by the same priest. He ends his chronicle where his source ended, without information on later popes. Before concluding his work, the weaver cites several quotations from scripture condemning human additions to pure scripture and the wicked clergy who led people astray by raising such human inventions about the letter of the bible. His critique of the human inventions of the papacy serves to draw attention to the papal office as potential Anti-Christ. The weaver follows Zwinglian theology to expose the church as a sacramental institution based on a

Ain hübsch Gespräch biechlein / von aynem
Pfaffen vnd ainem Weber / die züsamen kumen seind
auff der straß was sy für red / frag / vñ antwort / gegen
ainander gebraucht haben / des Euangeliums vnd anderer sachen halben:

Dez Rychsner Weber. 1524.

36 *A Nice Dialogue between a Priest and a Weaver, who meet on the road...to discuss
the gospel and other things. By Utz Rychssner, 1524.*

tradition of laws in addition to scripture. The bible must stand above
tradition. His papal chronicles reappear in future works, as he continues
to expose the human teaching of the popes for his polemical purpose.

When Matthias Kretz assumed the preachership at the cathedral in
Augsburg, his traditional theology, especially the publication of a book
defending the sacramental status of auricular confession, drew much
criticism from Lutheran sympathizers, and particularly from Utz Rychssner.
In his *Dialogue between a Priest and a Weaver*, the weaver reveals his

sacramental theology. Like Martin Luther, he only recognizes baptism, eucharist and penance as sacraments.[29] His views on the first two sacraments are very traditional. He makes no mention of a necessary baptism in the spirit. He insists on enjoying the eucharist in both kinds. His sacramental theology is Lutheran. He defends the real presence and the necessity of communion for future salvation. Confession, he thought, is best done by one layman to another. He vigorously attacks confession to a priest, not particularly because of the payment required to receive the yearly absolution (although he does not like this either), but because the scriptures are silent on the nature of confession and absolution. He proves that ordination and confirmation were human inventions, insisting that the only exclusive right belonging to the priesthood is celebration of the eucharist. He calls Innocent I ($+417$) 'the devil's pope' for requiring extreme unction as a means to obtain forgiveness of sins. He states that if marriage were a Christian sacrament, then Jews, Turks, and heathens would have a Christian sacrament as well. According to the weaver, the first priests were the Virgin Mary, eleven apostles and the seventy-two disciples at the pentecost. In his *Dialogue between a Tradesman and a Weaver*, the tradesman, who at the beginning of the dialogue considers going to confession, concludes after his discussion with the weaver: 'you have instructed me wisely and convinced me of your way. I will read the bible diligently...and I confess that I have always secretly liked you and I will throw Dr Kretz's book into the oven today and I won't go to his sermons anymore...'[30]

Compared to other lay pamphleteers, Rychssner is far less spiritual in orientation. It is not clear whether he himself felt called to preach, although he consistently defends the rights of other common people to do so. He states positively that: 'the common man is like the prophets in ancient times, whose job it was to remind the clergy of their sins. John the Baptist reminded Herod of the sin of marrying his brother's wife. St Stephen and all the apostles and prophets did this, just as Moses warned the people of Israel. Therefore we must warn the clergy and the pope.'[31] The importance of this brotherhood of all Christians and the universal priesthood of all believers, is something he dedicates an entire treatise to. Although on the surface such a treatise might seem to be typical Anabaptist polemic, this is still far too conservative to suggest that Christians are temporally equal. Rychssner is careful to remind his readers not to misuse scripture. He tells his readers: 'and the chair of the Anti-Christ has been powerfully built and reinforced...yet we must be careful about speaking of it and writing about it, for it is said that this serves to create rebellion among the people, even if it is the word of God.'[32] Our weaver criticizes the same abuses that Humanists attacked in their sermons: purchasing masses, indulgences, paying for sacraments. He reminds his audience: 'O' dear brother, see what their works are...They say they have the holy spirit...but the bible is as pleasing to them as a sow in a Jewish synagogue. For they prefer to preach indulgences, private confession, confirmation, last rites, holy salt, oil, spices...eternal lights, chalices, vestments.'[33] He tells his readers that reading scripture and hearing sermons should result in the imposition of Christian virtues in their hearts: faith, hope, and love, which result in humility, a quality which would prevent them from taking up arms against the establishment. Like Sebastian Lotzer, the weaver commends the eschatological necessity of the works of holy mercy described in Matthew 24, feeding and clothing the needy, ministering to the sick and prisoners. Unlike Lotzer, he is less interested in preparation for good works. He is much more an agitating propagandist than a spiritual theologian.

Rychssner exploits the divisions among the clergy to make a case for his pure, biblical religion. He notes: 'one group says that the learned [clergy] have heaven in the palm of their hands, and the other group says that if you listen to the learned clergy, no one will get to heaven.'[34] He states conclusively that there had not been a holy prelate or prince in three or four hundred years. In his *Dialogue between a Priest and a Weaver*, the weaver implies solidarity between poor priests and poor artisans. At the end of the dialogue, having heard the weaver's comments on the human inventions of the popes and the existence of only three biblical sacraments, the priest replies: 'what can we poor priests and laypeople do? Our situation is hopeless. Nothing can help or change it. I don't want to challenge your opinions. Hold fast to the holy scriptures...until the End comes.'[35] Earlier in the dialogue the weaver admonished the poor cleric: 'dear sir:...You know well what Luke says in the 6th chapter. A kingdom which is divided will be destroyed...And you poor priests, don't you see that in Matthew 24, "You will be hated for my sake by all people and many things will happen, and some will say that they are Christ and will hate each other." Now it is clear that the time is already upon us!'[36] The weaver was convinced that the Anti-Christ was already on earth in the person of the pope and his clergy. For this reason, he took up his pen to save the Reformation, a movement the weaver claims had been growing for the previous four hundred years. He found it necessary to defend this conservative scriptural religion, lest the forces of evil subdue the saved in the imminent return of Christ. Like Sebastian Lotzer, he called the *lex evangelica* the true tradition of the church.

Was Rychssner dependent on Luther for his ideas? It is difficult to trace his sources. On some occasions, he rises to Luther's defense since Luther taught what was based in scripture. There seems as much an indication that the German works of Erasmus were as influential as those of Luther. His arguments against the Petrine claims of the papacy are reminiscent of those arguments in Erasmus' works. Rychssner is the only pamphleteer who complains of the use of secular music, organs and pipes in churches. Like Erasmus, he writes: 'what kind of worshipful atmosphere do organs produce in churches? When during many a mass, I could hardly say one "Our Father" before the organ interrupted me. And at Strasbourg, they even bring pipes, horns, and drums into the church!'[37] The weaver's use of the human teaching vs. the gospel paradigm reflects a Zwinglian orientation. Much contained in the weaver's statements could also be Waldensian in inspiration. The continuity of arguments, especially the scriptural conservatism evident in his works, and his particularly vehement attack on auricular confession are both traditionally Waldensian and reformed. For Rychssner, as for many of his pamphleteer colleagues, common people had to take reform into their own hands, to write and publish, since the bitterly divided clergy had failed them, and secular authorities, dominated by their own thirst for money, were only interested in maintaining power. The weaver is careful not to involve himself in imperial–papal controversies and to admonish his readers to passive resistance against attempts to stop evangelical reform. Rychssner is probably the most potentially radical pamphleteer in this sample. Ironically, the humility that he assumed would naturally accompany faith, love, and hope, is hardly evident in his own works. His works contain more polemical critique than positive suggestion. He assumed reading the bible was all that was necessary to prepare mankind for the coming End. The good works would necessarily flow from that activity. Even though he respects the sacramental mission of the church, he is more concerned with practical, biblical piety and the unity of laypeople. His model for church reform is a church confessing, brother to sister, not to a priest, in anticipation of the equality in the millennial kingdom.

What Rychssner seems to lack in spiritual theology his pamphlet-writing colleague in Augsburg, Haug Marschalck gracefully supplies. Marschalck was apparently born in Memmingen, the son of a merchant, in 1491. As an imperial soldier accustomed to taking risks, he entered the campaign to save church reform he thought was in danger of being lost. Working from his imperial army division in Augsburg, Marschalck managed to publish theological treatises between campaigns. He addressed his pamphlets to the emperor, the knights, and his fellow common people. His often desperate appeal to the emperor to support evangelical reform and evangelical preachers, to integrate that reform into official imperial policy, reflect the difficult time he experienced as an avid supporter of both imperial and evangelical causes. As paymaster for the imperial troops in Augsburg, Marschalck was seldom supplied with sufficient funds to pay his soldiers. Still he was required to join his disgruntled, poorly paid soldiers on many imperial campaigns: against Duke Ulrich of Wuerttemberg in

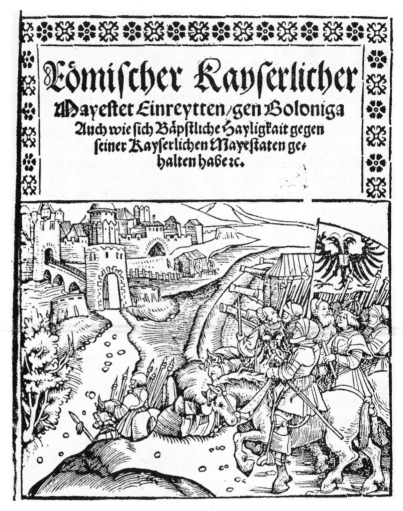

37 *His Imperial Roman Majesty's Entry into Bologna*, 1529. Haug Marschalck was
present when Charles V met Pope Clement in Bologna.

1519 and the revolting peasants in 1525. He saw service on the campaigns
against the French in Italy in 1525-26, and finally in the wars against
the Turks in 1529.[38] It is interesting that he was on close terms with the
influential mayor of Augsburg and leader of the Swabian League, Ulrich
Artzt, who shared his passion for theology. Marschalck achieved very few
of his goals. When he tried to publish a pamphlet on the eucharist in 1526,
the city council gave him a month's prison sentence. Marschalck often
attended sermons in the Franciscan church. He witnessed the disturbances

there in May, 1524. He helped to guard the city hall from possible insurgents in August–September of the same year. His six pamphlets were written between 1521 and 1525, a period when the city council was still tolerant of publishing laypeople.[39] Marschalck was admittedly a man of poor education. He gleaned his knowledge of biblical things from preachers he sought out in parishes and monasteries in Augsburg and on his travels. Local preachers, Urbanus Rhegius at the cathedral, the Carmelite Johannes Frosch at St Anne's, Johann Speiser at St Moritz's parish, and Johann Oekolampadius at the cathedral all helped to shape his theology, although Marschalck never acknowledges their inspiration in his works. The paymaster tells us that after hearing a sermon, he would return to his barracks to look up quotations from the bible himself. This helped him gain a superb knowledge of the bible, which he copiously cites in his pamphlets.[40] He dedicated one of his pamphlets to George von Frundsberg (+ 1528) a knight for whom Marschalck had much admiration and probably under whom Marschalck had personally served. Marschalck hoped that the support of reasonable soldiers and the emperor for evangelical reform would help to convince common people to avoid rebellion and surrender to the *lex evangelica*. Although he personally witnessed artisan protests, he was no friend of radicals and rebels. Poor, ill and disappointed, the paymaster died in Augsburg in 1535.

It is particularly difficult to trace the most important influences on Marschalck's theology. When he states that he learned just a little from evangelical preachers, he hardly exaggerates. His deep traditional spirituality reflects more the theology of medieval Nominalism, providing a context for the paymaster's own ideas about church reform. Contrition, mystical reunion, and the freeing of the human *synderesis* to ascend to God are the means by which he exhorts his readers to obedience. Like Sebastian Lotzer, he emphasizes the eschatological necessity of returning to the *lex evangelica*. Yet, unlike Lotzer, he could never excuse rebellious behavior. Marschalck's combination of deep affective piety, reformed ideas, critique of contemporary church practice, and trust in imperial leadership gives his theology a unique place among the lay pamphleteers in this study. The paymaster hoped that the emperor would soon be convinced of the righteousness of the evangelical party and lead it to battle against the papal Anti-Christ. In the meantime, before the emperor would accept reform and take on the battle against the pope, laypeople, 'the true, righteous, and Godly instruments of biblical music,' would assume the task of spreading the gospel in preparation for Christ's return.[41] Not surprisingly, he recommends that his fellow laypeople prepare themselves by reuniting their hearts with God, by lifting their *gemüthe* and by using the holy spirit available to them to preach the nearing kingdom of Christ. Reading scripture was not sufficient for Christians to fulfill their spiritual mission.

Marschalck complained that most people called themselves evangelical, but lacked the appropriate fire to realize an effective mission.[42] His pamphlets were intended to fan that fire, with a trust that obedience would result as the first fruit of faith.

The end of the world and the more recent resurrection of the gospel are important for Marschalck. Christ's return to save his elect would parallel Christ's historical mission, when he came to warn man of the End.[43] Evangelical reform was a sure sign of Christ's return; despite the turbulence of his own time, Marschalck insists that he enjoyed a particularly merciful generation, when the gospel, 'a great light which has been powerfully lit in the blind darkness of the world,' would warn mankind of the approach of Christ's kingdom.[44] Who could expect to be saved? 'Those who recognize and follow his heavenly teaching.' Who might be condemned? 'Anyone who would strive against his word and glory.'[45] Thus Christ had directly placed salvation in the hands of common people that they too might be apostles, for 'blessed are those who see what has been revealed to them.'[46] People must understand and grasp the word in order to be saved. At the last day, ignorance of the word would excuse no one: 'now there are other confounded and money-hungry people who shun the truth and refuse to read those honorable and useful evangelical pamphlets...At the last day their ignorance will not excuse them.'[47] The fact that preachers of the word had been persecuted by the authorities, who 'scorned them...driving them from village to village, because they stand for evangelical truth,' seemed to be a sign that Christ would return soon.[48]

Another powerful sign of the End is the rampant materialism which Marschalck sees everywhere in the world: 'the world is deeply rooted in temporal wantonness, with evil profit from temporal goods, with evil gains from unclean hope, and everything is overrun with evil greed. Some brutally seek the ruin of their fellow man and Christian brothers, in order that they might reap great profits and flaunt their great riches. This accounts for much sin...For there is a secular proverb: whoever can deceive the most is seen as the most praiseworthy.'[49] This materialism pervaded all levels of society. Young people were particular proof of this malevolence: 'look at the youth of today; no matter how small they are they must be surrounded with the richest things...This results in great pride, followed by both lack of chastity and lack of the fear of God. For we lose all humility, all patience, all propriety, and all our brotherly love.'[50] The parents of these impossible youth bear the responsibility for such behavior, 'for children are allowed to do as they please; they are dressed in silk clothes with gold beyond imagination.'[51] Marschalck attributes the general lack of Christian virtue to materialism. Parents, rather than teach their children, preferred 'to erect some great monument to their memory

stus der herz hat geredt. Jch wird mein glory voz den hoch
weiſen verbergē vnd wird es den kleinē verkünden vnd off
baren. Dañ ee mein glory vnd eer ſolt vndergon/es müſt
ent ee ſteyn vnd holtz reden lernen. Vff ſolichs iſt vffge-
richt anzüſchawē diſer Spiegel der Blinden.

38 *A Mirror for the Blind.* 1524, by Haug Marschalck. The title woodcut shows
a canon and a bishop looking for truth in a mirror held for them from a pulpit
by the Franciscan scholastic, John Duns Scotus. Because everyone is blindfolded
and even the mirror is covered, the truth is completely concealed. By contrast,
the common man on the right, presumably because he knows the gospel, can see
Christ and the angels in heaven clearly.

in the churches.'[52] The lust after material things prevented laypeople from
profiting by knowledge of the gospel: 'everyone returns home after the
sermon or discussion, continuing to sin as he did before, doing everything
just as before.'[53] Merchants and bankers ruined people by their 'unrea-
sonably ruthless behavior.' Artisans busied themselves with 'evil, wasteful
work.' Grocers tipped their scales. Wine purveyors watered their wine,
endangering 'the real warming power wine has in healthy blood and for

healthy members.' Bakers put plaster in their bread to make it weigh more. 'Even the nobility, who claimed to be evangelical do nothing but incite wars and thereby ruin poor people, making the streets unsafe.'[54] All this greed was a sign that Christ soon would return and that the last days were indeed nearing. 'Then your mass vestments, your chalices, your expensive paintings, your stone epitaphs and monuments will be washed away.'[55] To prepare for that day, people must be free of those temporal lusts which plagued their consciences and must be willing to forsake temporal riches for the riches of the kingdom of heaven.[56] Marschalck was seriously disturbed by economic change and the great discrepancy between rich and poor in Augsburg.

To prepare for Christ's return, common people must also do works of mercy, the six works of holy mercy that Christ commanded in the last days. Marschalck, motivated by eschatological necessity, admonished his fellow laypeople to 'house the needy, clothe the naked, give food and drink to the hungry and the poor.'[57] People who wanted to be saved must do four things to prepare for Christ's return: read scripture and evangelical pamphlets, preach the gospel, abandon worldly pursuits, and most importantly, seek an active ministry among the poor. The model for Marschalck's own brand of reformed Christianity is Mary Magdalen, 'who from the mouth of her heart lifted her soul to the word of God,' in order to unite her spirit with God. 'Thus the Lord has shown us that external things please him less, especially when we think we do God a favor by doing them: just like the Magdalen, we must sit at the foot of Christ diligently listening to the word of God, pushing all other cares from our mind, for Christ doesn't need your unnecessary troubles.'[58] Conversion of the heart is the essential spiritual preparation for works of mercy. Marschalck's theology is a combination of Protestant inspiration and the message of late-medieval reformers with its own ascetic tone, suggesting the influence of Oekolampadius. His use of Mary Magdalen as a model for laypeople is traditionally medieval.

As in the sermons of contemporary Nominalist theologians, the difference between man's and God's nature is never overemphasized in Marschalck's theology. Indeed, man and God seem to be similar species, by virtue of the *tau* (Marschalck's own term) planted in man. This *tau* is the mystical equivalent of the scholastic *synderesis*, that part of man, infused with grace at birth, that turns one naturally toward God. Yet man is weak, often susceptible to the intervention of evil from outside. Man's weakness is realized in the conscience: 'for many, through their cursed greed, risk the loss of that most sensitive part [i.e., the *tau*] and feel it in their conscience.'[59] The conscience can be freed by God's word when 'the common man receives understanding in his heart.'[60] The realization of the saving power of faith, received from God's word, is found in works, specifically in helping the poor. On the one hand, Marschalck attacks the works-holiness of the old church: 'Why should God need your counting and reading or your wax candles, or the icons you hang on your wall and adore?'[61] Because works of mercy are based on scripture, they may be meritorious. Here in Marschalck's theology as in Lotzer's theology, one notes the importance of mystical preparation for works. The eschatological element is the key. In general, Marschalck is far more positive than others in his glorification of the human condition. According to Marschalck, man could by his own nature turn to God, were it not for the limitations of his corruptible conscience. The holy spirit seems the best remedy for the weak conscience: 'the holy godly spirit working in people completes [God's] work, partially enlightening the weak spirit in order that the noble fruit [faith] can be inplanted and will continue to grow.'[62] Faith, according to Marschalck's understanding, is the key to meritorious action: 'Mary, worthy mother and spotless virgin, also lacked faith in the beginning, but she was strengthened and enriched by the holy Archangel Gabriel.'[63] This emphasis on the spirit is something he shares with earlier Waldensians and later Anabaptists.

Before examining the role he assigns the new evangelical Christian in the church and the world, one must understand Marschalck's view of the nature of society and man's place in that society. Visible in the paymaster's attitude toward social organization is a confirmed opinion that God's intention for society was decidedly hierarchical; never does he make any pretense of human equality. He imposes the human hierarchical ordering of society on heaven:

O' what a wonderful, lovely, holy imperial diet in which heaven and earth can rejoice! To preside over that imperial diet comes the all-powerful, invincible emperor, the most powerful, mild, and good Lord, word of God. He came as a little human baby from the heavens of the Godly empire. O' you honorable word of God, you held this marvelous imperial diet (at his birth) where princes in all their glory came and sought you, recognizing your powerful majesty.[64]

The social order of heaven is identical with the social order on earth. Christ is the emperor, the apostles and evangelists comprise the electors; the saints in heaven are the heavenly counterpart of the laity on earth, to whom Christ, the emperor, chose to reveal himself: 'You all powerful emperor, you dearest Christ, you assembled this marvelous diet on earth, revealing yourself to poor shepherds. How would our rich shepherds now detract from their honor?'[65] Christ would, however, return for another such diet. Just as the epiphany personified that first earthly diet, so the last judgment would realize the second. The second time, Christ would invite artisans and the poor to share his kingdom, 'poor fishermen, carpenters, rug makers, all ignorant people.'[66] At this diet, the position of the Holy Roman

39 The lay estate, led by the emperor attacks a canon lawyer and a bishop, while all the churches are destroyed. Woodcut from Joseph Grünpeck's *Spiegel*, 1522.

Emperor on earth assumes special importance. Imperial mythology in the image of Frederick II is not far removed from Marschalck's historical assumptions. A vision of a papal Anti-Christ doing battle with a good noble emperor in the last days is explicit in Marschalck's first pamphlet: 'oh wise emperor, it is right that you show the pope and his host by using holy scripture that he is truly a vicar of the devil and the Anti-Christ, for indeed, papal law has no good foundation beyond that which humans have managed to dream up, nothing more than the stinking fish of the devil.'[67] His use of Christ as the good emperor (not a model for a good pope) constitutes an 'imperial piety' of the highest order!

Because Emperor Charles V was reluctant to acknowledge the same 'evangelical truth,' common people needed to assume a new role. They would have to prepare themselves. First they ought to read holy scripture: 'So read all the books... in which the righteous good teaching is contained for the instruction of the long misled common people... as well as the bible, the true foundation of Godly teaching.'[68] At the same time, spiritual inner conversion is necessary to understand what is revealed in scripture: 'it won't help you here to read books and hear sermons if you live your life in such an evil manner, disputing and arguing all the time. We must stick our hands into the proper dough and hold on. What is the true dough? Love God with all your heart, with all your soul and your *gemüthe*, then love your neighbor as yourself...When we do that, then the good evangelical sermons can do us some good.'[69] He encouraged his readers/ listeners to read scripture, to love God, to offer their hearts and souls, and lastly to do works of charity, to prepare the way for the second coming.

The devil might intervene in his salvific formula. He interrupts God's natural harmony with mankind, continuing to misdirect humans from the real road to salvation. Christ disputed with the devil in Marschalck's *Sharp Axe against Those who call Themselves Evangelical, yet are opposed to the Gospel*: 'Devil: "No, no, I have bound them on their oath; they cannot escape me!" Captain of the King of Glory: "Get out of here, Devil! Whatever men swear against the honor of their king, against the trust and love of their neighbor, and against the salvation of their souls, they are not bound to keep!"'[70] It would be easy to see the ideal emperor in Marschalck's earlier works in the role of captain in this dialogue. Here the emperor as captain of Christ, slayer of the Anti-Christ, and defender of the *lex evangelica* personifies the great imperial hero of medieval legend. Thus the evangelical movement seems not only to represent what people like Marschalck would call the 'real' tradition of the church, but it also actively fulfills a medieval prophetic tradition. Not surprisingly, Marschalck casts the entire program of redemption in pseudo-military context. Sin, the weapon of the devil, continues to attack man. God, man, and the devil are all part of a great battle scheme, where eventually a triumphant Christ and his great army of saints would destroy the devil, really and historically: 'there are two cities or castles, God's and the devil's. God's castle is walled and fortified with love to the point of almost unrequited love. The devil's castle is walled in with self love, to the point of scorning God's love...God's castle has a secret battle slogan: unity and peace. The devil's castle has one too: rebellion and disturbing the peace.'[71] The devil encourages man to rise up against authority. Indeed, man often can not distinguish between the devil's castle and God's castle, since the fortifications look identical. Thus, man could justify rebellion in the name of the gospel, while in reality, he follows the devil. The gospel is clearly a bearer of peace and concord – this is where enthusiasts and Anabaptists are mistaken.

The paymaster aggressively opposed the Peasant Wars. Unlike Lotzer, who could excuse some violence, if committed in the interest of promoting the word of God to the point of martyrdom, Marschalck cannot defend rebellion: 'do you think that you can be holy and evangelical and at the same time lend your support to those who promote rebellion and disturb the peace? No, indeed; as soon as you come to a truly evangelical man with your rotten complaints, he will avoid you and will put no trust in you. Why? In your heart you know what Isaiah says: The godless cannot tolerate peace.'[72] It was the devil acting on earth that caused people to rebel against authority. Marschalck describes the actions of the devil thus: 'He poisons human hearts and tears out the noble heavenly *tau*.'[73] The *tau* represents the capacity of man's reason to discover God. If left alone by the devil and unclouded by human teaching, that ability to reason can bring man to God: 'Give in to your nature; seize the reason in your soul, look, experience, and read what God has put into your heart...Now use that reason to benefit your dear Christian neighbor.'[74] Divine reason has its origin with God, but there is also a parallel, less reliable human reason: 'we cannot hope or put trust in humanity, nor in human reason, human trust, human teaching, human ceremonies, and all that is not born of the word of God.'[75] Yet the *tau* is in every man, and must be nurtured, be allowed to grow and to bear fruit, that is, good works.[76] Obviously, reason is capable of meritorious works, providing the word of God conditions the *synderesis*. Here Marschalck adapts an evangelical concept to his mystical, Nominalist-inspired, late-medieval piety. The overall assessment of man's possibilities is positive. The focus remains, however, on the Christ-figure as material word. Marschalck's theology is by all means Christocentric. The material *Verbum Dei* is the true object of faith: 'in him we put our trust and in him alone; we should call on him when we are in need. We need no advocate other than him'.[77] Christ is more than an historical figure; the atonement is much more than a simple historical event: 'for he not only suffered for us in his body, but, to some extent, he still suffers for us in our body.'[78] Marschalck's image of Christ is still influenced by a medieval picture of Christ as vengeful judge: 'you let yourself down from on high and put yourself in this poor vale of tears to warn us of the horrible day of the gnashing of teeth, and of the joy of your great honor in the kingdom of your father.'[79] Following a Renaissance tradition, Marschalck casts Christ as a loving, tender, merciful man: 'our king gave up his power, his justice, and his riches to the father, and took on human weakness, sin, and poverty, and sought us in dust and all uncleanliness, in order that he might bring honor to you, and therefore you should desire to be evangelical, seeking the Lord and returning that honor.'[80] He combines both images of Christ, though the Christ operative in this world is no longer quite as merciful as he once had been; when he returned he would vindicate his elect.

Reconstruction of the ecclesiological perspective of these pamphlet writers in the sixteenth century can be an extremely difficult endeavor, especially since the overwhelming importance of eschatological ideas often precludes thoughtful development of a theology for the church militant that is marking time until the second coming. Since many pamphleteers saw the Protestant reformers as part of the fulfillment of eschatological prophecy, they were seldom willing to deal with concepts of temporal authority or tradition. Their conception of lay apostleship is shaped by that sense of immediacy, lest Christ return and find his flock unprepared. Caught in the general economic upheaval of the sixteenth century, it is not surprising that downwardly mobile members of society would find consolation in the hope of an immediate final reckoning.

Marschalck's criticism of contemporary clergy reflects his own negative appraisal of more recent economic developments. When particularly provoked, he calls the Roman clergy 'vipers and snakes,' or 'simple bad shepherds with the bark of wolves';[81] when less offended, Marschalck attributes their corruption to general economic materialism: 'oh venomous, damned penny! The root from whence you have sprung is poison, indeed!' exclaimed the paymaster.[82] Marschalck insists that lay activity was part of the genuine tradition of the church and that the Roman concept of tradition as revelation through holy fathers and councils was in reality only a means of protecting the financial interests of the Roman clergy. Like Humanists he heard preach, Marschalck contrasts his 'high and noble German homeland,' with the depravity of Roman courtesans.[83] The Roman church had abandoned the word of God. The church from apostolic times through the patristic period has remained true to the word, according to Marschalck, until the Romans submitted to the temptations of the secular world and 'had covered the spiritual fathers with lies.'[84] Marschalck saw himself and his evangelical mentors as martyrs for the word against idolatry and heresy. He found historical precedent for such martyrdom: 'the pious bishop Polycarp showed the Romans that the heretic Arius was a son of the devil, just as the holy martyrs destroyed idols for Christ's sake.'[85] One can imagine how Humanist reformers fed this fire of anti-Roman sentiment, giving the polemical propaganda in favor of the Reformation a particularly biting edge. Marschalck himself had very little knowledge of the church fathers. He may have heard about them from Rhegius, who often cited Augustine, Cyprian, and John Chrysostom in his sermons. The source for Marschalck's mysterious combination of Polycarp and Arius is anyone's guess! He obviously links Arius to Rome in order to show some precedent for Roman heresy. He emphasizes Peter's denial of Christ to discredit the Roman see, a device not uncommon in reformers' sermons.[86] Romans had added human teaching to God's word and had subsequently raised this human teaching to Godly commandment. Thus, they had been able to successfully suppress the lower clergy: 'the lower clergy has no time to read the writings of great prelates and courtiers, since they must depend on their poor families. They have no great titles; most of them have to cut wood or learn difficult crafts. They have no time to study any more. For the proverb holds true here, "the greatest in title conceal the lowest craftiness in their velvet cloaks"'.[87] Marschalck calls the Romans 'apostates and treasure hunters,' who refuse to recognize their error: 'they don't want to be corrected in their evil abuses; for what happened in the beginning was that they used Latin language for right and proper reasons, but now they use Latin to keep laypeople ignorant.'[88]

Since God no longer wanted 'human invention' mixed with the truth concealed in his word, church reform was necessary. The *lex evangelica* is Marschalck's answer to clean up Roman pollution, since it was 'the oldest, most righteous, and healthy teaching of Christ.'[89] Christ had defended his father's honor on earth; why should laypeople fail to take their apostleship seriously and follow him? Because the authority of the Roman church was grounded in human rather than godly teaching, Christians were not bound to obey it: 'for whatever has been added to the word of God from human teaching is nothing, is invalid, accomplishes nothing, and will be swept away.'[90] The Wittenberg theologians received praise from Marschalck because they based their teaching on the gospel through the 'inpouring of the holy spirit.' Marschalck contrasts Luther's acceptance of the pure gospel with the confoundedness of the Roman authorities who wanted to persist in their abuses.[91]

The image of the Roman church is not a treasury of spiritual merit in Marschalck's theology, but a corrupt institution designed to rob poor people. The parish clergy could no longer make do with their benefices; yet the great prelates had so many benefices that it became necessary to appoint vicars who could themselves hardly make do with the paltry stipends given them by the bishops who received the income from these benefices.[92] Financial oppression left mendicants no time to read; instead they were forced to 'herd pigs, thresh wheat, work in the fields, or even run away.'[93] Bishops no longer wanted to write, for they were too tired for writing and publishing after a long day's hunt: 'they cannot think up any respectable teaching because of the crude harshness of their condition, for they are too old, too drunk and too lazy.'[94] The church's financial holdings had forced it to hire 'procurators, lawyers, solicitors, and other beggars.' Thus, the sacraments themselves were offered for money: 'what is there in our temple that is not sold for money and exchanged for benefices and God's gifts? The Jews sold only doves..., but our pastors sell the holy sacrament of the body of Christ, and the holy sacraments of baptism and penance, too, together with heaven itself for filthy money!'[95] Like Sebastian Lotzer, Marschalck vigorously opposes the offering of money on the altar. He condemns it as a 'pagan or Jewish custom' not commanded by Christ.[96] The Roman church had taught people to offer money: 'if we would give them money, they would help us into heaven with indulgences and take care of the souls of the dead in exchange for a large offering.'[97] These offerings seemed contrary to

40 The world turned upside-down. Woodcut from Joseph Grünpeck's *Spiegel*, 1522. A farmer celebrates mass in a church, while priests and monks are forced to plow the fields.

those Christ demanded from man in the gospels. Christ wanted a different sort of offering: 'thus Matthew says in the twelfth chapter, "I want mercy, not offerings." And from that I understand what I should offer...Should I desire to offer money for a dead relative, or a friend's dead relative, I would not lay it on the altar, but instead give it to the poor, since I understand that this is the sort of offering God desires and will accept no other.'[98] Marschalck, like Lotzer and Rychssner, recommends the six works of holy mercy as the safest means to salvation. The poor as the treasury of the church offered all people a means to achieve eternal life. Marschalck objects less to the concept of praying for the souls of the dead than he does to the kind of offering required.

Spiritual offerings in accordance with scriptural directives presuppose some form of communication between God and man. Communication is a sign of reconciliation. In Marschalck's piety, spiritual reunion becomes a sacrament: 'instead of lighting candles we ought to enlighten our hearts with faith, and we should offer our hearts up to God, not that candles at mass or honoring the holy sacrament are essentially wrong, but their use is an evil pagan and Jewish custom.'[99] The importance of the reunion of the heart with Christ as an extra-sacramental act of faith is the core of Marschalck's message. It is this act which these pamphleteers see as a special sacrament of the third age, an age of the spirit. Because the paymaster's theology presupposes a nearing End, the essential pious teaching of the late-medieval reformers is raised to pseudo-sacramental status. Since, in the third age, all the traditional sacraments of the church would pass away, a new and special reunion might replace them. Faith is the sign of this new 'sacrament' and the holy spirit is its substance: 'God doesn't want your money and your possessions, but wants your heart and your soul,' in order that he might infuse the saving faith of the Holy Spirit, 'so that body and soul might be saturated!'[100] The *Sursum Corda* of the great thanksgiving in the mass has a special significance for Marschalck: '*Sursum Corda*. Our lord God does not want you to suffer from heavy burdens in your heart and conscience. For we are all flesh and blood, ordinary weak creatures, yet it is not necessary that we fall to things of the flesh, since with the help of God's holy spirit, we can overcome them.'[101] The holy spirit infuses in people the all important faith, 'for nothing but strong powerful faith in him can help us, since faith comes from God himself. This faith cannot fail, and will bring good fruit and works to him.'[102] Grace is mediated, therefore, from God, via the holy spirit, to people in the form of faith, which allows people to do good works commanded by and acceptable to God. This grace is mediated by scripture and also by contemplation as in the following figure:

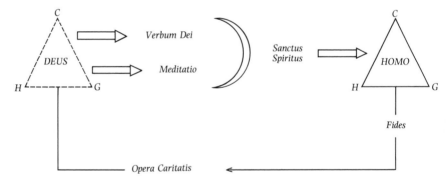

Figure 4. The Economy of Salvation in Haug Marschalck's Pamphlets

When speaking of faith, Luther is probably the paymaster's inspiration.

Sebastian Lotzer reduces the mediators of grace common to late-medieval pious works to one single medium, scripture. Marschalck preserves contemplative elements (in the form of simple meditation), in his explanation of the Lord's Prayer:

Holy be your name. O that we might attain that good spirit from the mercy of God; that his name become holy in us; that we never cease to praise him, and never again speak evil things, or be deceitful, either to God or to our neighbor, but only seek to sow God's praise. Just as is written in Psalm 48: 'Praise the Lord from the heavens; praise him in the highest; all the angels praise him; the heavenly host praises him; all the stars, the sun, the moon and other lights praise him; all the heavens shall praise him, etc.'[103]

Marschalck's description of the life of Christ expresses a special tenderness: 'consider the pure, chaste, Mary, chosen from among all other creatures on earth, a woman poor in terms of material possessions, yet rich in honor, in purity, in wisdom, and in holiness. Consider then Joseph, a poor carpenter, yet also rich in wisdom, purity, and holiness.'[104]

What we find in his theology is a strong scripture-based piety, complimented by an equally deep mystical, affective piety. He preserves not only the contemplative aspects of affective piety, but also the Nominalist *synderesis*, the force which naturally turns man toward God. The holy spirit conveys God's grace to man in Marschalck's theology. This grace may be obtained by reading scripture, contemplating Christ's life and passion, and by receiving the holy eucharist which, according to Marschalck, is the only force which links the heavenly and earthly cities. The eucharist is a sign of God's affection for man: 'he left us an important inheritance as he departed this earth, dear children, which is the most noble, precious inheritance and possession which could be in heaven or on earth...his most holy and tender body and his rose-colored blood, which he ordered us to take and receive.'[105] As that link between heaven and earth, the real presence of Christ in the eucharist is preserved to demonstrate the bridge between both cities, or, in Marschalck's terminology, both enemy camps! Marschalck's attitude toward church reform is determined by his extremely legalistic and formal vision of society, combined with a deep, intensely mystical medieval spirituality. He projects the hierarchical organization of society and its legal systems on the heavenly host to create an ideal model for people on earth as a standard for reform.

Marschalck's works did not go unnoticed. They went through several editions in various cities and can be found scattered throughout archives in Southern Germany. They even attracted the attention of Michael Hug, reading master to the Franciscans in Lindau, who dedicated a pamphlet to the paymaster in 1524. The pamphlet, entitled *A Brief, but Christian Sermon on True and Righteous Faith...*, takes its tone and its theology from St Paul's epistles.[106] Hug addresses Marschalck in recognition of his reputation as 'an especially diligent follower of the gospel.' The Franciscan sought to add to and develop further the lay theologian's emphasis on the necessity of good works in the last days by discussing the importance of faith. Preaching salvation by grace alone in this Lenten sermon, Hug

41 Imprisonment in a Tower (*Turmstrafe*). Woodcut from Ulrich Tengler's *Laien-spiegel*, 1508. When Haug Marschalck attempted to publish a pamphlet on the importance of the eucharist in 1525, the city council in Augsburg sentenced him to one month in prison in a tower in Augsburg's city wall.

commends the works which must flow from faith, as well as the transcendental nature of the faith inspired by the spirit, which he suggests 'goes far beyond any historical faith.' It is the trust in Christ alone, praised in his saints, which can insure Christians grace and reconciliation with God. The Franciscan deplores any attempts to seek grace by the invocation of saints: 'for Christ promised to grant what was asked in his name, not in the name of SS. Peter, Nicholas, Sebastian or any other.' Hug also disliked the denotation of the Virgin Mary as 'font of grace.' According to him, all the epistles of Paul disprove such theories. He ends his sermon dedicated to Marschalck, 'Praise be to the holy spirit which leads us to Christ through scripture.'[107]

Marschalck, like Lotzer and Rychssner, advocates a lay apostolate, although he does not make this apostolate the sole object of his polemic. His goal in reforming the church is the creation of an actual elect, to form a holy army against the works of the devil, as he attacked the human teaching of the apostate Roman church. His theology is reminiscent of Taborite theology, but closer to Waldensian models, since Marschalck avoided any suggestion of social revolution or armed uprising. His pamphlets are essentially scriptural and pastoral showing Lutheran and perhaps Erasmian influence. They reflect both a naive understanding of contemporary power politics and a vision of an ideal church in a less corrupt society of the future. Marschalck, like his contemporary pamphleteers, makes it clear that he as a layman had every right to speak, since God had always in the past revealed himself through simple pious laymen and would continue to do so in the future. The rebirth of the gospel among common people was a sign of progress toward the last judgment, an image never far removed from the paymaster's thoughts. Inevitably, the works of holy mercy seem more important than preaching as the means by which laypeople could effect Christ's return. Common to these pamphleteers is the necessity of obedience to temporal law without losing sight of an ultimate spiritual law, the *lex evangelica*. Laws of human design seemed opposed to eternal law in the scriptures, another sign for these pamphleteers that Christ's return was imminent.

Perhaps the pamphlets of Marschalck and Rychssner did help to stir artisans to violent protest in the churches, but not necessarily against civic authority. In Augsburg, the pamphleteers were careful to admonish their readers to obedience to civil authority. The shouting baker at a sermon and the weavers who interrupted the baptism in Augsburg were engaged in the same sort of protest action we saw in Memmingen, when protestors demanded immediate, uncompromising conformity to the *lex evangelica*. It is possible, as Scribner feels, that pamphlets were responsible for such active protest, as for instance, abolitionist literature was responsible for motivating citizens like John Brown to violent protest in pre-civil war

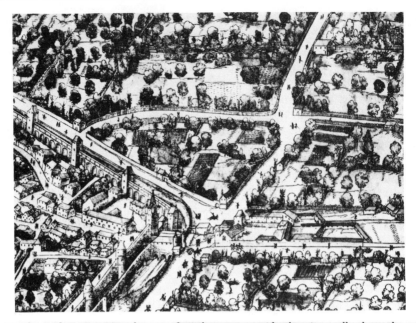

42 The Red Gate in Augsburg and settlements outside the city wall where the weaver Utz Rychssner lived. Poorer artisans lived outside the city walls. Detail from the 1521 city plan by Andreas Seld.

America. Yet, unlike abolitionist propaganda that focused on a single, clear, moral issue, the pamphlets of our sample highlight different kinds of complaints. Still, the definition of the opposition in these pamphlets is clear: the decadent clergy who prefer human law to eternal law, lead others astray, and exclude themselves from Christ's nearing kingdom.

Historians like Tentler and Ozment may point to confession as the single greatest flaw in the old church as an institution, but the objects of protest in Augsburg are more varied. Rychssner does mention confession as a particular problem and prefers that sinners confess to each other, rather than take absolution from a priest. This is a constant theme in Waldensian documents since the twelfth century and exemplifies what Lionel Rothkrug noted as a 'shift to a new collective responsibility.' This new collectivity is demonstrated, too, by the popularity of brotherhoods, which played such an important role in late-medieval lay piety.[108]

In Augsburg we have two very different conceptions of the Reformation in the works of two pamphleteers, writing from the same city at the same time, who witnessed the same events. Rychssner is more political propagandist than spiritual Christian. He emphasizes the brotherhood of all Christians, the activity of the spirit, and the necessity of works of mercy in the last days, as did many Waldensians before him and Anabaptists after him. He has less in common with Sebastian Lotzer and Haug Marschalck. Haug Marschalck discussed his universe in imperial, military terms. God fought the devil and won; man must fight the devil to conquer sin, to be made worthy to be saved; the gospel must be used to fight materialism and corruption, because it would logically defeat human teaching. The paymaster's spirituality is mostly medieval, relying on a reconciliation of the human heart with God in order to prepare for the eventual battle. Marschalck uses traditional mystical terminology to describe the nature of this reunion, a step beyond the spirituality of Sebastian Lotzer. By employing the technical terminology of medieval mystics, he puts himself in touch with a long medieval tradition, once confined to monasteries, but brought to the world by reforming Humanists. He provides us with an excellent example of what one could call imperial piety. At the core of Lionel Rothkrug's thesis is the assumption that a well entrenched imperial piety in Bavaria, crusading and Marian in character, prevented the adoption of Protestantism in that region.[109] The Virgin Mary still plays an important role for Marschalck, as model, but not as mediatrix. Marschalck's imperial piety was no roadblock to Protestantism. He reconciled his decidedly hierarchical, aristocratic attitudes toward religion with the needs of his own society to combat foreign ideas and growing materialism. The result was an imperial Protestantism. The principles of collective responsibility so common to Lotzer and Rychssner are entirely missing in Marschalck's works.

As different as Marschalck and Rychssner are in their attitudes toward preparation for reform, both have many things in common. Divisions within the clergy were too apparent for them. Their common search for order brought them to an image of the church awaiting the last judgment based on a conservative, but not necessarily fundamentalist interpretation of scripture. The result of the infiltration of Renaissance ideas into German society had caused both frustration with the present situation and a desperate longing for a romantic millennium, when evil, material or otherwise, would be destroyed once and for all. The political impotency of common people to effect change is reminiscent of the plight of early lay movements, caught up in the midst of rapid economic change. Increasing literacy and the possibility of bringing their ideas to a broader public gave these laypeople an advantage earlier laypeople did not enjoy. The earlier movements had to rely on a charismatic leader; they might find a patronizing bishop or city council if they wanted to succeed. The printing press opened a new route for our laypeople to the forefront of major theological controversy, on a level never before open to them.

The activities of radical mendicants, in particular Franciscans like Johann Schilling and Michael Hug, encouraged solidarity among artisan

protesters in Augsburg. Unlike other pamphleteers in this sample who are
so critical of mendicant monks and their pretensions, both Marschalck and
Rychssner are reluctant to single out the mendicants for their vehement
critique of the failure of the church. The fruits of observant reform in
Augsburg led by Johannes Faber (+1531) were apparently positive in
the eyes of many common people. Pamphleteers in Augsburg profited too
from tensions within the political system in the city. Unity in the city
council was difficult to achieve because of different economic and political
interests. The divisions between the *novi homines* and lower guildsmen were
no help in creating a united front against strong political forces within
the church: bishop, cathedral chapter, Benedictines, mendicants, all
hoping to retain and preserve ancient privileges. The tensions within the
city council are set against a battle between city council, cathedral chapter,
mendicants, and the evangelical preachers. The course of reform in the
city was predictably confused; some of the preachers who called themselves
evangelical, e.g. Rhegius and Oekolampadius, seem more influenced by
Zwingli than Luther at times, but as Humanists in their own right they
provided an individual program for reform. Speiser and Frosch may have
been more Lutheran in their theological ideas. These divisions within the
evangelical clergy were at least as important as the divisions between
old-church and evangelical parties: one cannot perceive these divisions,
however, in the theology of Marschalck and Rychssner. They expected an
evangelical reform that would prepare the way for the End, based on the
lex evangelica; in Marschalck's works this reform would come finally with
the armies of the emperor who would go to battle against the papal
Anti-Christ. For Rychssner this reform would come from his brother and
sister Christians who would use the bible to remodel their own lives in
preparation for the second coming. Like Lotzer, they both tend to view
reform of the church in Zwinglian colors of opposition, of human teaching
and the church of the gospel. Their sacramental theology remains
essentially Lutheran in the number of sacraments and in preserving the
integrity of the real presence in the eucharist. The city as community of
equals, the preservation of a *bonum communis* is important in determining
the direction of Rychssner's works. Marschalck's conception of society is
hierarchical, military, and dynamic, certainly in terms of leadership; yet,
his theology on a more personal level is democratic, spiritual, mystical,
and affective. Friedwart Uhland noted that their pamphlets prepared the
ground for the Anabaptism that came later in Augsburg: 'the Lutheran
reformation was important because it gave impetus to people to reform
their lives strictly according to Christian commandments. The ideal life
was one lived in humility and service to one's neighbor, in simplicity and
without want. The imperfect reality of the situation was measured against
this ideal vision.'[110] Uhland is correct in his assumption, but narrow in

assigning the roots of this reformation to Luther. The demands for conformity to the *lex evangelica* were as old as the great lay and mendicant movements of the twelfth century. The *sola gratia* solution for salvation and the practical works holiness of lay pamphleteers is as medieval as it may be reformed. Zwingli, Luther, Rhegius, Erasmus, and Schappeler were seen by our pamphleteers as important prophets, whose ideas were integrated into that vision of an ideal life based on the letter of scripture. The chaotic state of society was proof that Christ would soon return. Since the priesthood and church hierarchy had failed them, common laypeople would have to assume the mission to the poor and simple, that Christ commanded in Matthew 25.

CHAPTER V

Nuremberg: a shoemaker, a painter, and an inquisition

Nuremberg was different from other imperial cities in at least three respects: first, members of the city council in Nuremberg were better educated and more powerful than in any other municipal government in the German speaking part of the empire. Among its councilors could be counted first-rate Humanists and wealthy patricians, who were as well acquainted with the theological issues of the Reformation as they were aware of trends in an international economy. Artisan unrest was somewhat less a problem in Nuremberg, since the city council had effectively excluded artisans from participation in its government: there had been no guilds in Nuremberg since 1394, when after an uprising they were forcefully dissolved.[1] The city council maintained its own representative in Rome to lobby the papal curia. The council controlled appointments of the provosts to the two major parishes in the city, St Lawrence's and St Sebald's. In the fifteenth century the council obtained these appointment rights through its representative at the curia.[2] Secondly, after Cologne, Nuremberg was the next most populous city in the empire: by 1450, the city had a population of over 30,000, among whom could be counted nearly 5,000 artisans and 446 clergy. By the Reformation, the city may have housed as many as 40,000 people, however poorly: a city chronicler noted that Nuremberg was a city 'so populous, that people live on top of each other, some under the steps because there is a terrible shortage of apartments.'[3] The city council controlled commerce and production within its territories. It set the number of apprentices each master could take on, fixed prices, forbade religious brotherhoods and private taverns, where artisans might organize.[4] Thirdly, Nuremberg played a very important role in imperial government. The city housed the crown jewels and most sacred relics of the empire in its Holy Spirit Hospital. The imperial supreme court met in Nuremberg, as did imperial diets. The city's international commercial ties were extensive. Nuremberg was in many ways the most important city in the empire, certainly more prosperous than many other cities. Its churches and altars could be counted among the loveliest in Europe.[5]

43 View of Nuremberg, showing the two parish churches, St. Lawrence's and St. Sebald's. From Hartmann Schedel's *Weltchronik*, 1493.

Yet, however large and important Nuremberg might have been, its social structure was not unlike that of other imperial cities. Most recent scholarship argues that wealth was not quite so concentrated in Nuremberg's upper class as in other cities, that some wealth was shared by more prosperous artisans. Nearly 450 citizens in Nuremberg could be considered rich in 1500, a greater percentage of the city's population than in Augsburg. Nuremberg's artisans were not nearly as poor as many in other cities, which helps to explain the great immigration to Nuremberg in the depression of the late fifteenth century. Still, like other imperial cities in the late Middle Ages, nearly one third of the city's population in 1500 could be considered poor. These poor were mostly artisans and day laborers who did not own enough to be taxed and who, as early as 1522, were dependent on the city poor-chest for relief. Public support of the poor had an early history in Nuremberg.[6] The political impotence of Nuremberg's artisans had few serious consquences, since the paternalistic attitudes of the city council and a generally healthy economy reassured the lower classes that things were improving. The council provided important social services for artisans. Councillors were also apparently willing to listen to and redress grievances. City government was more effective in dealing with real centers of political power, which helped it to extend control over the clergy and the poor. Nuremberg's city council even seems to have increased wage levels to meet inflation. As a result, the city experienced none of the artisan unrest that plagued other cities in the early sixteenth century.[7]

The political acumen of Nuremberg's city council gave it decided advantages in dealing with both the Bavarian dukes and church officials. The Bishop of Bamberg, in whose diocese the city was located, often complained about the council's intentions to gain control over all clerical appointments, its desire to inventory monastic foundations in the city, and attempts to try clerical offenders in municipal courts. But the council was able to use imperial connections to circumvent the power of the local nobles and bishop. The council's enthusiasm for reform of its monasteries was well known in Rome. Reforming popes granted extraordinary concessions to the council in Nuremberg. The city lobbied in Rome for indulgences for the pilgrimage to its own St Sebald. To commemorate St Sebald, a parish church of St Mary was detached from its mother church in Furth and rededicated to him. Pope Sixtus IV raised the pastors of both SS. Lawrence's and Sebald's parishes to provosts in 1477. In a contested appointment to St Sebald's in 1512, the Bishop of Bamberg sent his own troops to take control of the church. By negotiation in Rome, city councilor Willibald Pirckheimer gained full rights of appointment for both parishes for the city council in exchange for a yearly payment to Rome of one hundred gold florins. The Bishop of Bamberg suffered the first of several important defeats.[8]

The mendicant houses in Nuremberg – Augustinian hermits, Franciscans, Dominicans – all reformed themselves at city council initiative. In 1452, St John Capistran preached in Nuremberg on his mission to Germany. A day after his sermons (11 August 1452), jubilant citizens carried their chess boards, dice and playing cards, even their elaborately painted sleds to the marketplace, where they were ceremoniously burned. Many miraculous healings were reported after his sermons; the city council agreed to help the Franciscans with the canonization of St John

44 St. Sebald, patron saint of Nuremberg. Sebald is shown dressed as a pilgrim, with pilgrim's hat, purse, staff, and rosary, holding the parish church re-named after him.

Capistran after his death, in exchange for use of their Roman connections to help further the cause of St Sebald. Only the Dominican nuns seemed to be out of favor with the council: they refused to reform. So in 1429, thirty-five recalcitrant nuns were forced to leave their convent and were replaced by the same number of properly reformed nuns from a convent in Alsace. By 1483, all churches, monasteries, and hospitals had wardens appointed by the city council to supervise their business ventures and examine their records.[9]

The city council was well on its way to reform before 1517. Evangelical sermons could be heard at several of the monastery chapels on the eve of the Lutheran reformation. The Augustinians in Nuremberg maintained close contact with Johann von Staupitz (+1524), close friend and advisor to Luther and prior of the German province of Augustinian hermits. Interested members of the city council met weekly with the Augustinians at their monastery for lively theological discussion.[10] In 1516, Staupitz preached to the citizens of Nuremberg on predestination, dedicating the sermons to city councilor Jerome Ebner (+1533). Christoph Scheurl (+1542), legal advisor to the city council and sometime colleague of Luther brought copies of the ninety-five theses to Nuremberg and had them translated into German by another city councilor, Kasper Nützel (+1529).[11] It was with a sense of genuine Humanistic collegiality that the translated theses were circulated. Councilor Pirckheimer sent copies to fellow Humanists and other clergymen in Heidelberg and Cologne, and to John Eck at Ingolstadt, popular among wealthy patricians for his positive attitudes toward the taking of interest.[12] The same city councilors served as wardens to supervise the activities of monasteries and convents. Pirckheimer's sister, Charitas, was prioress of the Poor Clares. Councilor Nützel was their warden. It came as a matter of some surprise and great embarrassment when in 1520, among those excommunicated by the papal bull *Exurge Domine* were two Nuremberg councilors, Pirckheimer and the council secretary Lazarus Spengler. The council tried to obtain an absolution for them through the Bishop of Bamberg and the Dukes of Bavaria, neither of whom had sufficient influence on John Eck, to whom the right of absolution had been entrusted. The council had to send its secretary and two councilors to the imperial diet at Worms in 1521 to meet with the emperor to arrange the absolution for its excommunicated members.

Unlike other city councils, the Nuremberg council seemed less concerned with the possibility of urban revolt as a consequence of evangelical reform. They had the religious question firmly in hand. When in 1520, the provost of St Lawrence's parish died, the council called a young patrician and student of Luther, Hector Pömer (+1541) to the post. For preacher at St Lawrence's, they chose Andreas Osiander (+1552), who after his studies in Ingolstadt had taught Hebrew to the Augustinian hermits in Nuremberg. Most members of the city council stood clearly on Luther's side. In the early years of the Reformation, the councilors of Nuremberg saw no reason why they might not remain thoroughly Catholic, loyal to the emperor and still continue reform of the church.[13] At Easter, 1523, the prior of the Augustinians, Wolfgang Volprecht (+1528) gave communion to the citizens in both kinds. The two provosts received permission from the Bishop of Bamberg to distribute communion in both kinds at Easter, 1524. Still, as the city council carried out an orderly reformation of the church, conservative clergy complained in Rome. At the Nuremberg imperial diet (14 January–19 April 1524), the Roman cardinals politely refused to be received by the clergy of the city. The city council hoped that the diet would commend its efforts to reform the church, but instead, the representatives meeting in Nuremberg appealed to a future church council and asked the cities to enforce the Edict of Worms, which forbade further discussion of religious issues in the press until that council, 'as much as possible.' When the imperial supreme court was moved to Esslingen, the Nuremberg theologians assumed that they would be able to carry on with reform.[14] They were wrong: in September, 1524, Volprecht and the provosts of both parishes were excommunicated in Rome.[15] The city faced a probable interdict.

Events in 1524 forced the city council to reconsider the cost of reform; an interdict would surely have international commercial consequences. In April of that year, broadsheets posted on churches declared artisan solidarity with rebellious peasants over the question of the tithe. Stones were thrown at monasteries. Osiander began to preach against enthusiasts. The city council was worried about the future of monastic orders, as monks and nuns left their monasteries for a newly proclaimed evangelical freedom. City councilors had a special interest in Nuremberg's monastic orders: not only did the monasteries house the sons and daughters of many councilors, individual councilors were also personal patrons of the monasteries. As in Augsburg, the orders themselves were divided on the subject of reform. The Franciscans, Dominicans and Carmelites opposed the process in Nuremberg. Members of the Augustinians, the Benedictines, and the Carthusians supported it. The only solution could be a disputation between the dissenting parties. Margrave Casimir of Brandenburg (+1527) (in whose territory Nuremberg was located) sent articles prepared by his court theologians for discussion. Despite the emperor's warnings to forbid open theological discussion between the parties, on 3 March 1525, the council held its own disputation chaired by legal counsel Christoph Scheurl and the two provosts of the city's parish churches. The monastic orders could not come to agreement. Scheurl recommended that the council forbid preaching in the mendicant monasteries that opposed reform. His motion was subsequently adopted by a majority of the council members. In the meantime, the council accepted an offer by the Augustinians to put their revenue at the disposal of the city council for poor relief; the council capitalized on dissension within the monasteries. When the prior of the Carmelites, Andreas Stoss (+1540), refused to hand over the monastery to the council, he was banned from the city. In May, 1525

45 Andreas Osiander by Georg Pencz, 1544.

the city assumed control of the monastery. In July 1525, the Benedictines
followed suit and turned over their revenues. In November, the Carthusians
transferred their holdings to the city poor-chest. Other monastic houses
held out longer. Convents that refused reformation were denied the right
to take new novices, and, as in other parts of the empire, monks who
wanted to leave their cloisters were given a pension by the city council
to live as private citizens. Some monks and nuns, however, continued to
live in their convents until their deaths. The last cloistered nun died in

1596. Already by May, 1525, the clergy of the city were incorporated into the citizenry to become citizens like everyone else, by order of the council. The clergy lost their former privileges and their courts. The Bishop of Bamberg lost all jurisdiction over the clergy in the city. In the future, the city council would control all appointments.[16]

In Nuremberg, reform of the city's churches and monasteries was clearly in the hands of the city fathers. Neither the Bishop of Bamberg nor the mandates of the emperor could affect the council's reforming zeal. However, the city council found itself in a peculiar position: having intervened in theological matters, it would have to be prepared to defend reformed orthodoxy in the face of 'sects' and the conservative opinions of councilors like Pirckheimer, who refused to abandon the old church entirely and grew even more skeptical of reform. The city council was forced to define and defend Protestant orthodoxy, with the help of its evangelical preachers and legal advisors.

Heresy had a long history in Nuremberg. The city council was traditionally lenient. In 1332, a Nuremberg pastor, Hermann von Stein, recommended ninety people to be investigated by the city council for Waldensian heresy. Since both lower and upper class people were accused (among them members of the important Tucher family), the council simply exiled some people; convicted heretics could either leave or be executed by drowning. In many cases, the exile was later lifted and the citizens were permitted to return.[17] Nuremberg's citizens were in contact with Bohemian Hussites between 1421 and 31. This was possible because merchants generally ignored imperial mandates to stop trading with Bohemia. In 1427, two Nuremberg citizens were found among the Hussites in Prague. In 1431, a manifesto from the dwellers on Mount Tabor was addressed to the Nuremberg city council, hoping to enlist the aid of the city in defeating their papist opponents. The city council never persecuted those who were in contact with the Hussites.[18] Anti-papalism had a long history in Nuremberg. A wealthy merchant and city councilor, Hans von Plauen and his colleague, Friedrich Reiser (possible author of the *Reformatio Sigismundi*) were both open Waldensians and sought a union of German Waldensians and Hussites from within the city walls. Both eventually left the city to preach to Waldensians in other parts of Germany in order to encourage this union. Reiser journeyed to Prague and Tabor; his Waldensian ideas were influenced by the radical principles of the Taborite community during his visit there in 1434. Reiser was given the title 'Head and Bishop of the faithful of the Roman church, who deny the Donation of Constantine.'[19] The enthusiast was eventually captured, tortured and burned with a colleague, Anna Weiler at Strasbourg.[20] The city council in Nuremberg remained generally tolerant of religious dissent. One could predict that the city council would be lenient with the 'heretics' of Lutheran orthodoxy.

On 20 May 1524, rumors that farmers in Forchheim, a village belonging to Nuremberg had refused to pay their tithe provoked the following warning from the city council: 'that every Christian has been made free in his conscience through the blood and death of the savior, yet this does not release them from their external responsibilities.'[21] When new notices appeared in the parish churches, urging the poor to refuse to pay their tithe, the city fathers responded, 'that the poor were well cared for in city hospitals, that the common man was better off in Nuremberg and its territories than in any other city.'[22] Like in Augsburg, as an example to enthusiasts, the council beheaded a weaving apprentice and an innkeeper for conspiring to incite rebellion.

Enthusiasts in and around Nuremberg did not have to look far for inspiration. Both Thomas Müntzer (+1525), and Andreas Carlstadt (+1541) had been in Nuremberg, publishing their treatises against Luther and encouraging open rebellion against secular authority. On 2 November 1524, the city council fined printers for publishing Müntzer's work: *A Well Documented Apology and Answers to the Spiritless, Weak, Living Flesh of Wittenberg . . . which has burned Christendom by its theft of Holy Scripture.* Associates of Müntzer sent a translation of four articles of the Taborites to councilors Jerome Ebner, Anton Tucher, and Willibald Pirckheimer.[23] To ensure orthodoxy, the city council set up its own inquisition. The examinations of citizens that followed seemed to uncover a conspiracy among poor journeymen painters. But how would a city council, historically tolerant of heresy (even among its own councilors) deal effectively with a new sect, when Lutherans themselves were schismatic? The council chose to rely on the advice of the most popular preacher in the city, Andreas Osiander.

Artists were among the first to be accused. Their economic position was particularly precarious. Their profession had been degraded by the prejudice of evangelical theologians and Humanists. Artists and sculptors were highly prized citizens in the Middle Ages. If they were good, they often amassed a fortune very quickly. The Nuremberg artist, Veit Stoss (+1533) had over 1,000 Guilders to invest in a local trading company. Albrecht Dürer (+1528) was wealthy enough to buy his way into the patrician ranks in Nuremberg, rich enough to sit on the city council.[24] The expectations of younger artists were shattered by the Reformation. Evangelical reaction to the cult of saints was enough to reduce sculptors and painters to poverty. Only those artists with talent as engravers could survive by working for the burgeoning publishing industry. Most sculptors had to turn their attention from adorning churches with statues to carving epitaphs for the rich. The despair among younger journeymen artists may have made the acceptance of radical theological ideas by this group more likely. Nuremberg city council investigations document the popularity of

Hussite and other radical ideas among young journeymen and apprentice painters. Their situation may have been much like the journeymen printers in other parts of the empire. Frustration with their own difficult economic situation led them to accept more radical attitudes toward the reform of the church and society.

Between October 1524 and January 1525, several artists in Nuremberg were accused of evangelical heterodoxy and imprisoned by the city authorities. The city council's advisor on theological matters, Andreas Osiander, became the unlucky inquisitor. The council charged painter Hans Greiffenberger with painting blasphemous pictures of the pope and holding wrong opinions about the eucharist. Osiander investigated. The painter submitted a written *confession* to the council, one of the most interesting documents of the Nuremberg Reformation. The painter, when questioned about his views on the sacrament, insisted that Christ could in no way appear on the altar. He claimed that he didn't want to deny God's power, but tried to avoid sacramental abuses of the real presence by the old church. (It is interesting that unorthodox eucharistic theology is not evident in the printed works he published.[25]) He wrote that he didn't think his eucharistic theology central to his ideas: 'for I believe, the gospel should be and will be preached to awake the hearts of men to faith in Christ's promise; for the Anti-Christ has not taken it upon himself to preach the gospel to people, but instead, to hold them captive.'[26] After personally examining the painter, Osiander wrote to the city council that he found little dangerous in his teaching and that the artist was willing to be instructed. Greiffenberger makes no reference to influence from either Müntzer or Carlstadt, something Osiander as inquisitor certainly would have noted. Osiander recommended his release, with a warning not to be so easy on him if he were accused a second time.[27] The content of his pamphlets, seven in all, was not questioned by inquisitor or council. The investigation did not end with Greiffenberger. On 31 December, another painter, Hans Platner, was accused. Two more accusations followed in January: the journeymen painters, Sebald and Barthel Beheim. When examined, they answered only that they had been led astray by the sermons they heard. They in turn incriminated two additional people, another painter Georg Pentz and the school-master of St Sebald's, Hans Denck. Sebald Beheim was prepared to recant his error; his brother Barthel, however, refused, going beyond the now customary definition of reception of the eucharist by faith, which made bread and wine only signs of future salvation. He called both baptism and the eucharist 'human inventions.' When asked if he denied secular authority, he answered that he knew of no authority but God's. When asked if he supported equal distribution of wealth in society, he stated that all Christians were equally brothers and sisters, who shared the responsibility of reminding one another of sin. He made no mention of temporal wealth. It is difficult to discern whether or not his ideas were inspired by Müntzer or Carlstadt, especially since these same answers could have been expected from a Waldensian heretic thirty years earlier. None of the painters indicated a particular mentor. They only mention connections with Hans Denck (+1525), the school-master of St Sebald's parish.[28]

Since June 1524, Denck had forbidden his students from taking part in liturgical ceremonies in the parish, normally an important part of their training. Denck was a friend of Oekolampadius; he knew close associates of Müntzer. Denck was ordered by the Protestant inquisition in Nuremberg to submit his theological ideas to Osiander in writing. In January, 1525, he presented his confession to the city council. The work is deeply mystical and intensely personal in its spirituality. Denck emphasized what the holy spirit had done for him: how the spirit helped him to believe, and how without inspiration, he could not have understood the bible. He mentions how a light from within him had helped him to transform what he read and heard in scripture into active faith. 'Because of divine immanence through the word, real contact between God and man had never been lost, but ignored.'[29] Lutheran *sola scriptura* salvation was empty and dead. Salvation needed cooperation between human beings and God. A union between Godly and human wills was necessary to consummate the love God had shown for man historically. Christbirth in the soul was the only means to achieve reunion with God, something that could not be done without the help of the spirit. Power to do good came not from man, but from God. In discussing the eucharist, he wrote: 'the believer receives the saving word of God, the logos in human form, which is invisible in the visible bread, which is nothing other than bread, as it is the invisible word of the visible body, conceived by the holy spirit, born of the Virgin Mary.'[30] It was the *nova lex Christi* that one needed to internalize in order to achieve salvation. A recent historian has noted that Denck is both late-medieval Christian, a *homo spiritualis* and potential Anabaptist, perhaps even an 'ecumenical Anabaptist.'[31] The similarities in the theology of Denck, Lotzer, Marschalck, and Ryschssner are remarkable. They share a common theology, even though they were probably never in contact with each other. The mystical, affective tradition that permeates Denck's theology, his emphasis on the conscience, the importance of the bible as a medium of grace, made active in works are hallmarks of an independent lay theology; the ideas did not originate with Müntzer or Carlstadt or Oekolampadius, but were propagated by Humanists interested in a reformation of the church as a means to producing a more virtuous society. Denck's confession was rejected by the council on Osiander's advice, not so much because his theology was unorthodox, but because of Denck's conviction that the holy spirit was responsible for the enlightenment of his conscience. Osiander particularly disliked Denck's insistence that he had a font of natural good within him, which could be activated by the spirit, through the word. The city council banned Denck from the city. He went to Augsburg, where he was long active among Anabaptists there.[32]

The painters Georg Pentz and Barthel Beheim received six simple questions to answer. Their responses are confusing: they answered that they didn't believe in God or Christ, nor in sacraments; they denied that the city council of Nuremberg was the secular authority to whom they owed obedience. Their answers were more likely prompted by the simplicity of the questions asked or their imprisonment and torture during the hearings.[33] Denck's confession shows the depth of thought to be expected from a learned man. It demonstrates as well how tenacious the affective mystical piety was: the voice buried in the soul calling to repentance is reminiscent of a long medieval tradition. It seems ironic that the men who sat in judgment on Denck and the painters defended a Lutheran *sola scriptura* orthodoxy that had scarcely been formulated, condemning a system of pious theology which had prepared the way for their own vocation. One wonders if Denck attended the sermons of Wenzel Linck (+1547) at the Augustinian church in Advent 1518. Note what Linck (one of Luther's closest associates) had to say about the spirit:

First, a sign of the presence of the holy spirit makes holy people feel a persistent longing for salvation from God. Second, there is a sign that salvation is near... Then the bridegroom will bid the bride to rise and come to him when the voice of the turtledove is heard, that is the longing in the heart. Third, there is a sign of deep Christian faith...In those people whose memory has thus been cleared of sin by mercy, it follows that they take on others' sins, transforming evil with sure faith...As a result, they give alms to the poor, visit the sick, help save prisoners.[34]

Like Denck, the 'Godless' painters were banned from the city. As in the past centuries, the exiles were eventually lifted. Scarcely nine months later, at the request of the provost of St Sebald's parish, the Godless painters were re-admitted to the city, reminded that their activities would remain under surveillance.[35] Hans Greiffenberger was not exiled, probably because he agreed to be instructed by Osiander. It seems peculiar that the city council did not ask Osiander to examine the seven works Greiffenberger had published before his hearing. They could shed important light on the theology of the individuals accused of heresy by the city council.

Hans Greiffenberger is one of the more prolific pamphleteers in our sample. He published seven pamphlets, two in 1523 and five in 1524.[36] The theology in his pamphlets demonstrates another version of medieval mystical spirituality. He is by no means an Anabaptist protagonist: there is no mention of baptism in the spirit or an opposition to secular authority. There is no clear appeal to a communal society. Yet already in 1523, the artist highlights the importance of the spirit and what he felt it had already accomplished as a result of Luther's reform. In his pamphlet, *Some say they see no Improvement among those who call themselves Lutheran*, published in 1523, he declares his purpose at the beginning of the work 'to teach a little bit about the true improvement of man who is reborn of the spirit of truth.' He cites John 3:5 'unless one is born of water and the spirit, he cannot enter the kingdom of God.'[37] He refers to the Reformation as that rebirth of the spirit, a kind of extraordinary grace given to mankind in the last days, reminiscent of much medieval eschatological expectation. He, like Denck would confess later, insists that natural man cannot have knowledge of salvation without the spirit. Natural man does false works out of blindness: lighting candles, honoring statues, buying masses and joining brotherhoods. A true enlightened Christian does works of mercy. This person does not need to count prayers or light candles; there is another light in the conscience that does not require trumpets to announce good works. The painter was unhappy with the attitude of some Lutherans: 'it is a peculiar state of affairs, when one does not have to pray any more, or visit churches, or fast, as if faith were enough. Now people need not do any works!'[38] He presents a vision of an ideal evangelical reform, that neither Lutherans nor old church believers yet understand. He insists that the spirit has nothing to do with the clergy and their claim to be the 'spiritual class.' For this painter, the spirit belongs to all Christians: 'learned people say the common man should not speak of the gospel because it is not appropriate. A shoemaker shouldn't go about with pen and ink, but with leather and shoepolish...These people are ignorant.'[39] People who remained loyal to the old church party spent their time kissing statues, while the Lutherans craned their necks like geese and insisted that all others were fools. There were people, however, who for a long time had not kissed statues, not because they had any particular argument against it, but because they simply didn't want to do it, or because those who did it only wanted to be seen doing good works. 'These Lutherans eat, drink, and fornicate to excess just as they did before...worse now, because they curse all those who don't do as they do.'[40] He compares Lutherans with members of his own profession: 'they are no better than someone who has a business or a workshop and uses this to annoy his neighbor, like the sculptors, painters, who create whores and knaves for profit...because now the saints are out of fashion.'[41] He notes that there was little real improvement among Lutherans, but recommends that 'every Christian man should practice the law and word of God day and night...Dear brothers in Christ, let God call us in spirit and in truth to tell us of his power and our salvation, that we may happily suffer according to God's will.'[42] Here Greiffenberger appeals to an alternative group of pious Christians, whose bible-based piety predates the Lutheran reform. Neither Carlstadt nor Müntzer seem particularly influential here.

The painter addresses his second pamphlet, *On the False and Learned Beggars* to the 'common man' so that he might recognize the wolf in sheep's clothing. Greiffenberger wanted to expose the Anti-Christ so that the simple man could protect himself. First he gives advice on how to pray. He asked his readers to pray with a simple, childlike heart: one Our Father is sufficient. Long prayers without attention and diligence are useless. Like Haug Marschalck he complains about those who oppress the poor, 'interest and banking houses who destroy widows and orphans...monks, priests, and praying sisters who don't want to be your brother and sister or have anything to do with you.'[43] Secondly, he insists that no priest can say mass for the benefit of another. No one could benefit from the mass, except the person who receives the eucharist in true faith for the forgiveness of sins. He was convinced that long prayers and masses would bring the judgment day soon. Thirdly, he tells his readers that no works could make a man holy, no rosaries or psalters. People who wished to continue to practice as their parents were blind. One ought to hear the word preached to be saved and forget the past.

Greiffenberger devotes an entire treatise to necessary good works, *A Short Summary of Good Works.* His recommendations sound very much like the sort of pious advice given people in sermons before the Reformation. Only God could make people holy and only 'in the spirit' could one do meritorious good works. Only when people believed internally, would they then stop drinking beer, 'for lechery is rooted in the bottle.' Then they would do works according to God's plan, not their own thoughts. People will begin to keep the sabbath. Their own will will die as they give up temporal goods, to become obedient and patient. Only after man has received the spirit does man become like God to do nothing but God's works, because man knows that his own ability to reason, his flesh, nature and good will are worth little. Only after man has the spirit will people stop waging war (an opinion Greiffenberger could have taken from Erasmus). He tells his readers to first believe and trust to 'help your fellow men to become living saints.'[44]

Greiffenberger's model of an evangelical church working toward the End is based on the gospel alone. He even wrote a short pamphlet, *A Christian Answer to those who say the Gospel has its Power from the Church,* to specifically explain scriptural primacy in the church. He insists that the church was born of the gospel, not the gospel of the church. Those who rely on Augustine put their trust in a doubting Thomas, who can only believe what he touches and sees: 'no heart or *gemüthe* can understand the word of God unless God has taught it and enlightened it. When this happens a man will become strong and sure in God's word.'[45] His theology is nearly identical to Hans Denck's. Greiffenberger takes up the same theme in *A Consoling Admonition to those Bothered in Conscience*, also published in 1524: the gospel ought to be preached to the poor because it gives peace to consciences burdened by sin. Using a familiar flesh–spirit contrast, the painter presents a formula for salvation similar to that in the theology of his pamphleteer colleagues:

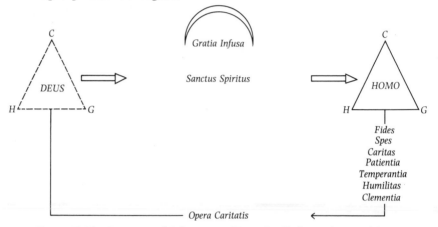

Figure 5. The Economy of Salvation in Hans Greiffenberger's Pamphlets

Greiffenberger's conception of the term 'spirit' is nearly identical to Denck's. He even cites seven traditional gifts of the spirit one could expect to receive: faith, love, charity, hope, gentleness, humility, and temperance. He notes that people who had received God's grace and believed the word were not entirely free in their conscience. He attributes this to the lingering sin of Adam, the fleshiness that continues to plague mankind. He notes: 'oh, how we have searched to repent of our sins, yet had we had Peter, Paul, John and the others, we would have recognized Jesus, his cross and loved it. Instead we prayed to saints who keep the cross far from us.'[46] He reassures his readers: 'when we follow the spirit, we abandon our reason, nature and good intentions and change our life according to God's commands and teaching.'[47] Denck, too, uses the flesh–spirit contrast in his *Confession*. The painter never mentions Erasmus, but he does recommend that his readers read pious works, especially Luther's *Exposition of the Our Father* and his works *On the Mass*, both published as pamphlets in 1522.

Greiffenberger wrote two apocalyptic treatises which he published in 1524. They are similar to Marschalck's *A Sharp Axe against those who call themselves Evangelical*. Where Marschalck presents two military camps, one of the Anti-Christ and one of the evangelical Christians, Greiffenberger

Ein warnüg vor

dem Teüffel/der sich wider
übt mit seinem dendelmarckt/vnter
einem gleissenden schein/in merck=
lichen stückenn/des Christen=
lichen lebens betreffen.

Hans Greyffenberger
1 5 2 4

46 *A Warning to beware of the Devil*, 1524. By Hans Greiffenberger.

depicts the pope as the captain of the devil, and the poor souls, robbed of the gospel as the group which will triumph. He notes: 'Satan the beast has taken his own people and these people have chosen their own king, the pope, the true living Anti-Christ, with his hellish, deceitful, screaming master, the cursed pagan Aristotle.'[48] The Anti-Christ had power over simple, pious Christians because he had taken away the 'sweetest burden of Christ and replaced that with heavier burdens, which serve to feed his greed and imprison miserable consciences.'[49] He makes reference to auricular confession, in particular, as the means by which the Anti-Christ exercised his power. The chalice of holy communion was meant for the forgiveness of sins, which the pope had taken from the people. The Anti-Christ had put fear, rather than hope in the hearts of common people. 'The poor have to be afraid if they eat fat or eggs on a day the Anti-Christ commanded to be a fast.' The apocalyptic themes, the contest between the gospel and its opponents in the last days, are familiar motifs in the works of these pamphleteers. Greiffenberger cites the same scriptural passages, the predictions of true Christians being led astray by the Roman church, that had been part of the rhetorical tradition of lay movements since the twelfth century. Like the dwellers on Mount Tabor, the painter exclaimed: 'come most praiseworthy king Christ, with your blessed advent and destroy this desert!'[50]

As biting as Greiffenberger's rhetoric might be, he is not entirely anti-clerical. He even admits that some good had been done 'by saying masses, founding monasteries, and lighting candles.' But these were not the works of the gospel commanded in the last days. There are similarities between his pamphlets and those of other lay pamphleteers. Like Sebastian Lotzer, in his discussion of the veneration of saints, he gives his readers an example of how to pray to saints: 'O' almighty God, I praise you, honor you, and thank you for all the holy, Godly works, which you have accomplished in your dear saints. I ask you, on account of your great love which you have shown to them, to grant me the same mercy and grace which worked through them, that I might work for your glory just as the saints have done.'[51] Singing litanies, the painter assures his readers, will do them no good in the last days. He tells people to avoid those vicars, bishops, and monks who serve the great beast. The painter gives some credit to preaching monks, who he admits had done some good from the pulpit, but 'many have two tongues, one in the pulpit and another in their houses.'[52] He is less critical of the fiscalism in the church than the usury of great banking houses. Like other pamphleteers, who were not happy with Lutheran reform, he wanted to maintain a devotion to the saints, a role for monasticism, and make the church as well as the state into institutions loyal to the gospel in service to the poor. Greiffenberger makes only one genuinely political statement about his own times. He tells his readers: 'pay no attention to king, emperor, or Anti-Christ, when they say wait until the council, as if they alone had the holy spirit...The Turks are not the Anti-Christ as they so proudly announce from their pulpits...but instead bishops, princes, vicars, pastors, and monks.'[53] Greiffenberger's model of the evangelical church, working to meet the last judgment, is very much the same as models presented in the pamphlets written by Lotzer, Rychssner and Marschalck. He too appeals to an earlier church that had only become corrupt in the past four hundred years, abandoning the *lex evangelica*. Although he puts more emphasis on the necessary spirit to accomplish conversion in heart and conscience, his theology is in many ways the same as theirs. The mystical influence of the Bernardine affective tradition in the late Middle Ages is also present in his works as it continued to inspire clergy and common people alike. This does indicate a consensus among these pamphleteers, afraid that real substantive personal reform had lagged behind enthusiasm for change. They are evangelical Christians, expecting a reform of the church in the last days, but somehow the reform which had occurred was not entirely satisfactory. They acknowledge few sources of inspiration beyond the gospel, the *lex evangelica*, or *nova lex Christi* which they insist is the only means to salvation. Greiffenberger like Denck was no *sola scriptura* Lutheran. His use of the 'spirit' and emphasis on practical personal piety is similar to recommendations in mystical works by approved Catholic authors before the Reformation.

Although Greiffenberger was released with a warning in 1524, he apparently became more radical. In 1525, he was accused of giving his own wife the eucharist and was banned from the city.[54] From Nuremberg he went to Pforzheim, where subsequent editions of his works were published. How substantial the accusation against him was is not clear. Many were accused as enthusiasts in 1525–1526. Among those people charged as enthusiasts in a list prepared for the city council on 9 August 1526 was the shoemaker, Hans Sachs.[55]

Sachs is no stranger to historians of the Reformation. Even in his own century he was known for his hymns and chorales that gave new life to the Lutheran liturgy. Editions of his works were published as early as 1612. How curious that the works of a shoemaker who had little formal education, and was accused as an enthusiast, might place him among the most important figures in the Nuremberg Reformation. His fame rests on his ability to translate complicated theological ideas into forms understood by common people. His own understanding of the issues of the Reformation is still a subject of debate.

Although Sachs pretended to some erudition, there is very little evidence that he ever achieved more than a rudimentary grammar-school education, certainly a German, not a Latin education. While he wrote in his autobiographical poem composed in 1567: 'when I was seven years old, I attended the Latin school, where I learned my grammar and music; I have forgotten everything;' there is no indication anywhere that he spent much time in Latin school. His works certainly produce no evidence of Latin knowledge.[56] Sachs more likely received his education in the city schools that taught in German. Most children of artisans – Sachs' father was a tailor – attended these schools.[57] The Sachs scholar Edmund Goetze called the shoemaker's reference to Latin education in his autobiographical poem 'poetic license.'[58]

47 Hans Sachs, woodcut by Michael Ostendorfer, 1545.

Sachs' family were likely recent emigrants from Saxony (hence the family name) who had come to Nuremberg seeking their fortune from the poorer rural areas. At age fifteen, Sachs was apprenticed to a shoemaker; during his apprenticeship he came in contact with a weaver, Lienhardt Nunnenbeck, who was busy trying to restore the *Meistersinger* competition in Nuremberg. Nunnenbeck gave the shoemaker the musical education that provided him with an outlet for his literary talent. In 1511, Sachs travelled to Bavaria, the Rhineland, and other German cities as a journeyman shoemaker: his talents as a songwriter and singer (not apparently his ability to make shoes) were recognized in Frankfurt and Munich. During these years he composed his first series of hymns to the Virgin Mary. Sachs returned to Nuremberg in 1517 to marry his first wife.

She died of the plague and all seven of their children were dead by 1567. He remarried and survived all but one of his children. He died at age 81 in 1576. His own personal and family tragedies did not prevent him from producing hundreds of poems and several pamphlets which he published in Nuremberg. By his death Sachs had personally experienced most of the political and religious events in the Reformation in Nuremberg.[59]

Andreas Osiander probably had the most direct impact on Sachs. It was Osiander who convinced him to read pamphlets, several of which are listed in the inventory of Sachs' library.[60] Sachs, like other pamphleteers, read Luther's *To the Christian Nobility of the German Nation* and *On the Freedom of the Christian Man*.[61] There is also evidence that he read pamphlets by Eberlin von Günzburg.[62] Osiander may have been a personal friend of Sachs, despite his elevated position in the city and his scholarly tastes. Osiander and Sachs collaborated on a pamphlet, *A Miraculous Prophecy on the Future of the Papacy*.[63] Osiander provided the introduction, Sachs the text, and an anonymous artist (perhaps Greiffenberger?) the illustrations for the work that predicted the papacy's downfall.[64] Martin Luther was impressed with the work and planned to have an edition of it published in Wittenberg. The city council in Nuremberg was less enthusiastic. To express their disapproval, the Nuremberg city council reminded Osiander of the agreement reached at the 1524 Imperial Diet not to publish anti-Roman propaganda.[65] Sachs was never brought to trial like Greiffenberger and other artists. Perhaps his friendship with Osiander provided him with a special immunity. Osiander often befriended laypeople. He was a friend of Argula von Grumbach and corresponded with her, for instance.

It is not certain when Sachs decided to favor the Lutheran party in Nuremberg. Unlike Jörg Vögeli, he mentions no particular conversion experience. In 1519, the shoemaker composed his last traditional hymn to the Virgin Mary. Between 1520 and 1523, he stopped writing works in praise of the saints, and began to set different accounts of the passion to music and rhymed verse, focusing on Christ as the central figure. His first polemical work in favor of the Reformation was composed in 1523, *The Wittenberg Nightingale*. In the poem, he praises Luther as the great prophet of a new age: 'as the sun descends in the west, a new day dawns from the east; the red bursting sunrise breaks through the gloomy cloudbank, from which the bright sun gleams.'[66] Perhaps Sachs meant to associate Luther with the long-awaited prophet from the East, expected before the End. The poem is a vigorous defense of Luther and his teaching. It was composed just at the point when city council members, many of whom had been early fans of mendicant reformers, began to cool their former enthusiasm.

In 1524, Sachs prepared a series of seven dialogues, at least four of

48 A Shoemaker's workshop in the early sixteenth century.

which were published as pamphlets. These dialogues are the best source for understanding his theological ideas. They reflect the opinions and attitudes of a layman deeply concerned with the progress and direction of the Reformation. Some historians have tried to classify Sachs among radical protesters and revolutionaries. Because he was among radicals accused by the city council he has been included with alleged social-revolutionaries. Ingeborg Spriewald noted, 'the harshness of his denunciation of social repression and injustice in the background of social–political unrest among Nuremberg's population.'[67] Other historians associate Sachs with Anabaptists. Joseph Beifus tries to link Sachs with Hans Denck, although there is little evidence to substantiate this.[68] Unlike Greiffenberger, the spirit plays no major role in his theology. The shoemaker was no friend of popular uprising. In his poem, *The Poor Common Ass* (1526), Sachs chided the peasants: 'Ass! You have been blinded by reason, when you think to oppose the authorities; for God has established them to punish your sins. So do not be obstinate and bear your cross in your distress. Be patient until the End, for whoever succeeds will be saved...Leave vengeance in God's hands'.[69] Bernd Balzer calls Sachs a loyal servant of the city council, suggesting that the shoemaker served as a propaganda mouthpiece for the city fathers. Sachs therefore produced Lutheran propaganda in order to present an image of the Lutherans as guarantors of order and security.[70]

Sachs defended Luther for the same reasons Greiffenberger defended him: Luther was a prophet, a sign that the world was near its end and the gospel reborn, thus signaling the return of Christ. Sachs' hymns composed during that period echo that spirit: 'arise from your sleep in God's name, oh worthy Christendom! give praise and thanks to your bridegroom, for he has resurrected his word, which one hears clearly proclaimed, in many towns of this German nation.'[71]

In 1526 Sachs translated Luther's psalms into rhymed verse for liturgical use. He also joined Luther in attacking Zwinglians and Anabaptists: 'here we see a serious error, when they say one should not baptize children because they have no power to reason, as if one needed reason in order to have faith.'[72] Sachs opposed both Zwinglians and Anabaptists for their use of reason in theological matters. The Zwinglians used reason, according to Sachs, to detract from Christ's presence in the eucharist. Sachs, like our other pamphleteers, worked assiduously for the establishment of the church of the gospel, willing to abandon all of church tradition not explicitly set forth in the bible. He demonstrated that all works, fasting, confessing, joining religious orders were meaningless; 'only works of mercy which spring from faith are acceptable to Christ.'[73] He admonished the city council to dispense with the old church and usher in the new.

The determining factor in Sachs' theology is his anticipation of the imminent end of the world. His works are colored with new testament predictions of the last days. Most convincing for Sachs was his own witness of Luther's plight. It made the predictions in Paul's letter to Timothy seem very real: (cf. I Tim 4:1f) 'In the fourth chapter of Timothy he says: "the spirit says clearly that in the last days some would give up the faith and join the league of the devil, when people would be forbidden to marry, and food which God had created and commanded to be eaten with thanksgiving would be forbidden." I think this is clear enough.'[74] Luther admonished people to return to the gospel, which (so it seemed to Sachs and other pamphleteers) did not command fasting and celibacy, but other works in the last days. The shoemaker particularly associated the end of the world with the state of the papacy in his own century: 'Daniel tells us truly (in the ninth chapter) all the signs of the end. The papacy is Babylon, the same to which John referred. Therefore O' Christians wherever you may be, leave the desert of the papacy for our shepherd Jesus

49 Two versions of the prophet to appear to herald the return of Christ. Compare
(a) woodcut from Grünpeck's *Spiegel*, 1522, and (b) title woodcut from Eberlin von
Günzburg's pamphlet, *A Friendly Warning to all pious Christians in Augsburg, where
it will be shown that Dr. Martin Luther was sent from God*, 1524.

Christ.'[75] As in Utz Rychssner's works, for Sachs the papacy becomes an important focal point for all that was wrong with the old church. His vehement anti-papalism may indicate the influence of Andreas Osiander.

Osiander's sermons (unfortunately none of which survived him) are a very likely source for Sachs' eschatological anti-papalism. We know from other sources that on 15 March 1524, Osiander preached against the pope as the Anti-Christ. Even the 1524 city council proposal for church reform in Nuremberg, prepared by Osiander, affirms his conviction that the sixteenth century was perhaps the last in human time: 'therefore we must be aware that the time (about which St Paul speaks in II Timothy, 4: "there will come a time when men will not tolerate the holy teaching and will follow their own desires and hire their own teachers; after that their ears will itch and they will turn from the truth and prefer myths...") has been fulfilled.'[76] The preacher spent much of the 1520s researching eschatological prophecies. After discovering copies of Joachim of Fiore's works in the Carthusian library, Osiander wrote: 'few people have understood the art of prophecy, since it is the nature of prophecy to remain obscure until it comes to pass.'[77] He continued to pursue this interest in prophecy. In the summer of 1527, the preacher produced yet another tract, revealing the prophecies of St Hildegard of Bingen.[78] Sachs adapted Osiander's eschatological discoveries to fit his own purpose in a poem entitled *A Miraculous Prophecy*: 'for God himself will choose a faithful son of his people and will strengthen him with his spirit, in order that he might harvest well, and honor all Christian people; he will teach Christ clearly and his noble heavenly treasure, without human teaching or other additions.'[79] Clearly, Luther the prophet, 'established by God', assumes the role of the mendicant, depicted with his scythe to cut down the weeds and harvest the crop of true believers.

Sachs' dialogues are filled with eschatological texts taken from scripture: in Dialogue I, he cites Matt 10:14–15, Matt 23:4, Joel 2:28, Matt 23:31f. Dialogue II uses Matt 25, Revelations 21:27, Matt 12:36.[80] Dialogue III opens with an eschatological text: 'with their debates and writings they have accomplished little; they accomplish even less with their countless pressures, and lapse into sinful life, which I hope will soon fall by a blast from the evangelical trumpet, as the walls of Jericho.'[81] Dialogue IV reiterates the same theme: 'Dear Brother: The end has been described to us through Christ. Read Matthew 10, Mark 12, Luke 21, and John 16: here we see the promised persecutions, which have begun now to overtake Christians.'[82] All of Sachs' writings are colored by eschatological convictions. Like other lay pamphleteers, he prefers texts from Matthew. He cites Matthew more than any other gospel, a continuing medieval preference in the works of these pamphleteers.[83]

The further the Reformation progressed, the more convinced the shoemaker became that he was living in the last days. The imperial wars against the Schmalkald League, the imposition of the Interim, were for Sachs signs that the End was near. In February 1545, he published a poem entitled: *The Gospel: The Last Judgment and Signs to Precede It*: 'and thus you will hear of war and the clamor of war, but be not afraid. For all this must come to pass in preparation for the End. For the authorities and people will rise against each other and each kingdom will rage against the next.'[84]

In Southwest Germany eschatological literature and antipapalism enjoyed particular popularity. In the chronicles published in German in the sixteenth century, the end of the world is prominent in the mind of the historians. Reform and opposition to the pope were important aspects of the progress to the End. The church expectant was not waiting in purgatory, but on earth. This attitude may have convinced some common people to support the Reformation. Our pamphleteers, at least, saw Luther not so much as the man to battle the Anti-Christ but as a predicted prophet, the standard-bearer of the reform, who represented the gospel, pure and uncorrupt. The emperor was expected to lead the battle against the pope. Pamphleteers writing in the early sixteenth century appealed to what they perceived as an even older tradition, insisting that in the twelfth century popes had abandoned the *lex evangelica*, the church's true tradition.

Sachs compares Martin Luther with the nightingale who announced the end of darkness in preparation for Christ's return: 'doctor Martin Luther, Augustinian at Wittenberg, awakened us from the night, in which the light of the moon had enraptured us. Moonshine is human teaching, promoted by the sophists here and there for the past four hundred years, who made judgments according to their own reason, hence leading us astray from the teaching of the gospel.'[85] The shoemaker reveals a great conspiracy between sophists and papists: 'the lion is the pope and the desert the clergy, which have been led astray by human invention evident everywhere.'[86] He relentlessly carries through his simplistic scheme as propaganda for the Reformation.

Zwinglian attacks on human teaching also find a place in his theology. Sachs' critique of human teaching concentrates on two separate effects of such teaching on the church; the clergy and the laity had each been led astray in different ways. The clergy had been seduced, 'by becoming monks, nuns, and pastors, wearing habits, tonsure, screaming day and night in church at matins, prime, terce, vespers, and compline; with vigils, fasting, lengthy prayers, with flagellation, kneeling, bowing, nodding, genuflection; with ringing bells, organ playing, relics, candles, carrying flags,...blessing bells, lighting lamps, selling grace; blessing churches, wax, salt, and water.'[87] Laypeople had been led away from the gospel: 'with offerings and lighting candles; with pilgrimage and worshipping saints; fasting in the evening, then celebrating the next day; confessing routinely; with confraternities and rosaries, indulgences, missing mass, the kiss of peace, viewing relics; by buying masses and building churches; equipping the altar with expensive vessels, making French votive images, velvet vestments, golden chalices, monstrances, silver figures.'[88] Not only was human teaching contrary to God's commandments, but it advocated salvation by works not found in scripture, a double blasphemy: 'they say you can earn heaven with them [works], and so erase the tinder of sin; all this has no foundation in scripture. It is conceited human concoction, which doesn't please God.'[89] In the pamphlet *Dispute between a Shoemaker and a Canon* (Dialogue I), Sachs notes:

Shoemaker: Paul tells us, in Romans V, that man is justified by faith without any works of the law, and told the Romans that they will be judged according to the way they live their faith.

Canon: Yet James says, in the second chapter, that faith without works is dead.

Shoemaker: A genuine Godly faith does not need to be demonstrated, since by its own virtue it yields good fruit, as in Matthew VII: 'a good tree cannot produce bad fruit.' However, such good works are not done out of desire to earn salvation, which Christ has already earned for us, nor are they done out of fear of hell, since Christ has freed us from that, nor are they done because we must offer them to God. They are done out of Godly love as a thanksgiving and to benefit our neighbor. Well, how do you like Luther's fruits?[90]

Here Sachs exclusively divides works of the law from works of the gospel. Only the works which Christ commanded in the last days are pleasing to God: 'for Christ commands nothing else of us in the last days than the works of holy mercy.'[91] Only the works of mercy are meritorious. God will indeed reward these works, according to Sachs. His solution to the economy of salvation, despite insistence on justification by faith, is similar to that of other pamphleteers: works of mercy are only meritorious for people *in fide*, still preserving the medieval concept of the poor as a gate to heaven. But only the works commanded by Christ in the last days can be in any way meritorious.

Sachs, more than Greiffenberger, vehemently attacks monastic orders, since in Nuremberg the strongest opposition to reform came from the Franciscan and Dominican orders; the friars' preachers vigorously opposed Lutheran reforms. As more and more monks left their monasteries, monastic opposition to reform became more adamant. Osiander preached against monks. To avoid the wrath of the city council (many of whom had sons and daughters in monastic orders), Osiander published his *How Monasteries and Convents May Become Christian through God's Grace* under a pseudonym in 1524.[92] Shortly thereafter, Sachs published his own attack on mendicant monks, (Dialogue II) *A Treatise on the Vain Works of the Clergy and their Vows, which they assume will save them, but really insult the Blood of Christ.* Monastic hypocrisy is the substance of Sachs' critique:

> *Hans*: Yes, outside the cloister you have your collectors and your distributors, like the princes, and collect great treasures (under the guise of voluntary poverty), purchasing cardinals' hats for many thousand ducats, building expensive monasteries like palaces... If that is not taking money, then I don't know what it is!
>
> *Peter*: It is greed hiding under the hat which is being played... And everyone is taken care of in terms of necessity their whole lives long, and no one knows anything of real poverty, yet they take the very bread from the mouths of the poor.[93]

He argues, too, that monastic houses served no purpose, worldly or heavenly. In Nuremberg the poor were cared for from the city chest. The shoemaker draws a distinction between real poverty and hypocritical monks' poverty. As monks continued to oppose the reform in Nuremberg, Sachs found it very easy to exclude them from his vision of the new church. He has an eschatological reason for this: 'for indeed you do service to God and good works, yet you lack the most necessary works, which Christ commands at the last judgment (Matt 25) namely the works of mercy: "I was hungry and you fed me not".'[94] In Dialogue II when Sachs begins to attack the validity of monastic vows as a saving work, the monk starts to break down: 'if I knew that I could not attain eternal life by my life in the monastery, I would hang my habit on a fence and throw stones at it.'[95] Sachs offers the monk a final admonition: 'see here, dear brother Heinrich, this is hypocrisy! Do not read Scotus or Bonaventure, but the bible. Then you will be enlightened by his Godly word, and won't despise us.'[96] The shoemaker helped to keep up pressure on monasteries to hand over their revenues for relief of the poor to the city, even though many councilors opposed the dissolution of monasteries.

Sachs, like Marschalck, was also critical of church bureaucracy: 'this is Roman extortion; see what it is like among the bishops, and what happens at their courts, with notaries, officials, in citing and lifting text from their false canon law, with which they deceive both men and women.'[97] The direction of Sachs' critique is similar to that of his colleagues. The church had no power to make laws contrary to God's laws or to make any laws which might impair the freedom given a Christian by his baptism. He scolds the church for its imposition of fast days and clerical celibacy in the same manner as Lotzer and Marschalck do: 'fasting is not commanded of us but left free. They consider eating meat on Friday a greater sin than adultery; and if a priest has a legal wife, it is a greater sin than if he kept one or two whores!'[98]

Sachs' theological anthropology is almost as simple as his general attitude toward God and the church. After creation and man's fall, man lost all his original grace: 'thus we are all children of wrath, cursed, damned, and lost.'[99] Only via the gospel can man recognize his sinfulness and unworthiness, and consequently turn to God: 'then we can become completely humble, as the glory of the day looms in the future, when the gospel shows Christ to the man, as the only son born of God.'[100] Through Christ one enters both the church and heaven: 'and when the man hears the trusting word proclaimed by Jesus Christ, and believes and builds on that faith, awaiting in his heart what Christ has promised, the same man is born again, from fire and the holy spirit, and is cleansed of his sins, lives in the word of God alone.'[101] Sachs is the only pamphleteer in this sample to take up the pentecostal theme. For him the pentecost was not a dead historical event, but a continuing action that occurs each time a person turns towards Christ through the gospel.

One finds no glorification of human nature in Sachs' theology. The influence of Lutheran Augustinianism is stronger than in Greiffenberger's works. Man can only be changed on earth by faith: 'when such faith is enjoyed, the same man is already saved.'[102] The faith is nevertheless only the medium of grace; it is not the efficient cause of salvation. His conception of faith and grace is essentially *sola scriptura* Lutheran. But he goes one step further. Grace comes to man from God by his word, both metaphorically and substantially; it is transformed into faith, which, active in works of mercy, can save man. Here he adopts Lutheran justification by faith and integrates it into the medieval affective system.

Our shoemaker makes a clear distinction between the old church and the new. Like other pamphleteers, he insists that the *lex evangelica* was part of a tradition that the popes had interrupted: 'therefore wolves and snakes have carried us in their hats for the past 450 years, harassing us with papal power, until Dr Martin began to write in opposition to such abuse.'[103] A reform of the church would reinstitute the gospel as the sole rule of Christian faith. The word would affect the consciences of individual Christians: 'such preaching and writing is done out of necessary Christian love, in order that the common people who have been led astray may be freed from their troubled consciences.'[104] The effect of the word is twofold. First it enters the soul to clear the conscience: 'let the word live in you in all wisdom, and teach each other.'[105] Then the word has a justifying effect: 'for the law does not make the heart righteous before God, but prepares the heart for justification by the gospel. The gospel changes the heart with lively trust in Christ through whom God works, in order that righteous fruits may follow.'[106] The heart is of primary importance here, 'for God judges according to the heart.'[107] The transition is affected by faith; 'salvation is ours through faith in Christ.'[108] Only when man has this free conscience, however, can faith be effective and can man hope for salvation: 'let us all be satisfied when our conscience is free and unburdened by human teaching, clearing the path to salvation.'[109] However, only in works of mercy is the faith fulfilled and the action of conscience-clearing complete and effective.

Unlike other lay pamphleteers, Sachs is reluctant to bridge the gap between the action of grace on the human soul and the good works which may be meritorious. He does so by a secondary *gratia gratum faciens*, a new kind of reason, which comes to man through faith; 'faith makes one blessed and pious, and reason reveals to man, consequently, that good works must be helpful.'[110] He distinguished this reason from 'blind human reason.' Sachs described the creation of right reason along mystical trinitarian parallels. Blind human reason denotes man's relationship to the law of the old testament. Faith in the gospel brings a second kind of reason. Yet, the fulfillment of God's action is only accomplished by the spirit: 'when man is baptized in the spirit, then blind reason leaves him, with its disobedience, death, and sin; also the evil conscience disappears.'[111] The coming of the spirit brings man to repentance. Sachs preserves and elevates the contrition process common to German late-medieval pious writers and he orders it in a trinitarian model:

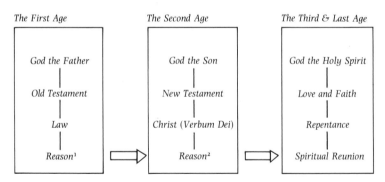

Figure 6. Revelation, History, and Salvation in Hans Sachs' Pamphlets

In the new church laypeople would play a new role. That role consisted of active studying, living, and preaching the gospel. Sachs defended the right of laymen to read the bible:

Shoemaker: And with what holy scripture can you deny the right of baptized Christians to research, read, and write about scripture?...as Paul teaches us in Ephesians VI, 'Oppose the temptations of the devil with the word of God', which he calls a sword. Sir, how might we stand before God if we knew nothing of the Scriptures?

Canon: Like a goose in a storm!

Shoemaker: You mock us! Jews know their law and prophets by heart. Should we
  Christians not also know the gospel of Jesus Christ, which is the power of
  God by which we shall all be saved?[112]

When the canon attempts to confine the preaching of the word of God
to the ordained priesthood, Sachs answers him:

Shoemaker: Christ says in Luke X, 'the harvest is great yet the workers are few;
  pray to the Lord that he might send laborers for the harvest.' For this reason,
  vocation is not something external, but internal; for externally we are all
  called to preach, the evil as well as the righteous.[113]

When the canon suggests that laypeople are too ignorant to understand
the gospel, Sachs replies: 'at what great university did John, who wrote
so impressively . . . study? He was only a simple fisherman.'[114] The substance
of Sachs' lay apostolate is the daily learning, living and preaching the
gospel, not in a formal sense from the pulpit, but in admonishing one's
brother against sin and warning him to repent. His model for this new
active layman conforms to the pattern common to many of the other lay
pamphleteers. Sachs even doubts the sufficiency of Luther's reform. To
address this problem he composed his fourth dialogue: *A Conversation
between an Evangelical Christian and a Lutheran, in which the annoying
Circumstances among those who call themselves Lutheran are exposed and
reprimanded.* Many scholars have had considerable difficulty in placing the
last two dialogues in context with Sachs' earlier works. Beifus and Keller
saw the change in themes in Dialogue IV as a sign that Sachs openly
acknowledged his sympathy for the developing left wing of the Reformation. Wernicke and Kawerau saw this change as a sign that Sachs had
changed the object of his criticism from the Roman church to rebellious
peasants and artisans.[115] Bernd Balzer, although noting a change in the
direction of Sachs' critique, sees more continuity with Sachs' earlier
Wittenberg Nightingale and his first two dialogues. Rather than a change
in personal convictions, Balzer indicates a change in the direction of Sachs'
propaganda to discredit enthusiasts, directly in conformity with the desires
of Luther and the Nuremberg city council. Balzer does agree, however,
that the sudden change in the latter dialogues has yet to be appropriately
explained.[116] Perhaps the terminology Sachs employs in his fourth
dialogue can provide a key. Scholars continue to be confused by Sachs'
terminology, specifically the contrast made in the title of Dialogue IV
between 'evangelical' and 'Lutheran.' Kawerau sees both terms as simple
Protestant variations, each with no specific meaning.[117] Beifus assumes
that the use of the term 'evangelical' is proof enough that Sachs was an
Anabaptist.[118] Wernicke explains the use of the term as a description

50 Woodcut from *A Dialogue between an Evangelical and a Lutheran Christian*, 1524.
By Hans Sachs.

of 'the internal and external aspects of Protestantism.'[119] The modern
Marxist historian, Ingeborg Spriewald described the two terms as illustra-
tive of 'different opinions...within the Protestant camp.'[120] Bernd Balzer
notes a preference for the term 'evangelical' rather than 'Lutheran' in
city council records.[121] Sachs is not the only pamphleteer to contrast
Lutherans with evangelical Christians. We note the same criticism of those
who call themselves Lutherans in works by Lotzer, Marschalck, and
Greiffenberger.

Both terms are used to contrast the insufficiency of Lutheran reform
with the evangelical model of our pamphleteers. Sachs' dialogue is
designed to present the ideal church of the gospel in its form closest to
the *lex evangelica*. To him, Lutheranism had accomplished little substantive
improvement in individuals. Those people who scorned the old catholics
for their superstitions and sinful behaviour were no better Christians
themselves, using Lutheranism as a license to abandon fasting and praying
altogether. Implicit in the contrast between 'evangelical' and 'Lutheran'
is an important critique of civic authorities and their leadership in the

reformation of monasteries and churches. Church authorities had failed to lead an effective reformation of the old church, but had civic authorities been any more successful in preparing the bride of Christ to meet the bridegroom in the nearing judgment?

The effect of evangelical preaching also fell short of most lay pamphleteers' expectations. It had produced hypocritical Lutherans instead of true children of the gospel. In Dialogue IV Sachs compares the ideal situation, common to the expectations of other lay pamphleteers, with the abuse of newly acquired freedom:

> they all want [all who call themselves Lutheran] to use the pious Luther as a cloak for their indecorous behavior, not living by his teaching. For despite the fact that Luther suggests the use of Christian freedom to help poor captive consciences, he also warns in his writings and sermons to beware of deceptive, troubled un-Christian behavior, and not to use the gospel and word of God as a precedent for uprising and to stir up the ignorant.[122]

Over and over again, Sachs admonished his readers to do works of mercy, rather than to ridicule those who cannot accept the change that evangelical reform implies. Sachs advises his fellow Christians (as does Lotzer) still to refrain from eating meat on Fridays and in Lent: 'it is far better not to eat meat and drink wine, when it bothers your brother, angers him, and offends him. If you have faith, then keep it to yourself before God...If my food were to offend my brother, I would stop eating meat forever.'[123] Here the tradition of evangelical reform hoped for by Waldensians, Hussites and many others before this generation of pamphleteers, shines through the customary rhetoric of Protestantism. Sachs only justifies the most peaceful protest: 'when you hear the truth of the gospel being offended, put down this idle human babbling with the word of God and do nothing by means of rumors or screaming, especially because this is wrong and offensive to the common man.'[124]

Bernd Balzer emphasizes Sachs' role as a propagandist, who could use his polemic to manipulate his readership. Balzer follows the traditional historical assumption that Sachs was dependent on Luther for his ideas and suggests that the works of Eberlin von Günzburg may have had an even more direct effect on the shoemaker. By downplaying Sachs' personal theology in his pamphlets, Balzer envisions a man who closely followed the directives of Luther and the city council. To what extent was Sachs a manipulating propagandist? By comparing Sachs with his fellow pamphleteers, we note similar concerns for the direction of the evangelical movement, but different from the concerns of the Nuremberg city council. Even if Sachs, Greiffenberger, Lotzer, Marschalck, and Rychssner do not speak for an evangelical consensus in 1524, they certainly reflect the traditional demands of laypeople for reform of society and the church since the twelfth-century heretical movements. They anticipate a church of the coming judgment based on an active *vita apostolica* and the *lex evangelica*. It is nevertheless true that much of Sachs' own theology is obscured by his personally creative rhetoric, giving less evidence of a clearly expressed personal theology than many of his colleagues. Certainly this led Balzer to his conclusions.

Lay pamphleteers were seldom very sophisticated propagandists. They wrote from a personal vocation, not simply a desire to manipulate their readers. They did understand their audience, and they directed their ideas to them in terms they would understand, a polemic painted in black and white with occasional hints of satire. Their pamphlets contain personal theology, propaganda, and occasional economic grievances. One cannot say (as Balzer does) that Sachs did not aim his works at the left wing of the Reformation.[125] Nor can one assume that Sachs is more propagandist than lay theologians. There are goals in these pamphlets beyond mere hopes of herding common people into the Lutheran sheepfold. Earlier Sachs scholars were careful to note the shoemaker's personal convictions, even if they did not fully appreciate his skills as a propagandist. The crisis situation in 1523 created by a growing suspicion of lay involvement in the Reformation, by predictions of a nearing End, and the growing unrest among peasants and artisans brought Sachs and Greiffenberger to the publishers. They tried to rescue a vision of reform close to the design of imperial reform proposals of the late Middle Ages.[126] Their demands for reform were far less dependent on magisterial theology for their direction than on the inspiration of medieval mystical theology, so often present in medieval lay heretical movements. In these early written documents of lay piety and theology, we see the core of the lay movements that survived underground and were never acknowledged officially by the established church authorities. City councils tolerated some lay activity, at least as long as they could supervise it. They seldom burned the many heretics accused by the church. In Nuremberg as in other cities accused heretics usually received light sentences, perhaps banishment for a year from the city. In these pamphlets we have proof of a popular, tenacious, biblical lay piety, proved in countless citations that show these pamphleteers well-schooled in the bible. Their theology was not produced by reading a few Lutheran pamphlets or hearing sermons. Their piety was urban, but not exclusively so. It was not entirely mystical, since mysticism is evident in varying degrees in their works. The aims of our pamphleteers were the same as the aims of earlier heretical movements: an active role for the laity in the church, an apostolic life defined by biblical works of mercy, an admonition to suffer persecution and martyrdom if necessary, to help the true flock of Christ persevere to the End.

Balzer also suggests a tendency in Lutheran propaganda 'to stylize its image as guarantor of order and security' in 1524.[127] This is not the most obvious goal in our broader survey of pamphlets earmarked as Lutheran propaganda, nor is this Sachs' main intention. Our evidence seems to confirm, not deny, Joseph Lortz's assessment that, 'in the actual situation, many people were not entirely sure to which group or to which teachings he or she belonged.'[128] In the midst of the confusion of political and religious issues, our pamphleteers promoted a generally older and more comprehensive proposal for reform of church and society: they were not confused in their theology, but aimed at creating a theological consensus based on the progress of the gospel among the common people that would guide the reform of church and society until the End. Underlying their assumption was often a mystical biblical theology that developed under the influence of Humanism. Their abstention from Anabaptist activities does not automatically clear them of enthusiast sentiment nor does it put them on the right wing of the Reformation. Although they paid lip service to their respective civic authorities, they noted that the gospel was the final authority against which obedience might be measured and declared themselves willing to be martyred for the gospel. Some pamphleteers noted the importance of the spirit as the bearer of Godly grace.

In Nuremberg, both Sachs and Greiffenberger shared common interests. The city council was unable to successfully direct the Lutheran reformation to meet their personal expectations. At the same time, we find a desperate quest for unity, a restoration of medieval collective principles important to common people. Sachs and Greiffenberger warned those who had not yet made up their minds where they stood, to relinquish the faith of their parents in hope of salvation at the nearing judgment. Their yearning for unity and the assurance of a nearing judgment played directly on the emotions of readers and listeners who longed for an end to their political and economic plight. Both pamphleteers tried to document an evangelical tradition as the real tradition of the church. Reform meant return to original principles. The importance of the *lex evangelica* as the earliest principle cannot be over emphasized. Even the Nuremberg city council insisted that its reform was 'evangelical', not Lutheran.[129] Our pamphleteers were not so certain.

Although the constitution of civic government in Nuremberg was different from other imperial cities discussed in this work, the nature of that constitution which excluded artisans from an important role in the city council seems to have had little bearing on the attitudes and opinions of artisan–pamphleteers. Erich Maschke's statement that reformation generally occurred in imperial cities where artisans were represented in the city council does not hold true for Nuremberg.[130] Even in the city where the city council had practically replaced the functions of the episcopal ordinary, making the path to reformation smoother, artisans maintained similar opinions about church reform to their colleagues in cities where the path to reform was not so smooth. Nuremberg did not experience such violent disruption of church services as did other cities. Few of the individuals accused as enthusiasts could be classified as levellers: certainly none of these pamphleteers sought to abolish social distinctions by a re-distribution of wealth. The city council dealt with potential enthusiasts in much the same way and for the same reasons they had dealt with Waldensians and Hussites centuries before. The role of Andreas Osiander as preacher is critical to the understanding of the Reformation in Nuremberg. As a Humanist in sympathy with Lutheran reform, he encouraged Sachs and perhaps Greiffenberger, who was set free after his trial on Osiander's advice. Osiander preached against enthusiasts and the pope. Like Schappeler in Memmingen and Rhegius in Augsburg, he befriended, encouraged, and if necessary, defended the role of active laypeople. Yet, Osiander did not hesitate to condemn Hans Denck. Greiffenberger was a mystic like Denck, but Osiander probably considered him less dangerous since he was a simple layman.

Steven Ozment's conclusions in his *Mysticism and Dissent* (Yale, 1973) suggest a direct connection between personal mysticism, individualized religion and active protest. Yet, even the most mystical of our pamphleteers, Haug Marschalck, indicates that a personal union with God must make man subject to, not above the gospel: the *vita apostolica* to which laypeople were called was already outlined for them in the six works of holy mercy required at the End. Marxist historians argue that economic discontent was at the root of active protest. These works of popular propaganda are intensely theological; economic grievances are aired in hope of a reform of society and church in these pamphlets. Robert Scribner insists that the stereotypical expression in the polemic of these pamphlets, codified in a litany of opposites, moved people to protest. These pamphlets provide something more than the traditional root paradigms of church critique, more than propaganda for Lutheran reform, more than mystical theology. They present documentary evidence of the survival of a lay piety, common to cities since the twelfth century and every bit as tenacious as the lay piety William Christian documented in the Spanish countryside.

This evidence agrees in part with John Dahmus' conclusions in a recent essay on Johannes Nider, O.P., whose *Twenty-Four Golden Harps* Dahmus analyzes. Dahmus discovered a very unsympathetic view of the laity in the Dominican's sermons, preached in Nuremberg in the late fourteenth century. One can imagine how welcome encouragement from Osiander was for so many laypeople seeking an active life in the church. Dahmus suggests that the alienation of laypeople might have been avoided if 'the late medieval church offered the laity a conception of their state as a vocation, a way of life that would bring them salvation.'[131] These pamphleteers felt that the laity already had a vocation of its own, that this vocation was in harmony with fifteenth-century imperial proposals for reform, but that the clergy, old church and Protestant, had no way of effectively integrating that vocation into established visions of the church. Their vocation and appeal to an evangelical tradition seems as much a challenge to the sixteenth-century church as St Francis' demands for apostolic poverty seemed to the twelfth century.

Dahmus is also critical of Ozment's thesis that the late-medieval church overburdened laypeople with religious demands. Dahmus feels that religious burdens were the result of a refusal to sanction lay vocations. Although the preference of the old church for human teaching above the gospel was a hindrance to more effective mystical communication with God, in their pamphlets the laity sought a more active, sanctioned role in the church. They seemed to want more work for themselves, not less. Confession and penance, which Ozment sees at the root of the burdens, were hardly the center of their complaints. They needed to work more actively in the face of a nearing End. In preparation for that End, the *nova lex Christi* became the hard and fast rule to which church and society needed to conform. The *lex evangelica* provided a model for apostolic behavior until the second coming. For nearly all of the pamphleteers thus far, *sola fide* and *sola scriptura*, the traditional hallmarks of Lutheran religion are less influential in directing the course of their theology than eschatological necessity of works of mercy, that would be meritorious inevitably, because of God's action in them through the spirit. These lay pamphleteers were convinced that leaders could inspire and certainly Luther, Zwingli, Geiler von Kaisersberg, Oekolampadius, Rhegius, and Erasmus played an important prophetic role, providing the context for their propaganda and even the subjects for discussion in their pamphlets.

Classification of this lay theology within the traditional labels of the contemporary period or subsequent Reformation history is impossible. Our pamphleteers were propagandists, but not enthusiasts. They could not and did not encourage open rebellion. They are not really *Schwärmgeister*, since the spirit comes as the bearer of grace to liberate the conscience in bondage, not to liberate the individual to extraordinary Christian license: they saw their calling to humility, obedience to the gospel, and active works as self-justifying, since it was based on the firm promises of Christ.[132] They are not Anabaptists, since a peculiar baptism in the spirit is not necessary, nor do we find any particular emphasis on the importance of baptism in their works: sacramentally, they are eucharistic Christians, who emphasize the forgiving power of the eucharist and the importance of the real presence. Yet the means to union with God was not eucharistic, but meditative: the gospel provided the means to union, not sacraments. Their theology certainly proves a medieval continuum, the effect of Humanism and a tenacious, affective, mystical tradition. Our pamphleteers do not want to see secular and religious authority destroyed, but reformed according to the principles of the gospel.

CHAPTER VI

Female pamphleteers: the housewives strike back

Whether or not piety can be 'masculine' or 'feminine' is dictated by both gender and role. Of the two aspects of definition, role is probably the more important: acceptable behavior by males and females in society, measured against appropriate role models, differentiates deviant from acceptable behavior. Pauline exhortations to women, recommending obedience and silence in the presence of men, have always provided a peculiar contrast to expectations of equality at the last judgment, certainly pre-figured by women as disciples in the presence of Jesus: Mary Magdalen, important model for all medieval laypeople, was the first to announce the resurrection to the apostles; the Virgin Mary shared pentecostal priesthood with the other apostles and disciples. Very soon after that pentecost, societal definitions of appropriate female roles reduced women's roles in the church and its developing theology. As martyrs women were venerated as equals, since martyrdom was a means to an assured place at Christ's right hand at the final judgment. Throughout most of the Middle Ages, women with an interest in theology could be nuns, and at least since the thirteenth century, those nuns might prophesy and even publish: convictions of a nearing end of the world called attention to daughters as well as sons, who were remarkable in their theological vocation. Just as the first apostles were from the lowest classes, so might the last prophets be from the subordinate sex.[1]

Only three of our sample of eight pamphleteers were women. Together they published eleven of the thirty-nine pamphlets, representing about 30 per cent of the pamphlets in this survey. How remarkable was their religious vocation? Their vocation was both expected and feared. Martin Luther might commend Argula von Grumbach for defending him in her letter to the university faculty at Ingolstadt, in 1523, but later joked about what would happen if even the women in a church might want to preach.[2] Reformers' attitudes toward women reflect the general attitudes toward appropriate female roles in their society. Unless women were powerful, well-educated, aristocratic ladies in positions of political power in the sixteenth century, they ought to be silent in the presence of men. Married

51 Women attack the clergy (detail). By Lucas Cranach, 1526.

women had even fewer rights than single women. For women with religious vocations, the appropriate place for them was in a convent. If women had no religious vocations, they belonged in the home, where they would serve their families and be obedient to their husbands. The female pamphleteers in this survey were all married. They lived in cities and villages far apart from each other: Argula von Stauffen (+after 1563) was herself of noble rank and was married to Friedrich von Grumbach on ducal estates at Dietfurt and Lenting in Bavaria. Ursula Weyda (+c. 1550) lived in the prosperous Eisenberg, a mining town in Saxony. Catherine Schütz (+1562) was married to a priest, the reformer Matthew Zell and lived in Strasbourg. She was among the first generation of artisans' daughters to marry a priest.[3]

Despite much societal prejudice against active women outside convents, there were some role models for married women in the ranks of venerated saints. St Elizabeth of Hungary (+1231) and St Birgit of Sweden (+1375) were married and lived an active, holy life in the world. But both Elizabeth and Birgit were powerful noble women: had they come from the poorer classes of married women, they would probably have been accused of heresy, tried, burned, or at least silenced. Women tertiaries and Beguines were always liable to be investigated by heresy hunters.[4] St Angela Merici (+1540) defied authorities as a Franciscan tertiary to live a life of charity and later founded the order of Ursuline nuns.[5] If a woman claimed an active vocation, the more she looked and lived like a nun, the more likely her vocation might be commended by church and society.

There were few models for married women with religious vocations. There was no shortage of female contemplatives, however, who served as models for medieval women. Women came into their own in a flourish of contemplative activity in the thirteenth-century church. Caroline Bynum notes that for the first time in Christian history, a distinctive 'female piety' emerged, described as devotion to the human side of the lives of Christ and the Virgin, special devotion to the wounds of Christ, and to the eucharist.[6] In her study of the nuns of Helfta, Bynum describes the importance of visions, spiritual marriage and ecstatic experience for her Cistercian nuns. The imitation of Christ carried with it potential for women to be more than contemplatives, pilgrims, and visionaries: a new interest in the gospel and a new 'evangelism, preaching the gospel by life...as well as the word', inevitably transformed the ecstatic experience of contemplatives into a calling to redeem society and the church.[7] St Catherine of Sienna (+1380) is a good example of a mystic who led an active life, advising popes and princes, preaching and caring for the poor.

The number of active, urban women in late-medieval society increased disproportionately to the civil rights granted them in towns. The fathers of the *Devotio Moderna* had a calling to motivate women as well as men. It was difficult to restrain women with a vocation to redeem society and to demonstrate their sanctity outside the institutions of traditional society. Margery Kempe (+c. 1439) was a laywoman who abandoned her marriage and family to lead the life of a pilgrim. She was respected, but continually annoyed officials, who found her behavior bizarre and hysterical. Called several times before the Archbishop of York's inquisition, she always cleared herself of any heretical suspicion. Kempe's piety was 'female', because it was inspired by female models as visionaries and contemplatives. Certainly, men too might experience visions and be called to redeem society beyond the walls of the monasteries. The secular priests of the *Devotio Moderna* were also inspired by female models, but were distinguished from women like Margery Kempe by their education: Margery Kempe was illiterate.[8]

Education for women improved with general education for guildsmen in the fifteenth century. Women in convents were more likely to be literate. Cut off from the life of the world, they enjoyed certain advantages, like education. They were active in *scriptoria*, copying and editing manuscripts. Many women tertiaries were instructed by Franciscan reading-masters. As guilds would occasionally admit women, they would also let them in their schools. Private school teachers in cities instructed both male and female pupils. Literate laywomen soon provided an important market for devotional literature. Contemporary paintings of the Virgin Mary show her not only holding a prayer book, but with a tiny library behind her.[9] Soon

52 St. Verena, Anchoress; from the parish church in Ditzingen, near Leonberg, 1524. St. Verena was a virgin and hermit, who left Egypt with a Roman legion and came to Zurzach in Switzerland. She washed poor people, combed their hair, and fed them. Her cult was particularly popular in Southwest Germany.

women could write their own chronicles, letters, and devotional literature. They no longer need a male secretary to write for them and to advise them. Within the walls of convents, literate women posed no threat.

Recently, feminine piety has been a special subject of investigation for historians of the Reformation. In his survey of pilgrimage sites in late-medieval Germany, Lionel Rothkrug identified essentially two kinds of pious behavior related to the distribution of sites. In Northern Germany, where there were fewer pilgrimage sites, Rothkrug pinpointed a special *mentalité collective*, a strong Christocentric piety, influenced by 'feminine devotion of a previous age.'[10] He noted that feminine religious activity was weakest in the Southwest of Germany, where there were many pilgrimage sites and 'where the spiritual significance of war and the hunt were more strongly established.'[11] Thus, one found a more personal, meditative, individualistic, feminine piety in the North, that prepared the way for an easy acceptance of the Protestant Reformation. By implication (though not by statement) the South of Germany was dominated by a more 'masculine' kind of piety: 'a patriotic, imperial religiosity, that prevented the infiltration of Protestantism in Bavaria.' But what about Southern imperial cities, where Protestantism was readily accepted? There Rothkrug describes 'a Southern artisanal tradition characterized by a militantly anti-patrician, anti-aristocratic, and anti-imperial form of public worship.'[12] Rothkrug indicated that the tradition of the lay activity was much more firmly rooted in the North than in the South, which encouraged people to accept the Reformation. In the South, Beguine houses were overshadowed by a preference for their more cloistered sisters, where brotherhoods were closely supervised and poor relief was controlled by city councils. As we have already seen, the situation in each German imperial city was different, which tends to refute some of Rothkrug's thesis. It will be interesting to see whether or not the female pamphleteers from the Southwest of Germany display anti-aristocratic, anti-imperial tendencies in their theology. Will they be closer to Northern models of feminine piety?

The Reformation presented women with new challenges. New roles for women as leaders in church and society were created by the new position of the pastor's wife. The Reformation also provided women with some different role models. About 1522, a pamphlet was published in Augsburg by an anonymous author entitled, *A Little Book for Women*. Rare in the annals of pamphlet literature from the early years of the Reformation, this treatise presented some alternative models for married women. Most of these models were from the old testament: Esther, Sarah, Deborah, Judith, mostly married women active both at home and in theological discussion. Only two models from the new testament were included in the pamphlet.[13] These old testament women were not model nuns; they had families and parents to care for; they did not spend most of their lives contemplating.

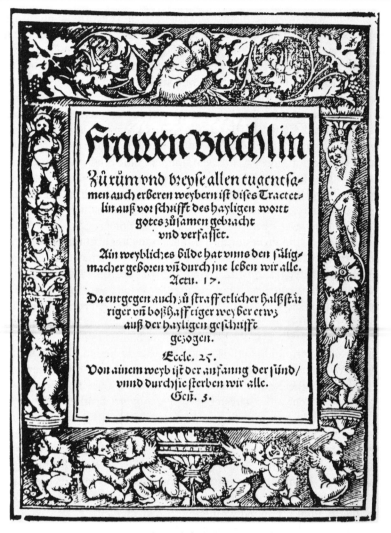

53 *A Little Book for Women*, c. 1522.

As a result of these new models for laywomen, literate housewives were bold enough to take their letters and treatises to publishers.[14] Encouraged by local pastors they sought a more active life in the church and society. For many, this burst of female activity in 1523–24 was a sign that the world was nearing its end. Daughters were finally beginning to prophesy.

The pamphlets published by female pamphleteers in this sample offer an interesting comparison with the works of male contemporaries. Is their theology and piety distinctly 'feminine'? Do they follow active medieval models, like Elizabeth of Hungary in a calling to do works of charity to redeem the world? Do they use old testament models to justify their vocation to publish? Are they interested in preaching, like many of their male contemporaries? Sebastian Lotzer applauded Argula von Stauffen's pamphlets: 'not only you [Schappeler] and those like you so boldly proclaim the word of God...but, for example, the noble, well-born woman, Argula von Stauffen, who has written to the university faculty like the holy virgin, St Katherine, who defeated fifty learned men...Here the spirit of God works miracles. May God bless her and all of us with firm faith. Amen.'[15] Andreas Osiander compared von Stauffen with Judith and Esther in the old testament.[16]

Argula von Stauffen was common only because she had common education. Unlike other high-born women of her time, she had no opportunity for Latin education. She lost her parents to the plague about 1505 and was sent by her uncle, Hieronymos von Stauffen (+1516) to the court of Duke Albrecht IV of Bavaria (+1508) in Munich. At court she was cared for by the Duchess Kunigund (+1520), a patroness of Humanists, sister of the Emperor Maximilian, and friend of Johann von Staupitz (+1524).[17] Argula von Stauffen had been given a copy of the 1483 Coburg bible by her father in 1502 and instructed to read it diligently, but had been discouraged from doing so by Franciscans, who taught her as a young girl that it might lead her to heresy.[18] At court the Duchess saw to it that she not only read the bible, but was provided with lives of the saints and other devotional works for her edification. Young Duke Wilhelm (+1550) promised her continuing personal patronage and together with his brother Duke Ludwig (+1545) found a suitable husband for her: Friedrich von Grumbach (+1532) had been caretaker of Duke Ludwig's estates at Dietfurt since 1515. Argula von Grumbach inherited virtually nothing from her own family. Her uncle aided the wrong side in the war of the Bavarian succession. He was captured and beheaded in 1516; as punishment all of her hereditary lands were confiscated by the Bishop of Würzburg. Her family name (from the powerful Hohenstauffen line) still meant something to nobles in the German Southwest, despite her impoverished state. She always used it when she published. Argula von Stauffen maintained her interest in theology after she moved to Dietfurt. Duchess Kunigund gave her a copy of Staupitz's *Sermons on the Love of God* (1518) to take with her to her new home.[19] Von Stauffen began to correspond with reformers; Osiander in Nuremberg, Paul Speratus (+1551) in Würzburg, Luther and Spalatin in Wittenberg. Her younger brother Marcellus brought her news of the Luther–Eck controversy from the university faculty at Ingolstadt where he was a law student.[20]

It was probably her brother who first informed her of the Arsacius Seehofer affair at Ingolstadt. Seehofer was a young instructor charged with

Lutheran heresy. He had been Melanchthon's student in Wittenberg. His earlier letters suggest an even closer relationship to Carlstadt. Seehofer left Wittenberg during the student revolts that called Luther out of hiding in 1522. He returned to university studies only under pressure from his parents. He had written them at one point while still at Wittenberg that there was no need to seek a Master of Arts degree, because Carlstadt taught that such distinctions among Christians were unnecessary and artificial.[21] Ingolstadt's university hardly provided the best atmosphere for aspiring young evangelical thinkers: the university senate insisted on a strict interpretation of the 1521 Edict of Worms and the 1524 Nuremberg Edict, both of which admonished preachers to 'continue to preach the plainer, purer Word of God according to the interpretation contained in the teaching and writings accepted by the Christian church.'[22] At the university in July 1523, complaints were heard that young students were being introduced to the *Colloquies* of Erasmus and to lectures on St. Paul tainted with Lutheran ideas. On 11 August, Seehofer was called before the rector, where he managed to respectably clear himself of suspicion, that is, until a search of his quarters turned up a number of contraband Lutheran pamphlets and letters written while at Wittenberg. The university senate decided to make an example of him, a less dangerous move probably than attacking a major professor with the means to defend himself. Seehofer, though bailed out by his relatives, was sent to the Benedictine monastery in Ettal after he had recanted all his former teaching as heresy and the work of the devil.[23] The exile at Ettal was not made public; many observers, including Argula von Stauffen, assumed that he was still in prison, awaiting the stake. Furious at the possible demise of such a young evangelical partisan, von Stauffen took up her pen to write the university senate.[24] Although she was not acquainted with Seehofer personally, she felt the university's action to be flagrant violation of the spirit of the Nuremberg Edict; she interpreted the edict as a practical license for evangelical preachers and teachers to continue to teach and preach until a future council might determine the status of their ideas.[25]

In her letter to the faculty, she exclaimed: 'the word of God is constantly before my eyes, reminding me of my obligation to confess Christ, an obligation from which neither man nor woman is excluded.' Quite convinced that the word of God prevails even against popes, emperors and princes, she admonished the university faculty to recognize their error, not just for condemning Seehofer, but also for condemning Luther and Melanchthon who, she felt, truly represented the word of God, on which she was willing to stake even the salvation of her own soul. Her aim in writing the letter was not just to obtain mercy for Seehofer, but to defend the evangelical movement. Although she emphasizes the necessity of obedience to secular authority, only the word can represent spiritual

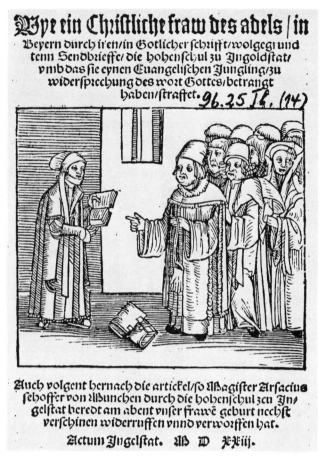

54 *A Christian Noblewoman from Bavaria's Missive to the Faculty in Ingolstadt, in which she uses holy scripture to defend an evangelical young man, 1523.*

authority, certainly not papal decrees or Aristotle. She claims to have it on good authority that Aristotle was never a Christian. Long moved by a desire to debate such matters with churchmen, she had restrained herself. 'I have never attended a university and do not know Latin but you know German', she wrote to the faculty senate. She would have liked to discuss with them personally in German. Quite aware of what scriptural citations might be brought against her as a woman, she cited St Paul's reference to the place of women in the church in his letter to Timothy (I Tim 2:12) and commented: 'I find no capable man and think of the references in the Psalms: "whoever confesses me I shall take for my own; I shall send children and women to the princes and the women shall rule over them".'

Hopeful that the faculty would return her compliment, she wrote, 'I beg you to let me know if you think I err.' She even cited examples of active women from the history of the church – Jerome himself was not ashamed to write to women, 'Plessila, Paula and Eustacia – even Christ himself instructed women, for example Mary Magdalen or the woman at the well.'[26]

Von Stauffen was apparently not aware that Seehofer had been released on bail and sent off to Ettal, an action taken by the university to prevent an official trial and investigation by the Bishop of Eichstett. Without hesitation she attacked the 'false prophets and wolves in sheep's clothing', a common metaphor in these pamphlets. She warned the university that it had been founded by princes and that the faculty were still dependent on princely support. Perhaps overestimating the amount of political pressure she personally might bring to bear on the situation, she upbraided them: 'how the princes have been deceived by you...Perhaps this is because they often made the poor among you rich, yet you have made their university a world-wide scandal! After all, when Peter denied Christ, he wasn't threatened with burning.' (She was under the impression that Seehofer would be burned.) Only once does a mother instinct break through her driving biblical polemic: 'he is, after all,' she added, 'only eighteen years old, a mere child.'[27]

In the midst of Argula von Stauffen's rather haphazard rhetorical style, it would seem that the major theological opinion underlying her voluminous biblical quotations is *sola scriptura* salvation. Unlike Sebastian Lotzer and others who saw scripture and active works as a means to conversion and a new society in anticipation of the second coming, her vision of reform in the church and its goals seems rather limited; preaching and hearing the word are the absolute center and means by which man might be saved excluding all other possible channels of grace. Like her pamphleteer colleagues she insists that the reading of scripture is necessary for every Christian. She was willing to admit some guilt on Seehofer's part and even suggests that Luther's translation of the new testament was not the best; however 'if Luther were to recant, it wouldn't make any difference to me, because I build my arguments on no human foundation, but on Christ the rock himself!' Rome and the pope were responsible, according to her, for creating that chain of delusion which had confused the princes and placed the German nation in such chaos. She follows a German tradition in her appeal to a holy Christian (not Catholic) church. She states that in the bible there was no mention of any Roman church. The Roman church had produced 'little good'; it had prevented people from reading the bible. The university by damning Seehofer had foolishly proceeded against God's word and advocated the use of force against the gospel. The princes (a reference to the Dukes of Bavaria) were led by the Roman church to do the work of the devil. That surprised her less: 'most of the sainted martyrs whose lives I have read were killed by the Romans.'[28] With 'limbs trembling and her heart palpitating', she ended her appeal to the faculty: 'I haven't written you about women's matters, but about God's word as a member of the Christian church against which the gates of hell may not prevail. The Christian church will even stand up to the Romans.'[29]

Rather than comment on Argula von Stauffen's appeal, the university instead sent a published copy of her treatise (which Osiander had encouraged her to publish in early October 1523) to the Dukes of Bavaria. Von Stauffen was not to be upstaged; she drafted a letter to Duke Wilhelm of Bavaria the very same day she completed her letter to the university. As willing to remind the duke of his Christian obligations as she was prepared to scold a university senate, she informed the duke that the innocent Seehofer had been condemned to the fire without any justification from scripture for alleged heresy in the case brought by the university; even worse, Seehofer had been forcd to deny the gospel. (She writes the prince as if he were unaware of the contest between the university and Lutheran partisans.) Instead of concentrating on the Seehofer problem, once again she took up the general cause of reformation, telling the duke to free himself from the evil academics and submit to the 'rule of the gospel.' In the spirit of Luther's address *To the Christian Nobility*, she asked the prince to take reform into his own hands to punish useless monks and money-hungry priests. She admonished the duke that he, not the pope, carried the sword of punishment and could reform the church because the priests had refused to do their duty and preach the gospel. In order that tax burdens be shared to support a crusade against the Turks, the prince ought to tax monasteries and parishes: 'take their registers and bring them into court to see how much they really earn and see that the money is put to some common use, so that the poor man is not quite so overburdened. Stop absentee priests with benefices they never visit, filling them with foolish vicars who know nothing! The rector in Voburg, receives 800 guilders income from his benefices but in a whole year never gave a sermon.'[30] It was the duke's Christian duty to reform the church, just as it was her Christian duty to preach the word when priests had refused. She promised the duke 'good fortune and victory' if he would see that the gospel was preached to the poor; hearing mass, she told him, was of less value. She published her letter without delay.

Von Stauffen like other pamphleteers vehemently attacked the contemporary clergy. Failing to preach the gospel was enough to condemn any priest; she claimed that celibacy was not humanly possible. 'Celibacy is as possible for a man as it is possible for me to touch heaven with my finger or perhaps to fly!'[31] Monks ought to be driven from their monasteries; canon lawyers stole from the poor in order to get rich, never even paying for as much as a glass of wine when they were students; they would not tolerate God's word and had been responsible for Seehofer's condemnation. She reminded the duke of her former days at court and of his promise to comfort her at the death of her parents. She apparently expected him to return the favor in ordering Seehofer's release.

Argula von Stauffen feigned a certain naivety. Her political acumen aided her in directing her propaganda to the general population. Certainly the dukes of Bavaria were well aware of the gravity of the problem and the divisions caused by Lutheran adherents. Not exactly 'unadvised' in the matter, the two dukes, Wilhelm and Ludwig, tried to put pressure on Friedrich von Grumbach to silence his wife. In Nuremberg, rumors circulated that Grumbach had been ordered to hack off two of his wife's fingers to prevent her from writing. By October 1523, feeling some pressure from above, Argula von Stauffen addressed yet another letter to the mayor and city council of Ingolstadt, another channel by which she might be able to obtain mercy for Seehofer and vent her fury. She insisted in her letter to the city council (probably written about mid-October 1523) that she belonged to the universal priesthood of believers by virtue of her baptism and was every bit as in possession of the spirit as a learned doctor, despite her lack of formal learning. She complained that the university 'sophists' had set the Roman church above the holy Christian church, the true church based on the word of God alone. Feeling the pressure placed on her husband to forbid her to write and publish, she turned her attention to Christian martyrdom. Seehofer like the early martyrs must die for the church like Christ, because the city council had acted like the Jews before Pilate; 'so let him be martyred...and may God do with me what he will...I presently seek the grace to suffer death for his name, that many hearts might be awakened: then perhaps a hundred women will write against them!' Content that her faith would save her as it saved her forefathers she proclaimed: 'for even if I die, the word of God remains to eternity.'[32]

With her letter to the city council already at press, Argula von Stauffen diverted her attention to another theater. With Osiander's continuing encouragement she sought to use her influence at the coming Nuremberg Diet which would discuss the Protestant issue. Despite the apparent silence of all her correspondents in the press, the publication of her letters did not go unnoticed. Dr Georg Hauer, preacher at St Mary's, Ingolstadt, used the occasion of the Feast of the Conception of the Blessed Virgin to comment on the 'pompous children of Eve.' He called activist women 'bitches and scoundrels' who suggest 'that just as Christ lived in Mary, so he might live in any Christian.' Luther had been responsible for such heresy; he had manipulated these women as Montanus did Prisca and Maximilla. Housewives ought not to meddle in the affairs of the church.[33]

On 1 December 1523, Argula von Stauffen addressed yet another letter, this time aiming at a higher level than the Bavarian dukes: she wrote to Elector Frederick the Wise of Saxony. He was a man certainly sympathetic to her cause, who would play an important role in the Nuremberg Diet. Her letter (also published) is a brief reminder to 'keep the word of God before your eyes' at the important diet. She begged him to see that the word of God not be taken from the poor, something pagan princes tried to do, as they continued to crucify Christ again and again by supporting the old-church party. Evil princes pursued evangelical preachers in their territories. She promised to write his colleague the Count Palatine the same day to remind him of his duty. Indeed, she did and also published her letter. She asked him to 'without fear confess the word of God at the diet to see that the kingdom of God is not shut to the poor', which would then result in everyone's destruction.[34] The increasing number of poor people and the suppression of true biblical preaching are the center of her concern, although she never develops these concerns as part of a mystical theology or a works-holiness, as did other pamphleteers. The word and the poor are linked together in her imagery of the last days, when God-fearing poor Christians would be justified and the wolves and false teachers of the old church would be condemned to hell. Curiously missing in von Stauffen's pamphlets is a means by which a utopian Christian kingdom might be realized on earth, which absorbs much of other pamphleteers' energy. One finds no theology of works-holiness defined by acts of love and charity. It would seem that only preaching accomplished the infusion of grace necessary for salvation. She never develops this theme very well, because her concerns are political. She knew that the Count Palatine was the hereditary enemy of the Bavarian dukes. In a bitter war over the inheritance of Duke George of Bavaria (+ 1503) he had been disinherited in favor of the sons of Duchess Kunigund, sister of the Emperor Maximilian. Von Stauffen knew well that Frederick the Wise was an ardent supporter of evangelical reform.

Invited by the Count Palatine to discuss her ideas, Argula von Stauffen saddled her horse to attend the imperial diet at Nuremberg. Whether or not she had direct contact with other princes and representatives of the free cities is not clear. Her trip to Nuremberg was certainly courageous: she owed her early education and support to the Duchess Kunigund; her husband's position depended on the favor of the Bavarian dukes. Unfortunately, we know little about her activity at the diet. She did comment on the behavior of the princes at that diet, who seemed more interested in hunting and whoring than theology. In her next letter (also published) to her cousin Adam von Törring, she responded to rumors she had heard in Nuremberg that the Bavarian dukes had ordered her husband to cut off her fingers. She had heard too, that her cousin had advised her husband to wall her up alive and forget about her. She told her cousin that he need not worry: her husband was doing his best 'to persecute Christ' in her. In self-defense she insisted that she had only sought to reason with the university faculty at Ingolstadt on a Godly, not a human basis. Besides, as a baptized Christian who had vowed to deny the devil, she had received the holy spirit and had been reborn through the death of Christ. Quick to separate herself from enthusiasts, she added: 'only when one confesses Christ can one call oneself a Christian, even if one has been baptized a thousand times.' Besides, why should people worry abut her and her fate, since in the nearing last days she would have to give account for herself. Aware that her husband's job and her marriage were in jeopardy, she reminded her cousin that to follow Christ one must be willing to abandon father, mother, husband and family, must be prepared to lose everything. God would watch over her four children, should she have to suffer martyrdom, and in that spirit, she would suffer any slander against her. 'I am not a Lutheran,' she insists: 'I confess Christ, not Luther.'[35] Argula von Stauffen considered herself part of an evangelical church like other pamphleteers, a church which pre-dated Luther.

Probably in reference to her own education, she reminded her cousin of a parent's duty to teach children the bible. Aware that most parents had failed to do so, she commented: 'the people know the word of God about as well as a cow knows how to play chess!' Because her cousin wanted to remain in the old church, true to the faith of his parents, she told him that he would have to answer for himself, not his parents, at the last judgment. Besides, had his parents gone to school, they would have learned about whoring and sex from Terence and Ovid; they would not have learned the bible. In hope of converting her cousin to her cause, she reminded him of what had happened to her family at the hands of the Bavarian dukes and the priests in Würzburg. She begged him to read the four gospels and to see that pastorates and preacherships, over which he exercised the right of appointment, were filled with learned men. In conclusion, to clear herself of any charges of enthusiasm, she said that she had not wanted to make her letters public; that was God's doing and she was willing to accept the consequences.

Because of his wife's publishing, Friedrich von Grumbach lost his position. He had to leave Bavaria with his family and return to his family home in the Rhineland. Von Stauffen was somewhat successful at rallying support among evangelically minded relatives, in order that she and her family might return to their home. This time she returned not to Dietfurt, but to Lenting, where she spent the rest of her life.[36] On returning to Bavaria in the spring of 1524, she took the opportunity to write to the city council of Regensburg. The council's decision to procede against Protestants was not to her liking. She published her letter in June, 1524. Von Stauffen insisted that the council mandate was the work of Satan. She was not ashamed of the gospel and would continue to confess it, even if people

55 A medal with a likeness of Argula von Stauffen (+1564?), probably commissioned by her sole surviving son, Gottfried, after her death. The reverse side of
the medal reads, 'Lying, envious tongues condemned me to suffering and pain.'

laughed at her because she was a woman. She warned the council: 'take
care that the souls in our lands have not been purchased with silver and
gold...but with the precious rose-colored blood of Jesus.'[37] The council
should use the word of God instead of weapons and see that they show
love for their neighbors in peace, not procede against them. With this last
letter she ended her published correspondence. One more curious work
appeared under her authorship, though it is not clear whether or not she
was the author. The work, *A Poetic Answer to a Poem written by a Student
of Ingolstadt*, may have been set to verse by Hans Sachs. The ideas are
certainly from Argula von Stauffen. A student had accused her of
forgetting 'all proper feminine conduct', and her proper place by 'scolding
princes, lords, and even a university.' All who followed Luther were 'full
of lechery and knavery..., who broke their marriage vows, spreading
slanderous gossip.'[38] Von Stauffen returned the compliment: God didn't
withhold his spirit from either peasants or women. At the End women
would be called to prophesy, 'besides, at what university did the apostles
study?' If she did not understand the word of God, why did the student
not explain it to her? Though she admitted that she might not speak openly
in churches, there was nothing to prevent her from doing so in her own
home and in the streets. She supported herself with old testament models.
'Like Judith and Deborah, God will produce many women to punish your
stupid arrogance...God did indeed order me to spin wool and keep house,
but let the university faculty not forget that God also called me to hear
his word!'[39] Insisting that she still continued to serve her husband, she
reminded the student that all Christians must be prepared to leave child
and husband to serve Christ. 'I remain obedient to my God and my
husband', she ended her poem, 'and my soul could be no more dear to me
than that.'[40]

It is difficult to speculate on the actual effect of her propaganda. The fact that she had enough weight with important family members to influence the duke of Bavaria to allow her husband and family to return is certainly significant. It seems that the interest of dynasty superseded the actual religious issue in this case. Neither the university at Ingolstadt nor the city council of Regensburg would listen to her. Although she retired from publishing her work, she did not disappear. Argula von Stauffen disassociated herself from Anabaptists and enthusiasts, through her close contact with Spalatin, Luther and Osiander, which continued throughout her life. Even Luther's arch-enemy John Eck entrusted her with some of his personal family business on one occasion. Luther clearly had approved her activities, though somewhat tacitly. She wrote to encourage him to marry and reported the deaths of martyrs to the evangelical cause in Bavaria. She sent her sons to school in Nuremberg, where Osiander looked after them, and later to study in Wittenberg with Melanchthon. When Luther was in Coburg in 1530, she paid him a visit and had supper with him. She wrote Spalatin in Augsburg after her visit: 'fear not in matters concerning God; what he has begun in us, he will continue to nurture and protect; though he may appear to sleep, he still protects his Israel. Leave it to God to settle theological arguments.'[41] Friedrich von Grumbach died in 1532. She remarried in 1533 and remained in Lenting. Her new husband died a year later. In May, 1563, she apparently began to officiate at funerals in cemeteries. She was briefly put in prison, but released later on the advice of the Regensburg city council.[42]

When we try to compare the theological content of her works with medieval predecessors or contemporary fellow pamphleteers, several problems are presented, many of whch arise from her haphazard style; she often gives answers to questions never defined and in no order of importance. She persists in giving unsolicited advice. This tends to confuse and complicate her message. Yet, she does share the conviction that a new age of the gospel had begun with other pamphleteers. She was convinced that Luther, Melanchthon and other magisterial reformers gave an early warning to common people to assume their own evangelical responsibility, since the church had refused to do so. The economy of salvation in her theology appears to be much simpler than that of her colleagues:

Figure 7. The Economy of Salvation in Argula von Grumbach's Pamphlets

Her theology is close to a Lutheran *sola scriptura* formula for salvation. Missing in her theology is an emphasis on works of mercy necessary in the last days. There is also no well-developed reference to the effect of the word on the conscience of the individual Christian. Characteristic of Argula von Stauffen's works is her political sensitivity. She knew the value of propaganda and how to use letters to important people to that end. From her own political experience she was aware of how such matters were handled by princes. She feigned naivety and manipulated arguments for decidedly propagandist purposes. Like our other pamphleteers, she collected a list of abuses; she despised canon lawyers, mendicant monks, and Roman leadership in the church. Canon lawyers had robbed her of her own inheritance; mendicant monks had tried to prevent her from reading the bible; the Roman church prevented evangelical preaching of the word of God and substituted inferior human teachings and traditions. She expresses no opposition to the cult of saints; she continued to read the lives of the saints and martyrs. Her vision of a church of the future lacks the mystical richness of other lay pamphleteers. In her works we see neither a clear element of contemplative 'female piety', nor even a hint of the imperial piety of Bavaria, so dominant in her region according to Rothkrug. She speaks of the ability of women and peasants to be inspired by the spirit. She is among the few pamphleteers to have speculated on baptism and its spirit-lending effect, which adds additional support to someone who had to accept Pauline statements on the status of women in the church. Luther approved of her efforts: he called her *instrumentum singulare Christi*![43]

Argula von Stauffen was not the only woman involved in the events that surrounded the theological controversies of 1523–24. The wife of the tax collector of Eisenberg in Saxony, Ursula Weyda, took up her pen as well to attack Simon Plick, Abbot of Pegau, a Benedictine monastery near Leipzig. A member of anti-Lutheran forces, he published a pamphlet entitled: *The Horrible Destruction of Land and People in Possessions, Person, and Honor and their future Salvation at the Hands of Luther and his Friends* in 1524.[44] In his treatise, the abbot stated that he would hate to be called either Lutheran or 'evangelical' since neither Luther nor the evangelists could accomplish his salvation. Lutheranism, he claimed, had not only put people's souls in danger by breaking the unity of the church, but also ruined the professions of sculptors, painters, and goldsmiths who had so long worked in the name of the church, its saints, and Jesus Christ. Among the Lutherans only devilish printers had profited from Luther's teachings. Luther unfairly discredited pagan philosophy as the work of the devil, as universities stood speechless against his rhetoric; Luther dared call universities synagogues of the devil and whorehouses of the pope.

Ursula Weyda responded to the abbot's treatise with her own *Against the Unchristian, Slanderous Work of the Abbot of Pegau*, published in the summer of 1524. She repaid the abbot with her own, not so subtle, mockery. The abbot published a pamphlet that was so badly written, she would have assumed it had been written by a half-witted drunk! She never spares the opportunity to curse the abbot in her earthy language which actually breaks the boredom of this very lengthy treatise against abbots, monks, and nuns: 'the abbot knows as much about the word of God as a great stupid oaf!...You stupid, ignorant abbot: you know as much about scriptures as a sow about harvesting a field of beets!...You know less about scripture than a cow about dancing!...' She called the Pegau Benedictines and all religious orders 'stupid, greedy, hungry dogs!' She even thought Eck to be more tolerable, if not a bit more intelligent: 'Eck and his followers have more intelligence in their little fingers than you have in your whole body and soul, you rude abbot!'[45]

Beyond her blasphemous polemic, the treatise is constructed around several theological propositions taken from the abbot's pamphlet. She answers the abbot's appeal to the unity and tradition of the church: 'the word of God alone is important, but monks and priests know nothing of this. They use lies, which the false and devilish papal church tells them.' Besides, the church wasn't made up of the pope, bishops, priests and monks. The church was the church of holy scripture, the holy Christian church, infallibly resting on scripture alone, through faith, where the holy spirit was contained. Councils had nothing to say in the matter. They had legislated against the word of God, e.g. Constance, whose bishops were not of Christ but the devil (probably a reference to the Huss affair). Popes, bishops, and priests didn't build on the true rock, but on their human wills. 'When a pope goes to bed he dreams up another bull and makes it an article of faith.' Turks and Jews were as Christian as popes, she insisted, for they relied on their human wills and sought only to make a great show.[46]

Ursula Weyda assigns scripture a particular role in society like Lotzer, Marschalck, Greiffenberger and Sachs: 'God's word nourishes the narrow consciences and sin-laden hearts to erase our human wills. See to it that God's word be in your heart at all times. Where God's word is missing, there is an indecisive heart and a fear-filled conscience. If it is not, then the pope is directly responsible, for the pope is a man who can err.'[47] Since the abbot often referred to Luther and his followers as runaway monks and nuns, even adulterers who had broken their vows, she devotes much of her treatise to attacking the nature of monastic vows, which she calls useless for salvation. She makes it quite clear: chastity is a supernatural gift possessed by very few and is given only to those with a *gemüthe* prepared to accept it, not to normal human beings. She exclaims: 'oh, if only God could show the nobility how their children's and friends' salvation is in danger in a monastery.'[48] Intoning the eschatological necessity of her appeal she tells monks to leave their monasteries and vows behind. 'Help, help! It is time to escape God's anger before it suddenly descends upon us...Leave the old church and return to your baptismal vows, for in baptism we all vow to believe his word and follow it...Break the bond of your monastic tonsure and take off your habits with free and certain conscience, even if you have taken a thousand oaths.'[49] The sad condition of the contemporary church had been predicted in the last days: the clergy tried to purchase God's grace with good works. Bishops were riders, rabbit hunters, and drunkards, better at playing pipes and drums, gaming and chess than as shepherds. Like Argula von Grumbach, she had to justify her audacity to write the abbot: she insists that Christ commissioned all his disciples to bear persecution for their willingness to speak out. 'Besides,' she adds, 'the children of God weren't monks and nuns, but children of the great patriarchs.'[50] Although her pamphlet is longer and better organized than any of those written by Argula von Stauffen, it emphasizes the same themes with the addition of an extravagant number of biblical citations.

Ursula Weyda's pamphlet did not go unanswered. The abbot's brother, Dr Wolfgang Plick, city councilor in Leipzig probably composed the answer entitled: *An Answer to the Unchristian Blasphemy of Mrs. Weyda, wife of the tax collector of Eisenberg*, published in the fall of 1524. Plick thought Weyda's husband must be a fine 'milk-toast', allowing his wife to write about such important matters so scandalously. Not the monks, but those 'who serve their stomachs first' were responsible for the divisions in the church and among the princes; Lutherans praise princes sympathetic to their cause, and good princes, loyal to the church suddenly become vicious tyrants. The electors of the empire were like the seven hairs on Samson's head for Delilah. As one by one the electors were converted to the Protestant cause, the church lost its power to enforce morality, creating schism and division, just as St Paul predicted that false teachers would lead men astray. 'What comes of your so-called evangelical freedom, ...Children don't obey their parents; pupils don't obey their masters...Your bearded preachers swagger through the streets in loudcolored clothing with a sword at their side like any other man, pretending to open wide the doors of heaven, when Christ himself tells us that the way to heaven is narrow.'[51] An anonymously authored apology appeared to rebuff councilor Plick, perhaps written by Weyda herself. The work, entitled *Apologia for the Wife of the Tax Collector of Eisenberg*, presents by far the most avid defense of women's activism in the church. 'Had Mary not spoken of faith and Godly works in her Magnificat?' If all women were forbidden to speak, how could daughters prophesy as Joel predicted? Although St Paul forbade women to preach in churches and instructed them to obey their husbands, what if the churches were full of liars? So long as they be loyal to their husbands, they might certainly speak out on theological matters. Popes, bishops, monks and priests had erred when they taught people that to get into

Straßburg

56 Strasbourg. From Hartmann Schedel's *Weltchronik*, 1493.

heaven, they ought to pray, fast, give alms, build churches, fund altars, purchase indulgences. 'The scriptures told us only to believe and love our neighbors.'[52] Since Ursula Weyda only spoke from the word of God, she could not be a heretic. After 1524, Ursula Weyda never published again. Reports about her later life are scanty. After her husband's death in 1541, she remarried; she died in Altenberg about 1550.[53]

Catherine Schütz was in a visible, public position as the wife of a priest and evangelical reformer, Matthew Zell (+1548). She was the daughter of an Alsatian carpenter. Very little is known about her life before her marriage in 1523. Among the first women to marry a priest in Strasbourg, she came under attack by the bishop, who had excommunicated her husband, and was subject to criticism by conservative members of the city council. In 1524, she published a pamphlet to defend herself, *An Apology...for her Husband, Matthew Zell*. She claimed that her husband did not know of her intentions to publish an apology for their marriage; she said that he would have tried to prevent her from publishing. She answered specific charges against clerical marriage made by Thomas Murner (+ 1537), Johann Cochleus (+ 1552), and Conrad Treger, OESA (+ 1542) Aware that she must be persecuted for her righteous act, she insisted that her conscience would not allow her to be silent about angry attacks on her and her husband.[54] As a Christian, she was under obligation to help her neighbor, in particular her husband and to warn the general populace of the outrageous lies spread by her enemies, 'the devil's mailmen.' She charged that 'evil teaching is more dangerous than an evil life', because teaching was ultimately more harmful to others, whereas an evil life only affected the individual. Her critics were not only damned because they lived wicked lives, but because they used their offices to spread lies.[55] In denouncing Cochleus, she chided: 'Cochleus? I almost wrote wooden spoon! (*Kochlöffel*.) Like a wooden spoon in an empty pot, he makes a lot of noise, but is of such inferior wood, that one could hardly stir a child's gruel with him!'[56] She called Murner, 'guildmaster of the guild of fools', and Treger, 'an enemy of Christ's cross.' She grouped them with the bishop and city councilors of Strasbourg who had condemned her marriage. Why had the bishop so vehemently attacked her marriage? Because the bishop collected more money from priests and monks who kept whores and therefore paid to be released from their sins, than he could collect from decent married people. The city council feared clerical marriage because they expected that the property they had given to churches and monasteries would be passed to the children of married clergy. 'They all condemn married priests,' she said, 'but none of them attack the worst sin of all, sodomy, which they have conspired to protect.' She was prepared to suffer martyrdom, if necessary. 'And if the princes of the world are enlisted to drive us out, we must suffer death; so we must remember that when we suffer, Christ suffers in us.'[57]

Not long after her apology was published, she took pity on a particular group of suffering women in the tiny city of Kenzingen, not far from Strasbourg. In June, 1524, Archduke Ferdinand of Austria, the Dukes of Bavaria and the South German bishops meeting in Regensburg joined forces to help enforce the Edict of Worms in their own territories. Kenzingen was not a free city; it lay in the Habsburg territory, subject to the control of the Austrian Archduke. The city council in Kenzingen tried to steer a moderate course between their support for an evangelical preacher, Jacob Otter (+ 1547) and the demands of their prince. An

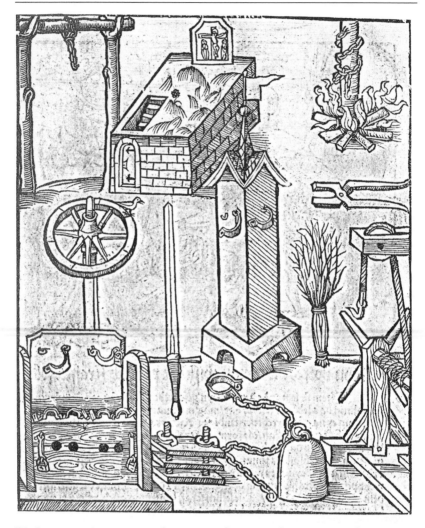

57 Customary instruments of torture in the sixteenth century, used to restrain prisoners and test heretics, among them neck irons. From *Bamberger Halszgericht*, 1506.

unsympathetic archduke sent troops; rather than risk destruction of the city, the city council asked Otter to leave the city. His dramatic departure from the city with two hundred armed citizens to insure his safety, seemed even more tearful when the armed men returned to find the city occupied and the gates locked. Shut out of their city, the men went to Strasbourg, where they stayed in the home of Matthew and Catherine Zell. Schütz housed eighty of them the first night and fed sixty of them for another three weeks. To console their wives, Schütz published *To the Suffering Women of Kenzingen Parish.*[58] The pamphlet was designed to give examples of heroic women of the past, most of them from the old testament. Abraham is her most frequently used model, since he, like the Kenzingen wives, nearly had to sacrifice his own flesh and blood, but was eventually rewarded for his faith and patience. She advised her sisters: 'take on a manly spirit, like Abraham, and when you fall into trouble, have the faith to suffer all sorts of trials, slander, and pain; even if they put neck rings on you, drown you, exile you, or kill your husbands, you must remain faithful to Christ.' If she were given the opportunity for martyrdom, she wrote her sisters in Kenzingen, she would be 'happier and more glorious than all the nobles of Strasbourg in their golden necklaces at the fair or even the wife of the emperor, who can sit on his throne.' The women ought not to grieve for their 'fleshy loss', for St Paul reminded them to 'suppress...fleshy desires and lift their spirits.' Like a medieval preacher, she reminded them that pain was the untimely inheritance of Christ's sacrifice; her readers ought to rejoice in potential widowhood, 'doing outward works as sure signs of faith.'[59] She ended her letter of consolation with a re-statement of the beatitudes, to comfort the sad and persecuted. Schütz's theology is boldly and clearly stated: God's word and the promise of salvation to all believers ought to be enough to sustain the Kenzingen wives. That promise rested on Christ's outpouring of his own blood. Until the return of their husbands, they should continue in the good works that were required of every Christian.

Unlike many of her pamphleteer colleagues, Catherine Schütz continued to be active in writing and publishing long after 1525. When peasants camped outside the city walls, Schütz went to them to ask them to lay down their arms and negotiate peacefully. In her home she nursed the wounded and refugees after the bloody battle. She entertained Zwingli and Oekolampadius on their way to Marburg for two weeks in 1529. She wrote Luther of her disappointment, when Zwingli and Luther failed to reach an agreement. She reminded Luther that love was stronger than any small point of theological controversy. She constantly defended Anabaptists, convinced that they shared the same conception of an evangelical church as other Protestants. She often visited Melchior Hoffmann (+c. 1543) in prison. She became a close friend and defender of Casper Schwenckfeld (+1561). When a city councilor was diagnosed a leper and was forced to live enclosed outside the city, Catherine Schütz visited him. At her husband's graveside in 1548, after the formal eulogy by Martin Bucer, she herself addressed the mourners: 'I am like the dear Mary Magdalen, who with no thought of being an apostle, came to tell the disciples that she had encountered the risen lord.'[60] She published her own edition of psalms and dedicated a meditation on the Lord's Prayer to her leper friend.

Catherine Schütz did not just write about the works of holy mercy: she spent her life performing them.

In examining the female contribution to the theological controversies in this pamphlet literature, generalization is difficult. Even the women themselves are difficult to integrate into patterns sought by historians to describe the role of women in the late Middle Ages. Yet, in comparison with their male publishing colleagues, certain aspects of their works are remarkable. We find more blaspheming for public attention, described by Joseph Schmidt as the easiest and most common means to get the attention of the 'common man.'[61] The rudeness of Ursula Weyda's work, and to some extent Catherine Schütz's polemic, stand out among their more decorous male colleagues. Argula von Stauffen was a propagandist of the first rank, using family connections and letters to powerful political figures, not only to remind princes of their evangelical responsibility, but to bring the Seehofer controversy directly to the people in her challenge to the university and city council of Ingolstadt. Although she was common in her education, she was aware of both intrigue and political negotiations at the highest levels in the Bavarian court. She deliberately overstated, feigned naivety, and manipulated in order to gain support for the evangelical cause. As a result of such sensitivity to audiences, we can say that the women in this study seem more concerned with their reader/hearership. There are few hints of traditional 'female piety' in their works. Only Catherine Schütz wrote a meditation on the Lord's Prayer. Catherine Schütz stands out among her colleagues as a pious model, not only because her early works contain a more detailed theological outline, but also because we know more about her intentions and activities from later works. She provided a model for the pastor's wife that left a stamp on later generations, perhaps as important as Kate Luther's. She consoled the wives of Kenzingen; she heroicly defended Casper Schwenckfeld before the authorities. She fed exiles in her home. She visited the sick. She exemplified the new role to which active women in the church laid claim. Unlike St Angela Merici she needed no benevolent patron: she had her husband for support and advice. His influence gives her theology an exemplary coherence and integrity. She strove for unity in the church: the failure of the Marburg Colloquy and subsequent attempts at Protestant intercommunion were as much a burden to her as was the imposition of the Interim in 1549.[62]

The activity of these women was hardly revolutionary. Putting themselves in print was, however, a challenge to contemporary society: if men laid spurious claim to universal priesthood, women had even less a claim in church tradition. Husbands were worried about the dangers of their publishing wives. Catherine Schütz noted that her husband would not approve of her publishing an apology for their marriage. Friedrich von Grumbach lost his post as warden on the ducal estates in Bavaria because

58 A woman performs works of holy mercy. Taken from *Bruder Klaus* (Nuremberg, 1488). The woodcuts were used to explain a mystical vision of the Swiss hermit, St. Nicholas von der Flühe (+1487), who sometime between 1474 and 1478, saw a head, wearing a papal crown and a beard, with six swords projecting from the face. The vision was interpreted by the author of *Bruder Klaus* to be a sign of Christ coming in judgment. Each of the swords pointed to a work of holy mercy, required in the last days before the End.

of his wife's activities. Certainly the fact that women's social position was inferior to males and their education was equal, or even better, than many males added extra frustration. They were quick to call forth old testament models for their activities, to confront Pauline theology with apocalyptic prophecy. The Virgin Mary no longer provided their most important behavioral model. Probably because of her general passivity in the gospel accounts of Jesus' life, these women needed stronger, more forceful models.

Was their piety essentially feminine? Certainly to the extent that they called forth female models. Lionel Rothkrug's conclusions about 'feminine' piety present a peculiar challenge. As a quantitative historian, Rothkrug is accustomed to counting numbers and certainly our three women cannot claim to be representative. Their piety includes a vigorous defense of lay activity, but their spirituality is not especially meditative, something that Rothkrug uses as a characteristic of feminine piety. These women demonstrate a form of active piety justified by old testament models for women. They are not particularly anti-aristocratic, certainly not Argula von Stauffen. Rothkrug's thesis is based on the contrasts that existed between North and South Germany. However, when he speaks of piety, he seems to ignore the importance of the affective tradition of late-medieval piety in all parts of Germany. Whether one read devotional literature or rode one's horse before the exposed sacrament (as was the custom in Bavaria) in the late Middle Ages, both activities were expected to result in good works, be those works defined as service to the poor or a pilgrimage to a holy shrine. Both men and women did them, both male and female saints shared that tradition. If we can call piety either 'masculine' or 'feminine', we must pay attention to role models. There is nothing peculiarly feminine about meditation or tears. A form of worship may be anti-aristocratic and we can certainly explain this by emphasizing the importance of the last judgment as levelling agent in the theology of lay pamphleteers. The women in this study used both male and female models for active laypeople, certainly crossing the boundaries of sexuality in pious behavior. The piety of women in this sample is oddly not close to Rothkrug's North German models; it is not even particularly affective (except perhaps in the works of Catherine Schütz). The males in this sample of pamphleteers are closer in many ways to Rothkrug's model for feminine piety than the women considered here.

In the pamphlets published by women, the appeal to an elect community of believers performing works of mercy required in the last days is a less determining factor for their theology. There are hints of the importance of works of mercy in the last days, of a purely evangelical church united in its goals in Catherine Schütz's works.[63] Because of these women's generally more propagandistic intentions, we have less evidence of personal theology and spirituality. Argula von Stauffen would seem to be a *sola scriptura* Lutheran, but we have no evidence of a developed theological anthropology or eschatological thought to substantiate such a statement. Convictions that the world was nearing its end are implicit in women's calling to speak out, to teach, preach and prophesy. It is clear that like their fellow male pamphleteers, they felt that their vocation to write and publish was part of a new birth of the gospel in their own time. They employ the same hackneyed paradigms as the males to criticize the failures of the old church, adding particularly blasphemous attacks on their personal enemies. In the works by women, suffering, persecution, and a willingness to be martyred stand out against pressure brought on their husbands to silence them. Certainly the plight of women seeking an active vocation in the church was every bit as acute as, if not more acute than, that of males. Weinstein and Bell suggest that the 'Protestant Reformation had the indirect effect of curtailing the role of women as leaders of Catholic piety.'[64] Catherine Schütz would be a useful example to refute this suggestion. Wives of pastors as leaders in church and society provided new models for active laywomen. Protestant women lived in the world, not in enclosed convents, where they had to more actively fight the social conventions of their own time.

Conclusions

The pamphlets in this study contain much more than propaganda for the Reformation. The evidence presented by this sample of lay pamphleteers demonstrates both a depth of religious feeling and a vision of church reform linked to a peculiar sense of immediacy. The 'new theology' of Luther, Zwingli, and other reformers was adapted to and integrated into an expected constitution of the elect, preparing to meet the coming judgment. Historians who frequently dismissed pamphlets as simple Protestant propaganda must take another look at these very personal documents of lay piety and theology. Marxist scholars, who use pamphlets as examples to illustrate socio-economic grievances that underlay the Reformation movement, must come to terms with the deep, in some cases traditionally medieval piety of the common people who wrote them. More recent historians of political propaganda must re-examine the personal motives of the individual writers for that vision of the church marking time until the End in a new call to prophesy and perform holy works.

As a group, the pamphleteers from various parts of Southwest Germany demonstrate a new vocation to redeem the world, foreshadowed in the medieval heretical movements, usually condemned by church authorities, and seldom encouraged by civic officials. As individuals, they responded to different stimuli, signs that the progress of church reform was in danger. Sebastian Lotzer wrote to support a wandering preacher he had never heard. Argula von Stauffen wrote to defend a scholar she had never met. Ursula Weyda scolded an abbot, whose anti-Lutheran pamphlet she happened to read. Catherine Schütz saw it as her own pastoral responsibility to comfort the Kenzingen wives. Marschalck, Sachs, Rychssner, and Greiffenberger all responded to indecisive city councils and others, who failed to see the importance of a real reformation of church and society. They all commented on growing divisions within the Protestant camp, that seemed to be leading the Reformation in a direction far removed from their personal hopes. They expected a reform of the church and society to meet the second coming of Christ. Their own self-righteous vocation to warn the common man to stand by the gospel in the last days has its roots in

late-medieval heretical movements that defined the true flock of Christ as
the poor and simple. Although our writers were neither especially poor nor
very simple, they insisted that they were called to awaken the common man
to his coming election.

Humanists and their studies, by education more sophisticated than these
common people, provided them with the means to enter the debate on the
Reformation by ennobling the simplicity of the poor and ignorant. They
encouraged our pamphleteers to take part in the religious controversy by
publishing their works. By their own pious treatises and sermons,
Humanists introduced common people to the effective vehicles of propaganda: apologia, warnings, expositions and dialogues. Our pamphleteers
understood common people better than their Humanist inspirators: they
repeated the age-old criticism of a lazy, decadent, ignorant, and corrupt
clergy. They did not hesitate to scold and upbraid their betters with crude,
often brutal curses. Fortunately, for us, their pamphlets as early documents
of lay piety and printed propaganda provide some insight into the reasons
why these people accepted the Reformation. We see the way in which the
ideas of several reformers were taken up and adopted. We note how Luther,
seen by many historians as the focus of the early Reformation movement,
was one among many others who influenced them. Luther was yet another
martyr for the older cause of reform, like John Huss, and perhaps even that
expected last prophet, a light in a long dark tunnel. Local parish preachers
(most of them Humanists) Schappeler, Rhegius, Osiander, Zell, Oekolampadius, Eberlin von Günzburg had a more immediate effect on our pamphleteers. Erasmus continued to be a cultural hero for them, despite his
later opposition to Luther. The old assumption that people were more
influenced by Zwingli and Luther depending on relative distance from
Zürich and Wittenberg is both false and misleading. The early Reformation
was local in character. People were concerned and involved in debate on a
local level. The crisis of 1523–24 helped to reveal a medieval watershed of
theological ideas, conceptions of the church, and its mission in society.
These ideas survived several centuries of oppression and persecution, as
the laity sought a more active recognized role in the life of the church to
redeem society.

The mystical theology that underlies the thought of some of our
pamphleteers, the exhortation to works of mercy in the last days and the
traditional critique of the clergy are neither entirely medieval nor entirely
Protestant. It would seem to be a last gasp of a lay subculture, with its own
theology, ideas, and expectations for reform. Our pamphleteers used
propaganda not just to convince others of Luther's virtue, but to spread
their own suggestions for constructive change. They encouraged personal,
individual activity, perhaps because lay corporate activity in the past had
always been suspect by authorities. Brotherhoods seemed too exclusive and

cared more for the souls of the dead than the fate of the poor. A theology of the poor as the gateway to heaven was apparently so deeply rooted in medieval piety, that even these first Protestants could not so easily dispense with it. Their theology bears closer resemblance to the theology of Waldensian communities and sects active in Southwest Germany in the fourteenth century.

Closer examination of this sample of pamphleteers not only reveals their lack of Latin education, but also their very brief period of activity. Only one of the writers published after 1525. The fact that four of our authors were artisans links them to a long tradition of protest. Artisans not only were active as leaders of religious and political protest in the late Middle Ages, but also supported the peasants in 1525. Their solidarity with peasants, their acceptance of the *lex evangelica* as the final authority in law, and their vision of the world turned upside down – where the common man knew theology better than the cleric – show the acceptance of the Reformation as a step toward the final judgment and a final justification. This sample of lay pamphleteers is significant because it provides early, personal, documentary evidence for the religious ideas of common people in the sixteenth century. Our writers did not need scribes to record and edit their ideas. They wrote their own works and brought them to the printers for publication. Our sample of pamphleteers can and does provide us with the kind of information Hans-Joachim Köhler hoped might be found as the result of a revival of interest in pamphlets: 'detailed information about opinions, convictions, and values of an epoch...insights into the social dynamics of the sixteenth century.'[1]

Did these lay pamphleteers speak for the proletarian masses? Hardly! Using Erich Maschke's classification system, they would belong to the lower ranks of the middle class, since they are occasionally listed in tax lists and paid taxes, but never paid enough to rank with merchants or patricians. Utz Rychssner was listed in a tax list, but he may never have paid his taxes. He lived outside the city walls in Augsburg, where most poorer artisans lived. Hans Sachs, by contrast, paid taxes, acquired a large library, and property. Maschke concludes that many of the people in the lower ranks of the middle class were socially stagnated, if not downwardly mobile in the economic decline of the early sixteenth century. The concern they express for the poor in their cities may be the result of frustration with their own immobility.[2] Perhaps some of our authors were in danger of falling to the level of the 'have-nots,' beggars, day laborers, and unemployed artisans. They often call themselves poor, but there are few indications that they were really very poor. The term 'poor' *per se* was not very significant. Even the documents of journeymen brotherhoods refer to their members as 'we poor people.' For Christians in general in the Middle Ages, it was always more advantageous to call oneself poor, than rich.[3]

What prompted our writers to begin publishing in the early years of the Reformation? The years 1522–23 present a period of serious crisis. Luther had disappeared. Monks and nuns fled their convents. Clergymen said mass in German and abandoned their ecclesiastical dress. Students rioted in the streets. In Augsburg, altars and epitaphs in churches were found spattered with blood. The world seemed to be turned upside-down. Despite the Edict of Worms, the Lutheran and Catholic parties were still trying to rally common people to their respective sides. Church reform was not the only debate on the horizon. Parallel to the debate over church reform was the controversy over the signs of the nearing end of the world. The publishing market was flooded with practical almanacs and *Prognostica* predicting 1524 as the End. Humanists tried to dispel the alarmist literature of many astrologers; astrologers saw the chaos in church and society as sure signs of the End. As theologians vied to capture popular support for their ideas, the astrologers predicted extraordinarily heavy rains for February, 1524, a second flood. Luther, too, was convinced that the End might be near. Preaching in December 1522, Luther declared that peculiar changes in the heavens were not due to natural causes, but were intentional signs from God. He could use this to encourage people to accept the Reformation as the true church of the gospel which would constitute the elect at the end of the world. He noted: 'Let the ungodly doubt and dismiss God's signs and say, "These are just natural events"; but you must hear what the gospel says: This and more signs from heaven...like plagues, inflation, earthquakes confirm Luke 17 and Matthew 24.'[4] As early as March 1521, Luther wrote to Spalatin, that he hoped an anti-papal picture-book pamphlet, *The Passion of Christ and the Anti-Christ*, would reach all the people, even illiterate peasants.[5] Reformers did their best to exploit the fears of common people. Humanists of the old church party scarcely had much of a chance. Besides, heavy rains in the summer of 1523, flood warnings and the conjunction of Jupiter with Pisces constellation on 31 January 1523, 3 and 5 February 1524 sent many astrologers speculating. The prospects in the German *Prognostica* are grim for 1524; flood, cold, hunger, pestilence, wars between princes, a church in chaos. In early 1524 much of Vienna was in panic. Roman nobles fled to the hills for shelter from the coming flood. Papal advisors tried to dispel the fears of the public. The Humanist Augustine Nifo published *Consolationes* and a treatise *De Falso Diluvio* relying on the scientific theories of Aristotle and Albertus Magnus to explain the coming events as natural, not divine in origin.[6] Translations of Nifo's works fell on deaf ears. The language of the German almanac, *Practica Deutsch* (Leipzig, 1522) was more familiar and convincing, since it went beyond the gospel predictions of the End: the almanacs predicted that changes in the heavens heralded the angelic shepherd, who would put an end to the tithe, prohibit luxurious display of clothing in the streets, put an end to licentious singing and dancing, dishonesty, and the immodesty of women.[7]

Common people would be more likely to believe the *Practica* above the learned works of Nifo, because the *Practica* relied on the gospel for its proof, not pagan philosophers, and it predicted an end to problems, many of which had been created by economic change as well as the introduction of Renaissance ideas and fashions north of the Alps. Economic and intellectual discontent are evident in the writings of Haug Marschalck and Argula von Stauffen. Marschalck condemned the luxurious display of fashion in Augsburg, parents dressing their children in velvet, while the poor man walked the streets in rags; he objected to the obvious dishonesty in market practices. Von Stauffen opposed the school system of her parents' day, where people knew the pagan ideas of Terence, Ovid, and Livy better than the simple truths of the bible.

Did our pamphleteers see Luther as the angelic shepherd of the *Practica?* Sachs' poem *The Wittenberg Nightingale* gives the reformer just such a role. But our pamphleteers were influenced by other reformers and preachers, whose message they thought in concord with the church of the gospel they anticipated. It was Luther's persecution by church authorities rather than his views on justification that interested them. Their vision of the End was more strictly biblical than influenced by Joachim of Fiore's angelic shepherd. The appeal of our pamphleteers (particularly Lotzer, Rysschner, Greiffenberger, Marschalck, Schütz, and even Sachs) to a more substantial reform of society beyond what Luther had begun and based on the *lex evangelica*, best explains their expectations from reform. Their brief advent on the publishing scene in 1522–23 was prompted by a conviction that Lutheran reform had been insubstantial, incomplete, and incapable of producing the required works and spiritual disposition necessary to prepare for the End. Their eschatological solution was encouraged by a sense of immediacy. The pattern of their thought seems to follow the eschatological thought of Franciscan Peter Olivi (+1298), a disciple of Joachim of Fiore who divided the world into three advents: Christ came first in the flesh to redeem, second in the spirit of evangelical reform to renew, and finally in judgment.[8]

The second reason why the year 1523 prompted their response was the decision of the imperial diet to enforce the Edict of Worms. Rumblings of peasant revolts forced city authorities to tighten security, to imprison wandering preachers, and stop alarmist propaganda. This disturbed our pamphleteers: they considered their calling to write, to preach, and to publish necessary to prepare a new lay apostolate in the wake of clerical failure and secular decadence. Our writers grouped civic officials with the lazy, corrupt clergy, who would not be saved at the end because they did not encourage their apostolate. Such persecution was a predicted sign of the End. Preaching simple people, the Karsthans and preaching women were expected and promised as signs of the End in the gospel. German almanacs provided proof that prophesy had been fulfilled and that the last days were already at hand.

Secular authorities considered this enthusiasm extremely dangerous. It might provoke another *Bundschuh* rebellion in the countryside or a bloody artisan revolt in the cities.[9] The decision of Archduke Ferdinand, the Bavarian Dukes, and the South German bishops to stop popular enthusiasm for reform at Regensburg in 1524, waved a red flag in the face of these common people, who were convinced that their work was necessary to prepare the bride of Christ. Still, our activist pamphleteers restrained themselves. They had to acknowledge the right of the secular authority to whom they had sworn loyalty and who were supposed to protect them. Like generations of protestors before them, they limited the extent of the obedience owed to the dictates of the gospel. Authority which acted contrary to the gospel was suspect. Our writers might speculate about the age of the spirit to come, but they could not encourage their readers and hearers to articulate that spirit in armed resistance. Only a working, suffering, lay apostolate might prepare the way to the End through works of mercy. The direct challenge to individual Christians to bear witness to the gospel in preaching and in print both encouraged them and reassured them of their own righteousness.

Thirdly, our pamphleteers responded to changes within the Protestant camp in 1523, which many scholars have seen as a developing criticism of the left wing of the Reformation, namely enthusiasts and Anabaptists. Bernd Balzer noted a change in the direction of Hans Sachs' critique from the old church to the Protestant movement itself. In this study, that change in direction is more difficult to document, since the anti-Roman polemic continues concurrently with criticism of those within the Protestant movement who misused their Christian freedom. Sachs, Greiffenberger, Lotzer, von Stauffen, and Marschalck all address those who used the new Christian freedom discovered in the gospel as an excuse for sinning. This critique is directly linked to their personal expections, not to the directives of secular authority or a specific reformer. Our pamphleteers expected that the gospel would bring about a real reform of society on the most micro-cosmic level, that would eventually result in the greater reformation of society. They were also less willing to entirely reject the medieval traditions of the church that could be justified by their ultimate authority, the gospel. Because these pamphleteers do not belong on the left wing of the Reformation, there is hardly a justification for placing them on the right wing, loyal to Luther and city councils. Over and over again our writers insist that the *lex evangelica* is the final authority, like earlier Waldensians and later Anabaptists. Raising arms against secular authority, rejection of oaths, etc., receive few comments from our pamphleteers. They were more interested in their apostolic vocation which both secular and ecclesiastical authority, Protestant and Catholic were reluctant to recognize. They wanted to actively preach, not necessarily in churches, but in houses and marketplaces and to do the six works of holy mercy required before the End. It is here that we have proof of a vigorous, thriving lay piety that historians like Davis, Rothkrug, and Christian point to, or proof of the sub-culture that Peter Burke, Josef Schmidt, and Herbert Grundmann describe, which had existed since the twelfth century and survived the heretical movements of the late Middle Ages.

The grievances expressed by these pamphleteers – their complaints of an overfed, lazy, decadent clergy, their anti-Romanism, the protest against selling grace in sacraments for money – are typical of lay movements in Europe since the twelfth century. The demand for the preservation of the *bonum communis* was a typical response to urban crisis: 'the individual loses his traditional bonds and becomes aware of the social reality of such lack of power, which is compensated by a vision of the future without differences between rich and poor...convinced of their righteousness, the group seeks a mass basis of support. Inner group consciousness is maintained by the creation of an opposition stereotype.'[10] When our writers saw the future of the Reformation in danger they both demanded a new lay apostolate and grasped for traditional bonds: they proved that the *lex evangelica* was the true tradition of the church, in some cases by giving historical examples. They proved that Romans had always betrayed and persecuted Christian martyrs. Their vision of a future without differences between rich and poor was also common to protest groups in the Middle Ages. However, our authors did not separate themselves from their cities, but instead worked to convert those around them by their publishing, by preaching, and doing works of mercy. This evidence confirms a statement by Thomas Brady, Jr.: 'the movement of the little people in the cities, in the small towns and on the land absorbed the propaganda of Luther and his disciples into a pre-existing program of social transformation in which the restoration of the true Christian gospel was to ring in a new order of divine justice, peace, and brotherhood.'[11] Yet, they were not particularly critical of the feudal order, nor did they wish to see all the hierarchy abolished. Christ himself would take care of that on his return.

The importance of the preservation of the *bonum communis* in these pamphlets reinforces Bernd Moeller's theories in his *Imperial Cities and the Reformation*. Their sense of collective responsibility for the city as sacred corporation echoes Moeller's statements: 'the town was not...a purely utilitarian association but was rather the place to which the life of each citizen was bound. Whenever the town was endangered, a burgher felt his very life threatened.'[12] Oaths of loyalty which were often sworn in churches symbolized the bond between citizen and the urban corporation. These pamphleteers adapted not just Luther's ideas to their own ends, practically ignoring the importance of justification by faith alone, but also the ideas of their local parish preachers. As early as 1523–1524, the *bonum communis* absorbed and selected from the varied corpus of reformed ideas, guided by an existing medieval vision. Their ideas of collective religious responsibility were not especially new: most earlier medieval heretical movements had drawn their zeal from just this conviction. This confirms Thomas Brady, Jr's statement that summarizes Moeller's early work: 'justification by faith alone gave way to an emphasis on sanctification through an ethically formed faith operating in a social context, in a word, love.'[13] One wonders how firmly rooted justification by faith alone ever was in the early years of the Reformation. It is interesting that church unity and a comprehensive view of church history remained important in their writings. Unity of the church and its history, a characterically medieval theme, has major significance. Our writers were part of an 'evangelical' movement. They did not want to be called Lutheran. They insisted that the gospel defined the limits of the real tradition of the church.

Theological inspiration in these pamphlets cannot be reduced to a single source. Luther and Zwingli were not more important than their local preachers. Great preachers were great heroes and models for our writers. Jacob Otter in Kenzingen was as important in 1523 as Geiler von Kaisersberg had been a decade earlier and St John Capistran had been half a century before. There is no indication that our writers saw the theology of the magisterial Reformation as either very new or effecting great changes in their own bible-centered piety. They seem to have no difficulty in combining biblical conservatism, an important hallmark of Reformation theology with a mystical anthropology and a vision of the city as sacred community that are very medieval. Their scriptural knowledge, encouraged by their preachers, is certainly remarkable. Our writers profited from the preaching they heard. Although they rhetorically abhorred Aristotle, they eagerly used his methods to prove their own points, just as their Humanist preachers had done. They divided everything into spiritual and physical attributes. The church consisted of an imperfect collection of sinners in its physical form; the elect were the true *ecclesia spiritualis*. The clergy had a responsibility to provide good sermons for the laity for meditation. Meditation mediated God's grace. In a sense, meditation and spiritual union became an extraordinary sacrament, a foretaste of heaven in sign and substance, a presage of eternal election. The flourish of bible printing in the late Middle Ages, the thirst for knowledge about the scriptures, and the popularity of sermons are given ample testimony here: they needed holy food for their spiritual ascent.

It is important that radical Chiliasm had no place whatsoever in the theology of these pamphleteers. Unlike many Brethren of the Free Spirit or later Anabaptists, their Christian freedom, acquired as a gift from meditation on Christ, made them subject to, not superior to, the gospel. Some pamphleteers wrote about the importance of the spirit, but their interpretation of the spirit still seems 'orthodox' by contemporary standards. Many early Anabaptists shared their activism. Friedwart Uhland noted a certain common program among the early Anabaptists in Augsburg: 'in general, we notice a common spirit in works by laypeople. It is the demand for a new evangelical life. The Lutheran Reformation only made sense if it sought to reorder life according to Christian commandments. The ideal model was a simple, uncomplicated life, lived in humility and service to God and one's neighbor. They were impatient when they compared their model with the real world. This provided the perfect fertile ground for the spread of Anabaptism.'[14]

Elsa Bernhofer-Pippert in her study of German Anabaptist trials saw a discrepancy between the missionary zeal of Anabaptists and their conviction that they were living in the last days.[15] Among our pamphleteers one finds the same ambiguity and tension in their rigid insistence on restoring a *status quo ante* and their knowledge that in the last days things would be turned upside-down. They expected martyrdom, yet paradoxically didn't want to isolate themselves as an elected community. They desperately grasped at a tradition, the *lex evangelica*, to which they could appeal, however insubstantially they might support this.

Although scriptures were spiritual food for our pamphleteers and a guide to the works necessary in the last days, their formula for salvation would most likely be *solo Christo, sola gratia, solis operibus evangelii*. This formula of salvation is dependent on a mystical anthropology, in form, a lay spirituality that approximates what Werner Packull has called the Cistercian/Franciscan tradition, 'affective, penitential, and Christocentric.'[16] The Bernardine Renaissance in the late Middle Ages provided the spiritual substance of this piety, the Franciscans a penitential emphasis, and the new biblicism a focus on the lives of Christ and Mary. At least two of the pamphleteers in this sample expressly acknowledged the importance of the *synderesis* and several others described the spirit as it affected the part of the human soul that is 'like God': Godly reason, not human reason could bring man closer to divine mystery. Christ as *logos* or embodiment of Godly reason came to people through scripture, heard, read, meditated on. Godly works, not human works might be meritorious, because they rest on Christ's promise in the gospel. Unlike the mysticism of the *Theologia Deutsch*, fulfillment does not come from the union of human and divine will, but in the church militant, working toward a nearing second coming. Here Franciscan-inspired mysticism seems more influential than Dominican.[17]

This Franciscan-inspired mystical thought parallels the important Franciscan eschatological influences that were equally significant in shaping the lay theology of these writers.[18] Werner Packull concluded: 'early South German Anabaptism inherited much of its theological inspiration from an earlier medieval, more specifically popularized mystical tradition. To put it most bluntly, the protagonists in our narrative represented a medieval mystical legacy within the Reformation context.'[19] The pamphlets written by this sample of authors provides additional documentation for that medieval, popularized mystical tradition within a specific eschatological context.

Why were these pamphleteers not Anabaptists? Schooled by the disciples of the *Devotio Moderna*, they insisted on an active life in the secular world, marked by acts of charity. Some eagerly used old testament models to justify this activity: the holy figures of the old testament were not all priests, but often common men and women. Their use of the universal priesthood argument was not so much directed against the clergy, as it was a means to both embarass a lazy, incompetent clergy and justify their own vocation. Our pamphleteers had no call to celibacy or particular asceticism, like Margery Kempe a century earlier. They rejected both isolation from society and monastic interment. None of our pamphleteers emphasized the importance of baptism as a sacrament, except Argula von Stauffen, who used it as a means to justify her vocation as a woman. The eucharist and the real presence were important to them because they effected the forgiveness of sins, based on Christ's promise. Only Hans Greiffenberger, who may have given his wife the sacrament, perhaps took the universal priesthood argument as license to make sacraments. Nearly all the writers in this sample recognize the importance of a penitential sacrament: they wanted to confess to each other and receive absolution, not to priests.

These pamphlets are probably the first important documents of Protestant piety. As piety, its form is alien to Lionel Rothkrug's descriptions of popular piety in Southwest German cities. Rothkrug suggests that Southern urban piety was 'militantly antipatrician, anti-aristocratic, and anti-imperial,' the result of deep differences in a sense of corporate belonging; in the North, individualistic lay activities were far more popular than in the South.[20] For Rothkrug, even the different theologies of the eucharist in North and South were signs of an essential disparity between the two regions. These assumptions cannot be substantiated by our lay pamphleteers, all from the Southwest. Haug Marschalck from Memmingen and Augsburg was aristocratic and imperial in his ecclesiology and piety. Yet, Marschalck's piety was deeply spiritual and affective, his theology mystical, almost Nominalistic. His conception of the eucharist was very much 'Lutheran,' maintaining the integrity of the real presence. This earliest Protestant piety could best be described as a combination of meditation and lay activism, shaped by convictions that the world was near its End. Yet, in the case of each individual pamphleteer, the emphasis is different. Medieval affective spirituality can be found in the works of Marschalck, Lotzer, Greiffenberger, and Schütz. Each of these writers emphasizes the importance of a liberation of conscience for a righteous Christian to do genuinely meritorious works. Marschalck and Lotzer accept a Nominalist definition of the *synderesis*. In their works, meditation on the models presented in scripture could activate the *synderesis* to unite the human will to God. In the state of grace achieved by this action, good works could be meritorious. Such speculation is entirely missing in Rychssner's works and the pamphlets of our female authors. Earlier and later lay movements would use mystical reunion and the liberation of the conscience from sins as Antinomian license. The biblical conservatism and social activism of our pamphleteers kept them close to a fundamentalist interpretation of the gospel. Few of our writers say much about the action of the holy spirit. Rychssner, von Grumbach, and Greiffenberger all speculate on the work of the spirit as an agent of grace. But the spirit moves man to conversion and works of mercy, to create a special (but not exclusive) brotherhood of Christians. All of our pamphleteers appeal to the *lex evangelica*, which called them to a life of service to the poor.

Did our writers want to preach from the pulpits of churches? Probably not. Only one author, Sebastian Lotzer, published a sermon. To most of them, preaching and prophesying meant the same thing. Like St Stephen, they wanted to bear witness to the gospel in houses and marketplaces. Sachs described this activity as 'admonishing one's brother against sin and warning him to repent.' Like early wandering Franciscans, they wanted to take to the roads and markets to prepare the bride for Christ's nearing return. When our writers speak of preaching they mean critique, warning, admonition to repentance, and works of mercy. They would have applauded Margery Kempe's statements before the Archbishop of York's inquisition: 'I shall speak of God...unto the time that the pope and holy church hath ordained that no man shall be so bold as to speak of God.'[21]

Since their general theological orientation is part medieval, part reformed in character, so is their attitude toward the saints. Marschalck, Rychssner, and Lotzer confine the objects of their meditation to biblical saints. Because they awaited Christ's final coming, the saints of the new testament become important prophetic models in their theology. They wanted to be like them, not to pray to them. John the Baptist is their ideal prophetic model. Mary Magdalen is the appropriate penitent and lay apostle.[22] The Virgin Mary is the ideal contemplative, humble and obedient, something civic authorities would probably have enjoyed. Old testament women were obviously more important for the women in this sample, since they needed more forceful models to justify their vocation. It is particularly interesting that the soldier

Haug Marschalck would encourage his readers to be humble and penitent, pure and chaste like Mary, and Catherine Schütz wrote the women in Kenzingen to be strong and virile like Abraham. This sexual cross-fertilization defies attempts to categorize their piety as either masculine or feminine, male or female.

As Bernd Moeller noted, the theology of the Reformation in Southwestern cities emphasized sanctification, rather than justification by faith. This sanctification occurs within a particular eschatological context. Because our writers anticipate the church of the elect, the works Christ commanded in the gospel must be meritorious. Just as he promised forgiveness of sins by the eucharist, so would the works of the gospel be meritorious. They held themselves responsible for the salvation of the commune. They began to publish their works for precisely that reason. They found adequate justification for their call in scripture: at his first advent, Christ called ignorant fishermen, not scholars; shepherds, not princes; the poor not the rich. He would do the same at his final advent. Their piety must be understood in light of the second coming. As they adapted reformed theological ideas and amended the more traditionally medieval affective system, the life of Christ assumed the place of lives of the saints as an object of meditation and emulation; the bible took the place of relics for veneration; works of mercy replaced pilgrimages and indulgences. Our writers would not effectively distinguish reformed piety from medieval piety, beyond their determination to avoid all things not mentioned in scripture. Their own personal devotions were still varied: Argula von Stauffen continued to read the bible, lives of the saints, Staupitz's sermons, and Luther's pamphlets. She even remained friendly with John Eck, because she was convinced that the gospel represented the real tradition of the church and whoever preached the gospel, Luther or Eck, represented the true church.

As documents of early Protestant piety, these pamphlets provide evidence for comparison with the conclusions of other scholars who rely on other kinds of sources. Steven Ozment points to a flawed piety in the late Middle Ages and a church that imposed an oppressive, complicated system of canon law on the conscience of the individual, from which people sought liberation. Protestantism was the ideal remedy because it abolished the confessional, teaching people to rely on the merits of Christ for spiritual grace.[23] Part of the problem in discussing the conscience of the individual in the Reformation period is the tendency to view the conscience as a post-Freudian moral mechanism, planted in the rational mind, which can mediate between the rational and irrational soul, allowing the individual to distinguish between good and evil. To have pangs of conscience is for most modern people to be troubled by guilt.[24] For Ozment Protestantism made people feel less guilty. Our pamphleteers meant something else when they spoke and wrote of a burdened conscience. When our writers use the word 'conscience,' they refer to the smaller mechanical part of a soul, the spiritual part of man. This spiritual soul was not irrational, but reflecting original grace, was divided into conscience (where sin was realized), heart (where love was felt), and *gemüthe* (where God's presence could rest). Sin was realized in the conscience because of the malfunction or malpreparation of the other parts of the soul. Man was confused because of Adam's sin in the loss of original grace. The gospel could help restore the right orientation and eliminate confusion. Thus correctly focused, the cleared conscience could help the other parts of the soul see God, united with him (by the *gemüthe*), and do works of mercy (from the heart). To clear one's conscience was not to remove guilt, but sin, in order to allow the soul to reunite with God. Then a vision of Christ could be planted in the heart, to help man do works of the gospel. Here the clearing process was ended. Unlike many medieval mystics, a special state of ecstasy is not the object of clearing the conscience and uniting the soul with God.[25] When our writers speak of clearing the captive conscience, they seek a purer, more inward vision of Christ, not liberation from the confessional. They often complain that Lutheran liberation from the confessional was used as an excuse to sin, though none of them had much love for contemporary confession practices. They preferred to confess to each other, as Luther had recommended in one of his printed sermons.[26]

Four of the pamphleteers in this sample were artisans, a furrier, a shoemaker, a weaver, and a painter. Do they demonstrate anti-patrician, egalitarian, revolutionary sympathies? Marxist historians would like to see their protest as part of the early capitalist revolution. Erich Maschke suggested that in cities where guilds were represented in the city council, the Reformation caught on first.[27] Although this sample of four cannot represent any majority opinion, there is little in their works nor in the histories of various city reformations to substantiate such conclusions. Even in Nuremberg, where there were no guilds, Sachs and Greiffenberger were active in encouraging church reform. These authors are ambiguous about the future role of secular leaders and the clergy, who had failed them. None of the artisans advocate particularly radical activities, nor do they suggest that anywhere outside the church were Christians equal. There is some confusion that results from their assumptions about the essential nature of the city as Christian community; they praise a church confessing, brother to sister. They rail against the exclusiveness of the old church clergy. Yet, they were required to swear loyalty by the gospel to their urban corporation and defended the secular authorities to secure their freedom to publish. Confusion results when they use the *lex evangelica* as the final authority in all law, civil and church. Since their vision of the future is determined by convictions of a nearing End, the artisans in this sample tend to ignore distinctions of the present in anticipation of the future *unum ovile*, the sheepfold of the elect. Such hope for an egalitarian society without distinctions is not unusual in history. Marjorie Reeves noted that 'in the very age when religious and national divisions were hardening irrevocably, men so often turned back to the apparently irrelevant ideal of the *unum ovile*. This must be recorded, since men's dreams are as much a part of history as their deeds.'[28] Our artisans, like the other four pamphleteers in this sample could not directly oppose secular authority and because they were willing to suffer martyrdom as a sure passport to heaven, they did not need to call down the wrath of heaven on their betters. Sachs may have thought Luther to be the angelic shepherd, predicted to usher in the age of the spirit, but he was reluctant to develop this theme further. Our pamphleteers do not point to any particular individual who would come to lead the elect. When forced to deal with the authority of the state, they used an old medieval solution to the problem: the state might rule what pertained to the physical property of people, man's body and possessions, but not the soul. Because the future of souls was in question, they insisted that the *lex evangelica* took precedence in principle over any other law. Obedience was owed to the state for all things related to keeping order, but state interference in the affairs of the church, especially imprisoning evangelical preachers and calling crusades against the Turks and Jews, they opposed. Only two pamphleteers were aristocratic in their attitudes: Argula von Stauffen took Luther's cue from his pamphlet *To the Christian Nobility of the German Nation* to encourage her relatives to reform the church. Marschalck invited the emperor to champion the evangelical reform. Other pamphleteers had their own mission to convert sinners, Turks, and Jews before Christ's final advent. If that mission came into conflict with the state, they would remind their leaders that they, too, were subject to the gospel. Because they expected martyrdom, our writers could not give up their devotion to the saints. They felt close to the martyrs and approved of a veneration of saints. They prayed for grace to be like saints, to emulate saintly courage and perseverance. Prayers to saints for favors they rejected, since this distorted the unity of the *unum ovile*. Their brotherhood could not be exclusive or recognize the rights of some over others. So when the state took upon itself to dissolve monasteries and confiscate church property, our pamphleteers raised no objection. Monasticism claimed an exclusivity they could not admit, even if preaching monks had done some good.

The lay piety expressed in these pamphlets is neither urban nor rural. One does note a lack of tolerance for the excesses of the medieval church, for festivals and the traditional practices of the countryside in these pamphlets. French historians would see these as proof of a creative *mentalité urbaine* that helped to usher in Protestantism in cities.[29] The dense settlement pattern in Württemberg and in parts of Franconia makes it difficult to distinguish clear points of demarkation between urban and rural. Some of our pamphleteers came from more rural areas, like Sebastian Lotzer, yet he chose to live in a city. Argula von Stauffen came from Munich to the countryside. Natalie Davis' examination of journeymen printers in Lyons suggests that artisan printers used Protestantism as a vehicle to express economic grievances. Our pamphleteers sought to maintain a peculiar and traditional vision of church reform in their own sub-culture. Economic and social grievances in that context simply indicate the ills of society that reform was expected to rectify. Their hopes for reform are best found in the spirit of imperial reform mandates of the late Middle Ages and more immediately in the Peasant Articles of 1525. All of these reform mandates were based on a medieval assumption that reform in head and members would result in an eventual redemption of society. The greatest enemies of our writers were not particularly patricians, masters, the pope and his bishops, but all who hindered the progress of the rebirth of the gospel.

It is easier to pinpoint the more traditionally medieval aspects of their piety in these pamphlets, than it is to denote the reformed aspects of their theology. Our pamphleteers were convinced that the reformed theology they read about and heard about was part of a longer and greater reform movement. They took many cues from Luther, Zwingli, and Eberlin von Günzburg. Respectively, their attitudes about confession, fasting regulations, and monastic vows can be traced to pamphlets published by any of these reformers. For most of the pamphleteers, the wrongs in the church began about the year 1100. Reform had begun with the great preachers of the late Middle Ages, and more immediately in their own calling to debate matters of theology.[30]

The audience addressed by our pamphleteers is difficult to define. It is impossible to say that they aimed their works at a particular social group, right wing or left wing, literate or illiterate. Instead, they addressed the rather difficult to define 'common man.' Their style is too haphazard to have profited much from either the organization of sermons listened to or devotional tracts read. They learned little from the developed style of Luther or Eberlin von Günzburg.[31] Their pamphlets were not even well illustrated. Only occasionally does a woodcut grace the cover page of a pamphlet in this sample. The themes of those woodcuts are simple: Christ carrying a lamb or perhaps a group of blindfolded clergy looking into a mirror, in the case of Marschalck's *Mirror for the Blind*. There are no catchy verses that might be sung to confirm Robert Scribner's alternative ways the Reformation message may have been communicated.[32]

The years after 1525 and the shape of the Reformation in the hands of princes must have been a bitter disappointment to our pamphleteers.

Marschalck died poor and disappointed in Augsburg in 1535. Lotzer disappeared in Switzerland. Greiffenberger and Rychssner were never heard from again. Argula von Stauffen stopped publishing, although she remained in contact with Osiander, Luther, and Eck. Catherine Zell lived the gospel and carried out the six works of holy mercy for the rest of her life, defending Anabaptists, visiting the sick and people in prison, and even publishing.

The groundswell of ideas that gave rise to the 'evangelical movement' continued to inspire Anabaptists and even Catholic saints like Angela Merici. Catholic laypeople were encouraged to take up an active life of service by clergy like SS. Vincent de Paul (+1660) and Charles Borromeo (+1584). The great saints of the Catholic Reformation, SS. Theresa of Avila (+1582) and John of the Cross (+1591) shared a mystical anthropology and interest in the works of the gospel that may have been inspired by the same 'evangelical movement.'[33] Whether or not the church in any century has been ready for active participation by the laity on a scale that our sample of lay pamphleteers demanded is a matter for debate. In the Southwest of Germany, their brief period of activity can be called the last breath of lay activity and affective piety before forced submission to a Reformation defended by princes and shaped by the great magisterial reformers. Our pamphleteers' demand for a lay apostolate forms a missing link between Franciscans, Beguines and Hussites of earlier centuries and the Anabaptists who followed them.

Notes

Wherever possible, abbreviated forms of citation have been used to save both space and printing costs. Secondary works are cited fully once in the endnotes and thereafter in abbreviated form, with the page numbers at the end of the citation. Critical editions of pamphlets are cited in the following manner: 223, 14–16 = page 223, lines 14–16. Few of the pamphlets cited in this work have appeared in critical edition. For pamphlets still in their original form the traditional method of pamphlet citation has been used. Developed in the nineteenth century by scholars, it was used as a means to separate editions, e.g.

> Ein trostliche ermanung// den angefochtn im gewissen/ von we =//gen gethoner sünd/ wye vn wa// mit/ Sye getrost werden/// Den Sathan/ sich nit// erschrecken las =//sen u. 1524 (SFB-Zl, Nr. 3051)

The single slash [/] indicates a pause in the sentence, serving the same function as a comma might in English. The double slash [//] was invented by bibliographers to indicate the end of a printed line, which helped to distinguish the various editions of the pamphlets. The double hyphen [=] indicates a broken syllable within a word. The triple slash [///] indicates both a pause and the end of a printed line. Since scholars may wish to obtain a copy of the original pamphlet, the source and call number are indicated. Other markings have not been included in the citations. Students of German will note missing letters in words. Early printers used customary Latin abbreviation method, indicating a missing letter by placing a hyphen over the preceding letter. The German umlaut appears in various forms, sometimes in the familiar modern form [ü or ö or ä], but more often with a [c] inserted over the letter. These markings have not been included in the citations. For frequently cited pamphlets, full citations with source can be found in the bibliography. For other pamphlets not available in critical edition, the full citation appears in the endnote. Students of German will note the imprecise grammar and style of these pamphlets: Sentences seem to run together; spelling is hardly uniform; the familiar rules of capitalization are not followed. One must remember that this text is early-new high German (*Frühneuhochdeutsch*) or more appropriately early sixteenth century regional German. Neither a standard German to be based on Luther's bible translations, nor accepted rules of grammar had been developed when these pamphlets were written. Common people (and others who might have been better instructed) wrote down their ideas as they occurred. These ideas were not organized in paragraphs with topic and concluding sentences. The best dictionary available for early-new high German is Alfred Goetze, *Frühneuhochdeutsches Glossar* (Berlin, 1967) 7th edition. Translations of the pamphlet titles and contents are generally my own. The translations are intended to present the ideas of the pamphleteers in modern English, rather than an attempt at literal rendition. Translations for biblical passages were made using the revised standard version of the bible. Some of the pamphleteers used Martin Luther's translation of the new testament; others used earlier translations.

ABBREVIATIONS

ADB	*Allgemeine Deutsche Biographie* (Leipzig, 1875–1912), 56 vols.
AK	*Arbeiten zur Kirchengeschichte* (Berlin and Leipzig, 1927f.)
ARG	*Archiv für Reformationsgeschichte* (Leipzig and Gütersloh, 1903f.)
BBKG	*Beiträge zur bayerischen Kirchengeschichte* (Erlangen, 1895–1925)
BWKG	*Blätter für württembergische Kirchengeschichte* (Stuttgart, 1886–90, new series, 1897f.)
CR	*Corpus Reformatorum* (Berlin, 1834f; Leipzig, 1906f.)
EKB	*Einzelarbeiten aus der Kirchengeschichte Bayerns* (Munich, 1927f.)
HZ	*Historische Zeitschrift* (Munich and Berlin, 1859f.)
KS	*Kirchengeschichtliche Studien* (Leipzig, 1888; Münster, 1896f.)
MVGSN	*Mitteilungen des Vereins für die Geschichte der Stadt Nürnberg* (Nuremberg, 1879f.)
RGG	*Die Religion in Geschichte und Gegenwart*, 3rd edition (Tübingen, 1957–1962)
RST	*Reformationsgeschichtliche Studien und Texte* (Münster, 1906f.)
SFB-Zl	Sonderforschungsbereich der Universität Tübingen, Spätmittelalter und Reformation, Projekt-Zl, Flugschriftenkatalog. Numbers which follow indicate references to the greater catalogue.
SVRG	*Schriften des Vereins für Reformationsgeschichte* (Halle, 1883–1892)
SW	*Hans Sachsens Werke*, eds. A. Keller, E. Goetze (Tübingen, 1870–1902) 26 vols.
WA	*D. Martin Luthers Werke*: Kritische Gesamtausgabe (Weimar, 1883f.)
WA:BW	*D. Martin Luthers Werke: Briefwechsel* (Weimar, 1883f.)
ZA	*Ulrich Zwingli: Eine Auswahl aus seinen Schriften*, eds. G. Finsler, et al. (Zürich, 1918).
ZH	*Zwingli Hauptschriften*, eds. E. Blanke et al. (Zürich, 1959f.), 8 vols.
ZHVSN	*Zeitshrift des historischen Vereins für Schwaben und Neuburg* (Augsburg, 1874f.)
ZKG	*Zeitschrift für Kirchengeschichte* (Stuttgart, 1876f.)
ZW	*Zwingli Werke*, eds. M. Schuler, J. Schulthess (Zürich, 1829–1942)
ZKWKL	*Zeitschrift für kirchliche Wissenschaft und kirchliches Leben* (Leipzig, 1880–89)

INTRODUCTION

1 Thomas Brady, Jr., 'Social History,' in S. Ozment, ed., *Reformation Europe: A Guide to Research* (St. Louis, 1982), 161.

2 cf. Robert Scribner, 'Is there a Social History of the Reformation?,' in *Social History* 4 (1977), 483–505, also Lawrence Buck and Jonathan Zophy, eds., *The Social History of the Reformation* (Columbus, 1972), 12f, Steven Ozment, 'The Social History of the Reformation; What can we learn from Pamphlets?,' in Hans-Joachim Köhler, ed., *Flugschriften als Massenmedium der Reformationszeit* (Stuttgart, 1981), 171f. (Cited hereafter as Köhler, *Flugschriften*.)

3 cf. Ernst Barth, *Probleme der frühbürgerlichen Revolution* (Karl-Marx-Stadt, 1975), 55f.

4 Peter Burke, *Popular Culture in Early Modern Europe* (New York, 1978), 36f.

5 Jean Delumeau, *Naissance et Affirmation de la Réforme* (Paris, 1965), 47f.

6 Jean Delumeau, *Catholicism between Luther and Voltaire: A New View of the Counter-Reformation* (London, 1977), 129f.

7 Steven Ozment, *The Reformation in the Cities* (New Haven, 1975), 49.

8 Steven Ozment, 'The Social History of the Reformation,' in Köhler, *Flugschriften*, 175.

9 Thomas Tentler, *Sin and Confession on the Eve of the Reformation* (Princeton, 1977), 155f.

10 Robert Muchembled, *Culture Populaire et Culture des Élites dans la France Moderne* (Paris, 1978), 209f.

11 Natalie Davis, *Society and Culture in Early Modern France* (Stanford, 1975), 13f.

12 Lionel Rothkrug, 'Popular Religion and Holy Shrines: Their Influence on the Origins of the German Reformation and their Role in German Cultural Development,' in James Obelkevich, ed., *Religion and People, 800–1700* (Chapel Hill, 1979), 58. See also by the same author, *Religious Practices and Collective Perceptions: Hidden Homologies in the Renaissance and Reformation* (Waterloo, Ont., 1980), 91f.

13 William Christian, *Local Religion in Sixteenth Century Spain* (Princeton, 1981), 167f.

14 Donald Weinstein and Rudolf Bell, *Saints and Society* (Chicago, 1982), 6.

15 Steven Ozment, 'The Social History of the Reformation,' in Köhler, *Flugschriften*, 176.

16 *Ibid.*, 172. It is somewhat ironic that Ozment himself indulged in a bit of reductionism in his work on the Reformation in the city, focusing on penance and confession as the key to understanding the popular success of Protestantism.

17 Hans-Joachim Köhler, 'Die Flugschriften. Versuch der Präzisierung eines geläufigen Begriffs,' in *Festgabe für Ernst Walther Zeeden zum 60. Geburtstag* (Münster, 1976), 50.

18 Richard Cole, 'The Reformation Pamphlet and the Communication Processes,' in Köhler, *Flugschriften*, 139.

19 Hans-Joachim Köhler, 'Fragestellungen und Methoden zur Interpretation frühneuzeitlicher Flugschriften,' in Köhler, *Flugschriften*, 1.

20 Funded through 1984 by the German Research Foundation, the present project publishes regular installments on microfiche as *Sixteenth Century Pamphlets in German and Latin, 1501–1530* (Zug, Switzerland, 1978f.)

21 Hans-Joachim Köhler, 'Das Tübinger Flugschriftenprojekt,' in *Wolfenbütteler Notizen zur Buchgeschichte*, 9/1 (1984), 5.

22 Robert Scribner, *For the Sake of Simple Folk: Popular Propaganda for the German Reformation* (Cambridge, 1982), 5.

23 Hans-Joachim Köhler, 'Fragestellungen,' in Köhler, *Flugschriften*, 26–27.

24 Bernd Balzer, *Bürgerliche Reformationspropaganda: Die Flugschriften des Hans Sachs in den Jahren 1523–25* (Stuttgart, 1973), 14f.

25 *Ibid.*, 135f.

26 Josef Schmidt, *Lestern, lesen, und lesen hören* (Bern, 1977), 9.

27 *Ibid.*, 44, also 140f.

28 Monika Rössing-Hager, 'Wie stark findet der nichtlesekundige Rezipient Berücksichtigung in den Flugschriften?,' in Köhler, *Flugschriften*, 77f.

29 Robert Scribner, *For the Sake of Simple Folk*, 58.

30 Berndt Hamm, 'Laientheologie zwischen Luther und Zwingli: Das reformatorische Anliegen des Konstanzer Stadtschreibers Jörg Vögeli aufgrund seiner Schriften von 1523/24,' in Josef Nolte, et al., eds., *Kontinuität und Umbruch. Theologie und Frömmigkeit in Flugschriften und Kleinliteratur an der Wende vom 15. zum 16. Jahrhundert* (Stuttgart, 1978), 232.

31 *Ibid.*, 294–5.

32 Cited in Hans-Joachim Köhler, 'Fragestellungen,' 19.

33 See Monika Rössing-Hager, 'Wie stark findet der Nichtlesekundige Rezipient Berücksichtigung in den Flugschriften?,' 84f.

34 Robert Scribner, 'Flugblatt und Analphabetentum: Wie kam der gemeine Mann zu reformatorischen Ideen?,' in Köhler, *Flugschriften*, 66f.

35 Steven Ozment, 'The Social History of the Reformation,' 172.

36 *Ibid.*

37 Peter Burke, *Popular Culture*, 38–42.

38 For a complete list of the thirty-nine pamphlets see bibliography, Printed Primary Sources, pp. 266–269.

39 Paola Zambelli, 'Fine del Mondo o Inizio della Propaganda? Astrologia, filosofia della storia e propaganda politico-religiosa nel dibattito sulla congiunzione del 1524,' in L. Olschki, ed., *Scienze, Credenze occulte, Livelli di Cultura* (Florence, 1982), 291f.

40 Cited by Robert Scribner, *For the Sake of Simple Folk*, 2.

41 Rolf Engelsing, *Analphabetentum und Lektüre. Zur Sozialgeschichte des Lesens in Deutschland zwischen feudaler und industrieller Gesellschaft* (Stuttgart, 1973), 34.

42 See Peter Burke, *Popular Culture*, 37.

43 Sebastian Lotzer makes reference to Argula von Grumbach, see Chapter 3, n46.

44 Paul O. Kristeller, *Medieval Aspects of Renaissance Learning* (Durham, NC, 1974), 18.

45 Rolf Engelsing, *Analphabetentum und Lektüre*, 37.

46 Monika Rössing-Hager, 'Wie stark findet der nichtlesekundige Rezipient

Berücksichtigung in den Flugschriften?' 135f., cf. Josef Schmidt, *Lestern, lesen, und lesen hören*, 77f.

47 Josef Schmidt, *Lestern, lesen, und lesen hören*, 41.

48 *Ibid.*, 43.

49 Siegfried Wernicke, 'Die Prosadialoge des Hans Sachs' (Dissertation, Berlin, 1913), 8.

50 Kurt Kasser, *Politische und soziale Bewegungen im deutschen Bürgertum des 16. Jahrhunderts* (Berlin, 1899), 186f.

51 Werner Lenk, *Die Reformation im zeitgenössischen Dialog* (Berlin, 1968), 33f., also Siegfried Epperlein, *Der Bauer im Bild des Mittelalters* (Jena, 1975), 21f., and Helmar Junghans, 'Der Laie als Richter im Glaubenstreit der Reformationszeit,' in *Lutherjahrbuch*, 39 (1972), 31–54.

52 Barbara Otwinoska, 'Der ''gemeine Mann'' als Adressat der volkssprachlichen Literatur in der Renaissance,' in R. Weimann, et al., eds., *Renaissance Literatur und frühbürgerliche Revolution* (Berlin, Weimar, 1976), 194–202.

53 Franz Falk, *Die deutschen Sterbebüchlein* (Cologne, 1890), 16f. cf. Peter Baumgart, 'Formen der Volksfrömmigkeit – Krise der alten Kirche und reformatorische Bewegung,' in Peter Blickle, ed., *Revolte und Revolution in Europa*, HZ, Beiheft 4 (Munich, 1975), 195: 'Sie [die Religiösität] wurzelt teils in der Bedrohung der einzelnen Existenz...die nach Ausweis einer umfangreichen Erbauungsliteratur bisweilen die rechte Todesvorbereitung, die *ars moriendi*, zum wichtigsten Lebensinhalt werden lässt.'

54 cf. Johannes Geffken, *Bilderkatechismen des fünfzehnten Jahrhunderts* (Leipzig, 1855), 43f., and Franz Falk, 'Das Unterricht des deutschen Volkes in den katechetischen Hauptstücken am Ende des Mittelalters,' *Historisch-Politische Blätter für das Katholische Deutschland*, 108 (1891), 552f., 682f.

55 *WA*, 6, 203, 8–10.

56 *Ibid.*, 6, 184, 8–10.

57 See Siegfried Wieland, 'Vom Lesen und Schreiben im späten Mittelalter,' in *Festschrift für I. Schröbler zum 65. Geburtstag* (Tübingen, 1973), 322f., and the older work by Friedrich Paulsen and R. Lehmann, *Geschichte des gelehrten Unterrichts* (Leipzig, 1919–21), I, 15f.

58 See Lawrence Buck, 'Toward a Definition of the Common Man,' unpublished paper presented to the Ohio Academy of History, 1978. The closest attempt at a practical definition of the 'common man' in the sixteenth century can be found in Peter Blickle, 'Thesen zum Thema ''Der Bauernkrieg'' als Revolution des ''gemeinen Mannes,''' in Peter Blickle, ed., *Revolte und Revolution in Europa*, 125f. Note in particular the studies in the series *Veröffentlichungen der Komission für geschichtliche Landeskunde in Baden-Württemberg*, vol. 41: Erich Maschke, Jürgen Sydow, eds., *Gesellschaftliche Unterschichten in den südwestdeutschen Städten* (Stuttgart, 1967), and vol. 69 by the same editors, *Städtische Mittelschichten* (Stuttgart, 1972). Maschke's important essays have been collected in Erich Maschke, *Städte und Menschen* (Wiesbaden, 1980).

59 Peter Blickle, 'Thesen zum Thema ''Der Bauernkrieg,''' 127. The 450th anniversary of the 1525 uprisings revived interest in the Peasant Wars: NB Günther Franz, *Der Deutsche Bauernkrieg* (revised, Darmstadt, 1977), Heiko

Oberman, ed., *Deutscher Bauernkrieg, 1525, ZKG/2* (1974), Bernd Moeller, ed. *Bauernkriegsstudien, SVRG,* 189 (1975), Peter Barton, ed., *Sozialrevolution und Reformation* (Vienna, 1975), Rainer Wohlfeil, ed., *Der Bauernkrieg, 1525–26: Bauernkrieg und Reformation* (Munich, 1975), Janos Bak, ed., *The German Peasant War of 1525* (London, 1976).

60 Peter Blickle, 'Thesen zum Thema "Der Bauernkrieg,"' 129–30.
61 Robert Lutz, *Wer war der gemeine Mann? Der dritte Stand in der Krise des Spätmittelalters* (Munich and Vienna, 1979), 95f.
62 Erich Maschke, 'Die Unterschichten der mittelälterlichen Städten Deutschlands,' in *Städte und Menschen,* 344f.
63 Paul Russell, '"Your sons and your daughters shall prophesy . . ." (Joel 2;28) Common People and the Future of the Reformation in the Pamphlet Literature of Southwestern Germany to 1525,' *ARG,* 74 (1983), 128.
64 Adolf Laube, 'Zur Rolle sozialökonomischer Fragen in frühreformatorischen Flugschriften,' in Köhler, *Flugschriften,* 207f. cf. Gerard Walter, *Histoire des Paysans de France* (Paris, 1963), 186.
65 See A. G. Dickens, *The German Nation and Martin Luther* (New York, 1974), 106f.
66 Peter Burke, *Popular Culture,* 213–14.
67 Lionel Rothkrug, 'Popular Religion and Holy Shrines,' 72.
68 See Robert Scribner, 'The German Peasants' War,' in Steven Ozment, ed. *Reformation Europe: A Guide to Research,* 108. cf. E. Werner, H. Steinmetz, eds., *Städtische Volksbewegungen im 14. Jahrhundert* (Berlin, 1960), 42f.
69 Steven Ozment, 'The Social History of the Reformation,' in Köhler, *Flugschriften,* 177.
70 cf. Adolf Laube, 'Die Volksbewegungen in Deutschland von 1470 bis 1517,' in Peter Blickle, ed., *Revolte und Revolution in Europa,* 84f., and Alfred Eckert, 'Waldensisches Bekenntnis, Motive hussitischer Revolution und lutherischer Reformation in Böhmen bis nach dem "Prager Blutgericht, 1521,"' in Peter Barton, ed., *Sozialrevolution und Reformation,* II 97f.
71 Steven Ozment, *Mysticism and Dissent* (Yale, 1973), 21f.
72 Donald Weinstein and Rudolf Bell, *Saints and Society,* 5.
73 Robert Scribner, 'Flugblatt und Analphabetentum,' 69f.
74 Bernd Balzer, *Bürgerliche Reformationspropaganda,* 126f.
75 cf. Heiko Oberman, 'Tumultus rusticorum. Vom "Klosterkrieg" zum Fürstensieg. Beobachtungen zum Bauernkrieg unter besonderer Berücksichtigung zeitgenössischer Beurteilungen,' in *ZKG* 85 (1974), 315.

I: THE CALL TO PROPHESY: PIETY AND DISCONTENT IN THE URBAN
COMMUNITY OF LATE-MEDIEVAL GERMANY

1 A. G. Dickens, *The German Nation and Martin Luther,* 216f.
2 Robert Muchembled, *Culture Populaire et Culture des Élites,* 137f.
3 Erika Uitz, 'Die europäischen Städte im Spätmittelalter,' *Zeitschrift für Geschichtswissenschaft,* 21 (1973), 402.
4 *Ibid.,* 403.

5　Gerhard Pfeiffer, 'Stadtherr und Gemeinde in der spätmittelälterlichen Reichsstädten,' in W. Rausch, ed., *Die Stadt am Ausgang des Mittelalters* (Linz, 1974),
203f. (Hereafter, W. Rausch, *Die Stadt*)

6　Rudolf Endres, 'Zünfte und Unterschichten als Elemente der Instabilität in den
Städten,' in Peter Blickle, ed., *Revolte und Revolution in Europa*, 154f.

7　Erich Maschke, 'Deutsche Städte am Ausgang des Mittelalters,' in W. Rausch,
Die Stadt, 22.

8　Erich Maschke, 'Die Unterschichten der mittelälterlichen Städten Deutsch-
lands,' in Erich Maschke, *Städte und Menschen*, 312.

9　Gerhard Pfeiffer, 'Stadtherr und Gemeinde,' 213.

10　Erich Maschke, 'Deutsche Städte,' 14f.

11　Erich Maschke, 'Die Unterschichten,' 349.

12　Rudolf Endres, 'Zünfte und Unterschichten,' in Peter Blickle, ed., *Revolte und
Revolution in Europa*, 161.

13　*Ibid.*, 170.

14　Erich Maschke, 'Deutsche Städte,' 2.

15　See A. Laube, 'Volksbewegungen in Deutschland von 1470 bis 1517,' in Peter
Blickle, ed., *Revolte und Revolution in Europa*, 85., also Rudolf Endres, 'Zünfte
und Unterschichten,' 160.

16　Erich Maschke, 'Deutsche Städte,' 18f., also 163 n45.

17　Rudolf Endres, 'Zünfte und Unterschichten,' 162.

18　Erika Uitz, 'Die Europäischen Städte,' 402.

19　Ernst Benz, *Ecclesia Spiritualis* (Stuttgart, 1934), 265f.

20　Steven Ozment, *The Reformation in the Cities*, 38f.

21　Erich Maschke, 'Deutsche Städte,' 22–23.

22　Caroline Bynum, *Jesus as Mother: Studies in the Spirituality of the High Middle
Ages* (Berkeley, 1982), 170f.

23　F. Paulsen, R. Lehmann, *Geschichte des gelehrten Unterrichts* (Leipzig, 1919),
I, 18–19.

24　Bernd Moeller, 'Frömmigkeit in Deutschland um 1500,' *ARG*, 56 (1965),
8f.

25　Otthein Ramstedt, 'Stadtunruhen von 1525,' in W. Rausch, ed., *Die Stadt*,
252f.

26　Rudolf Cruel, *Geschichte der deutschen Predigt im Mittelalter* (reprint, Hildesheim, 1966), 496–7.

27　Otthein Ramstedt, 'Stadtunruhen von 1525,' 252f.

28　*Ibid.*, 254f.

29　*Ibid.*, 265.

30　Erich Maschke, 'Deutsche Städte,' 22.

31　Steven Ozment, *The Reformation in the Cities*, 41–42.

32　See J. Fearns, ed., *Ketzer und Ketzerbekämpfung im Hochmittelalter* (Göttingen,
1968), 38f., and K. V. Selge, *Die Ersten Waldenser* (Berlin, 1967), I, 34f., also
Richard Kieckhefer, *Repression of Heresy in Medieval Germany* (Philadelphia,
1979), 11f.

33　cf. Eva Neumann, *Rheinische Beginen- und Beghardenwesen* (Mainz, 1960),
22.

34　Richard Kieckhefer, *Repression of Heresy*, 13f.

35 Alfred Eckert, 'Waldensisches Bekenntnis, Motive hussitischer Revolution und lutherischer Reformation in Böhmen bis nach dem "Prager Blutgericht, 1521,"' in P. Barton, ed., *Sozialrevolution und Reformation*, II, 101.
36 Richard Kieckhefer, *Repression of Heresy*, 21. See also R. Lerner, *The Heresy of the Free Spirit in the Later Middle Ages* (Berkeley, 1972), 14f.
37 Richard Kieckhefer, *Repression of Heresy*, 24.
38 *Ibid.*, 76f.
39 See H. Kaminsky, *A History of the Hussite Revolution* (Berkeley, 1967), 359, and Richard Kieckhefer, *Repression of Heresy*, 83f., Robert Lerner, *The Heresy of the Free Spirit*, 45, and Otthein Ramstedt, 'Stadtunruhen von 1525,' 255: 'Der einzelne verliert durch die Krise seine traditionellen Bindungen und wird sich damit seiner Ohnmacht gegen die soziale Realität bewusst. Diese wird nun kompensiert durch den Glauben an eine widerspruchsfreie Zukunft und an eine unmittelbare Gemeinsamkeit. Die Angst vor der Disorientierung und die Verunsicherung des eigenen Handelns schlägt um in ein fanatisches Festhalten an Ideologie und Gemeinschaft... Überzeugt von der Richtigkeit ihrer Anschauung wird die soziale Bewegung versuchen eine Massenbasis zu finden, die zugleich als Beweis für die Richtigkeit ihrer Ideologie dienen soll. Das "In-group-bewusstsein" der sozialen Bewegung, das in seiner Herausbildung koreliert mit der Ausprägung eines Hetero-stereotyps, bedarf mit der Zustimmung zugleich auch der Ablehnung...'
40 H. Kaminsky, *A History of the Hussite Revolution*, 360.
41 J. Maćek, 'Villes et campagnes dans le Hussitisme,' in Jacques LeGoff, ed., *Hérésies et sociétés dans l'Europe pré-industrielle, 11ᵉ–18ᵉ siècles* (Paris, 1968), 243.
42 cf. H. Jedin, *Kleine Konziliengeschichte* (Vienna, 1969), 47f.
43 Clarissa Atkinson, *Mystic and Pilgrim: The Book and the World of Margery Kempe* (Ithaca, NY, 1983), 129–130.
44 See J. LeClercq, F. ven den Broucke, and L. Bouyer, eds., *La Spiritualité au Moyen Âge* (Aubier, 1961), 583f. Regarding the popularity of St. Bernard in the late Middle Ages see Giles Constable, 'Twelfth-Century Spirituality and the Late Middle Ages' in O. B. Hardison, ed., *Medieval and Renaissance Studies* (Chapel Hill, 1970), 31f., and an essay on a similar theme by the same author, 'Twelfth Century Spiritual Writers in the Late Middle Ages,' in Anthony Molho, John Tedeschi, eds., *Renaissance Studies in Honor of Hans Baron* (DeKalb, Ill, 1970), 14f.
45 See Johannes Hofer, *Johannes Kapistran: Ein Leben im Kampf um die Reform der Kirche* (Heidelberg, 1965, reworked edition) II, 154f.
46 See K. Ruh, 'David von Augsburg und die Entstehung eines franziskanischen Schrifttums in deutscher Sprache,' in C. Bauer, et al., eds., *Augusta, 955–1955* (Augsburg, 1955), 71f.
47 Otto von Passau, ofm., *Die Vier und zweintzig Alten* (ed., Dillingen, 1568) (Tübingen, Universitätsbibliothek Nr. Gb 352.4°)
48 See Franz Falk, *Die Deutschen Sterbebüchlein* (Cologne, 1890), 16f., and by the same author, 'Das Unterricht des deutschen Volkes in den katechetischen Hauptstücken am Ende des Mittelalters,' *Historisch-Politische Blätter für das katholische Deutschland*, 108 (1891), 552f.

49 Vincenz Hasak, ed., *Der Christliche Glaube des deutschen Volkes beim Schlusse des Mittelalters, 1470–1520* (Regensburg, 1868).

50 *Ibid.*, 396.

51 Ulrich Tengler, *Lajenspiegel// von rechtmässigen ordnungen in// Bürgerlichen vnd pein // lichen regim // ten* (Augsburg, 1509), pt. III, (Tübingen, Universitäts-bibliothek, Nr. Ha III. 27°). cf. I. Schairer, *Das religiöse Volksleben am Ausgang des Mittelalters nach Augsburger Quellen* (Leipzig, 1914), 83f.

52 William A. Christian, Jr., *Local Religion in Sixteenth Century Spain* (Princeton, NJ, 1981), 115f.

53 Lawrence Duggan, 'The Unresponsiveness of the Late Medieval Church: A Reconsideration,' *Sixteenth Century Journal*, 9 (1978), 14.

54 Peter Baumgart, 'Formen der Volksfrömmigkeit – Krise der alten Kirche und reformatorische Bewegung,' in Peter Blickle, ed., *Revolte und Revolution in Europa*, 186.

55 Vincenz Hasak, *Der Christliche Glaube*, and Johannes Janssen, *Geschichte des deutschen Volkes seit dem Ausgang des Mittelalters* (Freiburg, 1878–94), I, 62f.

56 Steven Ozment, *The Reformation in the Cities*, 15–17.

57 Bernd Moeller, 'Piety in Germany around 1500,' in Steven Ozment, ed., *The Reformation in Medieval Perspective* (Chicago, 1971), 57f.

58 Steven Ozment, *The Reformation in the Cities*, 21–22.

59 Peter Baumgart, 'Formen der Volksfrömmigkeit,' 195.

60 See Franz Boll, *Sternglaube und Sterndeutung: Die Geschichte und das Wesen der Astrologie* (Berlin, 1926), 15f., and Otto Schiff, 'Forschung zur Vorgeschichte des Bauernkriegs,' in *Historische Vierteljahresschrift*, 19/2 (1919), 189f., and Paola Zambelli, 'Fine del Mondo,' 293–4.

61 Robert Scribner, *For the Sake of Simple Folk*, 6. cf. Clarissa Atkinson, *Mystic and Pilgrim*, 108–9.

62 Robert Lerner, *The Heresy of the Free Spirit*, 231.

63 Robert Scribner, 'Flugblatt und Analphabetentum,' 68f.

64 Karl Schottenloher, *Flugblatt und Zeitung* (Berlin, 1922), 81f.

65 Herbert Grundmann, 'Der Typus des Ketzers in mittelälterlicher Anschauung,' in *Kultur und Universalgeschichte, Walter Goetz zu seinem 60. Geburtstag* (Leipzig, 1927), 105f.

66 Cited in Bernard McGinn, *Visions of the End: Apocalyptic Traditions in the Middle Ages* (New York, 1979), 31.

67 Klaus Arnold, *Niklashausen, 1476* (Baden-Baden, 1980).

68 *Ibid.*, 81.

69 Ernst Laubach, 'Zur Botschaft des Paukers von Niklashausen,' *Jahrbuch für fränkische Landesforschung*, 36 (1976), 93f.

70 Klaus Arnold, *Niklashausen, 1476*, 96.

71 *Ibid.*, 122.

72 *Ibid.*, 110.

73 Karl G. Veesenmeyer, ed., *Sebastian Fischers Chronik* (Ulm, 1896), 120.

74 See Otto Clemen, 'Der Bauer von Wöhrd,' in Otto Clemen, ed., *Beiträge zur Reformationsgeschichte*, 2 (1902), 85f., also Siegfried Epperlein, *Der Bauer im Bild des Mittelalters* (Jena, 1975), 203f.

75 cf. H. Öhler, 'Der Aufstand des Armen Konrad im Jahr 1514,' *Württembergische Vierteljahreshefte für Landesgeschichte*, 38 (1932), 401f.
76 *Ibid.*, 408, cf. Günther List, *Chilianism, Utopie, und radikale Reformation* (Munich, 1973), 9f.
77 cf. Josef Schmidt, *Lestern, lesen, lesen hören*, 130.
78 Bernd Hamm, 'Laientheologie zwischen Luther und Zwingli,' 240.
79 See Robert Muchembled, *Culture Populaire et Culture des Élites*, 219f.

II: REFORMERS AND LAYPEOPLE

1 H. Wayne Pipkin, 'Zwingli, the Laity and Orders: From the Cloister into the World,' *Hartford Quarterly* 8 (1968), 33.
2 Lewis W. Spitz, ed., *The Protestant Reformation* (Englewood Cliffs, NJ, 1966), 55.
3 cf. Hans J. Hillerbrand, 'The Origins of Sixteenth Century Anabaptism: Another Look,' *ARG*, 53 (1962), 152f., and Kenneth R. Davis, 'Erasmus as Progenitor of Anabaptist Theology and Piety,' *Mennonite Quarterly Review*, 52 (1974), 163f., and Werner Packull, *Mysticism and the Early South German–Austrian Anabaptist Movement, 1525–1531* (Scottdale, PA, 1977), 17f.
4 Cyril Eastwood, *The Priesthood of All Believers* (Minneapolis, MN, 1960), 241.
5 *WA* 5, 649, 12–13.
6 *WA* 2, 248, 11–12.
7 *WA* 6, 184, 8–10.
8 *WA* 6, 431, 9–13., cf. *WA* 2, 10, 19f.
9 *WA* 237, 19–21, cf. 625, 22–24.
10 *WA* 1, 238, 9–12.
11 *WA* 6, 563, 31–35. Trans. John Dillenberger, *Martin Luther* (New York, 1961), 345.
12 *WA* 2, 189, 27–28.
13 *WA* 6, 566, 16–21. Trans. John Dillenberger, *Martin Luther*, 348.
14 *WA* 10 III, 390, 25–27.
15 *WA* 1, 625, 33.
16 *WA* 6, 509, 36–37.
17 *WA* 10 II, 548, 17–31.
18 *WA* 6, 203, 8–10.
19 *WA* 26, 219, 4–7.
20 *WA* 2, 649, 1–2, 15–17.
21 *WA* 10 I, pt. 2, 150, 6–9.
22 *WA* 33, 352, 7–9.
23 *WA* 10, I, pt. 1, 69, 22–23.
24 *WA* 7, 315, 6–8. See Robert Scribner, *For the Sake of Simple Folk*, 168f.
25 cf. Wolfgang Stein, *Das kirchliche Amt bei Luther* (Wiesbaden, 1974), 114f.
26 *WA* 7, 58, 12–22. Trans. John Dillenberger, *Martin Luther*, 65.
27 *WA* 6, 408, 26–31. Trans. John Dillenberger, *Martin Luther*, 409.
28 *Ibid.*

29 *WA* 7, 633, 29–34.
30 cf. *WA* 6, 567, 17–22.
31 *WA* 6, 370, 16–27.
32 *WA* 10 III, 396, 14–19.
33 *WA, BW*, 3, 244: Luther an Spalatin.
34 *WA* 7, 647, 7–11.
35 *WA* 10 III, 96, 15–22.
36 *WA* 10 III, 522, 25–34.
37 *WA* 10 II, 396, 11–12.
38 *WA* 6, 566, 29.
39 *WA* 6, 299, 35–40.
40 *WA* 10 I, pt. 1, 262, 1–4.
41 *WA* 10 I, pt. 1, 263, 7–9.
42 *WA* 10 I, pt. 1, 494, 14–16.
43 *WA* 10 III, 97, 8–14.
44 *ZH*, 11, 337–8.
45 S. M. Jackson, ed., *Zwingli's Latin Works and Correspondence* (New York, 1912) II, 261.
46 *Ibid.*, I, 230.
47 Robert C. Walton, *Zwingli's Theocracy* (Toronto, 1967), xiiif., cf. Walter Jacob, *Politische Führungsschicht und Reformation: Untersuchungen zur Reformation in Zürich, 1519–1528* (Zürich, 1969), 12f.
48 *ZA*, 618.
49 S. M. Jackson, ed., *Zwingli's Latin Works*, I, 230.
50 *Antwurt eins Schwy//tzer Purens/über die vngegründte//geschrifft Meyster Jeronimi Geb//wilers Schulmeisters zu Stras//burg/ die er zu Beschirmung der// Römischen kilchen/ vnd iro//erdachten wesen/ hat las//sen vssgon. Ein Epistel Huldrich Zuinglis.* (1522) (Würburg, Universitätsbibliothek, Nr. Th dp. 1. 864.) 'Welcher a Ber sich uff die gotlichen warheit Bas verstand vnd das gots wort eigenlicher Bruche wirdst du in deym gleubigen hertzen jnnen... Also wen ir die vertriben han werden die hafner, müller, glaser, tuchschärer, schumacher vnd schnyder leeren.'
51 *ZH*, 11, 333.
52 G. W. Bromiley, ed., *Zwingli and Bullinger*, Library of Christian Classics, 24 (Philadelphia, 1953), 88.
53 *ZH*, 10, 17.
54 *ZH*, 10, 16.
55 *ZA*, 629.
56 E. Künzli, ed., *Huldrych Zwingli, Auswahl seiner Schriften* (Zürich, 1962), 311.
57 *ZH*, 10, 22.
58 *ZA*, 632.
59 S. M. Jackson, ed., *Zwingli's Latin Works*, I, 284, cf. *ZH*, 10, 142.
60 *ZH*, 10, 142.
61 E. Künzli, ed., *Huldrych Zwingli, Auswahl seiner Schriften*, 273.
62 *ZA*, 621.
63 See Bard Thompson, ed., *Liturgies of the Western Church* (Cleveland, 1962), 141f.

64 Christof Gestrich, *Zwingli als Theologe* (Zürich, 1967), 171.
65 *Antwurt eines Schwytzer Purens*...: 'Sich fromer Christ wie den himelsche
     vatter lustet siner gotliche wyssheit liecht vor den wysen vnd fürsichtige ze
     verbergen. Matt. II. Vnnd das den kindischen erscheinen da mitt er allweg
     jm selbs glych sye der da verderbet die wyssheit der wysen vnnd den verstand
     d fürsichtigen verschupfft.'
66 See Robert Scribner, 'The Social Thought of Erasmus,' *Journal of Ecclesiastical
     History*, 6 (1970–71), 5f.
67 cf. Alfons Auer, *Die volkommene Frömmigkeit des Christen: Nach dem Enchiridion
     militis Christiani des Erasmus von Rotterdam* (Düsseldorf, 1954), 71f.
68 *Erasmi Roterdami Pa //racelsis Teütscht wie ein teüerlich vn=//ausprechlich schatz
     vnd klainer sey das Euan=//gelium vnd haylig wort gottes* (1522) (SFB-Zl, Nr.
     00407) 'vn ich wolt selbst das ich gleich die warhait sage das all schuster
     weber hecker ackerknecht lesen das Evangelio vnd eplas pauli...Wolt got das
     der paur am pfluge redet vnnd sunge hirvon...das handwergsgesellen in der
     werckstatt der wulle weber bi seiner spumell der schuster bey seinen laysten
     die Botten auff dem felde singen.'
69 Alfons Auer, *Die volkommene Frömmigkeit des Christen*, 72.
70 See Robert Scribner, 'The Social Thought of Erasmus,' 5.
71 *hern Erasmi vo Roterdam//vormanung des heylige//Evangelin vnd der//heyligen
     zwelf//=bote schrifft// fleissig zu lesen// in kurtz verdeutscht.* (1522) (Würzburg,
     Universitatsbibliothek, Nr. Th. dp. g. 423.) 'Wiltu zu Christo de hern gehn
     so thu das du zu dir selbest geest dir ist nichts inwendigers oder das mehr
     inwindig yn dir ist als dein gemute do selbst zeuch dich gar hyn.'
72 Alfons Auer, *Die volkommene Frömmigkeit des Christen*, 116.
73 *herr Erasmus von Ro//terdam/ verteutschte ausslegung///über das gottlich trostlich
     wort// vnsers lieben herrn vnnd selig=//machers christi/ Nement auff//euch mein
     Joch/ vnd ler=net von mir* (1521) (SFB-Zl, Nr. 2671.) 'Dan das der Türck oder
     ein Tyrann mit emporung vnd zerstorung der ausgerichten stende vnd
     ordnung die Christenhiet widerumb in gutte ordnung bringe...'
74 Alfons Auer, *Die volkommene Frömmigkeit des Christen*, 139.
75 *Ibid.*, 147.
76 See *Erasmus von Roterdam von der ver=/bothen speyss des//fleyschs. An den
     erwirde vn durch// lauchten firsten vn herrn// Christoff Bischoffen zu Basell// en
     verantwortug Erasmi von Roterdam von verpotener speyss// des fleysches/ vnd von
     der gley=//chen/ aufsatzungen der menschen.* (Leipzig, 1523) (Würzburg,
     Universitätsbibliothek, Nr. 15a Th. dp. 423.)
77 Alfons Auer, *Die volkommene Frömmigkeit des Christen*, 144.
78 *herr Erasmus von Roterdam veteutschte auslegung*: 'Dan was sol ich sage
     von der beschwerung des menschliche gesetz vnd recht so sant Augustin vor
     vil hundert jaren in der Epistel zu de Januarius gezornt...Was wurd er jtzo
     thun vnd sagen wen er seh das das frey folick Christi mit sovil rechten vnd
     gesetzen beschwert, mit sovil cermonien od. kirche gepreng vnd sovil stricke
     verbunden. vn mit manchfeltiger wütlichen regierung der weltlichen Fürsten,
     der Bischöffen vn de Bäpste vn zu not derselbe trabanten vn diener
     vnterdruckt.'
79 *Her Erasmus von Roterdams// verteütsche Auslegung über// dise wort sant Paulo*

zu den// von Corinth/in der ersten Epistel am vierze=//tenden Capitel. Ich will lieber in meine// gemut fünff wortinn der kirchen reden// andere zu unterweysen/ dan zehentausent wort mit der zungen. Von gesang. (1521) (SFB-Zl, Nr. 01660) 'Und wir sollen mit grossem fleyes prophecieren das ist die hailigen Schrifft auslegen, verkleren, vnd erleütern.'

80 *Von Walfart// Erasmi Roterdami//vermanung wo Chri=//stus vnd sein reich// zu suchen ist.* (1522) (SFB-Zl, Nr. 2805) 'Wil ermanen alle christglaubigen mensche dz sy zu dem lautern vn rainen prunen Christi zu dem hailigin Ewangelio lauters gewissen vnnd raine hertzen bringen vnnnd sy noch nichts anderes durfte da allain noch diser lere.'

81 *Her Erasmus von Roterdams verteütsche Auslegung über dise wort sant Paulo:* 'Es erschallet als von Pasaunen Trumeten Krumhornern Pfeyffen vnd Orgelen vnnd dartu singt man auch darein. Do hort man schentliche vnd vnerliche Bulli leder vnd gesang dar nach die Huren vnd Buben tantzen.'

82 *Her Erasmus von Ro=//terdam verteutschte auslegung über//disen spruch Christi unsers herrn// Matthei um drey und zweintzigsten// Capitel/ von den Phariseyern/// Sie thun alle ire werck///das sie von den menschen// gesehen werden/ Vnd breyten// ir gebortzedeln auss. Vom heyltumb u.* (1521) (SFB-Zl, Nr. 2670)

83 *Herr Erasmus von Ro=//terdam verteutschte auslegung über// sant heironymus Allegation/ was// guts die Philosophi in der heyligen// schrifft schaffen.* (1521) (SFB-Zl, Nr. 2668)

84 Karl G. Veesenmeyer, ed., *Sebastian Fischers Chronik,* 18.

III: MEMMINGEN: A FURRIER, A PREACHER, AND A PEASANTS' WAR

1 W. Schlenck, *Memmingen im Reformationszeitalter, Memminger Geschichts-blätter,* 12 (1968), 21. cf. P. Eitel, *Die oberschwäbische Reichsstädte im Zeitalter der Zunftherrshchaft.* (Stuttgart, 1970) 121f.

2 W. Schlenck, *Memmingen im Reformationszeitalter,* 16.

3 *Ibid.,* 15.

4 *Ibid.,* 19.

5 *Ibid.,* 21f.

6 *Ibid.,* 24.

7 See Erich Maschke, 'Deutsche Städte,' 21–22.

8 W. Schlenck, *Memmingen im Reformationszeitalter,* 122, Anhang 3.

9 *Ibid.,* 25, 26.

10 *Ibid.,* 31f.

11 Karsthans is a late-medieval symbol for the rebellious peasant, who went about the countryside inciting peasants to revolt. This particular Karsthans (from *Karst* or hoe + *hans*) is first mentioned in an official complaint published by the Bishop of Strasbourg against the preacher Matthias Zell (+1548). The bishop refers to Karsthans as 'ein Laie und nachgültig schweisenden Menschen und als ein alleruffrürigster und der lutherischen Ketzerei anhangend, rumor und faction wider alles Erbvolck errengend,' *ADB,* 15, 432. This particular man, Hans Maurer is described in another

source as a short fat little man in a gray coat without arms, black pants, and a broad gray hat. Works attributed to him are of spurious origin. The 1521 *Karsthans* dialogue was written by Thomas Murner. The other, *Gesprechbiechlin neüw Karsthans* (1521) was probably the work of Martin Bucer. For texts of these see Werner Lenk, ed., *Die Reformation im zeitgenössischen Dialog* (Berlin, 1968), 67–127. For more information about this particular preaching Karsthans see: W. Vogt, 'Zwei oberschwäbische Laienprediger,' *ZKWKL*, VI (1885), 413f., and Adolf Laube, et al., eds., *Flugschriften der frühen Reformationsbewegung, 1518–1524* (Berlin, 1983), I, 262, n2.

12 Gustav Bossert, *Sebastian Lotzer und seine Schriften* (Memmingen, 1906), 74. (Reprinted from *BWKG*, II, 1887, 16f.)

13 W. Schlenck, *Memmingen im Reformationszeitalter*, 33.

14 *Ibid.*, 34.

15 *Ibid.*, 36.

16 *Ibid.*, 38f.

17 *Ibid.*, 37.

18 *Ermahnung*, 35, 36–37. (See note 28)

19 J. Schelhorn, *Kurtze Reformationshistorie von Memmingen* (Memmingen, 1730) 61.

20 Gustav Bossert, *Sebastian Lotzer*, 36. cf. Huldrych Zwingli, *Wer Ursache gebe zu Aufruhr* (1525) in *CR*, 90, 359: 'warlich ufrürigen sind die pfaffen die dz euangelion verbeten.'

21 For Memmingen's role in the peasant negotiations see: Wilhelm Vogt, ed., 'Die Correspondenz des schwäbischen Bundeshauptmanns Ulrich Artzt von Augsburg aus den Jahren 1525–27,' *ZHVSN*, VI, VII, IX, X (1897f.)

22 W. Schlenck, *Memmingen im Reformationszeitalter*, 39.

23 *Ibid.*, 45.

24 Gustav Bossert, *Sebastian Lotzer*, 52.

25 See Ludwig Baumann, *Die oberschwäbische Bauern im März 1525 und die Zwölf Artikel* (Kempten, 1871), 25f., and Martin Brecht, 'Der theologische Hintergrund der Zwölf Artikel der Bauernschaft in Schwaben von 1525,' *ZKG*, 85/2 (1974), 31f.

26 W. Schlenck, *Memmingen im Reformationszeitalter*, 50.

27 Gustav Bossert, *Sebastian Lotzer*, 62.

28 Lotzer published five pamphlets between 1523 and 1525, which are found in Alfred Goetze, ed., *Sebastian Lotzers Schriften* (Leipzig, 1902). For exact citations see bibliography, Printed Primary Sources. For convenience sake, they are cited as *Ermahnung*, 1523. *Sendbrief*, 1523. *Auslegung*, 1524. *Beschirmbüchlein*, 1524. *Entschuldigung*, 1525. The Peasant Articles, written by Lotzer, Schappeler, and Ulrich Schmid are cited, *12 Artikel*, 1525, and can be found in Günther Franz, ed. *Quellen zur Geschichte des deutschen Bauernstandes in der Neuzeit* (Darmstadt, 1963). Lotzer's works are cited in both the Goetze edition and in Franz by page and line.

29 Lotzer seldom uses correct Latin. He gives the plural of *concilium* as *concillii*, *actorum* as *actuum*. cf. Gustav Bossert, *Sebastian Lotzer*, 3. The rolls of the university at Tübingen include a 'Sebastianus ex Horv' in the matriculation

lists for 1505, but most scholars agree that this could not have been our furrier. See R. Roth, ed., *Urkunden zur Geschichte der Universität Tübingen aus den Jahren 1476 bis 1550* (Tübingen, 1877), 497.

30 *Beschirmbüchlein*, 52, 31f.

31 Gustav Bossert, *Sebastian Lotzer*, 3.

32 *ADB*, 30, 576f.

33 *Sendbrief*, 36, 41–42.

34 *ADB*, 30, 576. cf. Adolf Laube et al., eds., *Flugschriften*, I, 262 n2.

35 *Ermahnung*, 35, 36–37.

36 *Sendbrief*, 38, 24–25.

37 cf. Gerhard Ritter, 'Romantische und revolutionäre Elemente in der deutschen Theologie am Vorabend der Reformation,' in *Deutsche Vierteljahrschrift für Literaturwissenschaft und Geistesgeschichte*, 5 (1927), 364f. See also J. Rohr, 'Die Prophetie im letzten Jahrhundert vor der Reformation als Geschichtsquelle und Geschichtsfaktor,' *Historisches Jahrbuch*, 19 (1898), 32f.

38 There was a general preference for Matthew's gospel in medieval times, especially for its references to kingship and the kingdom of Christ. It was particularly important for its eschatological passages and the cult of the poor as a means to heaven in chapter 25. Lotzer used Luther's *Neu Testament Deutsch*. See *Beschirmbüchlein*, 75, 5f.

39 Several Zwingli works may have directly influenced Lotzer. There is no proof that he actually read Zwingli's pamphlets, but the following works are likely sources for his theology: *Von Erkiesen und Freiheit der Speisen*, 1522 (Lotzer on fasting); *Ein frundlich bitt und ermanung etlicher priester der Eidgenossenschaft*, 1522 (Lotzer on human teaching and the gospel); *Von Klarheit und Gewissheit des Wort Gottes*, 1522 (*Lotzer on lex evangelica*); *Die 67 Artikel*, 1523 (Lotzer on celibacy, fasting, sacraments). cf. Gustav Bossert, *Sebastian Lotzer*, 3: 'Seine [Lotzers] Schriften ziegen nirgends eine Spur von Zwinglis geistigem Einfluss.' If Lotzer did read Zwingli's works, when discussing identical topics, the furrier used his own scriptural citations; he did not copy verbatim from Zwingli. See Alfred Goetze, ed. *Sebastian Lotzers Schriften*, 20, 21.

40 cf. L. Enders, ed., *Eberlin von Günzburg, 15 Buntsgenossen, Neudrücke deutscher Literaturwerke des XVI and XVII Jahrhunderts* (1896), 164–5.

41 *Ibid.*, 17.

42 Christoph Schappeler, *Verantwortug//und auflösung etlicher//vermainter Argument vnd ursachen So// zu widerstandt vnnd verdruckung des // Wort Gottes vnd hailigen Evangelions. Von denen die nit Cris//sten sein vnd sich doch Chris//sten namens rumen/ tag//lich gebraucht//werden.* (1524) (SFB-Zl, Nr. 3013) 'Zum dritten kommen sie mit ainem argument vnnd sagen Luther vnnd andere wollen die hailigen geschrifft zu irem gefallen vnd wider der alten vater verstandt auslegen darumß sol inen billich kain glauß gegeßen werden.'

43 For further references to Lotzer see: E. Rohling, *Die Reichsstadt Memmingen in der Zeit der evangelischen Volksbewegung* (Munich, 1864), 35 and Justus Maurer, 'Das Verhalten der reformatorisch gesinnten Geistlichen Süddeutschlands im Bauernkrieg, 1525' (Dissertation, Tübingen, 1975), 122f.

44 cf. *Auslegung*, 76, 39f.

45 *Ermahnung*, 27, 35–31.

46 *Auslegung*, 76, 51–46.
47 *Beschirmbüchlein*, 48, 19–21.
48 *Ermahnung*, 34, 34–37, cf. *Sendbrief*, 31, 3f., and *Beschirmbüchlein*, 53, 6f.
49 *Ermahnung*, 34, 30–33.
50 cf. Natalie Davis, *Society and Culture in Early Modern France*, 13f.
51 *Sendbrief*, 40, 23.
52 *Ibid.*, 40, 8–10.
53 *Ibid.*, 37, 40–42.
54 This use of *gratia infusa* is not identical to the use in Nominalist terminology. It is not a reference to the event that takes place as a *gratia prima*. It is a special grace, infused by reading scripture, actually closest to the Nominalist *gratia gratum faciens*. It is acquired faith as *fides ex auditu*, not a *fides aquisita* dependent on human positive volition.
55 *Sendbrief*, 37, 32–33.
56 cf. *Ermahnung*, 31, 31–33.
57 *Sendbrief*, 39, 22f.
58 See Heiko Oberman, 'Facientibus quod in se est, Deus non denegat gratiam: Robert Holcot, O.P., and the Beginnings of Luther's Theology,' in Steven Ozment, ed., *The Reformation in Medieval Perspective*, 119–141.
59 *Auslegung*, 80, 30–86.
60 *Sendbrief*, 42, 26–29.
61 *Ibid.*, 42, 12–13.
62 *Ibid.*, 42, 7–15.
63 *Ibid.*, 42, 22–23.
64 *Ermahnung*, 33, 39f.
65 *Sendbrief*, 44, 1–3.
66 *Ermahnung*, 33, 28–32.
67 *Ibid.*, 33, 33–37.
68 *Beschirmbüchlein*, 38, 1., cf. *Auslegung*, 75–76, 45, 1–2.
69 *Beschirmbüchlein*, 65, 14; see also Zwingli's *Von Klarheit und Gewissheit des Wort Gottes*, 1522, CR, 88, 384: 'menschlich leer von der papisten und altkirche.'
70 *Ermahnung*, 29, 40–41.
71 *Beschirmbüchlein*, 56, 30–31.
72 *Ermahnung*, 32, 11–14.
73 *Ibid.*, 32, 23–27.
74 *Ibid.*, 34, 1–3.
75 *Beschirmbüchlein*, 54, 22f.
76 *Ibid.*, 64, 9–13.
77 *Sendbrief*, 29, 35–38.
78 *Beschirmbüchlein*, 71, 1f.
79 *12 Artikel*, 5, 13–17, cf. Zwingli's *Wer Ursache gebe zu Aufruhr*, 1525, CR, 89, 767. Lotzer's concession to the tithe in the Peasant Articles may have been a conciliatory measure to city authorities.
80 *Beschirmbüchlein*, 58, 42f.
81 *Ibid.*, 58, 43.
82 *Sendbrief*, 29, 33–35.
83 *Beschirmbüchlein*, 67, 37–41.

84 *Ibid.*, 70, 9. Several pamphlets by Martin Luther were certainly influential in Lotzer's theology. *De captivitate Babylonica*, 1520; *An den Christlichen Adel deutscher Nation*, 1520; *Magnifikatsauslegung*, 1521.
85 *Sendbrief*, 45, 46, 43–46, 1–3.
86 *Beshirmbüchlein*, 65, 18–21.
87 *Ibid.*, 67, 35–40.
88 *Ibid.*, 67, 22–26.
89 *Ibid.*, 22, 10–15.
90 *Ibid.*, 27, 5–9.
91 *Ibid.*, 67, 11–14.
92 *Ibid.*, 68, 20–24.
93 *Ibid.*, 66, 16.
94 *Auslegung*, 8, 24–26.
95 *Beschirmbüchlein*, 79, 2–4.
96 *Ibid.*, 74, 40.
97 *Ermahnung*, 33, 43–44.
98 *Ibid.*, 33, 12–17.
99 *Ibid.*, 28, 29, 45–46, 1–2.
100 *Sendbrief*, 46, 33–34. cf. Ludwig Enders, ed., *Eberlin von Günzburg, 15 Buntsgenossen*, 165: 'On zwyfel ist es durch des teufels rot und hindernuss geschahen, das die helge Bibel allein den pfaffen, münchen, und hoher schüler zu geaygnet ist, und den schlechten Christen als ein schedlich ding abgesprechen.'
101 *Ermahnung*, 33, 4–5, 8.
102 *Sendbrief*, 38, 21–22.
103 *Ermahnung*, 28, 21–22.
104 *Ibid.*, 28, 29, 24–25, 26–27.
105 *Sendbrief*, 38, 23–25.
106 *Ibid.*, 38, 25f.
107 *Ibid.*, 43, 1–3., cf. Christoph Schappeler, *Verantwortung und Auflösung*: 'dan was hundert jar vnrecht gewest ist würdet (nach gemainem sprichwort) nye kain stund recht.'
108 *Beschirmbüchlein*, 55, 45–47.
109 *Ibid.*, 60, 23–29.
110 *Ermahnung*, 31, 20–24.
111 *Sendbrief*, 45, 1–6.
112 *Ermahnung*, 31, 28–30. cf. Zwingli's *Christliche Antwort Zürichs an Bischof Hugo*, 1525, ZW, III, 179; 'Wir hangen solches Gut nicht an die Götzen, sondern den lieben Heiligen, die im Himel sind, zu ehren.' See also Walter Tappolet, *Das Marienlob der Reformatoren* (Tübingen, 1962), 221–260.
113 *Sendbrief*, 45, 1–6.
114 *Auslegung*, 81, 3–7.
115 *Sendbrief*, 38, 5–8; cf. *Beschirmbüchlein*, 55, 1–5.
116 *Sendbrief*, 37, 36–38.
117 cf. Clarissa Atkinson, *Mystic and Pilgrim*, 147f.
118 Alfred Goetze, ed., *Sebastian Lotzers Schriften*, 5–12.

119 *Beschirmbüchlein*, 63, 30–33.
120 *Ermahnung*, 35, 35, 53–56, 1–2.
121 *Beschirmbüchlein*, 72, 2–4.
122 *Ermahnung*, 35, 8–10.
123 *12 Artikel*, 15, 8–13.
124 *Entschuldigung*, 82, 32f.
125 *Sendbrief*, 38, 34f.
126 *Entschuldigung*, 83, 33.
127 W. Schlenck, *Memmingen im Reformationszeitalter*, 58.
128 Donald Weinstein and Rudolf Bell, *Saints and Society*, 161.
129 *Ibid.*, 104.
130 Adolf Laube, 'Sozialökonomische Fragen in Flugschriften,' 221.
131 Lionel Rothkrug, 'Popular Religion and Holy Shrines,' 38.
132 Bernd Hamm, who generally follows the tradition of Delumeau, traces only Luther and Zwingli's influence on Vögeli. See Gottfried Seebass, 'Zur Beurteilung des Reformatorischen bei Vögeli,' in Josef Nolte, et al. eds., *Kontinuität und Umbruch*, 299.
133 Bernd Hamm, 'Laientheologie zwischen Luther und Zwingli,' 292.
134 Robert Scribner, 'Flugblatt und Analphabetentum,' 73.
135 William Christian, *Local Religion in Sixteenth Century Spain*, 167–68.

IV: AUGSBURG: A WEAVER, A SOLDIER, AND A RADICAL FRANCISCAN

1 Erich Maschke, 'Deutsche Städte,' 4. cf. Joachim John, 'Die Augsburger Sozialstruktur im 15. Jahrhundert,' in G. Gottlieb et al., eds., *Geschichte der Stadt Augsburg* (Stuttgart, 1984), 188.
2 Rudolf Endres, 'Zünfte und Unterschichten,' 156.
3 Herbert Immenkölter, 'Kirche zwischen Reformation und Parität,' in G. Gottlieb, et al., eds., *Geschichte der Stadt Augsburg*, 392. cf. Erich Maschke, 'Deutsche Städte,' 15.
4 Friedwart Uhland, 'Täufertum und Obrigkeit in Augsburg im 16. Jahrhundert' (Dissertation, Tübingen, 1972), 15f.
5 Rolf Kiessling, *Bürgerliche Gesellschaft und Kirche in Augsburg im Spätmittelalter* (Augsburg, 1971), 294f.
6 Friedrich Schubert, 'Die Reformation in Augsburg,' in C. Bauer et al., eds., *Augusta*, 288.
7 *Ibid.*, 288, cf. Heiko Oberman, *Masters of the Reformation: The Emergence of a New Intellectual Climate in Europe* (Cambridge, 1981), 128f.
8 Martin Luther, *Von Kauffzhand//lung vnd wuch-//er.* (Wittenberg, 1524) (Herzog–August Bibliothek, Wolfenbüttel, Nr. C lb Helmst. 4° 8.)
9 Rudolf Endres, 'Zünfte und Unterschichten,' 161.
10 Erich Maschke, 'Deutsche Städte,' 21–22.
11 Rolf Kiessling, *Bürgerliche Gesellschaft*, 301.
12 *Ibid.*, 308.
13 Friedrich Schubert, 'Die Reformation in Augsburg,' in C. Bauer, et al., eds., *Augusta*, 290.

14 Rolf Kiessling, *Bürgerliche Gesellschaft*, 316.
15 Erich Maschke, 'Verfassung und soziale Kräfte in der deutschen Stadt des späten Mittelalters,' in E. Maschke, ed., *Städte und Menschen*, 180.
16 Rolf Kiessling, *Bürgerliche Gesellschaft*, 318.
17 Friedrich Roth, 'Die geistliche Betrügerin Anna Lamanit von Augsburg, 1480–1518,' in *ZKG*, 42 (1924), 355–417.
18 Rolf Kiessling, *Bürgerliche Gesellschaft*, 313f.
19 Friedrich Roth, *Augsburgs Reformationsgeschichte, 1517–1537* (Munich, 1881), I, 125f.
20 Friedrich Schubert, 'Die Reformation in Augsburg,' 290.
21 Friedwart Uhland, 'Täufertum und Obrigkeit in Augsburg', 38f.
22 For a complete list of Utz Rychssner's pamphlets see bibliography, Printed Primary Sources. For convenience sake, they are cited, *Papstchronik*, 1524; *Eine schöne Unterweisung*, 1524; *Gesprächbüchlein/ Weber–Krämer*, 1524; *Gesprächbüchlein/Weber–Pfaffen*, 1524. Ryschssner is mentioned in Friedwart Uhland, 'Täufertum und Obrigkeit in Augsburg,' 67–68. See also Adolf Laube, et al., eds., *Flugschriften der frühen Reformationsbewegung*, I, 439–440.
23 *Gesprächbüchlein/Weber–Pfaffen*: 'Es ist wol dreyundzwayntzig Jar da was ich zu Strasspurg an Doctor Kayserspergers predig Da sagt er an offner kantzel er wolt nit mer begeren von gott dann das jm des hymmelreych als gewyss wer als grossen Prelaten die hell bey drey oder vierhundert jaren...des glechen hort ich auch zu Ulm von aynem Doctor zu den predigern auch an der Kantzel...also schieden wir bayd von ainander bey dem Rottenthor vnd er ging in die Stat hyneyn vnnd ich auff dem graBen biss das ich auch haym kam.'
24 The edition of Jacob Twinger von Königshofen's 1382 chronicle, addressed to 'intelligent laypeople, who like to read about historical events as much as learned priests,' was published by Johann Bämler in Augsburg in 1478: *Heinach volget ein Cronica von allen Keysern//vnd künigen dye sei der Cristi geburt geregier//ret vnnd gereichsnet haben= wolche Cronica// gar kurtz weily nutzlich vnnd lieplich zuhern//vnnd zu lesen ist//* (Augsburg, 1478). cf. G. W. Panzer, *Annalen der älteren deutschen Litteratur* (Nuremberg, 1788), I, 73f., also Hermann Maschek, *Deutsche Chroniken* (Leipzig, 1936), 16, Klaus Arnold, *Niklashausen, 1476*, 111, and *ADB* 18, 525–26.
25 *Papstchronik*: 'damit das jr menschliche auffsatzung wider die satzung gottes allmächtigenn genug samlich erkennt werden in allem volck...auss den gesatzen der menschen darmit wir arme schaflein so hart vnd lange zeyt Beladen seyen gewesen vnnd noch kain end will nemen in vil hertzen der menschenn.'
26 *Ibid.*, 'Celestinus, was ain frumer ainfeltiger Bapst vnd der het ain Cardinal der macht ain ror vnnd ain loch durch ain wand in des Bapst schlaffkamer vnd redet durch das ror vnnd durch das loch iij necht dysse maynung. O Celestine, gib auff das ampt des Bapstumbs wiltu selig werdenn da menet der gut ainfeltig Bapst es wer ain stym von dem heiligen gaist vnd gab es auff vnd darnach ward der selb Cardinal zum Bapst erwolt der durch das ror mitt dem Bapst geret hett.'
27 *Ibid.*, 'Der satzt auff das priester vn nunnen nit Bey ainander in ainem kor

solten singen vn verBot auch beym ban das kain lay kain priester solt schlagen
vnd Bey des selben Bapstszeyten seynd vff gericht worden die ij bettelorden
als d Barfusser vnd prediger orden vnd der barfusser orden hat angefange
zu Assis iij tag rayss Rom nach Christus geburt tausent ij hundert jar. Vnd
der prediger orden fieng an zu Pannonia nach Christi geburt MCC vnd xj jar.'

28 *Ibid.*, 'Das kam mit schalckhait an das Bapsthumb vnnd machet vil gesatz
in das gaistlich recht vnd satzt auff das Jubel jar das man solt almal zu hundert
jaren ain Jubel jar haben. Also was die erst Romfart bey des Bapst zeyten da
man zalt nach Christi geburt 13 hundert jar er was hoffertig vn Benant sich
selb ain herren d gatzenwelt aber es wert nit lang da warde er vmb sein
myssthatt gefangen vnd zu hungers getodt daz er im selber die finger abfrass
darvon ward ain sprichwort von jm Er kam an das bapstumb wie ain fuchs
vnd regiert wie ain wutender leo vnd starb wie ain hund.'

29 *Gesprächbüchlein/ Weber–Pfaffen*: 'das wir nit meer dann zway oder drey
Sacrament haben Got verordnet. Der Tauff des Sacramentt des altars vnnd
die vergebung dr. sund. das ander acht ich als für mensche traem vnd
erdichung vn locknagel dem liebe seligen pfennig.'

30 *Gesprächbüchlein/ Weber–Krämer*: 'Ir hond mich warlich wol halb auff euren
wegg gebracht vnnd ich will mich Bosser fleyssen in der Bibel zu lesen wan
ich nye gethon hab...wan warlich ich haB ain haymlichen neyd zu euch
gehabt von des Mans willen Doctor Kretzen da ir also wider sein Buchlein hond
geredet aber ich wil es noch hewt in offen werfen...vn will auch an seyn
predig nymmer gon. er soll mich nit weytter hineyfüren.' cf. *Frag vnnd
Antwort etli//cher Artickel zwischen D.//Michaelen Kellern predi=//cante bey den
parfussern/// vnd D. Mathia Kretzen/ predicanten auff dem hohe stifft zu
Augspurg//newlich begeben. Anno XXV.* (Herzog–August Bibliothek, Wolfenbüttel, Nr. 135.6 Theol. 4° 11)

31 *Gesprächbüchlein/Weber–Pfaffen*: 'mey nerr ich wen ain yetlicher der da stat
an ofner kantzel der hab macht das übel zu straffen. man sol nit gar zu allen
sachen schweygen synd doch die propheten den künigen vnder ir angesicht
gestand vnd hand sy gestrafft vmb ir sünt doch die man wil in der geschrifft
sind...Johannes der tauffer strafft Herodem von wegen seins bruders
weyb...des gleychen sant Steffan vnnd alle Aposteln vnd lieb heyligen ja
Christus selb. Wie offt hat got befolhn Mosi vnd der andern propheten Israel
z straffen.'

32 *Eine schöne Unterweisung*: 'von der stul des Endtchrists gewaltig geBaut vnd
gesterckt worden ist...Nun es ware vil darvon zu reden vnnd zu schreyben
aber mer wurd sprechen es diente zur auffrur wie wol es die wort gottes
seynd.'

33 *Ibid.*: 'O lieben bruder, wir sehen wol wie jre werck schynen wie aim
esselsfeygen in ainer dornen högken. Sy sagent auch sy haben den hayligen
geyst das lass ich wol geschehen. wan sy in haben wolten so stunden sy jn
in der Bibel...aber die Bibel ist jnen also angenam als wann ain Sau in ain
judenschul kam...sy predigen Genad vnnd abplass, haymlich Beycht, ölung,
Fyrmung, saltz schmaltz krawt wurtz wasser vnd weyn weyen...ewig Jartäg
ewig messen styfften ewyg liechter, Messgewend kelch vnd zu allem dem das
ir nutz vnnd eer ist gewesen had sy es zugewendet.'

34 *Gesprächbüchlein/Weber–Pfaffen*: 'Auf aym tal sagent ir gelerte ir hab dz hymelreych in der hand. auf dz andern tyl sagent auch die geleerten es kum darbey ir kayner in hymel.'

35 *Ibid.*: 'aber was wollen wir armen pfaffen vnd arm layen darzu tun. vnser sach ist unerspriesslich. es wirt nichts helffen vnd ergeben. vn ich will euch ewre leste maynung nit abschlagen haben bey der hayligen geschrifft zu bleyben vnd ir mügent euch gegen got wol darmit befelhen biss das es ain andere gestalt gewint.'

36 *Ibid.*: 'Ir wisst wol wie Lucas am 6 Cap spricht Ain yetlich reych das in im selbs zertaylt ist wirt zerstort...Dunct euch nit es wol schier dem schimpf gleych sehe ewer macht dr zerstörng dann ir arm geystlichen wisst ir nit was mathei am 24. stat. Ir werdet gehasst umB meinen namen...vn werden wir geschent...dar maint jr nit die sachen seyen yetz all verhanden.'

37 *Papstchronik*: 'ich waiss aber das Bey mir selber wol was orglen in der kirchen mir für ein andacht hat bracht das ich Bey mengem ampt kaum ain vater vnser mocht sprechen das ich nu der orgel zuloset ich wil anderer andacht geschweygen vn sonderlich zu Strassburg wan sy mit den zincken schalmeyen vn mit d hortrumen oder baugken kamen so wolt ich lieber dantzet wan betet.'

38 See Friedrich Roth, 'Wer war Haug Marschalck gennant der Zoller von Augsburg?,' *BBKG*, 6 (1900), 229f., Otto Clemen, 'Haug Marschalck genannt Zoller von Augsburg,' *BBKG*, 4 (1898), 223f., and Adolf Laube et al., eds., *Flugschriften*, I, 150–151.

39 For a complete list of Haug Marschalck's works see bibliography, Printed Primary Sources. For convenience, his works are cited: *Trachtlein*, 1521; *Von dem Name Luther*, 1523; *Das Heilige Ewige Wort*, 1523; *Blindenspiegel*, 1523; *Die Scharf Metz*, 1525, in Otto Clemen, *Flugschriften aus den ersten Jahren der Reformation* (Halle, 1907), I, 94–130. A work entitled *Wer gern wolt wissen wie ich hiess* (Strasbourg, 1520), written by one Johann Schnewyl has been attributed to Marschalck, but the theological sophisitication of the text of this pamphlet is far beyond Marschalck's knowledge. The author of the work is familiar with scholastic theology at a level not evident in any of Marschalck's works. More likely from Marschalck is a work entitled: *Eyn hüpsch Cristliche// vnd Gotliche erinnerung vnd warnung-// so Kayserlicher Maiestat vo eynem//jren Kayserliche Maiestat ar//men Reuterlyn vnd vn//derthenigem diener beschicht.* (Strasbourg, 1521) in Hans-Joachim Köhler, et al., *Bibliographie der deutschen und lateinischen Flugschriften des frühen 16. Jahrhunderts* (Tübingen, 1978, test printing), 41. I include it among Marschalck's works citing it *Christliche Warnung*. cf. also Karl Schottenloher, *Philip Ulhart: Ein Augsburger Winkeldrucker und Helfershelfer der 'Schwärmer' und 'Wiedertäufer'*, (Nieuwkoop, 1967, reprint), 44f., and Fritz Redlich, *A German Military Enterpriser* (Wiesbaden, 1964–65), I, 42.

40 *Das Heilige Ewige Wort*: 'Ich armer unferstediger bewegt auss Christlichem gemudt...des edlen wort gots etlichen hochgelerten prediger alhie zu Augspurg nachgewander auss dere mund und leer ich den merentail dyss enpfagen un darbey aus irem willigen brüderlichn anzaigen in der geschryfft selbs auch nach gesucht.' Other pamphleteers mention returning home to look up biblical texts after sermons. Sebastian Lotzer did this. See Friedrich Dobel, *Memmingen im Reformationszeitalter*, 31.

41 *Blindenspiegel*: 'die rechten gottlichen instrumenten der Biblischen musick.'
42 *Ibid.*: 'ja wir spreche all wir seind gut Euangelisch, der titel were gut, es Bedarff aber einer guten hitz darbey die gat uns ab.'
43 cf. note 79.
44 *Ibid.*: 'yetzt in der blinden finstery der erden darein das liecht von dir geweltig angezündt wirdt.'
45 *Ibid.*: 'erkenner vnnd nachfolger deiner hymlischen lere...den widerstreßern deiner wort deiner eeren deiner glori.'
46 *Christliche Warnung*: 'Gott hat unss auss grosser syner barmhertzigkeit die augen auff gethan: das auch die kinder sehen mogten...so sehen wir das die Aposteln unseren herrn Cristum gesehen haben zu denen er gesprochen. Selig synt die di so sehent das ir sehent. u.'
47 *Blindenspiegel*: 'Nun sind sunst andere verstockte und gelsychtige mensche, die...vor der Warheit uffgehalten werden und der edlen nutzbarlichen Euangelischen Buchlin keins lesent...Nun werden wyr mit dieser unwissenheit zuletst nit entschuldigen mügen.'
48 *Ibid.*: 'durchachtet worden...unnd von einem ort zum andern vertriben umb der Euangelischen warheit willen.'
49 *Ibid.*: 'Die welt ist hart versticket in zeitliche wollust mit ubel gewinnung d zeitlichen guter mit Bosem gebracht mit unreyner hoffnug un ist alles mit Bosem geitz überleffen. Macher Beschwert und verderbt hart seinen eben meschen un christliche bruder dadurch er grossz gut zu im Bringt un uff ein hauffen zeuht darin er grossz sund wurckt...Dan es ist sunst ein weltlichs sprichwort, welicher am meysten betriegen kann, dan hellt ma für geschickt.'
50 *Ibid.*: 'Es sey die jugent yetzt, wie kleyn sye sey, so muss sye uffs kostlichst geziert sein...in grosser sund zu falle mit grosser hochfart mit unkeuscheit mit ungotzforchtigkeit. dan da weicht von uns alle demütigkeit, alle gedultigkeit, alle rechte erberkeit und alle bruderliche liebe.'
51 *Ibid.*: 'In solche kind un junge trage also die alte grossz gfalle dan sye verhenge kleine un grosseñ zu treibe was sye lust. un voruss mit kleyd eiden gewand un von gold über alle massz...' Marschalck disliked the introduction of Italian Renaissance fashion in Augsburg. In comparison with times past he states, 'das warlich die alten von uns nye haben düren gedecken.' He resented the fact that medieval clothing regulations among the various classes were not enforced.
52 *Ibid.*: 'Darnach wiltu dir selbs ein gedachtniss und spiegel in der kirchen uffrichten.'
53 *Ibid.*: 'Was wurckt es aber in der selbige? Es gaet ein yeder von solcher predig un disputatz wider heym...und was yeder für ein handel...vorlagher getriben hat, das treibt er fürhyn wie vor.'
54 *Ibid.*: 'Ein grosser teyl vom adel Behrumet sich auch gut euagelisch zu sein, sye richtet aber darbey grossz krieg uff und verderbet vil armer leut und machet grossz unsicherheit der strass.'
55 *Ibid.*: 'da kere dein messgewandt, dein kelch, dein kostliche tafelen, dein steynigreber und dein Epitahium hyn.'
56 *Ibid.*: 'Besorgt euch nit so hart ewer zeitlich Belonug zu verlieren.'
57 *Ibid.*: 'du solt den elenden herbergen den nackenden kleyden, den hungrigen und durstige speisen und trencken...unnd dyss daselbst mer auch Math am

xxiiii ca. wie er die sechs werck der heyligen Barmhertzigkeit so starck anzeucht und sogar streng wirt für sich nemen zu straffen.'

58 *Das Heilige Ewige Wort*: 'darumb lobedt er Magdalenam die ir seel mit dem wort gotes auss dem mund des herren waidnet un speyset un sprach Maria hat den bessern tail erwelt…sol wir mit Magdalenam zu den füssen Christi sitzen das wort gots fleyssigklich hören und all unnöttige sorg lassen faren. Christus bedarf unser unnöttigen sorg und unsers übrige gebrencks und umlaufens des gleisseden leychtens gar nit.' cf. Clarissa Atkinson, *Mystic and Pilgrim*, 132–133., also Victor Saxer, *Le culte de Marie Madeleine en occident, dès origines à la fin du moyen âge* (Paris, 1959), II, 132f.

59 *Ibid.*: 'das mancher durch seinen verfluchten geitz Besorgt zu verliere darin er empfindt in seiner gewissen gestrafft zu werden.'

60 *Ibid.*: 'Es were auch dem gemeynen menschen…stark zu hertzen vnnd in rechte verstentnuss komen.'

61 *Ibid.*: 'was bedarff er deines zelens und lesens, was bedarf er auch deiner wechsin kertzen mit denen du di wend und die hulzin Bilder Besudelst.'

62 *Blindenspiegel*: 'd heylig gottlich geist gross wurckug un arbeit volbringt un die schwache geist der mensche anrurt un zum teil entzündet, damit solich edel frucht ympflantzt wird un also still wurckt und ynfleusst.'

63 *Trachtlein*: 'Maria deiner wirdigen muter der rainen junckfraw beschahe die des glauBens vo erst auch mangelt und also gestarckt un im glauben bekrefftiget ward durch den heyligen Ertzengel Gabriel.'

64 *Ibid.*: 'O ein schoner lieblicher ein heyliger Reichstag des sich hymel und erden erfrewer haBen. Darauff ist kumen der Grossmechtig unuberwindtlicher Kayser der gewaltigst miltest und gutigst herr Verbu domini der ist kumen. Er kam in klainer menschlicher jugent auss der hohe des gottlichen Reichs…O du edles Verbu domini, bist du her auff diesen grossmechtige Reichstag zu herBerg gelegt welche fursten un mit was herlig kayt seind am ersten zu dir kumen, die disen hohen Reichstag bey dir vnnd mit dir haimgesucht haßen und die auch dein gewaltige Maiestat erkent haben.'

65 *Ibid.*: 'du grossmechtiger Kaiser du lieblicher Christus hast du diese zu dir auff einen Reichstag berufft, diese arme hyrten was wollen dann yetzt die grossen reichen hyrten der welt darbey abnemen…nun hastu ein andern Reichstag auff ain anere zeyt verkundt. O ein erschockenlichen strengen tag der letzten urtail.'

66 *Ibid.*: 'arme visher, wohnschlaker, teppichmacher frume handtwerker, groB ungelert leut.'

67 *Christliche Warnung*: 'O tugentlicher keyser dir wil auch gebüren den Babst vn die synen uss brüderlicher liebe zu diesem brunen zu leyten dem selbige kanstu mit grund d heilgen geschrifft anzeige das er warhafftig ein Vicary des teüfels vn Anticrist is vn das warhafftig die Bebstlich gesetz so durch die mensche ire kopff nach erdocht kein guten grunt haben vn das solichs nichts anders dan ein stinkend pffitz ist des tüfels.'

68 *Trachtlein*: 'so nym für dich die buchl…von rechte guten leer gemacht zu underrichten dem gemeynen lang verfürten hauffen…auch die Bibly…der recht brun der gottlich leer ist.'

69 *Blindenspiegel*: 'Es hilfft nit bucher lesen und predig horen allein und das selb feintlich loben un darin disputieren un vnsere zeitliche handlug danacht so

greuerlich übel brauch. wir mussen mit de hende den recht teyg auch starck angreifen. Was ist der recht teyg? Hab gott lieb uss ganzen hertzen, uss gatzer seel, uss gante gemut von deinem krefften und dem nechsten als dich selbs...wan wir das thund, so sind uns diese gute euangelische predig nutz und gut.'

70 *Die Scharf Metz*, 126, 1–9.
71 *Ibid.*, 105–106, 19–25, 1–9.
72 *Ibid.*, 111, 14–20.
73 *Trachtlein*: 'er vergifftet die hertzen der menschen unnd riss den Edelen hymlischen taw daraus sider dich.'
74 *Blindenspiegel*: 'gibt dir nun das dein natur yn, ach so nym die vernunfft deiner seelen und schaw und erfar und lyss was dir gott dein herz geben gethan... Nun nym dir yetzt in deiner vernunfft für die lieben christen mesch.'
75 *Das Heilige Ewige Wort*: 'Dyss hat er alles gethon damit er uns ain exempel geb dz wir auff menschlich wesen, mensch liebe vernunfft, menschlich vertrawen, menschliche erdychte gepot, menschliche Cerimonia, vn alles was nit den gepotn oder worten gots gemass ist unser hoffnung trost un beschyrmung der seel solten setzen besunder got in allendinge lassen wurcken vnd im die eer allain begehn.'
76 *Ibid.*: 'dartzu vnser fruch d glaubigen dirgird bey disem liepliche taw mit gotlicher feuchtikeit aufwachsen lassen, die selben pflantzen ym seyne vn behutn wie sol wir aber dise armensre pflantzug vn frucht beschirme un vor dem gewld bschodiger der seel verhütten.'
77 *Ibid.*: 'im allein vertrawen un sunst niemant dan in allein anruffen er allein wol uns helfen. wir bedurffen kains procurators vor im.'
78 *Ibid.*: 'Dan er hat nit allein in seine Leib gelitte für uns sonder leidet auch etlicher massz in unserem leib.'
79 *Trachtlein*: 'du liessest dich von der hohe unnd ergabst dich in disen armen iamertal zu wandern uns armen creaturn vor dem grimen grausamen tag der zahern zu warnen und die freud deiner grossen eren in deinem heyligen vaterlandt uns zu offenßaren und andern deinen nachfolgern und Befelchtragern zu underweysen weyter ausszuprayten und zu verkünden.'
80 *Die Scharf Metz*, 124, 6–12.
81 *Blindenspiegel*: 'viper nateren vnnd schlangen geschlecht...einfeltige schlechte hyrte welichs wolffs geschrey hat.'
82 *Ibid.*: 'O gysstigen verdapter pfennig die wurtzel ist vergyffts daruss du gewachsen bist.'
83 cf. Gerhard Ulhorn, ed., *Urbanus Rhegius, Leben und ausgewählte Schriften* (Elberfeld, 1861), 37; *Anzaygung das die Römische Bull mercklichen schaden in gewissen manicher menschen gebracht hat*, 1521: 'entweder der Papst schämt sich der heiligen Schrift oder erkennt sie nicht oder er will alles ohne Schrift mit seiner Gewalt thun. Er fürchtet die Schrift wie der Teufel das Kreutz. Wo er in die Schrift sieht, da sind alle Dinge wider ihn. Er findet Demütigkeit, Armuth, Verfolgung, predigen das Wort Gottes in widerwärtigen dingen, Gottes Lob, Kasteiung des Leibes, Hass dieser Welt, das ist ihm allzusammen zu wider, denn er sucht Reichtum, Glorie der Welt, gute Tag auf Erden.'
84 *Blindenspiegel*: 'Item nun sind sunst andere verstockte und geltsychtige

mensche auch mer die durch dise hye vorgenante geistliche vater mit lugen verfürt und vor der warheit uffgehalten werden.'

85   *Ibid.*: 'Der frum Bischoff Policarpus hatt Rom dem ketzer Ariu des teufels sun geheyssen auch die historien der heylige marterer sind um Christus willen die abgotter zerissen.'

86   *Trachtlein*: 'Lass unns nit fincken als Petrum...'

87   *Blindenspiegel*: 'Grossen prelate un Curtisane mussent sich bey iren vater armklich neere da sy nit gross titel mochtent haben und die zweyteyl holtzhacken oder schwere handwerck lerne, wo sye nit Bass studiere wollent den Bitzhar von in Beschen, dann warlich bey den grosten im titel ist die aller feichtest kunst im seiden kittel.' cf. Ernst Rhegius, ed. *Urbanus Rhegius, Deutsche Bücher und Schriften* (Nuremberg, 1562), xliii; *Ein Sermon vom dritten Gebott wie man Christlichss feyren soll mit anzeigung etlicher Miszbreuch gepredigt zu Hall im Intal*, 1522: 'Den es ist ein volck auf erden, die heissen Curtison, ist geschwind wo gelt stehet.'

88   *Blindenspiegel*: 'Die dann nit bestrafft wolten sein in irem yrthumb ires Bosen miszbrauchs das dan von ersten zymlich und freundtlich Beschach zu latein von den getrewen an sye dardurch es nit für den gemeyne leychen menschen ussgebreytet wurde.'

89   *Ibid.*: 'Des gleiche mer auch Den am xiij ca. vn Mat am v cap. wie gott der herr gar kein mensche gesatz nit under seine worte habe wil nit mit einem Buchstaben gemeret oder gemindert.'

90   *Trachtlein*: 'Wo sunst von menschen auffgerichtet gemacht zu dem word Gottes gehauffet und gesetzt ist, das ist nichts und gilt nichts un wirk und sol nichts bleyben.'

91   *Blindenspiegel*: 'des Euangelions eyn von ersten yber dise Wittebergische im anfang geschriben als menigklich weysset die sye gelesen hond, wie dan von den Romische gesellen Beschehen die dann nit gestrafft wolten sein in irem yrtumb ires Bosen misszbrauchs.'

92   *Ibid.*: 'Die selbigen mit ir arme kunst der mancher etwa wil pfrunde hat der nit ein halbe versehen künd. die setzent Vicari an ir stat und fordert so vil absentz das der vicar nit wol usskomen mag.'

93   *Ibid.*: 'mustent ir der meyst teil der schwein huten un tresche un zu acker gon oder entlauffen, damit wurde die arme menschen dester Bassz ernert werden.'

94   *Ibid.*: 'Ite so woll wir d Bischoff gar nit mer gedencke sye lesents gern od nit sye sind des schreibes und truckens gar zuvil mud worde.'

95   *Ibid.*: 'was ist yetzt in unserem tempel das man nit umb gelt verkaufft, un mit pfrunden und gots gaben verwechslet und vertauscht. Die juden verkaufften nur tauben...so verkauffent unsere seelsorger das horchwirdig sacrament den leib Christi und das heylig sacrament des tauffs und der bussz mit sampt dem hymel umb das schodgelt alle tag.'

96   *Ibid.*: 'Sunst mochten sye wol als dan Christus gethon hat ettwa vil vergeben und unnutz gebreng und heydnisch oder judisch gebreuch schelten und straffen.'

97   *Ibid.*: 'so wir ihn vil gelts gebe, so wollent sye uns mit Brieffen gen himel helfen und erledige die seele auch solle wir vil opffern.'

98 *Ibid.*: 'Item Matth. am xii capitel, Ich will die Barmhertzigkeit und nit das opffer. Un also da verstad ich nun wol was ich gott opfferen sol... Wan ich für mich oder yemants abgestorbnen wolt gott ein opffer uff den altar legen, aber es dem armen zugeben, dan ich wol verston das wil Gott und kein anders haben.'

99 *Ibid.*: 'also solen wir unser hertz im glauben anzunden für kertzen und sollen auch gedecken unsere hertze uffzuopfferren nit das die kertzen bey der messz zu noturfft un ere des heylige sacraments zu straffen seyend, aber sunst d Boss heydenisch und judisch missbruch.'

100 *Ibid.*: 'Gott wil dein gelt und gut nit von dir haben, er wil dein hertz und dein seel haben... Diss alles sollen wir wol bedencken wol zu hertze nemen und uns gantz in jnBilden mit Leib und mit seel.'

101 *Ibid.*: 'Sursum Corda. Gott d herr heysst euch nit schwere sorg in ewere hertze und gewissen leide. Wir sind alle blut und fleysch schwach creature nit müglich wir mussen im fleysch fallen aber mit der helf und dem geist gottes muge wir wider uffkomen.'

102 *Ibid.*: 'darumb hilfft uns nichts dann der starck krefftig glaub in jn. der selb wurckt darnach von im selbs. dan ein rechter glaub kan nit feyerer bringt all gut frucht un werck zu im.'

103 *Das Heilige Ewige Wort*: 'Gehailiget werde dein nam. O daz wir den guten gaist durch die gnad gottes in uns zehaben mochten erlangen, dz sein nam in uns gehailiget wurd so wurd wir unser lesstzen nimmer übelreden in kaine betriegliche lastern weder gege got noch wider unsern neben menschen dann nur allain daz lob gotts pflantzen. Als dan d 1. 48 psalm so schön auss streichtt lobend den herren von den himeln, lobend in in der hohe, all sein engel loben in, all sein krese lobend in, ir son vnd Mon all ir sternen und liecht vnd ir himel d himel lobend in u.'

104 *Trachtlein*: 'Besunder die raine keusche ausserwelt für alle Creaturn der erden Maria, ein arme tochter an zeytlichen gutern aber mer dan überflussig reich an eren an rainigkait tugent und heyligkait. Vnnd darzu mer ain armer zymmerman, Joseph auch reich von tugent rainigkait und heyligkait.'

105 *Ibid.*: 'Er hat sich verwiligt für uns zuleiden vnd zu sterben wz hat er uns zu aim erbteil hynder im verlassen sein zugedencken vns als seinen kinder vn erbn fürwar das aller edlest teurest erbtail vnd gut daz in himel vnd auf erden hat mugen sein; was ist nun das edel erbtail un gut das uns der getreuherr und vater gelassen hat? Es ist sein hailigster zarter leyb vn sein kosparlychs rosenfarbs blut wie hat er uns aber solichs verordnet anzunemen vnd zu enpfahen.'

106 *Ain kurtzer aber Christlich//er vnnd fast nutzlicher Sermon//von dem rechten waren/ vnd lebendigen//Glauben/ an den ainigen mitler vn//gnadenstul Christum. Durch Michel hug/ Lessmayster zu Lindaw bey den//Barfüssen// Geschikt an den Erberen//Haug Zoller zu Augsburg.* (1524) (SFB Zl, Nr. 10668)

107 *Ibid.*: 'Vnder andrem vil guts so ich von euch hor sagen wirt in sonderhait geprisen euwer sonder gunst fleyss vnnd eyfer des Euangeliums wollichs ich on sonder grosse freud nit schreyBen kann... Diser glaub aber von dem wir hie sagen ist nit ain lawer glaub oder ain Hystorischer glaub als wenn man ein Historei oder etwas sagt... Christus sagt was ir in meinem namen bittent

u. Nit in Sant Peters Niclaus Sebastians namen aber in meinem namen bitent...Der hailig gayst aBer durch die geschrifft weyset vns allain auff Christum von dem vn durch den vns alle ding vom vater zufliessenn des allain ist der preyss vnd herrlichkait in aller welt. Amen.'

108 Lionel Rothkrug, 'Popular Religion and Holy Shrines,' 38.
109 *Ibid.*, 26.
110 Friedwart Uhland, 'Täufertum und Obrigkeit in Augsburg', 69.

V: NUREMBERG: A SHOEMAKER, A PAINTER, AND AN INQUISITION

1 Rudolf Endres, 'Zur Lage der Nürnberger Handwerkerschaft zur Zeit von Hans Sachs,' *Jahrbuch für fränkische Landesforschung*, 37 (1977), 109. cf. E. Pitz, *Die Entstehung der Ratsherrschaft in Nürnberg im 13. und 14. Jahrhundert* (Munich, 1956), 155f., and Gerald Strauss, *Nuremberg in the Sixteenth Century* (Bloomington, Ind., 1966), vol. I, 85f.
2 Gerhard Pfeiffer, 'Das Verhältnis von politischer und kirchlicher Gemeinde in den deutschen Reichsstädten,' in W. Fuchs, ed., *Staat und Kirche im Wandel der Jahrhunderte* (Stuttgart, 1966), 79f.; the actual size of the city of Nuremberg in the sixteenth century is still a matter of dispute. cf. Gerald Strauss, *Nuremberg*, 36.
3 Rudolf Endres, 'Zur Einwohnerzahl und Bevölkerungsstruktur Nürnbergs im 15./16. Jahrhundert,' *MVGSN* 57 (1970), 249.
4 Rudolf Endres, 'Zur Lage der Nürnberger Handwerkerschaft,' 109.
5 Gerald Strauss, *Nuremberg*, 231f.
6 Rudolf Endres, 'Zur Einwohnerzahl und Bevölkerungsstruktur,' 255.
7 Rudolf Endres, 'Zur Lage der Nürnberger Handwerkerschaft,' 110.
8 Gerhard Pfeiffer, ed., *Nürnberg – Geschichte einer Europäischen Stadt* (Munich, 1971), 137f.
9 *Ibid.*, 140–141.
10 *Ibid.*, 146.
11 cf. Felix Streit, *Christoph Scheurl, Ratskonsulent von Nürnberg und seine Stellung zur Reformation* (Plauen i.V., 1908), 32.
12 cf. P. Drews, *Willibald Pirckheimers Stellung zur Reformation* (Leipzig, 1887), 87.
13 Gerhard Pfeiffer, *Nürnberg*, 147f.
14 *Ibid.*, 150.
15 *Ibid.*, 152.
16 *Ibid.*, 153.
17 Hermann Haupt, *Die religiösen Sekten in Franken vor der Reformation* (Würzburg, 1882), 19.
18 *Ibid.*, 36.
19 *Ibid.*, 46.
20 *Ibid.*, 47.
21 Theodor Kolde, 'Hans Denck und die gottlosen Mahler von Nürnberg,' *BBKG*, 8 (1902), 7.
22 *Ibid.*, 8.
23 Gerhard Pfeiffer, *Nürnberg*, 155.

24 Erich Maschke, 'Deutsche Städte,' 7.
25 See D. Wünsch, 'Schriften zum Fall Greiffenberger,' in G. Müller, ed. *Osianders Werke* (Gütersloh, 1975), I, 268, n5: 'Zwar wird in dem Büchlein *Die falsche Propheten* der Kelch als Zeichen der Zusage Christi apostrophiert, aber das schliesst ja die Realpräsenz keineswegs aus (vgl. Osianders *Kurzer Begriff*). Vielmehr deutet die in gleichem Zusammenhang geschehene Erwähnung des "kelches des Blutes Christi" darauf hin, das Greiffenberger hier noch ganz "korrekt" über das Abendmahl dachte.' After January 1525, Wünsch calls Greiffenberg the first disciple of Carlstadt in Nuremberg, cf. 272.
26 See Gerhard Pfeiffer, *Quellen zur Geschichte der Reformation in Nürnberg* (Nuremberg, 1977), Nr. 66, 298.
27 See Theodor Kolde, 'Hans Denck,' 31.
28 *Ibid.*, 4.
29 Werner Packull, *Mysticism and the Early...Anabaptist Movement*, 49.
30 Theodor Kolde, 'Hans Denck,' 58.
31 Werner Packull, *Mysticism and the Early...Anabaptist Movement*, 35f.
32 See Hans Dieter Schmidt, *Täufertum und Obrigket in Nürnberg* (Nuremberg, 1972), 6f.
33 Theodor Kolde, 'Hans Denck,' 66.
34 Wilhelm Reindell, ed., *Wenzel Lincks Werke* (Marburg, 1894), I, 78–79.
35 Theodor Kolde, 'Hans Denck,' 70.
36 For complete citations of Greiffenberger's works, see bibliography, Printed Primary Sources. For convenience sake, they have been cited: *Die Welt sagt sie sehe keine Besserung*, 1523; *Dieses Büchlein sagt von den falschen Kamesierern*, 1523; *Eine Christliche Antwort*, 1524; *Eine Warnung*, 1524; *Eine tröstliche Ermahnung*, 1524; *Ein kurtzer Begriff von guten Werken*, 1524; *Dieses Büchlein zeigt die falschen Propheten an*, 1524.
37 *Die Welt sagt sie sehe keine Besserung*: 'darauff ich fürgenummen mit der gnad Christi meines gottes ein wenig unterricht zu geBen was die recht warhaffte Besserung eines menschen sey der widerumB geBoren wirdt auss dem geyst der Wahrheit wie Cristus sagt Johannis am iij.'
38 *Ibid.*: 'O hie es ist yetzt ein seltzams ding man darff nit mer Betten vnd in kirchen geen vnd darff nit mer fasten man hat genug am glauBen man darff gar nichts guttes mer thun.'
39 *Ibid.*: 'Wiewol etlich gelert sagen der gemain man sol nit mit der geschrifft umB geen wan es zimB sich nit das ein Schuster das Ewagelion less oder mit feder vnd tinckten vmB gee sunder mit leder vnd schwertz...Blodern wissen nit was.'
40 *Ibid.*: 'sie sauffen fressen vnd Buben aber gleich als vor. das ist kain Besserung vnd seind erger dan vor. vrsach sie verachten vnd spotten aller der die noch nit ledig seind mit den sie sollen ein mitleyden haben.'
41 *Ibid.*: 'Der is auch nit geBessert der ein handel hat oder ein hatdtwerck damit sein nechsten Betrogen oder verergert wirt vnd nit darvon leBt wie etliche thun als Bildschnitzer Maler vnnd Forumbschneyder etc. Ey sagen die gelten die heyligen nicht so wil ich huren vnd Buben machen ob dei gelt gulten. das ist falsch vnnd unchristlich.'
42 *Ibid.*: 'DarumB sol ein yegklich Christenmensch sich tag vn nach üBen im

gesatz vnd wort gottes...Lieben Brüder in Christo. lasst uns got anrüffen (im geyst vnd in der warhait) das er uns mittail sein krafft an vnsere erlösung das wir die frölich leyden nach gottes willen. Amen.'

43 *Dieses Büchlein sagt von den falschen Kamesierern*: 'darauff merck du einfaltigs hertz was des Anticrists volckh gelernet hab vnd merck wer die dasigen seind die zinss güllt heüser der wittib vnd waysen fressen...nur Munch vnd pfaffen vnd petschwestern ich will aber nicht jr brueder sein oder tayl mit jnen haben.'

44 *Ein kurzer Begriff von guten Werken*: 'schau nur auf sein nechsten vnd lebendigen hailigen mit liecht vn klaidern. er soll vn darff nit mer.'

45 *Eine christliche Antwort*: 'Ja kein hertz oder gemüt mag sich des wort gotes oder handels verston. Es werd dann von got erleüchtet vnd gelert. Da aber das geschicht so wirt der mensch also sicher vnd dapffer auff das wort gotes hyn.'

46 *Eine tröstliche Ermahnung*: 'Auch got was haben wir gesucht dardurch wir die sünd hond büssen vnd bössern wollen. Hetten wir Paulum vnd Petrum Johanem vn ander gehört so hetten wir Christum vnnd das Kreütz leernen erkennen vnd es lieB gehabt. So haBen wir alle hailigen angerufft das das kreütz nur fern von vnns Bleybe.'

47 *Ibid.*: 'Aber nach dem gaist wander ist so der mensch absagt seiner vernunft natur vnnd gut duncken vnd sein leben rycht nach gottes wort bevelch vnd lere.'

48 *Dieses Büchlein zeigt die falschen Propheten an*: 'Das hat der Sathan die beste ersehen vn hat im ain volck ausserkorn...in dem selben volck ain grossen aufgeblassen kunig ausserkorn vnd verschafft...das ist der war lebendig Antechrist der Bapst mit seinem hellischen gleyssenden schreyenden herr ...des verfluchte hayden Aristotles.'

49 *Ibid.*: 'Aber der antichrist hat von uns aufgehept das aller suessest joch Christi vn hat vns dafür auffgeladen schwerer bürd die alle dienen zu seyne geytz vn zu gefencknus unser ellenden gewissen, nemlich die haimliche beycht.'

50 *Ibid.*: 'O kum du hochgelopter künig Christus mit diener zukuft vn stuntz disen wüst.'

51 *Ibid.*: 'O du hailiger ma oder fraw oder juckfraw. O almechtiger got ich sag dir gross lob err und danck deyner hailigen gottlichen werck die du gewürkt hast in deine lieben hailigen. Ich bitt dich durch der lieb willen die du zu im od er zu dir gehapt hat woellest mir auch dein barmhertzigkeit mittaylen vn dein gnad in mr wirken das ich müg deiner glory würcken das der oder diser hailig gewürkt hat.'

52 *Ibid.*: 'aber es haben ettlich zwo zungen, ayne auff dem Predigstul vn ain andere in den hausern.'

53 *Ibid.*: 'Acht nit könig kayser oder antichrist die sagen wartet zum konzilin als oB sy alayn den hailig geist haben...Dan ist namlich nit der Turck wie man yetz sagt vn sy bleren auff dem predigstulen der Antechrist... aber nemlich Bischöff, fürsten, pfaffen, pfarrer, münch.'

54 Theodor Kolde, 'Hans Denck,' 71. cf. Adolf Laube, et al., eds., *Flugschriften*, I, 268.

55 Ludwig Keller, 'Aus den Anfangsjahren der Reformation,' *Monatshefte der Comenius-Gesellschaft*, 8 (1899), 177.

56 A. Keller, E. Goetze, eds., *Hans Sachsens Werke* (Tübingen, 1870–1902), 21, 337, 1–2: 'Beschluss inn dises funffte und letzte buch. *Summa all meiner gedicht vom MDXIIII jar an biss ins 1567 jar.*' Keller–Goetze's critical edition of Hans Sachs' works is cited *SW* hereafter.

57 Klaus Leder, *Kirche und Jugend in Nürnberg und seinem Landgebiet, 1400–1800*, *EKB*, 52 (1966), 15f. See also Otto Barthel, *Die Schulen in Nürnberg, 1905–1960, mit Einführung in die Gesamtgeschichte* (Nuremberg, 1964), 25f.

58 Sachs described his *Wanderjahre* in *Summa all meiner gedicht, SW*, XXI, 338, 7–14. He describes many places he had visited, which scholars find to be exaggerated, cf. *ADB*, XXX, 114f.

59 Barbara Könneker, *Hans Sachs* (Stuttgart, 1971), 2.

60 Emil Weller, *Der Volksdichter Hans Sachs und seine Dichtungen* (Nuremberg, 1966, reprint) appendix, arranged by E. Carlsonn, 'Die Bibliothek Hans Sachs.'

61 The book of bound pamphlets contained this inscription: 'Diese püchlein hab ich Hans Sachs also gesamelt, got und seinem war zw eren vnd dem nechsten zu guet anpünden lassen, als man zelt nach Christi gepurt 1522 jar.,' *SW*, XXV, 9.

62 Siegfried Wernicke, 'Die Prosadialoge des Hans Sachs' (Dissertation, Berlin, 1913), 21f. cf. Bernd Balzer, *Bürgerliche Reformationspropaganda*, 112, 120, 130.

63 See Otto Clemen, 'Die Papstweissagungen des Abts Joachim von Flora,' *ZKG*, 48 (1929), 372f.; Gottfried Seebass, *Das reformatorische Werk des Andreas Osiander*, *EKB* (Nuremberg, 1967), 99f.; Marjorie Reeves, 'Some Popular Prophecies from the Fourteenth to the Seventeenth Centuries,' in G. J. Cuming and Derek Baker, eds., *Popular Belief and Practice* (Cambridge, 1972), 107f.

64 Otto Clemen, 'Die Papstweissagungen,' 375.

65 *Ibid.*, 378.

66 *SW*, VI, 368, 7–11.

67 Ingeborg Spriewald, ed., *Die Prosadialoge des Hans Sachs* (Leipzig, 1970), 25: '...aber es ist das Charakteristische seines dritten Dialogs, dass er in der Schärfe der Anprangerung sozialer Unterdrückung und Ungerechtigkeit die Nähe sozial–politischer Unruhen in der Bevölkerung Nürnberg deutlich spüren lässt.'

68 Joseph Beifus, 'Hans Sachs und die Reformation bis zum Tode Luthers,' *MVGSN*, 19 (1911), 12: 'Er suchte nach Art der Mystiker mit denen er sich angelegentlich beschäftigt hatte, Gott mit dem Gemüt zu erfassen. Die Formel der lutherischen Lehre, Rechtfertigung durch den Glauben allein, widersprach ihm.'

69 *SW*, XXIII, 14, 24–34.

70 Bernd Balzer, *Bürgerliche Reformationspropaganda*, 137–38.

71 *SW*, XXII, 94, 1–11.

72 *SW*, XXV, Nr. 227a.

73 Joseph Beifus, 'Hans Sachs', 23: 'Er erklärt, dass alle Werke, Fasten, Beichten, Kutte, Platte, Strick, ohne Bedeutung seien, allein die Werke der Liebe, die da dem Glauben entspringen, seien Christo angenehm.'

74 *SW*, VI, 373, 5–13. cf. Bernd Balzer, *Bürgerliche Reformationspropaganda*, 79f.

75 *SW*, VI, 835–836, 34–35, 1–6.
76 Gerhard Müller, ed., *Osianders Werke*, I, 320, 15–20.
77 Otto Clemen, 'Die Papstweissagungen,' 377.
78 Gottfried Seebass, *Das reformatorische Werk des Andreas Osiander*, 15.
79 *SW*, XXII, 135, 26–35.
80 The four dialogues are cited Dialogue I, II, III, IV. For complete citations see
    bibliography, Printed Primary Sources. In my collection I have another
    dialogue, published anonymously, which may have been one of the original
    seven: *Dialogus von der//zwitrachtung de hayligen// Christlichen glaubens new-
    lich// entstanden/ darum der men=//sch vnderricht virt/ wie er// sich in denen
    vnnd an=//dern yrrtumben//halten sol.* (SFB Zl, Nr. 3182) cf. Bernd Balzer,
    Bürgerliche Reformationspropaganda, 99, G. Niemann, 'Die Dialogliteratur der
    Reformationszeit nach ihrer Entstehung und Entwicklung' (Dissertation,
    Leipzig, 1905), 84f., and Werner Lenk, *Die Reformation im zeitgenössischen
    Dialog* (Berlin, 1968), 9f.
81 *SW*, XXII, 51, 17–21.
82 *Ibid.*, 76, 31–34.
83 Siegfried Wernicke, 'Die Prosadialoge des Hans Sachs', 25. The exact citation
    count for the dialogues is: Matthew, 58 times; Luke, 46 times; John 48 times;
    I Corinthians, 27 times; Romans, 22 times; Everything else is cited less than
    ten times, Mark's gospel only eight times.
84 *SW*, I, 301–302, 24–30, 1.
85 *SW*, VI, 370–371, 40, 1–9.
86 *Ibid.*, 371, 12–16.
87 *Ibid.*, 371, 19–30.
88 *Ibid.*, 372–373, 33–40, 1–6.
89 *Ibid.*, 372, 7–11.
90 *SW*, XXII, 24, 17–34.
91 *Ibid.*, XXIII, 22–23.
92 Gottfried Seebass, *Das reformatorische Werk des Andreas Osiander*, 7.
93 *SW*, XXII, 36–37, 23–30, 11–14.
94 *Ibid.*, 38–39, 34–35, 1–2.
95 *Ibid.*, 47, 5–8.
96 *Ibid.*, 50, 11–14.
97 *SW*, VI, 375, 1–8.
98 *SW*, XXII, 18, 22, 16–17, 24–26.
99 *SW*, VI, 377, 20–21.
100 *Ibid.*, 377, 26–30.
101 *Ibid.*, 378, 15–24.
102 *Ibid.*, 379, 1–2.
103 *Ibid.*, 376, 34–40.
104 *SW*, XXII, 78, 11–14.
105 *Ibid.*, 80, 19–20.
106 *Ibid.*, 65, 10–14.
107 *SW*, VI, 377, 18–19.
108 *Ibid.*, 379, 23–24.
109 *SW*, XXII, 72, 22–25.

110 SW, I, 395, 27–29.
111 Ibid., 396, 7–10.
112 SW, XXII, 10–11, 29–35, 1–13.
113 Ibid., 13, 12–14.
114 Ibid., 14, 27–29.
115 Siegfried Wernicke, 'Die Prosadialoge des Hans Sachs', 48., also W. Kawerau, Hans Sachs und die Reformation, SVRG, 26 (1889), 34.
116 Bernd Balzer, Bürgerliche Reformationspropaganda, 128–129.
117 W. Kawerau, Hans Sachs, 62–65.
118 Josef Beifus, Hans Sachs, 10–13.
119 Siegfried Wernicke, 'Die Prosadialoge des Hans Sachs', 48.
120 Ingeborg Spriewald, 'Die Prosadialoge des Hans Sachs', 26–27.
121 Bernd Balzer, Bürgerliche Reformationspropaganda, 132.
122 SW, XXII, 79, 10–19.
123 Ibid., 70–70, 32–35, 34–35.
124 Ibid., 77, 19–23.
125 Bernd Balzer, Bürgerliche Reformationspropaganda, 136.
126 See Gerald Strauss, ed., Manifestations of Discontent in Germany on the Eve of the Reformation (Bloomington, Ind., 1971), 3f.
127 Ibid., 138.
128 Joseph Lortz, Die Reformation in Deutschland (Freiburg i. Br., 1962) I, 201–210.
129 See Bernd Balzer, Bürgerliche Reformationspropaganda, 130.
130 Erich Maschke, 'Deutsche Städte,' 22.
131 John Dahmus, 'Preaching to the Laity in Fifteenth Century Germany: Johannes Nider's "Harps,"' Journal of Ecclesiastical History, 34 (1983), 66f. cf. Bernd Hamm, Frömmigkeitstheologie am Anfang des 16. Jahrhunderts (Tübingen, 1982), 146f.
132 Werner Packull, Mysticism and the Early...Anabaptist Movement, 18.

VI: FEMALE PAMPHLETEERS: THE HOUSEWIVES STRIKE BACK

1 cf. Clarissa Atkinson, Mystic and Pilgrim, 159f.
2 WA 10 III, 522, 31–34: 'Und zuletzt die Weiber auch wolten solch recht haben als 'die sitzerin' und die menner heissen schweigen, darnach immer ein weib das ander. O welch ein schöne kirchwey, dretzschmer und jarmarkt solt da werden!'
3 Bernard Vogler, 'Vie religieuse en pays Rhénan dans la seconde moitié du XVIᵉ siècle, 1556–1619' (Dissertation, Paris, 1972), I, 280f.
4 Richard Kieckhefer, Repression of Heresy in Medieval Germany, 105f.
5 Dorothy Latz, 'Feminine Lay Evangelism in Northern Italy: St. Angela Merici and Others.' (Unpublished paper given at the Sixteenth Century Studies Conference, Milwaukee, Wisconsin, 28 October 1983.)
6 Caroline Bynum, Jesus as Mother, 172.
7 Ibid., 250.
8 Clarissa Atkinson, Mystic and Pilgrim, 188.
9 Rolf Engelsing, Der Bürger als Leser, 10.
10 Lionel Rothkrug, 'Popular Religion and Holy Shrines,' 71.

11 *Ibid.*, 72.

12 *Ibid.*, 79.

13 *FrawenBiechlin// Zu rum vnd breyse allen tugentsa=//men auch erBeren weybern ist dises Tractet=//lin auss vorschrifft des hayligen wortt//gotes zusamen gebracht// vnd verfasset.* (Vienna, Nationalbibliothek, Nr. 78. R. 64. inc.)

14 Robert Stupperich, 'Die Frau in der Publizistik der Reformation,' *Archiv für Kulturgeschichte*, 37 (1955), 210.

15 A. Goetze, ed., *Sebastian Lotzers Schriften*, 76, 41–46.

16 Theodor Kolde, 'Arsacius Seehofer und Argula von Grumbach,' *BBKG*, 11 (1905), 64, and G. Müller, ed., *Osianders Werke*, I, 260.

17 Theodor Kolde, 'Arsacius Seehofer und Argula von Grumbach,' 60. The Duchess Kunigund was the sister of the Emperor Maximilian, to whom Staupitz dedicated his *Sermons on the Love of God* in 1518.

18 *Wie eine Christliche Frau des Adels in Bayern*: 'der Bibel...Wöliche mir mein lieber her vater so hoch bevalch zu lesen un gab mir dieselbig da ich zehen jar alt was habe jm aber layder nitt gevolgt auss verfürung der gaystlichen genanten sunderlich observantzer sagten ich verfuert mich.' Roland Bainton identified the edition of the bible as the 1483 Koburg edition. See Roland Bainton, *Women of the Reformation in Germany and Italy* (Boston, 1971), 98.

19 Theodor Kolde, 'Arsacius Seehofer und Argula von Grumbach,' 60, n5.

20 *Ibid.*, 64, n3.

21 *Ibid.*, 71f.

22 Heiko Oberman, *Masters of the Reformation* (Cambridge, 1981), 196, n28.

23 Theodor Kolde, 'Arsacius Seehofer und Argula von Grumbach,' 58.

24 *Ibid.*, 59.

25 Argula Von Grumbach published eight pamphlets. For full citations, see bibliography, Printed Primary Sources. For convenience sake they are cited: *Wie eine Christliche Frau*, 1523; *Eine Christliche Schrift*, 1523; *An den Rat zu Ingolstadt*, 1523; *An Friedrich von Sachsen*, 1523; *An den Pfalzgrafen*, 1523; *An Adam von Törring*, 1523; *Eine Antwort in Gedichtsweise*, 1524; *An den Rat zu Regensburg*, 1524.

26 *Wie eine Christliche Frau*: 'Soche wort von Gott selbs geredt seynd mir allzeyt vor meinen augen. Dan es werden weder frawen noch mann darinne ausgeschlossen...bin doch auf kainer hohenschul gewest...Ich kan kain Latein aber ir kündet Teutsch in diser zung geborn vnd erzogen...nun ich aber in mier art kain man sehe der reden wil noch darff dungt mich der spruch, Wer mich bekent wie ob angezaygt Vn nym für mich Psa. 3, Ich schick in kinder zu fürsten vnd weyber oder weybisch weren sy beherschen...Ich bit euch vnd begere Antwurt ob jr vermaynt das ich irret das ich ye nit waiss. Dann Jheronymus zu Plessila Paula Eutochia u. Ja Christus selbs hat sich nit geschempt sunder gepredigt Marie Magdalene dem frewlin bey dem brunne woelcher allain vnser aller mayster ist.'

27 *Ibid.*: 'Mich erbarmen vnsere fürsten, dass ir sy so jamerlich verfuert vn betrügt...Ist es darumb beschen das sy offt ain armen reich gemacht haben vnder euch was zeycht ir sy doch das ir sy vnd dise ire loblich gestiffte vniversitet also zu nachred der ganzen welt machent. aber ains habt ir

vergessen das er ist bey achtzehen jaren vnnd noch ain kind ander werns nit vergessen.'

28 *Ibid.*: 'Vn obgleich darzu kem davor gott sey das Luther widerrufft soll es mir nichts zu schaffen geben. Ich baw nit auff sein mein oder kaines menschen verstand sonder auff den waren felsen Christum selbs wolchen die Bawmayster haben verworffen...Jetzt aber nit von den Remischen Kirchen von vollicher Romischen kirchen ich kain wort in der Bibel fynd...Ich hab in den historien der hayligen gelesen das sy am maysten von derselbigen versamlung gemartert seynd worden.'

29 *Ibid.*: 'Ich habe euch nit weybs teding geschribe sunder das wort gotes als ain gelyd der Christlichen kirche vor wolcher die pforten der hell nit besteen mogen. Aber vor Romischen besteen sy wol.'

30 *Eine Christliche Schrift*: 'Wolt got es liessen sich die fürsten vn herren die gaystlichen genant nit lenger am affensayl fieren E. f. G. sunder wolt ain Turcken steuer so E. f. G. verordne wurde bey allen styfften Clostern auch Pfarren vnd Messen die Register auffzuheben ire leut die jnen zynss und gult geben in die gericht zu komen darin sy ligen vnd aygentlich ir vermogen erfaren hetten sy zu vil das man es an ainem gemain nutz brauchet. Der schwayss der armen wurt in aller dienstparkait des Teuffels verzert. Gestattet nit die schinderey der Absens dann man sich das sy die Pfarren auffs genawest verdingen das sich die so die herd Christi wayden sollen des hungers kaum erweren seynd auch selten mitt geschickten besetz dem lauter Narren die nichts kunnen nur auffs wolfaylist gedinget. Der freyberger Pfarrer zu Voburg hat mer dann achthundert gulden von Pfruenden that ain gaz jar kain Predig.'

31 *Ibid.*: 'Es ist gleych so ich gelobet keuschait als ich belob mit ainem finger an hymel zu rieren oder zu flyegen das steet nit in des mensche gewalt.'

32 *An den Rat zu Ingolstadt*: 'So geschech mir auch wie gott will hätte den Tod seines Namens willen zu leyden wurden gar vil hertzen dardurch erwekt ja wan ich allain schrib wurden hundert weyber wide zy schreiben...Wan ich sterbe bleibet das Wort in ewigekeyt.'

33 Theodor Kolde, 'Arsacius Seehofer und Argula von Grumbach,' 101.

34 *An Friedrich von Sachsen*: 'Geben damit das wort gottes den armen wider gepredigt vnd nit als ellendigklich mit gewalt durch etliche haydnischen fürsten verboten vnd den armen entzuckt wolch yetz auff ain news Christum creutzigen vnd veruolgen.'

35 *An Adam von Törring*: 'man hayst mich Lutherisch ich bin es aber nicht ich bin im namen Christus getaufft den beken ich vnd nit Luther aber ich benene das in Martinus auch als ein getrewer Christ bekent.'

36 cf. Roland Bainton, *Women of the Reformation*, 104–105.

37 *An den Rat zu Regensburg*: 'Nemet war der seelen in ewrem gepiet nicht mit silBer oder Goldt erkaufft sonder mit eynem theuren wehrt des rosenfarBen bluts des herren Jesu.'

38 *Ein Spruch von der Staufferin Ires disputierens halben* (Munich, 1524), cited in Theodor Kolde, 'Arsacius Seehofer und Argula von Grumbach,' 107.

39 *Eine Antwort in Gedichtsweise* : 'Johelis an dem andern stat, DaselBst findt jr also daruon, Nicht aussgeschlossen weiB noch man, Wie got sein gayst aussgiessen woll, Auff alles flaischs nit dass er stoll, Sein Gayst so in ain engen

stall, So ainer nur ain Blatten mal, Er das soll nur allayn verstan, Got redt gar vil anders daruon, Ewr son vnd dochter maydt vnd knecht Wern weyssagen lest die schrifft recht...Ist baur weib hie geschlossen daruon Zaigt mir wo findt jrs geschriben stan, Wer seind doch die Aposteln gewesen, Wo hands in hohenschulen gelesen, Joannes auch ain fischer war, der doch ye schreibt so hoch vnd klar...Dyser mayster von hohen synnen, Will mich lern hauszhaben vnd spinnen, Thu doch täglichs darmit vmbgan, Daz ichs nit wol vergessen kan, Auch Christus mir dabey erzelt, Sein wort zuhörn seysz best erwelt.'

40 *Ibid.*: 'So gebt vns auch noch ayn beschaydt, Zu dienen in gehorsamkayt, Vnd unser mann halten in eern, Es wer mir layd solt ichs verkern...Fidt ich Matthei gschriben stan, Am zehenden da lest daruon, Ja dasz wir miesten tretten ab, Von kindt, hausz, hoff, vnd was ich hab, Wers vm in liebt steet gar frey, Derselbig sein nit wirdig sey, So ich gotszwort verlaugnen solt, Ee ich das alles verlassen wolt, Ja leyb vn leben ergeben frey, Da mir mein seel nit lieber sey, Dann mir ist auch mein herr vnd got.'

41 Theodor Kolde, 'Arsacius Seehofer und Argula von Grumbach,' 170f.

42 Roland Bainton, *Women of the Reformation*, 108.

43 Otto Clemen, 'Die Schösserin von Eisenberg,' *Mitteilungen des Geschichts-und Alterthumsforschenden Vereins zu Eisenberg im Herzogtum Sachsen–Altenberg*, 13 (1898), 73.

44 Very little is known about Ursula Weyda beyond Clemen's article. Ursula Weyda wrote in response to a pamphlet entitled: *Verderbe vnd schade der Lande vnd leuthen am gut leybe, ehre vnd der selen seligkeit aus Lutherischen vnd seins anhangs lehre zugewant, durch Simonem Apt zu Begawe mit einhelliger seiner Bruder vorwilligug hirinnen Christlich angetzeigt vnd ausgedruckt.* (Leipzig, 1524). Apparently Ursula Weyda only composed one pamphlet in 1524. For a complete citation of that pamphlet, see bibliography, Printed Primary Sources. It is cited hereafter, *Wider das unchristliche Schreiben des Abts zu Pegau*, 1524.

45 *Wider das unchristliche Schreiben des Abts zu Pegau*: 'War nicht vom der nam des Apts zu Pegaw ausweyset, szo gedecht ich ein halpsynnich mensch guter bierbruder oder suns eyn vnuoschempter esels kopff als er den auch ist het es ertich...wie das du ein grober unverstendiger eselskopff bist vnd von der schrifft weniger weist den ein kue vom tantze...Meyn Apt dein buchlein das du wider Gotlich lere vnd das heylig Euangelium hast lassen ausgehe, ist mir auch zu handen kommen darin du reychlich eine vnverstand an tag gibst wie du in der schrift ya alss wenig weist alss ein grober vnbehawner klotz, hast du doch die schrift durch wuleth als eyn vnfeltige Saw...Es solt dich ye billich Eccius vnd sen angangt verstedigt gemacht haben die mehr kunst in eynem finger den du in leybe vn sele gehabt.'

46 *Ibid.*: 'Pfaffen und Münche...ohn Gotts wort allein mit eytel lauter lvege vn triege hadelt seyt alle betriege vorfüren un von der warheyt abwenden mit mehschlichen ertichten lügen dz tewer von Christo erkaufft volk Gottes... va wen der bapst die nohcht etwas getreumet vn darnach auff den abet eyn bulla des abetsreffens drauss macht was den diss volck beschleust sol balde eyn artikel des glawbens seyn.'

47 *Ibid.*: 'das ist ds wir das lebendige gotlich wort lasse sollen welchs trencken ist vnd erquicken die geengsten gewissen vnd von sunden beladene hertzen vnnd vns selbs eyn erdichte weyss furfassen durch vnser gutduncken darmit vnser seele hertz vn gewissen zu stillen vermeynen...Lieber wie kan doch anderss dyn hertz ruhe finden wo du nich gegrundt bist auff gottes wort vnd eyn gewiss verzugnäss gottes in dir hast gedenckt doch deyn hertz altzeyt (wo nicht gottes Wort ist) ey wie wenns nichtt war were denn dihe der babst hats gelert, so ist der babst eiyn mensch kann irren verfuret werden vnd mit sich ander auch verfuren.'

48 *Ibid.*: 'O wolt nu Gott das solchs der Adel zuhertzen fasset vn so kinder vn freundt yn klöstern haben die mit grosser gefare der seligkeit drinnen sein.'

49 *Ibid.*: 'Hilf, hilf. es ist zeit das vnss gottes zorn nicht plotzlich vberfalle weil zu helffen ist...Send auss mein eydigen wesen vn stricke des teuffels darein du etwan gefallen erledigst du dich vn kerest wider zu deine rechten eyde vn gelubde vormals got in der tauff gethan darvon du gefallen warst. Den wir haben got eins alle sampt in der tauf gelobet seinen worte zu glauben vn zu volgen daran seine aile geistlichen meineydig worden vn mensch ya teuffels wesen angenomen wider yre eyde vn vorschwenung vn darneben die gantzen wolt vfüret...so pring mit freye sichern gewissen auss vn loss klosterplatten, kappe ligen vn angesehen ob du tausent eyde gethan hest.'

50 *Ibid.*: 'Es wan wid much noch pfaffe kinder gottes warnss dz ist kind d heilige gotzforchtige patriarche wie sie noch die Jude ein sundlich volk gotes nenne.'

51 The work, *Antwurt wider das vnchristlich Lesterbuch Ursula Weydyn der Schosserin zu Eysenbergk. Auch vom Glauben vnnd Tauff eyn gegrundt Schrift Göttlichs wort Belangen de Durch henricum P.V.H.*, is cited in Otto Clemen, 'Die Schösserin von Eisenberg,' 77.

52 The work, *Apologia Fur die Schösserin zu Eysenbergk. Auff das gotlose Büchlin so fur Ern Simo So sich schreybt von Gots vnd dess Römischen Stuls gnaden Apt zu Pegaw*, is cited in Otto Clemen, 'Die Schösserin von Eisenberg,' 78–79.

53 Otto Clemen, 'Die Schösserin von Eisenberg,' 81.

54 For a complete Catherine Schütz bibliography see André Séguenny, ed., *Bibliotheca Dissidentium* (Baden-Baden, 1980), in the series *Bibliotheca Bibliographica Aureliana*, 97–125. See also Miriam Chrisman, 'Women and the Reformation in Strasbourg, 1490–1530,' *ARG*, 63 (1972), 143–168, Roland Bainton, *Women of the Reformation*, 55f, and Y.M. Ehrismann, 'Catherine Schütz, une Strasbourgeoise, remarquable au presbytère de la cathédrale,' *Bulletin de la Société de l'Histoire du Protestantisme Français*, 104 (1958), 94–106. Catherine Schütz's works published in 1524 are cited for convenience sake: *Entschuldigung*, 1524; *An die Weiber zu Kenzingen*, 1524. For complete citations see bibliography, Printed Primary Sources.

55 *Entschuldigung*: 'dann sy nit anders sind dann des teüffels postbotten...doch dweil ein Bose leer schedlicher ist dann ein bos leben.'

56 *Ibid.*: 'Joannes Cocleus ich hett schir gesagt kochleffel. Dann er eben thut wie ein kochleffel der vil geklappers in einm leren hafen macht vnd doch aus bosem thanne holtz gemacht ist do man nit ein kynds bäpp mit rüren möcht.'

57 *Ibid.*: 'Und aber die ee...die wollen sy verdammen vnd pennigen und materen

aber die unkeüsch keüschheit die sündtflüssisches Sodomitische Moezytische hurery strafen sy nit und habents nie gestrafft sunder die beschirmt... Vn ob sich dan auch der selb empört vnd die fürsten diser welt zu hülff nimpt das wir also verjächt vnd den todt darüber müsten leiden... vnnd so wir leyden so leydet Christus in vns dan wir sein glider sind.'

58 Hermann Sussann, *Kenzingen in der Reformationszeit* (Kenzingen, 1888), 14f.
59 *An die Weiber zu Kenzingen*: 'Also thunt ir auch bitt ich euch ir redlichen glaubhaftigen weyber nemen an euch ein männisch Abrahamisch gemut, so ir also in notten seynd in allerley schmach vnnd leydungen darmit ir werden geschmecht es sey gleych mit dürnen halsseysen ertrencken vertreyben vn was der gleychen auch begegnen mag, ja so euch ewer man werden getodt vnd ir selb... wolt ich fraydiger hochfertiger vnd frölicher darin sein dann aller Adel in Strassburger Mess in iren gulden ketten vn halssbanden seind gewesen, ja froelicher darin ston dan so ich des Roemischen Kaysers weyb wer vnd in seiyner hoechsten Kayserlichen mayestat sitz sass... Treten ewer flaysch nyder auffheben ewrn gayst vn sprechend ewern mannen froelich zu vnd auch euch die wort Christi so er selber geredt hat... Vn wirst nit trauig sein an deiner witwenschaft... die eusserliche werck der lieb machen uns gewiss das wir glauben.'
60 Roland Bainton, *Women of the Reformation*, 63f.
61 Joseph Schmidt, *Lestern, lesen, lesen hören* (Bern, 1977).
62 Roland Bainton, *Women of the Reformation*, 68.
63 *Entschuldigung*: 'Sie widerfechten den glauben damit sye meinen jre eigen vn nit gotts gute werck.'
64 D. Weinstein and R. Bell, *Saints and Society*, 225.

CONCLUSIONS

1 Hans-Joachim Köhler, 'Fragestellungen,' 26–27.
2 Erich Maschke, 'Die Unterschichten der mittelälterlichen Städten Deutsch-lands,' 312f.
3 *Ibid.*, 357.
4 *WA*, 1, II, 108.
5 Karl Schottenloher, *Flugblatt und Zeitung*, 80.
6 Paola Zambelli, 'Fine del Mondo,' 303f.
7 *Ibid.*, 317f.
8 cf. Werner Packull, *Mysticism and the...Early Anabaptist Movement*, 33, and Raoul Manselli, *La 'Lectura Super Apocalipsim' di Pietro di Giovanni Olivi* (Rome, 1955), 133f.
9 cf. H. Öhler, 'Der Aufstand des Armen Konrad im Jahr 1514,' *Württem-bergische Vierteljahreshefte für Landesgeschichte*, 38 (1932), 401f.
10 Otthein Ramstedt, 'Stadtunruhen von 1525,' 255.
11 Thomas Brady, Jr., *Ruling Class, Regime and Reformation at Strasbourg, 1520–1555* (Leiden, 1978), 199.
12 Bernd Moeller, *Imperial Cities and the Reformation* (Durham, NC, 1982), 45.
13 Thomas Brady, Jr., *Ruling Class, Regime and Reformation*, 5.
14 Friedwart Uhland, 'Täufertum und Obrigkeit in Augsburg', 69.

15 Else Bernhofer-Pippert, *Täuferische Denkweisen und Lebensformen im Spiegel oberdeutscher Täuferverhöre* (Münster, 1976), 157–158, and Bernhard Lohse, 'Die Stellung der Schwärmer und Täufer in der Reformationsgeschichte,' *ARG*, 60 (1969), 15f.

16 Werner Packull, *Mysticism and the...Early Anabaptist Movement*, 19–20.

17 *Ibid.*, 19. cf. Steven Ozment, *Mysticism and Dissent* (New Haven, 1973), 15f., also Giles Constable, 'Twelfth-Century Spirituality and the late Middle Ages,' in O. B. Hardison, ed., *Medieval and Renaissance Studies*, 27f.

18 cf. Bernard McGinn, *Visions of the End*, 260f.

19 Werner Packull, *Mysticism and the...Early Anabaptist Movement*, 176–177.

20 Lionel Rothkrug, 'Popular Religion and Holy Shrines,' 79.

21 Clarissa Atkinson, *Mystic and Pilgrim*, 108–109.

22 Victor Saxer, *Le culte de Marie Madeleine en occident dès origines à la fin du moyen âge* (Paris, 1959), I, 85f.

23 Steven Ozment, *The Reformation in the Cities*, 49. cf. Peter Baumgart, 'Formen der Volksfrömmigkeit,' 186.

24 cf. Sigmund Freud, *Civilisation and its Discontents* (London, 1961), 70–75, and P. Russell, '"Your sons and your daughters shall prophesy..." (Joel 2:28) Common People and the Future of the Reformation,' 132–133.

25 Heiko Oberman, 'Gabriel Biel and Late Medieval Mysticism,' *Church History*, 30 (1961), 272.

26 cf. *Drey schön Sermo// gepredigt zu Born durch Doct≠//Martinum Luther alle from//en Christglaubigen men//schen nützlich vnd// fruchtbar zu// wissen.* (Strasbourg, 1524) (Vienna, Nationalbibliothek, Nr. FO III 32. inc.) especially the sermon preached at Borna, 27 April 1522.

27 Erich Maschke, 'Deutsche Städte,' 22.

28 Marjorie Reeves, *The Influence of Prophecy in the Later Middle Ages* (Oxford, 1969), 448–49.

29 Robert Muchembled, *Culture Populaire et Culture des Élites*, 137f.

30 cf. Steven Ozment, *The Age of Reform, 1250–1550* (New Haven, 1980), 5f.

31 See Monika Rössing-Hager, 'Wie Stark findet der nichtlesekundige Rezipient Berücksichtigung,' 135f. and Roberta Adamcyk, 'Die Flugschriften des Johann Eberlin von Günzburg' (Dissertation, Vienna, 1981) 110f.

32 cf. R. W. Scribner, 'Flugblatt und Analphabetentum,' 69f.

33 cf. Brian Pullan, 'Catholics and the Poor in Early Modern Europe,' *Transactions of the Royal Historical Society*, 26 (1976), 21.

Bibliography

PRINTED PRIMARY SOURCES

A. Pamphlets written by authors in this sample

N.B. An asterisk indicates an anonymously authored pamphlet, probably written by and listed under a pamphleteer in this sample.

Greiffenberger, Hans

Die Welt sagt sy sehe//kain besserung vonn den//die sy Luterische nennen// was besserung sey///ein wenig hierin//begriffen. M.D. XXiij. (SFB-ZL, Nr. 629)

Diss biechlin sagt von// den falschen Kamesierern/ die sich auss//thund vil guts mit fasten/peten///messlesen für anndre/auff das// jn der sack/tasch vol werd//achten nit wo die seelen hinfare. M.D. XXiiij. (SFB-ZL, Nr. 3261)

Ein Christliche Antwordt//denen/ die da sprechen/ das Euangelio// habsein krafft vo der kirchen [Ver=//legt] mit gotlicher geschriff/auff//das kürtzist/ zu trost den Chri=sten/ inn Christo. M.D. XXiiij. (SFB-ZL, Nr. 20523)

Ein warnug vo//dem Teüffel/ der sich wider//uBt mit seinem dendelmarckt/ vnter// einem gleissenden schein/in merck=//lichen stückenn/ des Christen=//lichen lebens betreffen. 1524 (Nuremberg, Stadtbibliothek, Nr. Theo. ZW 914. Nr. 29)

Ein trostliche ermanung// den angefochtn im gewissen/ von we=//gen gethoner sünd/ wye vn wa// mit/Sye getrost werden///Den Sathan/ sich nit// erschrecken las=//senn. u. 1524 (SFB-Zl, Nr. 3051)

Ein kurtzer begrif//von gutten werckenn/dye// gott behagen/ vn der wel// ain spot seynt/ yetzt ein gro=//se klag/ wye nyemat mer// guts thu/ vnd aller Gotz// syenst vndergee/wie sy// geduncktin jrem syn// Eyn antwurtt wz// gutte werck// seynd. M.D. XXiiij. (SFB-Zl, Nr. 3006)

Diss biechlin zaigt an die Falschen// Propheten/ vor den vnss gewarnet hat Christus/ Paulus// vn Petrus/ vn sindt darin/ was vn wie wir uns Chri//sten halten sollen/ yetz in diser geferlichen//zeyt/ auff das kürtzest begriffen/ gemacht durch hanns Greyffenberger zu Pfortzhaym. n.d., in H.–J. Köhler, et al., eds., *Sixteenth Century Pamphlets in German and Latin, 1501–1530*, (Zug, Switzerland), Fiche 255, Nr. 715.

Lotzer, Sebastian

Works listed may be found in *Sebastian Lotzers Schriften*, A. Goetze, ed., (Leipzig, 1902):

Ain hailsame Ermanuge an die ynwoner zu horw das sy bestendig beleyben an dem hailige wort Gottes mit anzaigug der göttlichen hailigen geschrift. 1523. 27–36.

Ain christlicher sendbrief darin angetzaigt wirt, dz die layen mach vnd recht haben von dem hailigen wort gots reden, lern vn schreibe auch von der speiss vn dgleichen ander artickel grud auss der götliche hailigen schrift vast haylsam vnnd fruchbar. 1523, 36–47.

Ayn auslegung über dz Euangelium so man lysst vn singt nach brauch d kyrchen am zwayvntzigstn Sontag nach d hayligen Triualtigkait, wöllichs beschreibt Matth. am xxij. Capit. von einem Künig so seinem Sun hochtzeyt zuberayt hett. 1524, 75–81.

Ain vast haylssam trostlich christlich unüberwynndlich beschyrmbüchlin, Auff ainvnddreyssig Artyckel, Auss götlicher hailiger geschrifft, des alten vnd newen Testaments gegründt, mit antzaigug der Capitel, vn underschid, zu nutz trost vn hail allen gelyebtten brüdern in Christo, auch zu widerstandt de vervolgern Götlichs worts. 1524, 47–75.

Entschuldigung ainer Frumen Christlichen Gemain zu Memmingen mit sampt irem Bischoff, vn trewen Botten des Herren Christoff Schappeler, Prediger alda. Von wegen der emporungen so sich bey vns begeben u. Im jar 1525, 82–86.

Die grundlichen vnd rechten Hauptartikel aller Bauerschaft vnd Hindersessen der gaistliche vnd weltlichen Oberkaiten von wölchen sie sich beschwert vermeinen. 1525, in *Quellen zur Geschichte des deutschen Bauernstandes in der Neuzeit*, Gunther Franz, ed., (Darmstadt, 1963), 11–15.

Marschalck, Haug, gennant 'der Zoller'

Eyn Edles/Schoner//lieblichs Tracterlein///von dem rainen/hymlischen//wort [*Verbum Domini*] *zu lob Got dem schopffer//hymels vn erden vn zu eeren dem Christlichen diener des Gottliche worts*. 1521 (Tübingen, Universitätsbibliothek, Nr. Gi 9, H0°)

Von dem weyt/erscholle//Name Luther// wz er bedeut vnnd wie er wirt missbraucht. //Er heyst nit der trüber/vil mer der lauterer// Er heisst auch nit der lotter// vil mer der bewerer (Strasbourg, 1523) (Tübingen, Universitätsbibliothek, Nr. Gi 88.9.J.°)

Der hailig ewig wort gots///was dz in Kraft/ stercke/tugent///frid/fred/ erleuchtung vnnd leben// in aym rechten/Christen/zuerwecken vermag// Zu gestelt dem edlen/ gestrengen/ Riter vn kaiserliche/hauptman//Herrn Jorgen von Fronnsperg zu Mundelhain. (Augsburg, 1523) (Augsburg, Staats- und Stadtbibliothek, Nr. 5 Aug 884)

Ein Spiegel der Plinden//wan Christus der her hat geredt// Ich wird mein glory von den/hochweisen verberge/vnd//wird es den kleine//verkünden vnd offbaren.// Dann ee mein glory vnd eer solt undergon//es musten die steyn vnd holtz/reden lernen. Uff solichs ist vff=//gericht anzuschauwe dises Spiegel der Blinden. 1523 (Tübingen, Universitätsbibliothek, Nr. Gi 29. 7.°)

Die Scharf Metz wider die, die sich evangelisch nennen und doch dem Evangelio entgegen sind. 1525 in *Flugschriften aus den ersten Jahren der Reformation*, Otto Clemen, ed., (Halle, 1907), I. 94–130.

Eyn hüpsch Cristliche// vnd Gotliche erinnerung vnd warnung-// so Kayserlicher Maiestat vo eynem//jren Kayserliche Maiestat ar//men Reuterlyn vnd vn//derthenigem diener beschicht. (Strasbourg, 1521) (SFB-Zl, Nr. 955)

Rychssner, Utz

> *Ayn Ausszug/ auss der// Cronicka d Bapst vn// iren gesatze/ wie gleych// formig sy de gesatze gots// vn leer der apostel seyen// zu vergleichen/ auff das// kürtzest vn ainfaltigest/ zusamengefugt.* 1524 (Augsburg, Staats- und Stadtbibliothek, Nr. 4 Aug. 1132)

> *Ain schone vnderweysung///wie vnd wirin Christo alle gebruder//vn schwester seyen/ dabey angezaigt// nicht allain die weltlichen/ wie sy es//nennen/ sonder auch die gaistlichen// zu straffen/ wa sy anders in der leybe// dessen haubt Christus ist wolle sein// auff die geschrift gotes gegründt// vn darauss gezoge/ zu nutz//alle die das gotlich wort//lieben seindt.* MDXXiiij. (Augsburg, Staats- und Stadtbibliothek, Nr. 1964. 2379)

> *Ain gesprech buchlin/ von ainem Weber// vnd ainem Krämer über das Buchlin Doctoris// Mathie Kretz von der haimlichen Beycht///so er zu Augspurg vnnser frawen//Thum gepredigt hat.* im M.D. XXiij. (Augsburg, Staats- und Stadtbibliothek, Nr. 4 Aug. 1136)

> *Ain hübsch Geprechbiechlein/ von aynem//Pfaffen vnd ainem Weber/ die zusamen kumen seind// auf der strass was sy für red/frag/vn antwort/ gegen// ainander gebraucht haben/ des Euangeliums vnd an=//derer sachen halben.* 1524. (SFB-Zl, Nr. 00983)

Sachs, Hans

Sachs' dialogues are found in *Hans Sachsens Werke,* A. Keller, E. Goetze, eds. (Tübingen, 1870–1902), vol. 21.

> *Disputacion zwischen ainem Chorherren vnd Schuchmacher Darin das wort gotes und ain rech Christlich wesen verfochten wirt.* 1524, 6–34.

> *Eyn gesprech von den Scheinwercken der gaystliche vnd iren gelübdten, damit sy zu verlesterung des bluts Christi vermaynen selig zu werden.* 1524, 34–50.

> *Ein dialogus des inhalt ein argument der Römischen wider das christliche heuflein, den geytz, auch ander offenlich laster usw. betreffend.* 1524, 51–68.

> *Eyn gesprech eynes evangelischen Christen mit einem Lutherischen, darin der ergerlich wandel etlicher die sich lutherisch nennen angezaigt vnd brüderlich gestrafft wirt.* 1524, 69–84.

> **Dialogus von der// zwitrachtung de hayligen// Christlichen glaubens newlich// entstanden/ darum der men=//sch vnderricht virt/ wie er// sich in denen vnnd an=//dern yrrtumben//halten sol.* (SFB-Zl, Nr. 3182)

Schütz, Catherine

> *Den leyden-//den Christglaubigen//weybern der gemain zu//Kentzingen meinen// mit schwestern in// Christo Jhesu//zu handen.* M.D. xxiiij. (SFB-Zl, Nr. 4269)

> *Entschuldig=//ung Catherina Schütz// inn/ für M. Matthes Zellen/ iren Eege=// gemahal/der ain Pfarrher vnd dyener ist im//wort Gottes zu Strassburg. Von wegen// grosser lügen vffin erdiecht.//Darin ettlich stoltze Sophisten angriffen// sein/als D. Murnar. D. Jo. Cocleus// Bruder Conrad Treger/Augu//stiner ordens Prouincial//so iüngst mit vil lüge//die Christlichen//prediger vnd stande hat//zu verunglimpffen.* n.d. (New Haven, Yale University Library)

on Stauffen, Argula

> *Wie ain Christliche fraw des//Adels/ in Bayern durch jren/ in Gotli=//cher schrift/ wolgegründte Sendt//brieffe/ die hohenschul zu Ingoldstat//vmb das sy aynen*

Ewangelischen Jüngling/ zu widersprechug des wort Gottes/ be=trangt haben/straffet.
(1523) (Augsburg, Staats- und Stadtbibliothek, Nr. XXXM e. 44°)

Ain Christenliche schrifft//ainer Erbarn frawen/ vom Adel//darin sy alle Christenliche
stendt//vnd obrikayten ermant/ Bey der warhait/ vn dem wort// Gottes zu bleyben/
vnd//solchs auss Christlicher//pflicht zu ernstlich=// sten zu handt=//haben. M.D.
xxiii. (SFB-Zl, Nr. 1521)

An ain Ersamen// Weysen Radt der stat// Ingolstat/ain sandt// brieff/ von Fraw
Argula von Grun//bach geborne//von Stauf//fen. (1523) (Augsburg, Staats- und
Stadtbibliothek, Nr. XXM e. 42. 131)

Dem Durchleüchtigisten hoch//gebornen Fürsten vnd herren/Herrn Fri=//derichen/
Hertzogen zu Sachssen/ Des//hayligen Romischen Reychs Ertz=//marschalck vnnd
Churfürsten///Landtgrauen in Düringen// vnnd Marggrauen zu// Meyssen/mey-
nem// Gnedigisten herren. Argula Staufferin. (1523) (SFB-Zl, Nr. 974)

Dem Durchleüchtigen Hochge//bornen Fürsten vnd herren/ Herrn Jo=//hansen/
Pfaltzgrauen bey Reyn/// Hertzoge zu Beyern/ Grafen// zu Spanhaym u. Mey=//nem
Gnedigisten//herren. Argula Stauferin. (1523) (SFB-Zl, 10734)

Ayn Antwort in//gedichtss weiss/ ainem auss d// hohen Schul zu Ingol=//stat/ auff
ainen spruch/// nerrlich vo jm auss// gagen/welcher// hynde dabey// getruckt//
steet. Anno M.D. XXiiij. (SFB-Zl, Nr. 10738)

An den Edlen// vnd gestrengen her// ren/Adam vo Thering//der Pfaltzgrauen stat//
halter zu Newburg//u. Ain sandtbrieff// vo fraw Argula// vo Grunbach// geborne
vo// Stauf=//fen. (1523) (Augsburg, Staat- und Stadtbibliothek, Nr. XXXM 3.
43)

Ein Sendbrief der edeln// frawen Argula Staufferin/ An di// von Regensburg. M.D.
xxiiij. (Vienna, Nationalbibliothek, Nr. 20 T. 494.)

Weyda, Ursula

Wyder das vnchristlich schreyben vn// Lesterbuch/ des Apts Simon zu Pegaw vnnd
seyner// Bruder. Durch Vrsula Weydin Schosserin zu// Eyssenbergk/ Eyn gegrundt
Christliche//schrift Gotlich wort vnnd Ehe=//lich leben belangende. (SFB-Zl, Nr.
988)

B. *Pamphlets by other possible lay pamphleteers*

Anonymous:

Ain Sendbrieff von// Ainer erbern frawen im Eelichen stat an ain Klosterfrawen/ gethon
über berummung ettlicher hayliger geschrifft// in Sermon begriffen./ So die
Klosterfraw verbrent/ vnd darauff// ain lange vngesaltzne geschrifft zu vrsach erzelt
hat u. n.d. (SFB-Zl, 3290)

FrawenBiechlin// Zu rum vnd breyse allen tugentsa=//men auch erBeren weybern ist
dises Tractet=//lin auss vorschrifft des hayligen wortt//gotes zusamen gebracht// vnd
verfasset. (Vienna, Nationalbibliothek, Nr. 78. R. 64. inc.)

Ain schöner//Dialogus von Marti=//no Luther vnd der ge=//schickten Botschafft aus
der//helle die falsche geistlichkeit//vnnd das wort gots be=//langen gantz hüb=//sch
zu lesen. Anno. M.D. XXiij. (SFB-Zl, 3005)

Ain schoner/ dialo//gus von zwayen gutten ge//sellen genant Hanns Tholl. vnnd Claus//
Lamp. sagendt vom Antechrist vnd seynen jungern. (SFB-Zl, 3179)

Füssli, Hans

Antwurt eins Schwy//tzer Purens/ über die vngegründte// geschrifft Meyster Jeronimi Geb=//wilers Schulmeisters zu Strass//burg/ die er zu Beschirmung der// Romischen Kilchen/ vnd jro// erdachten wesen/ hat las=sen vssgon. n.d. (Würzburg, Universitätsbibliothek, Nr. Th. dp. g. 864)

Gerhardt, Hans

Schone Frag vnd// Antwort/ Was ain warhafftiger Christenn// der recht Glaub/ vnnd seyn frucht sey// Idem die zehen gebot Gottes/ wie er sie dem// Moysi auff dem berg Sinay angeBen hatt// vnd das Vater vnser u. den Jungen//fast nutzlich. Hans Gerhardt, Wegmaister zu Kitzingen. M.D.XXV. (SFB-Zl, 4289)

Haug, Jörg

Ain Christlich//ordenung/ aines war=//hafftigen Christen/ zu// verantwurtten die// ankunfft seynes//glaubens. Jorg Haugk von Juchsen. (1526) (SFB-Zl, Nr. 361)

Peringer, Diepold

Ain Sermon gepredigt vom//Pawren zu Werdt/ bey Nürmberg/ am Sontag// vor fassnacht/ von dem freyen willen// des menschen/ auch von anruf=//fung der hailigen. (1524) (Nürnberg, Stadtbibliothek, Nr. 4° Th. 2061)

Des Christliche Bawern// getrewer Rath.// Wie die ChristglawBig seel ain gesprech// mit dem menschlichen flaysch taglich// halten/ vn betrachten soll. (1524) (SFB-Zl, Nr. 3307)

Ein Sermon//von der Abgotterey/ durch den//Pawern/der weder schreyben// noch lesen kan/gepredigt zu// Kitzingin Francken=//land auff vnsers herren Fronleych-nams tag. M.D. XXiiij. (Augsburg, Staats- und Stadtbibliothek, Nr. Th. 10. 40)

Schwalb, Hans

Beclagung eines Ley//ens genant hanns schwalb// über vil missbrauchs christenlichs// Lebens/vnd darin begriffen kurtzlich von//Johannes hussen. M.D. xxi (SFB-Zl, Nr, 7371)

Staygmeier, Hans

Ain kurtze vn=//derichtung von der// waren Christliche bru=//derschaft/allen Chri// stenlichen men=//sche ser nutz//lich zu lee=//sen. Hans Staygmayr zu Reytlingen. M.D. xxiiij. (SFB-Zl, Nr. 9261)

Ain Schoner Dialogus oder// Gesprech/ von aynem Münch vnd// Becken/ wolcher die Oster//ayer Samlen//wolt. hanns Staygmayer/ Beck zu Reytlingen (1524) (SFB-Zl, Nr. 981)

C. Works by theologians and other clerical reformers:

Erasmus of Rotterdam

Erasmi Roterdami Pa//racelsis Teütscht wie ein teüerlich vn=//ausprechlich schatz vnd klainer sey das Euan=//gelium vnd haylig wort gottes. (1522) (SFB-Zl, Nr. 407)

Hern Erasmi vo Roterdam//vormanung des heylige// Evangelin vnd der// heyligen zwelf=//bote schrifft//fleissig zu lesen// in kurtz verdeutscht. (1522) (Würzburg, Universitätsbibliothek, Nr. Th, dp. g. 423.)

Herr Erasmus von Ro//terdam/ verteutschte ausslegung/// über das gottlich trostlich wort// vnsers lieben herrn vnnd selig=//machers christi/ Nement auff// euch mein Joch vnd ler=//net von mir. (1521) (SFB-Zl, Nr. 2671)

Erasmus von Roterdam von der ver=//bothen speyss des// fleyschs. An den erwirde vn durch// lauchten firsten vn herrn// Christoff Bischoffen zu Basell//en verant-wortug Erasmi von Roterdam von verpotener speyss// des fleysches/ vnd von der gley=//chen aufsatzungen der menschen. (Leipzig, 1523) (Würzburg, Universitäts-bibliothek, Nr. 15a Th dp. 423.)

Herr Erasmus von Roterdams// verteütsche Auslegung über// dise wort sant Paulo zu den// von Corinth/ in der ersten Epistel am vierze=//tenden Capitel. Ich will lieber in meine// gemut fünff wortinn der kirchen reden// andere zu unterweysen/ dan zehen tausent wort mit der zungen. Von gesang (1521) (SFB-Zl, Nr. 1660)

Von Walfart//Erasmi Roterdami// vermanung wo Chri=//stus vnd sein reich// zu suchen ist. (1522) (SFB-Zl, Nr. 2805)

Her Erasmus von Ro=//terdam verteutschte ausslegung über// disen spruch Christi unsers herrn// Matthei um drey vnd zweintzigsten// Capitel/ vonn den Phariseyern/// sie thun alle ire werck/// das sie von den menschen// gesehen werden/ Vnd breyten ir gebortzedeln auss. Vom heyltumb. u. (1521) (SFB-Zl, Nr. 2670)

Herr Erasmus von Ro=//terdam verteutschte auslegung über// sant hieronymus Allegation/ was// guts die Philosophi in der heyligen// schrifft schaffen. (1521) (SFB-Zl, Nr. 2668)

Gerson, Jean, *Oeuvres complètes*, ed. Palemon Glorieux (Paris, 1961f.), 14 vols.

Günzburg, Johann Eberlin, ofm, *Sämtliche Werke*, ed. L. Enders (Halle, 1896), 3 vols.

Hug, Michael, ofm.

Ain Kurtzer aber Christlich//er vnnd fast nutzlicher Sermon//von dem rechten waren/ und lebendigen//Glauben/an den ainigen mitler vn//gnadenstul Christum. Durch Michel hug/Lessmayster zu Lindaw bey den//Barfüssen//Geschikt an den Erberen//Haug Zoller zu Augsburg. (1524) (SFB-Zl, 10668)

Linck, Wenzel, *Wenzel Lincks Werke*, ed. Wilhelm Reindell (Marburg, 1894)

Luther, Martin, *Martin Luthers Werke: Kritische Gesamtausgabe* (Weimar, 1883f.)

Olivi, Peter, ofm., *Lectura super Apocalipsim*, ed. Warren Lewis (Tübingen, 1972).

Otto von Passau, ofm., *Die Vier und zweintzig Alten* (ed., Dillingen, 1568) (Tübingen, Universitätsbibliothek, Nr. Gb 352.4°)

Osiander, Andreas, *Osianders Werke*, ed. G. Müller (Gütersloh, 1975f.) 4 vols. t.d.

Rhegius, Urbanus, *Deutsche Bücher und Schriften*, ed. Ernst Rhegius (Nuremberg, 1562).

Schappeler, Christoph

Verantwortug//vnd auflosung etlicher//vermainter Argument vnd ursachen So//zu widerstandt vnnd verdruckung des// Wort Gottes vnd hailigen Evan//gelions/ Von denen die nit Cris//sten sein vnd sich doch Chris//sten names rumen/tag//lich gebraucht// werden. (1524) (SFB-Zl, Nr. 3013.)

Zwingli, Ulrich

Zwingli Werke, ed. M. Schuler, J. Schulthess (Zürich, 1829–42), 6 vols.

Ulrich Zwingli: Eine Auswahl aus seinen Schriften, eds. G. Finsler, et al. (Zürich, 1918)

Zwingli's Latin Works and Correspondence, ed. S. M. Jackson (New York, 1912) 2 vols.

Zwingli and Bullinger, G. W. Bromiley, Library of Christian Classics, vol. 24 (Philadelphia, 1953)

Zwingli Hauptschriften, ed. E. Blanke et al. (Zürich, 1959), 8 vols.

Huldrych Zwingli, Auswahl seiner Schriften, ed. E. Künzli (Zürich, 1962)

D. Printed Chronicles and other Incunabula:

Bämler, Johann

    Hienach volget ein Cronica von allen keysern// vnd künigen dye seit der Cristi geburt geregier//ret vnnd gereichsnet haben= wolche Cronica// gar kurtz weily nutzlich vnnd lieplich zuhern// vnd zu lesen ist. (Augsburg, 1497) (Zürich, Zentralbibliothek, Nr. ZT z. 112)

Fischer, Sebastian, *Sebastian Fischers Chronik,* ed. K. G. Veesenmeyer, *Mitteilungen des Vereins für Kunst und Alterthum für Ulm und Oberschwaben,* V-VIII (Ulm, 1896)

Tengler, Ulrich.

    Laÿen Spiegel// Von rechtmässigen ordnungen in// Burgerlichen vnd pein// lichen regim//ten. (Augsburg, 1509) (Tübingen, Universitätsbibliothek, Nr. Ha III 27°)

E. Primary Source Collections:

Clemen, Otto, *Flugschriften aus den ersten Jahren der Reformation* (Leipzig, 1907–11), 4 vols.

Cruel, Rudolf, *Geschichte der deutschen Predigt im Mittelalter* (Reprint, Hildesheim, 1966)

Falk, Franz, ed. *Drei Beichtüchlein, RST,* II (1907), 1–95.

Franz, Günther, ed., *Quellen zur Geschichte des deutschen Bauernstandes in der Neuzeit* (Darmstadt, 1963) reprint.

Hasak, Vincenz, ed., *Der Christliche Glaube des deutschen Volkes beim Schlusse des Mittelalters, 1470–1520* (Regensburg, 1868)

Köhler, Hans-Joachim, et al., eds., *Sixteenth Century Pamphlets in German and Latin, 1501–1530* (Zug, Switzerland, 1978f.), 7 vols. t.d.

Laube, Adolf, Schneider, Annerose and Looss, Sigrid, eds., *Flugschriften der frühen Reformationsbewegung 1518–1524* (Berlin, 1983), 2 vols.

Lenk, Werner, ed., *Die Reformation in zeitgenössischen Dialog* (Berlin, 1968)

Pfeiffer, Gerhard, ed., *Quellen zur Geschichte der Reformation in Nürnberg,* (Nuremberg, 1977)

Roth, R., ed., *Urkunden zur Geschichte der Universität Tübingen aus den Jahren 1476 bis 1550* (Tübingen, 1877)

Schmid, J. C., Pfister, J. C. eds., *Denkwürdigkeiten der württembergischen und schwäbischen Reformationsgeschichte* (Tübingen, 1817)

Schornbaum, K., Schmidt, W. F., eds., *Die fränkischen Bekenntnisse* (Munich, 1930), 2 vols.

Sehling, Emil, ed., *Die evangelischen Kirchenordnungen des XVI Jahrhunderts* (Tübingen, 1902–1969), 15 vols.

Strauss, Gerald, ed., *Manifestation of Discontent in Germany on the Eve of the Reformation* (Bloomington, Ind., 1971)

Thompson, Bard., ed., *Liturgies of the Western Church* (Cleveland, Ohio, 1962)

Vogt, Wilhelm, ed., 'Die Correspondenz des schwäbischen Bundeshauptmanns Ulrich Artzt von Augsburg aus den Jahren, 1525–27,' *ZHVSN,* VI, VII, IX, X (1879f.)

Wackernagel, Wilhelm, ed., *Altdeutsche Predigten und Gebete aus Handschriften* (Basel, 1876)

SECONDARY SOURCES

Adamcyk, Roberta, 'Die Flugschriften des Johann Eberlin von Günzburg, 1465–1533' (Dissertation, Vienna, 1981)

Ammann, Hektor, *Die wirtschaftliche Stellung der Reichsstadt Nürnberg im Spätmittelalter* (Nuremberg, 1970)

Andreas, Willy, *Deutschland vor der Reformation* (Stuttgart, 1932), 3 vols.

Arnold, Klaus, *Niklashausen, 1476. Quellen und Untersuchungen zur sozialreligiösen Bewegung des Hans Behem und zur Agrarstruktur eines spätmittelalterlichen Dorfes* (Baden-Baden, 1980)

Aston, Margaret, 'Lollardy and Literacy,' *History*, 62 (1977), 349–71.

Atkinson, Clarissa, *Mystic and Pilgrim: The Book and World of Margery Kempe* (Ithaca, NY, 1983)

Auer, Alfons, *Die volkommene Frömmigkeit des Christen: Nach dem Enchiridion militis Christiani des Erasmus von Rotterdam* (Düsseldorf, 1954)

Bainton, Roland, *Women of the Reformation in Germany and Italy* (Boston, 1971)

Bak, Janos, ed., *The German Peasant War of 1525* (London, 1976)

Balzer, Bernd, *Bürgerliche Reformationspropaganda: Die Flugschriften des Hans Sachs in den Jahren 1523–25* (Stuttgart, 1973).

Barth, Ernst, *Probleme der frühbürgerlichen Revolution* (Karl-Marx-Stadt, 1975)

Barthel, Otto, *Die Schulen in Nürnberg und seinem Landgebiet, 1905–1960, mit Einführung in die Gesamtgeschichte* (Nuremberg, 1964)

Barton, Peter, ed., *Sozialrevolution und Reformation* (Vienna, 1975), 3 vols.

Bauer, Clemens, et al. eds., *Augusta, 955–1955* (Augsburg, 1955)

Baumann, Ludwig, *Die oberschwäbischen Bauern im März 1525 und die Zwölf Artikel* (Kempten, 1871)

Baumgart, Peter, 'Formen der Volksfrömmigkeit – Krise der alten Kirche und reformatorische Bewegung,' in P. Blickle, ed., *Revolte und Revolution in Europa*, 186–204.

Beifus, Joseph, 'Hans Sachs und die Reformation bis zum Tode Luthers,' *MVGSN*, 19 (1911), 1–76.

Benz, Ernst, *Ecclesia Spiritualis* (Stuttgart, 1934)

Bernhofer-Pippert, Else, *Täuferische Denkweisen und Lebensformen im Spiegel oberdeutscher Täuferverhöre* (Münster, 1976)

Bezold, Franz von, 'Die "armen Leute" und die deutsche Literatur des Spätmittelalters,' *HZ*, 41 (1919), 1–37.

Blickle, Peter, ed., *Revolte und Revolution in Europa*, HZ, Beiheft 4 (1975)
  'Thesen zum Thema "Der Bauernkrieg" als Revolution des "gemeinen Mannes,"' in P. Blickle, ed., *Revolte und Revolution in Europa*, HZ, Beiheft 4 (Munich, 1975), 127–131.

Boll, Franz, *Sternglaube und Sterndeutung: Die Geschichte und das Wesen der Astrologie* (Berlin, 1926)

Bossert, Gustav, *Sebastian Lotzer und seine Schriften* (Memmingen, 1906)

Brady, Thomas A., Jr., *Ruling Class, Regime and Reformation at Strasbourg, 1520–1555* (Leiden, 1978)
  'Social History,' in S. Ozment, ed., *Reformation Europe: A Guide to Research*, (St. Louis, 1982), 161–181.

Brecht, Martin, 'Der theologische Hintergrund der Zwölf Artikel der Bauernschaft in Schwaben von 1525,' ZKG, 85/2 (1974), 31–64.

Buck, Lawrence, and Zophy, Jonathan, eds., *The Social History of the Reformation* (Columbus, 1972)

Burger, Gerhard, *Die Südwestdeutschen Stadtschreiber im Mittelalter* (Böblingen, 1960)

Burke, Peter, *Popular Culture in Early Modern Europe* (New York, 1978)

Bynum, Caroline, *Jesus as Mother: Studies in the Spirituality of the High Middle Ages* (Berkeley, 1982)

Cadet, Jean, *Le Laïcat et le droit de l'Église* (Paris, 1963)

Chrisman, Miriam, 'Women and the Reformation in Strasbourg, 1490–1530,' ARG, 63 (1972), 143–168.

   Lay Culture, Learned Culture: Books and Social Change in Strasbourg (New Haven, 1982)

Christian, William, Jr., *Local Religion in Sixteenth Century Spain* (Princeton, NJ, 1981)

Clemen, Otto 'Haug Marschalck genannt Zoller von Augsburg,' BBKG, 4 (1898), 223–230.

   'Die Schösserin von Eisenberg,' *Mitteilungen des Geschichts- und Alterthumsforschenden Vereins zu Eisenberg im Herzogtum Sachsen–Altenberg*, 13 (1898), 73–81.

   'Der Bauer von Wöhrd,' in O. Clemen, ed., *Beiträge zur Reformationsgeschichte*, 2 (1902), 85–84.

   'Die Papstweissagungen des Abts Joachim von Flora,' ZKG, 48 (1929), 371–379.

Cohn, Norman, *The Pursuit of the Millennium* (Oxford, 1957)

Cole, Richard, 'The Reformation Pamphlet and the Communication Processes,' in H.–J. Köhler, ed., *Flugschriften*, 139–162.

Constable, Giles, 'Twelfth-Century Spirituality and the Late Middle Ages,' in O. B. Hardison, ed., *Medieval and Renaissance Studies* (Chapel Hill, 1970), 27–60.

   'The Popularity of Twelfth Century Spiritual Writers in the Late Middle Ages,' in Anthony Molho, John Tedeschi, eds., *Renaissance Studies in Honor of Hans Baron* (Dekalb, Ill, 1970), 5–28.

Dabin, Paul, *Le sacerdôce royal des fidèles dans la tradition ancienne et moderne* (Paris, 1950)

Dacheux, Louis, *Un reformateur catholique à la fin du 15ᵉ siècle, Geiler von Kaysersberg* (Paris, 1876)

Dahmus, John, 'Preaching to the Laity in Fifteenth Century Germany: Johannes Nider's "Harps,"' *Journal of Ecclesiastical History*, 34 (1983), 55–68.

Davis, Kenneth R., 'Erasmus as Progenitor of Anabaptist Theology and Piety,' *Mennonite Quarterly Review*, 52 (1974), 163–78.

Davis, Natalie, *Society and Culture in Early Modern France* (Stanford, 1975)

Delumeau, Jean, *Naissance et Affirmation de la Réforme* (Paris, 1965)

   Catholicism between Luther and Voltaire: A New View of the Counter-Reformation (London, 1977)

   Un Chemin d'Histoire, Chrétienté et christianisation (Paris, 1981)

Dickens, A. G., *The German Nation and Martin Luther* (New York, 1974)

Dobel, Friedrich, *Memmingen im Reformationszeitalter* (Memmingen, 1877)

Douglass, Jane D., *Justification in Late Medieval Preaching. A Study of John Geiler von Kaisersberg* (Leiden, 1966)

Drews, P., *Willibald Pirckheimers Stellung zur Reformation* (Leipzig, 1887)

Duggan, Lawrence, 'The Unresponsiveness of the Late Medieval Church: a Reconsideration,' *Sixteenth Century Journal*, 9 (1978), 3–26.

Eastwood, Cyril, *The Priesthood of all Believers* (Minneapolis, MN, 1960)

Eckert, Alfred, 'Waldensisches Bekenntnis, Motive Hussitischer Revolution und Lutherischer Reformation in Böhmen bis nach dem "Prager Blutgericht, 1521,"' in P. Barton, ed., *Sozialrevolution und Reformation*, II, 97–149.

Ehrismann, Y. M., 'Catherine Schütz, une Strasbourgeoise remarquable au presbytère de la Cathédrale, 1597–1562,' *Bulletin de la Société de l'Histoire du Protestantisme Français*, 104 (1958), 94–106.

Eitel, P., *Die oberschwäbische Reichsstädte im Zeitalter der Zunftherrschaft. Untersuchungen zu Ihrer politischen und sozialen Struktur unter besonderer Berücksichtigung der Städte Lindau, Memmingen, Ravensburg und Überlingen* (Stuttgart, 1970).

Ellis, F. H., *The Early Meisterlieder of Hans Sachs* (Bloomington, 1976)

Endres, Rudolf, 'Zur Einwohnerzahl und Bevölkerungsstruktur Nürnbergs im 15./16. Jahrhundert,' *MVGSN*, 57 (1970), 242–71.

'Zur Lage der Nürnberger Handwerkerschaft zur Zeit von Hans Sachs,' *Jahrbuch für fränkische Landesforschung*, 37 (1977), 107–123.

'Zünfte und Unterschichten als Elemente der Instabilität in den Städten' in P. Blickle, ed. *Revolte und Revolution in Europa*, 151–170.

'Zur sozialökonomischen Lage und sozialpyschischen Einstellung des "gemeinen Mannes,"' in H.-U. Wehler, ed., *Geschichte und Gesellschaft* (Göttingen, 1975) 61–75.

Engelsing, Rolf, *Der Bürger als Leser, Lesergeschichte in Deutschland, 1500–1800* (Stuttgart, 1974)

Analphabetentum und Lektüre. Zur Sozialgeschichte des Lesens in Deutschland zwischen feudaler und industrieller Gesellschaft (Stuttgart, 1973)

Epperlein, Siegfried, *Der Bauer im Bild des Mittelalters* (Jena, 1975)

Fabian, Ekkehart, *Die Abschiede der Bündnis- und Bekenntnistage protestierender Fürsten und Städte, 1529–1530* (Tübingen, 1960)

Falk, Franz 'Das Unterricht des deutschen Volkes in den katechetischen Hauptstücken am Ende des Mittelalters,' *Historisch–Politische Blätter für das Katholische Deutschland*, 108 (1891), 552–560, 682–694.

Die deutschen Mess-Auslegungen von der Mitte des fünfzehnten Jahrhunderts bis zum Jahre 1525 (Cologne, 1889)

Die deutschen Sterbebüchlein (Cologne, 1890)

Fearns, J., ed., *Ketzer und Ketzerbekämpfung im Hochmittelalter* (Göttingen, 1968)

Fraker, C., 'Goncalo Martinez de Medina, the Jeronimos and the Devotio Moderna,' in D. West, ed., *Joachim of Fiore in Christian Thought* (New York, 1975), II, 611–631.

Franz, Günther, *Der deutsche Bauernkrieg* (Darmstadt, 1977) Eleventh edition.

Freud, Sigmund, *Civilisation and its Discontents* (London, 1961)

Fuchs, W., ed., *Staat und Kirche im Wandel der Jahrhunderte* (Stuttgart, 1966)

Gebhardt, B., *Die Gravamina der deutschen Nation gegen den Römischen Hof* (Leipzig, 1895)

Geffken, Johannes, *Bilderkatechismen des fünfzehnten Jahrhunderts* (Leipzig, 1855)

Gestrich, Christof, *Zwingli als Theologe* (Zürich, 1967)

Gottlieb, Gunther, et al. eds., *Geschichte der Stadt Augsburg, von der Römerzeit bis zur Gegenwart* (Stuttgart, 1984)

Grundmann, Herbert 'Der Typus des Ketzers in mittelälterlicher Anschauung,' in *Kultur und Universalgeschichte, Walter Goetz zu seinem 60. Geburtstag* (Leipzig, 1927) 91–107.

    Studien über Joachim von Flora, Beiträge zur Kulturgeschichte des Mittelalters und der Renaissance, 32 (Leipzig, 1927)

    Religiöse Bewegungen im Mittelalter (Berlin, 1935)

    'Literatur–illiteratus,' *Archiv für Kulturgeschichte*, 40 (1958), 1–65.

Hamm, Bernd, 'Laientheologie zwischen Luther und Zwingli: Das reformatorische Anliegen des Konstanzer Stadtschreibers Jörg Vögeli aufgrund seiner Schriften von 1523/24,' in Josef Nolte et al. eds., *Kontinuität und Umbruch. Theologie und Frömmigkeit in Flugschriften und Kleinliteratur an der Wende vom 15. zum 16. Jahrhundert* (Stuttgart, 1978), 222–295.

    Frömmigkeitstheologie am Anfang des 16. Jahrhunderts (Tübingen, 1982).

Hashagen, J., *Staat und Kirche vor der Reformation: Eine Untersuchung der vorreformatorischen Bedeutung des Laieneinflusses in der Kirche* (Essen, 1931)

Haupt, Hermann, *Die religiösen Sekten in Franken vor der Reformation* (Würzburg, 1882)

    'Waldensertum und Inquisition,' *Deutsche Zeitschrift für Geschichtswissenschaft*, 3 (1890), 337–411.

Helender, J., *Johannes Tauler als Prediger* (Lund, 1923)

Hillerbrand, Hans J., 'The Origins of Sixteenth-Century Anabaptism: Another Look,' *ARG*, 53 (1962), 152–180.

Hippe, Heinrich, *Das Schulwesen des Mittelalters* (Marburg, 1860)

Hofer, Johannes, *Johannes Kapistran: Ein Leben im Kampf um die Reform der Kirche* (Heidelberg, 1965, reworked edition), 2 vols.

Hoffmann, H., 'Reformation und Gewissensfreiheit,' *ARG*, 37 (1940), 170–185.

Immenkölter, Herbert, 'Kirche zwischen Reformation und Parität,' in G. Gottlieb, et al., eds., *Geschichte der Stadt Augsburg*, 391–402.

Jacob, Walter, *Politische Führungsschicht und Reformation: Untersuchungen zur Reformation in Zürich, 1519–1528* (Zürich, 1969)

Janssen, Johannes, *Geschichte des deutschen Volkes seit dem Ausgang des Mittelalters*, (Freiburg i. Br., 1878f.), 8 vols.

Jedin, Hubert, *Kleine Konziliengeschichte* (Vienna, 1969)

John, Joachim, 'Die Augsburger Sozialstruktur im 15. Jahrhundert,' in G. Gottlieb, et al. eds., *Geschichte der Stadt Augsburg*, (Stuttgart, 1984) 187–201.

Junghans, Helmar, 'Der Laie als Richter im Glaubenstreit der Reformationszeit,' *Lutherjahrbuch*, 39 (1972), 31–54.

Kaminsky, H., *A History of the Hussite Revolution* (Berkeley, 1967)

Karrer, Leo, *Von Beruf Laientheologe?* (Vienna, 1970)

Kasser, Kurt, *Politische und soziale Bewegungen im deutschen Bürgertum des 16. Jahrhunderts* (Berlin, 1899)

Kawerau, Waldemar, *Hans Sachs und die Reformation*, SVRG, 26 (1889).

Keller, Ludwig, 'Aus den Anfangsjahren der Reformation,' *Monatshefte der Comenius-Gesellschaft*, 8 (1899), 176–85.

Kieckhefer, Richard, *Repression of Heresy in Medieval Germany* (Philadelphia, 1979)

Kiessling, Rolf, *Bürgerliche Gesellschaft und Kirche in Augsburg im Spätmittelalter* (Augsburg, 1971)

Köhler, Hans-Joachim, 'Die Flugschriften, Versuch der Präzisierung eines geläufigen Begriffs,' in *Festgabe für Ernst Walther Zeeden zum 60. Geburtstag* (Münster, 1976), 36–61.

'Fragestellungen und Methoden zur Interpretation frühneuzeitlicher Flug-schriften,' in H.–J. Köhler, ed., *Flugschriften*, 1–27.

'Das Tübinger Flugschriftenprojekt,' *Wolfenbütteler Notizen zur Buchgeschichte*, 9/1 (1984), 3–22.

Köhler, Hans-Joachim, ed., *Flugschriften als Massenmedium der Reformationszeit* (Stuttgart, 1981)

Köhler, Hans-Joachim et al. eds, *Bibliographie der deutschen und lateinischen Flug-schriften des frühen 16. Jahrhunderts* (Tübingen, 1978, test printing.)

Könneker, Barbara, *Hans Sachs* (Stuttgart, 1971)

Kolde, Theodor, 'Zum Prozess Johann Denck und die drei gotlosen Maler,' *KS*, 1 (1888), 228–250.

'Hans Denck und die gottlosen Mahler von Nürnberg,' *BBKG*, 8 (1902), 1–72.

'Arsacius Seehofer und Argula von Grumbach,' *BBKG*, 11 (1905), 49–77, 97–125, 149–87.

Kristeller, Paul O., *Medieval Aspects of Renaissance Learning* (Durham, NC, 1974)

Kurze, Dietrich, 'Astrologie und Prophetie im spätmittelälterlichen Geschichts-denken,' in *Festschrift für Richard Dietrich zum 65. Gerburtstag* (Frankfurt, 1976), 164–86.

'Prophecy and History in Lichtenberger's Forecasts of Events to Come, their Reception and Diffusion,' *Journal of the Warburg and Courtauld Institutes*, 12 (1958), 63–85.

Lagarde, Georges de, *La Naissance de L'Esprit Laique au Déclin du Moyen Âge* (Paris, 1956–63), 5 vols.

Laubach, Ernst, 'Zur Botschaft des Paukers von Niklashausen,' *Jahrbuch für fränkische Landesforschung*, 36 (1976), 93–105.

Laube, Adolf, 'Die Volksbewegungen in Deutschland von 1470 bis 1517,' in P. Blickle, ed., *Revolte und Revolution in Europa*, 84–98.

'Zur Rolle sozialökonomische Fragen in frühreformatorischen Flugschriften,' in H.–J. Köhler, ed., *Flugschriften*, 205–224.

LeClercq, Jean, et al., eds., *La Spiritualité au Moyen Âge* (Aubier, 1961)

Leder, Klaus, *Kirche und Jugend in Nürnberg und seinem Landgebiet, 1400–1800*, *EKB*, 52 (1966)

LeGoff, Jacques, ed., *Hérésies et sociétés dans l'Europe pré-industrielle 11ᵉ-18ᵉ siècles* (Paris, 1968)

Lenk, Werner, *Die Reformation im zeitgenössischen Dialog* (Berlin, 1968)

Lerner, R., *The Heresy of the Free Spirit in the Later Middle Ages* (Berkeley, 1972)

Lier, A. H., 'Der Augsburgische Humanistenkreis mit besonderer Berücksichtigung auf Bernard Adelmann von Adelmannsfelden' *ZHVSN*, 7 (1880), 68–108.

List, Günther, *Chilianism, Utopie, und radikale Reformation* (Munich, 1973)

Locher, Gottfried, *Die Theologie Huldrych Zwinglis im Lichte seiner Christologie* (Zürich, 1952)

Lohse, Bernard, 'Die Stellung der Schwärmer und Täufer in der Reformations-geschichte,' *ARG*, 60 (1969), 10–32.

Lortz, Joseph, *Die Reformation in Deutschland* (Freiburg i. Br., 1962), 2 vols.

Lutz, Robert, *Wer war der gemeine Mann? Der dritte Stand in der Krise des Spätmittelalters* (Munich and Vienna, 1979)

Maćek, J., 'Villes et campagnes dans le Hussitisme,' in J. LeGoff, ed., *Hérésies et sociétés dans l'Europe pré-industrielle*, 243–256.

McGinn, Bernard, *Visions of the End: Apocalyptic Traditions in the Middle Ages* (New York, 1979)

McLaughlin, Eleanor C., 'The Heresy of the Free Spirit: A Study in Medieval Religious Life' (Dissertation, Harvard University, 1967)

Manselli, Raoul, *La 'Lectura Super Apocalipsim' di Pietro di Giovanni Olivi* (Rome, 1955)

Maschke, Erich 'Deutsche Städte am Ausgang des Mittelalters,' in W. Rausch, ed., *Die Stadt* 1–44.

'Die Unterschichten der mittelalterlichen Städten Deutschlands,' in E. Maschke, *Städte und Menschen*, 306–379 (1–74).

Städte und Menschen (Wiesbaden, 1980)

Maschke, Erich, and Sydow, Jürgen, *Gesellschaftliche Unterschichten in den süd-westdeutschen Städten* (Stuttgart, 1967)

Maschek, Hermann, *Deutsche Chroniken* (Leipzig, 1936)

Maurer, Justus, 'Das Verhalten der reformatorisch gesinnten Geistlichen Süd-deutschlands im Bauernkrieg, 1525' (Dissertation, Tübingen, 1975)

Moeller, Bernd, *Imperial Cities and the Reformation* (Durham, NC, 1982)

'Frömmigkeit in Deutschland um 1500,' *ARG*, 56 (1965), 5–31. See also an English translation, 'Piety in Germany around 1500,' in S. Ozment, ed., *The Reformation in Medieval Perspective* (Chicago, 1971), 50–75.

Moeller, Bernd, ed., *Bauernkriegsstudien*, SVRG, 189 (1975)

Mommsen, Wolfgang J., Alter, Peter and Scribner, R. W., *The Urban Classes, the Nobility and the Reformation: Studies in the Social History of the Reformation in England and Germany* (Stuttgart, 1979)

Monter, E. William, 'Reformation History and Social History,' *ARG*, 72 (1981), 5–12.

Mousnier, Roland, 'Saint Bernard and Martin Luther,' *The American Benedictine Review*, 14/3 (1963), 448–462.

Muchembled, Robert, *Culture Populaire et Culture des Élites dans la France Moderne, XVe-XVIIIe siècles* (Paris, 1978)

Naujoks, Eberhard, *Obrigkeitsgedanke, Zunftverfassung und Reformation. Studien zur Verfassungsgeschichte von Ulm, Esslingen, und Schwäb. Gmünd* (Stuttgart, 1958)

Nebelsieck, H., 'Ein fürstlicher Laientheologe des 16. Jahrhunderts, Graf Wolrad II von Waldeck,' *ARG*, 41 (1940), 38–93.

Neumann, Eva, *Rheinische Beginen- und Beghardenwesen* (Mainz, 1960)

Niell, S., and Weber, H., eds., *The Layman in Christian History* (Philadelphia, 1963)

Niemann, G., 'Die Dialogliteratur der Reformationszeit nach ihrer Entstehung und Entwicklung' (Dissertation, Leipzig, 1905)

Oakley, Francis, 'Religious and Ecclesiastical Life on the Eve of the Reformation,' in S. Ozment, ed., *Reformation Europe: A Guide to Research*, 5–32.

Oberman, Heiko A., 'Gabriel Biel and Late Medieval Mysticism,' *Church History*, 30 (1961), 259–287.

The Harvest of Medieval Theology: Gabriel Biel and Late Medieval Nominalism (Cambridge, MA, 1967)

'Facientibus quod in se est, Deus non denegat gratiam: Robert Holcot, O.P. and the Beginnings of Luther's Theology,' in S. Ozment, ed., *The Reformation in Medieval Perspective*, 119–141.

'Tumultus rusticorum. Vom "Klosterkrieg" zum Fürstensieg. Beobachtungen zum Bauernkrieg unter besonderer Berücksichtigung zeitgenössischer Beurteilungen,' in H. Oberman, ed., *Der Deutsche Bauernkrieg*, 301–316.

Masters of the Reformation: The Emergence of a New Intellectual Climate in Europe (Cambridge, 1981)

Oberman, Heiko A., ed., *Deutscher Bauernkrieg, 1525*, ZKG 2 (1974)

Oberman, Heiko, and Trinkaus, Charles, eds., *The Pursuit of Holiness in Late Medieval and Renaissance Religion* (Leiden, 1974)

Öhler, H., 'Der Aufstand des Armen Konrad im Jahr 1514,' *Württembergische Vierteljahreshefte für Landesgeschichte*, 38 (1932), 401–486.

Otwinoska, Barbara, 'Der "gemeine Mann" als Adressat der volkssprachlichen Literatur in der Renaissance,' in R. Weimann, et al. eds., *Renaissance Literatur und frühbürgerliche Revolution*, 194–202.

Ozment, Steven, *Mysticism and Dissent. Religious Ideology and Social Protest in the Sixteenth Century* (Yale, 1973)

Homo Spiritualis. A Comparative Study of the Anthropology of Johannes Tauler, Jean Gerson and Martin Luther, 1509–16, in the Context of their Theological Thought (Leiden, 1969)

The Reformation in the Cities (Yale, 1975)

The Age of Reform, 1250–1550: An Intellectual and Religious History of Late Medieval and Reformation Europe (New Haven, 1980)

'The Social History of the Reformation; what can we learn from pamphlets?' in H.–J. Köhler, ed., *Flugschriften*, 171–203.

'Pamphlet Literature of the German Reformation,' in S. Ozment, ed., *Reformation Europe: A Guide to Research*, 85–105.

Ozment, Steven, ed., *The Reformation in Medieval Perspective* (Chicago, 1971)

Reformation Europe: A Guide to Research (St. Louis, 1982)

Packull, Werner O., *Mysticism and the Early South German–Austrian Anabaptist Movement, 1525–1531* (Scottdale, PA, 1977)

Panzer, G. W., and Weller, E., *Annalen der älteren deutschen Litteratur*, fol. *Repertorium Typographicum* (Nuremberg, 1788f., 1864f.) 3 vols.

Paulsen, F. and Lehmann, R. *Geschichte des gelehrten Unterrichts* (Leipzig, 1919–21), 2 vols.

Pfeiffer, Gerhard, 'Stadtherr und Gemeinde in der spätmittelälterlichen Reichsstädten,' in W. Rausch, ed., *Die Stadt*, 201–223.

'Das Verhältnis von politischer und kirchlicher Gemeinde in den deutschen Reichsstädten,' in W. Fuchs, ed., *Stadt und Kirche im Wandel der Jahrhunderte*, 79–99.

Pfeiffer, Gerhard, ed., *Nürnberg – Geschichte einer europäischen Stadt* (Munich, 1971), 2 vols.

Philips, Gerard, *Le rôle du laïcat dans l'Église* (Tournai, 1954)

Pipkin, H. W., 'Zwingli, the Laity and Orders: From the Cloister into the World,' *Hartford Quarterly*, 8 (1968), 32–41.

Pitz, Ernst, *Die Entstehung der Ratsherrschaft in Nürnberg im 13. und 14. Jahrhundert* (Munich, 1956)

Post, R. R., *The Modern Devotion. Confrontation with Reformation and Humanism* (Leiden, 1968)

Pullan, Brian, 'Catholics and the Poor in Early Modern Europe,' *Transactions of the Royal Historical Society*, 26 (1976), 13–34.

Ramstedt, Otthein, 'Stadtunruhen von 1525,' in W. Rausch, ed., *Die Stadt*, 239–276.

Rausch, Wilhelm, ed., *Die Stadt am Ausgang des Mittelalters* (Linz, 1974)

Rauscher, Julius, *Württembergische Reformationsgeschichte* (Stuttgart, 1934)

Redlich, Fritz, *A German Military Enterpriser* (Wiesbaden, 1964–65), 2 vols.

Reeves, Marjorie, *The Influence of Prophecy in the Later Middle Ages* (Oxford, 1969)
 'Some Popular Prophecies from the Fourteenth to the Seventeenth Centuries,' in G. J. Cuming and D. Baker, eds., *Popular Belief and Practice* (Cambridge, 1972), 107–134.

Reinmann, G. J., *The Third Order Secular of St. Francis* (Washington, 1928)

Ritter, Gerhard, 'Romantische und revolutionäre Elemente in der deutschen Theologie am Vorabend der Reformation,' *Deutsche Vierteljahrschrift für Literaturwissenschaft und Geistesgeschichte*, 5 (1927), 342–380.

Rössing-Hager, Monika, 'Wie stark findet der nichtlesekundige Rezipient Berücksichtigung in den Flugschriften?' in H.-J. Köhler, *Flugschriften*, 77–137.

Rohling, E., *Die Reichsstadt Memmingen in der Zeit der evangelischen Volksbewegung* (Munich, 1864)

Rohr, J., 'Die Prophetie im letzten Jahrhundert vor der Reformation als Geschichtsquelle und Geschichtsfaktor,' *Historisches Jahrbuch*, 19 (1898), 29–55.

Roth, Friedrich, *Augsburgs Reformationsgeschichte, 1517–1537* (Munich, 1881f.), 4 vols.
 Die Einführung der Reformation in Nürnberg, 1517–1528 (Würzburg, 1885)
 Willibald Pirckheimer, ein Lebensbild aus dem Zeitalter des Humanismus und der Reformation, SVRG, 21 (1887).
 'Wer war Haug Marschalck genannt der Zoller von Augsburg?,' *BBKG*, 6 (1900), 229–234.
 'Die geistliche Betrügerin Anna Lamanit von Augsburg, 1480–1518,' *ZKG*, 42 (1924), 355–417.

Rothkrug, Lionel, 'Popular Religion and Holy Shrines: Their Influence on the Origins of the German Reformation and their Role in German Cultural Development,' in J. Obelkevich, ed., *Religion and People, 800–1700* (Chapel Hill, NC, 1979), 20–86.
 Religious Practices and Collective Perceptions: Hidden Homologies in the Renaissance and Reformation (Waterloo, Ont., 1980)

Ruh, K., 'David von Augsburg und die Entstehung eines franziskanischen Schrifttums in deutscher Sprache,' in C. Bauer, et al., eds., *Augusta*, 71–82.

Russell, Paul A., 'Lay Theology and Ecclesiastical Attitudes in Southwestern Germany 1450–1555' (Dissertation, Boston College, 1978)

'"Your sons and your daughters shall prophesy..." (Joel 2:28) Common People and the Future of the Reformation in the Pamphlet Literature of Southwestern Germany to 1525,' *ARG*, 74 (1983), 122–140.

Saxer, Victor, *Le Culte de Marie Madeleine en Occident, dès Origines à la Fin du Moyen Âge* (Paris, 1959), 2 vols.

Schairer, I., *Das religiöse Volksleben am Ausgang des Mittelalters nach Augsburger Quellen* (Leipzig, 1914)

Schelhorn, J. C., *Kurtze Reformationshistorie von Memmingen* (Memmingen, 1730)

Schiff, Otto, 'Forschung zur Vorgeschichte des Bauernkriegs,' *Historische Vierteljahresschrift*, 19/2 (1919), 189–219.

'Die Wirsberger,' *Historische Vierteljahresschrift*, 26 (1931), 776–786.

Schlenck, W., *Memmingen im Reformationszeitalter*, *Memminger Geschichtsblätter*, 12 (1968)

Schmidt, Hans-Dieter, *Täufertum und Obrigkeit in Nürnberg* (Nuremberg, 1972)

Schmidt, Joseph, *Lestern, lesen, und lesen hören. Kommunikationsstudien zur deutschen Prosasatire der Reformationszeit* (Bern, 1977)

Schottenloher, Karl, *Philip Ulhart: Ein Augsburger Winkeldrucker und Helfershelfer der 'Schwärmer' und 'Wiedertäufer,' 1523–1529* (Nieuwkoop, 1967, reprint.) *Flugblatt und Zeitung* (Berlin, 1922)

Schubert, Friedrich, 'Die Reformation in Augsburg,' in C. Bauer, et al., eds., *Augusta*, 283–300.

Scribner, Robert W. 'The Social Thought of Erasmus,' *Journal of Ecclesiastical History*, 6 (1970–71), 3–26.

'Is there a social history of the Reformation?,' *Social History*, 4 (1977), 483–505.

'Flugblatt und Analphabetentum: Wie kam der gemeine Mann zu reformatorischen Ideen?' in H.–J. Köhler, ed., *Flugschriften*, 65–76.

'The German Peasants' War,' in S. Ozment, ed., *Reformation Europe: A Guide to Research*, 107–133.

For the Sake of Simple Folk: Popular Propaganda for the German Reformation (Cambridge, 1982)

Seebass, Gottfried, *Das reformatorische Werk des Andreas Osiander, EKB* (Nuremberg, 1967)

'Zur Beurteilung des Reformatorischen bei Vögeli,' in J. Nolte, et al., eds., *Kontinuität und Umbruch*, 296–299.

Séguenny, André, ed., *Bibliotheca Dissidentium. Répertoire des non-conformistes religieux des dix-seizième et dix-septième siècles* (Baden-Baden, 1980)

Selge, Karl, *Die Ersten Waldenser*, (Berlin, 1967) 2 vols.

Southern, R. W., *Western Society and the Church in the Middle Ages* (Baltimore, 1969)

Spriewald, Ingeborg, *Die Prosadialoge des Hans Sachs* (Leipzig, 1970)

Stein, Wolfgang, *Das kirchliche Amt bei Luther* (Wiesbaden, 1974)

Strauss, Gerald, *Nuremberg in the Sixteenth Century* (Bloomington, Ind., 1966)

Strauss, Gerald, ed., *Pre-Reformation Germany* (New York, 1972)

Streit, Felix, *Christoph Scheurl, Ratskonsulent von Nürnberg und seine Stellung zur Reformation* (Plauen i.V., 1908)

Stupperich, Robert, 'Die Frau in der Publizistik der Reformation,' *Archiv für Kulturgeschichte*, 37 (1955), 204–233.

Reformatorenlexikon (Gütersloh, 1984)

Sussann, Hermann, *Kenzingen in der Reformationszeit* (Kenzingen, 1888)

Tappolet, Walter, *Das Marienlob der Reformatoren* (Tübingen, 1962).

Tentler, Thomas, *Sin and Confession on the Eve of the Reformation* (Princeton, 1977)

Thomas, Keith, *Religion and the Decline of Magic: Studies in Popular Beliefs in Sixteenth and Seventeenth Century England* (London, 1971)

Thompson, J. W., *The Literacy of the Laity in the Middle Ages* (New York, 1965)

Tüchle, H., *Kirchengeschichte Schwabens* (Stuttgart, 1950), 2 vols.

Uhland, Friedwart, 'Täufertum und Obrigkeit in Augsburg im 16. Jahrhundert' (Dissertation, Tübingen, 1972)

Uitz, Erika, 'Die europäischen Städte im Spätmittelalter,' *Zeitschrift für Geschichteswissenschaft*, 21 (1973), 400–425.

Ulhorn, Gerhard, ed., *Urbanus Rhegius, Leben und ausgewählte Schriften* (Elberfeld, 1861)

Verheus, S. L., *Zeugnis und Gericht: Kirchengeschichtliche Betrachtungen bei Sebastian Franck und Matthias Flacius* (Niewkoop, 1971)

Vogler, Bernard, 'Vie religieuse en pays Rhénan dans la seconde moitié du XVIe siècle, 1556–1619' (Dissertation, Paris, 1972), 2 vols.

    Le Monde Germanique et Helvétique à l'Époque des Réformes, 1517–1618 (Paris, 1980)

Vogt, W., 'Zwei oberschwäbische Laienprediger,' *ZKWKL*, 6 (1885), 413–425, 479–499, 537–545.

Walter, Gerard, *Histoire des Paysans de France* (Paris, 1963)

Walton, Robert C., *Zwingli's Theocracy* (Toronto, Ont. 1967)

Wehler, Hans-Ulrich, ed., *Der deutsche Bauernkrieg, 1524–1526* (Göttingen, 1975)

Weigelt, Horst, *Sebastian Franck und die lutherische Reformation*, SVRG, 186 (1972).

Weimann, R., et al., eds., *Renaissanceliteratur und frühbürgerliche Revolution* (Berlin and Weimar, 1976)

Weinstein, Donald and Bell, Rudolf, *Saints and Society* (Chicago, 1982)

Weller, Emil, *Der Volksdichter Hans Sachs und seine Dichtungen* (Leipzig, 1868; reprint Nuremberg, 1966)

Werner, E., and Steinmetz, H., eds., *Städtische Volksbewegungen im 14. Jahrhundert* (Berlin, 1960)

Wernet, Karl F., *Handwerksgeschichtliche Perspektiven* (Münster, 1963)

Wernicke, Siegfried, 'Die Prosadialoge des Hans Sachs' (Dissertation, Berlin, 1913)

Wieland, Siegfried, 'Vom Lesen und Schreiben im späten Mittelalter,' in *Festschrift für I. Schröbler zum 65. Geburtstag* (Tübingen, 1973), 309–327.

Winkler, Hannelore, 'Zum sozialogischen Aspekt von Flugschriften aus der Zeit der Reformation und des Bauernkriegs,' *Beiträge zur Geschichte der deutschen Sprache und Literatur*, 94 (1971), 37–51.

Wohlfeil, R., ed., *Der Bauernkrieg, 1525–26; Bauernkrieg und Reformation* (Munich, 1975)

Wünsch, Dietrich, 'Schriften zum Fall Greiffenberger,' in G. Müller, ed., *Osianders Werke*, I, 266–274.

Zambelli, Paola, 'Fine del Mondo o Inizio della Propaganda? Astrologia, filosofia della storia e propaganda politico–religiosa nel dibattito sulla congiunzione del 1524,' in L. Olschki, ed., *Scienze, Credenze occulte, Livelli di Cultura* (Florence, 1982), 291–368.

Zorn, Wolfgang, *Augsburg, Geschichte einer deutschen Stadt* (Munich, 1955)

Index

absenteeism, 195
affective piety, see piety
Albertus Magnus, St., 215
Albigensians, 35
Albrecht IV, Duke of Bavaria (1501–08), 191
almanacs, 48, 215
Altenberg, 204
Anabaptists, 17–18, 64, 71, 158, 169, 183, 217, 220, 221, 226
Angela Merici, St., 186, 208, 226
Annales school of historical research, 5
Anthony, Hospital Order of St., 82, 89
anti-clericalism, 97, 137, 164, 174
Aristotle, 78, 193, 215
Arius, 137
Ars Moriendi, (see also Jean Gerson), 13, 45
artisans, see guilds
Artzt, Ulrich, 128
astrology, 215
atonement, 93, 103
Augsburg, 16, 28, 30, 80, 112f., *113*, *144*, 149,
    214, 221; guilds, 26; imperial diet,
    1518, 118; city government, 26, 115f.;
    bishops of (see also Christoph von
    Stadion), 85, 115
Augustine, St., 77, 137, 161, 175
Augustinian Canons (CRSA), 117
Augustinian Hermits (OESA), 150, 153, 172
authority, civic, 106–07, 125, 135, 217;
    papal, 98, 122f., 138,195

bakers, 119, 132
Bamberg, bishop of, see Weigand von
    Redwitz
Bad Windsheim, 30
Bämler, Johann, 121
baptism, 157, 176, 198
Barbara, St., 102
Basel, 83

Bavaria, Dukes of (see also William IV and
    Ludwig X), 26, 115, 150. 195, 196,
    198, 205
Beguines and Beghards, 21, 35, 48, 64,
    186, 189, 227; in Augsburg, 114f.
Beheim, Barthel, 157, 159
Beheim, Hans, *51*
Beheim, Sebald, 157
Benedictines, (OSB), 78, 81, 114, 121,
    153, 192
Bernard of Clairvaux, St., influence on
    late-medieval piety, 39, 45
Berthold von Regensburg, O. Min., 39, 117
Biberach, 121
Birgit of Sweden, St., 186
Black Death, 23
Bonaventure, St., 174
Boniface VIII, Pope (1298–1303), 123
Brethren of the Free Spirit, 220
brotherhoods, see confraternities
Brülinger, Hans, 31
Bucer, Martin, 207
Bundshuh, *49*, 217

Cajetan, Cardinal Thomas de Vio, 117
Carlstadt, Andreas, 156, 157, 158, 161,
    192
Carmelites (O. Carm.), 115, 117, 153
carnival practices, 4, 114
Carthusians (O. Cart), 153, 154
Casimir, Margrave of Brandenburg
    (1495–1527), 153
Catherine of Sienna, St., 187
Celestine V, Pope (1294), 122
celibacy, clerical, 100, 169, 174, 195,
    202, 221
Charles IV, H.R.E. (1355–78), 26, 35
Charles V, H.R.E. (1519–58), 119, 134
Charles Borromeo, St., 227
Chiliasm, 220
Cistercians (OCR), 187
city councils, see individual cities

Coburg, 200
Coburg bible, 191
Cochleus, Johann, 205
Cologne, 58, 152
'common man', 16, 90, 160, 226, 223,
    n58; definition of, 13–15
confession, see penance
confraternities, 26, 33, *59*, 92, 96, 148, 160,
    213
Conrad von Marburg, O.P., 35, 39
conscience, 160; liberation of, 44, 93,
    102, 175, 202, 224
Constance, 110
councils, ecumenical, 98, 164; Lateran
    IV, 37; Constance, 37, 202
Cranach, Lucas, *186*

David von Augsburg, O. Min., 39
Deichsler, Heinrich, 31
Denck, Hans, 157–58, 162, 182
Devotio Moderna, 30–31, 37, 42, 46, 54,
    76, 105, 187, 221
Dietfurt, 186, 191, 198
Dominic, St., *40*, 42
Dominicans (O.P.), 54, 78, 117, 119, 123,
    151, 153, 173, 182, 220
Duns Scotus, John, OFM, *131*, 174
Dürer, Albrecht, 156

Eberlin von Günzburg, Johann, 8, 91, 110,
    167, 179, 226
Ebner, Jerome, 152, 156
Eck, John, 115, 118, 202
economics, medieval, 23f.
education, 25, 30–31, 60, 187, 216
Eichstett, Bishop of, see Gabriel von Eyb
Eisenberg, 186, 201
Elizabeth of Hungary, St., 186, 191
emperors, holy Roman (H.R.E.), see
    individual entries
Emser, Jerome, 62
enthusiasts (*Schwärmgeister*), 18, 156, 183
Erasmus of Rotterdam, 60, *74*; *Enchiridion*,
    75–76; *Colloquies*, 192; *On Pilgrimage*,
    75, 76; attitude towards laypeople, 74f.;
    influence on pamphleteers, 97, 111, 127
eschatology, 72, 102, 127, 130, 137, 140,
    167, 180; influence on piety, 47–50,
    160, 162, 171f., 176
Esslingen, 153
Ettal, Benedictine abbey at, 192
eucharist, 19, 59, 98–99, 125, 139, 157,
    161, 164, 183, 187
excommunication, 98, 152
exegesis, 100–01
Exurge Domini, 1520, see Pope Leo X
Eyb, Gabriel von, Bishop of Eichstett
    (1496–1535), 194

Faber, Johann, O.P., 146
fasting (see also Lenten fast), 77, 97, 106,
    122, 164, 169, 172, 174, 179, 204, 226
Ferdinand, I, Archduke of Austria
    (1521–64), 205, 217
Fischer, Sebastian, 52, 78
Forchheim, 156
Francis, St., 42, 183
Franciscans (OFM & O. Min.), 78, 115,
    117, 120, 123, 141, 143, 153, 173,
    191, 220–221, 227; Third Order, 21,
    35, 48
Frankfurt, 25, 80, 166
Frederick II, H.R.E. (1220–1250), 123,
    134
Frederick III, H.R.E. (1452–1493),
    Reformatio, 109
Frederick, 'the Wise,' Elector of Saxony
    (1486–1525), 197
freedom, Christian, 94, 104, 217, 220
free will, 48, 103
Freiburg im Br., 28
friars, see individual orders
Frosch, Johann, 117, *119*, 129
Frundsberg, Georg von, 129
Fugger, Jacob, 112, 115
furriers, 84f.
Füssli, Hans, 54, 68, 73, Il. 22

Gay, Jodokus, 83
Gebwiler, Jerome, 68, *69*
Geiler von Kaisersberg, Johann, 41, 118,
    121, 122, 219
George, Duke of Bavaria (1479–1503),
    197
Gerson, Jean, 13, 37, 42, 46, 60, 64; *Little
    Work in Three Parts*, 41
gravamina, 31–33, 107, 110
Greiffenberger, Hans, 10, 16, 157, 221;
    trial of, 157; theology of, 159f.;
    Confession, 157
Grünpeck, Joseph, *47*, *134*, *139*, *170*
Grumbach, Argula, see Argula von
    Stauffen
Grumbach, Friedrich von, 191, 200
Gugy, Georg, 107
guilds (see also individual cities), 31, 33,
    77, 80, 113; role in city government,
    24–28, 148–52; revolts led by, 26, 115,
    148, 153
Günzburg, Eberlin von, see Eberlin von
    Günzberg, Johann

Hadrian VI, Pope (1522–23), 119
Hagenau, 30
Hanseatic League, 28
Haselbach, Thomas von, 31

Heidelberg, 152
Heilbronn, 28
Heltzlin, Hans, 86
Henneberg, Berthold von, Archbishop of
  Mainz (1464–1504), 31
heresy, 1, 11, 36–37, 118, 155, 235 n39
Hildegard of Bingen, St., 171
Hoepp, Paul, 85, 88
Hoffmann, Melchior, 207
Holbein, Hans, *32*
Horb am Neckar, 11, 83, 90
Hubmeier, Balthasar, *29*
Hug, Michael, 141, 145
Hugo von Trimberg, *46*
Humanists, 11–12, 45, 54, 70, 78, 125,
  137; in Augsburg, 114–15; in
  Nuremberg, 158; influence on
  pamphleteers, 11f., 181, 213, 219
human reason (*ratio humana*), 93, 136,
  176
human teaching (*doctrinae hominum*), 97,
  103, 137–38, 172, 173, 201
Huss, John, 36, 58, 202
Hussites, 18, 37, 56, 157, 164, 227; in
  Nuremberg, 155f., 182; in Augsburg,
  114f.

imperial cities, see individual cities
imperial diets; Augsburg, 1518, 118;
  Worms, 1521, 152; Nuremberg,
  1522–24, 153, 167, 197; Speyer, 1526,
  107
imperial edicts: Worms, 1521, 119, 153,
  192, 215; Nuremberg, 1524, 192
indulgences, 45, 126, 172
Ingolstadt, 191
Innocent III, Pope (1198–1216), 123
Innocent VIII, Pope (1484–1492), 123
inquisition, 35–36, 51, 157f.
Interim, 172, 208

Jerome, St., 78
Jews, 28, *29*, 64, 78, 94, 96, 125, 126,
  138, 140, 202, 225
Joachim of Fiore, 171, 216
Johann II, von Simmern und Sponheim,
  Count Palatine (1508–1557), 197
Johann von Freiburg, O.P., *116*
John Capistran, St., 39, 117, 150–51
John of the Cross, St. 227
Julius II, Pope (1503–13), 83
justification, 109, 173, 175, 214

Karsthans, 14, *49*, 83, 217, 240 n11
Katherine of Alexandria, St., 102
Kempe, Margery, 187, 221–22
Kenzingen, 205

Kretz, Matthias, 119, 124
Kunigund, Duchess of Bavaria (1501–20),
  191, 197

laity: reformers opinions of, 56–79; role in
  medieval church, 33f.
Laminit, Anna, 118
Leipzig, 201, 203
Lenten fast, 98, 106, 114, 122, 179
Lenting, 186, 198
Leo X, Pope (1513–21), 45; *Bulla Exurge
  Domine*, 152
lex evangelica, 53, 76, 96, 98, 101–02,
  105–06, 129, 138, 143, 164–65, 172,
  175, 178, 180, 181, 183, 214, 217,
  222
Linck, Wenzel, 159
Lindau, 141
Lord's Prayer, explanations of, 60,
  141–42, 207–08
Lotzer, Sebastian, 10, 16, 54, 222, 226;
  theology of, 89f.; negotiations with
  peasants, 87–88
Louvain, 58
Ludwig X, Duke of Bavaria (1508–45),
  191, 196
Luther, Martin, 1, 56, 125–26, 160, 172,
  183, 185, 191, 194, 199, 200, 216; *95
  Theses*, 58; *On The Babylonian Captivity*,
  57, 109; *To the Christian Nobility*, 56,
  167, 195; *On the Freedom of the
  Christian Man*, 61, 167; *Explanation of
  the Magnificat*, 104, 109; *Explanation of
  Our Father*, 162; *On the Mass*, 162;
  attitude toward the laity 56f.; attitude
  toward lay preachers, 62–63; influence
  on pamphleteers, 98, 111, 219
Lyons, 33, 80, 82

Mainz, 28, 31, 83
Marburg Colloquy, 1529, 208
Margaret, St., 119–20
marriage, 100, 125, 169, 205
Marschalck, Haug, 10, 16, 121, 221, 225,
  226, 248 n39; mystical theology of,
  129f.; role in imperial campaigns,
  127–8; imprisonment, 128, *142*
martyrdom, 94, 100, 185, 196, 207
Mary, St., The Blessed Virgin, 41–42, 52,
  104, 125, 133, 141, 143, 145, 166,
  167, 185, 187, 196, 203, 210, 220,
  222
Mary Magdalen, St., 132, 185, 194,
  207
materialism, 31, 130–31, 137, 161, 174
Maulbronn, Cistercian abbey at, *40*
Maurer, Hans, 90

Maximilian H.R.E., elect (1493–1519), 83, 115, 191, 197
Megerich, Jacob, 85–86, 90
Melanchthon, Philip, 192, 200
Memmingen, 10, 25, 28, 30, 80f., *81, 84, 85, 87, 221*
mendicants (see also individual orders), 30, 117, 138
millenarianism, 48, 127
ministeriales, 4, 18
Munich, 11, 166
Müntzer, Thomas, 17, 156, 157, 158, 161
Murner, Thomas, OFM, 205
music, in churches, 78, 127
mysticism, 44, 158, 180, 184, 213, 220; in Sebastian Lotzer's works, 92f., 99; in Haug Marschalck's works, 129f.

Nicholas von der Flühe, St., *209*
Nider, Johann, O.P., 182
Nifo, Agostino, 215
Niklashausen, Drummer of, *51–52*
Nominalism, 129, 141, 222
novi homines (see also patricians), 25, 80, 146
Nunnenbeck, Lienhardt, 166
Nuremberg, 25, 26, 28, 30, 80, 112, 117, 196, 224; city council, 19, 148f.; imperial diets, 153, 167, 197; guilds in, 148f.; Edict of, see imperial edicts
Nützel, Casper, 152

Oekolampadius, John, 118, 129, 183, 207; influence on pamphleteers, 132
Olivi, Peter, OFM, 216
Osiander, Andreas, 54, 152f., *154*, 191, 196; influence on pamphleteers, 167, 171, 182
Otter, Jacob, 205, 219
Otto von Passau, O. Min., 39

painters, 120, 158f., 201
Palatine, Count, see Johann II, von Simmern und Sponheim
pamphlet collections, 6
papal authority, see authority
patricians (see also *novi homines*), 26, 112, 189
Peasant Articles, 1525, 88, 97, 105–06, 226
peasants, 105, 168
Peasant Wars, 1, 2, 5, 14–15, 19, 32, 64, 135
Pegau, Benedictine abbey at, 201
penance, 44, 47, 53, 99, 125, 127, 163, 226
Pentz, Georg, *154, 157, 159*

Peringer, Diepold, *frontispiece, 53*
Pforzheim, 165
piety, medieval, 104; female (feminine), 18, 185f., 201; Protestant, 18, 221; affective, 37, 77, 129, 141, 165, 184; lay, 76, 105, 140, 162, 176, 200, 225
pilgrimage, 18, *29*, 30, 45, 96, 172, 187
Pirckheimer, Charitas, OSC1, 152
Pirckheimer, Willibald, 150, 152, 155–56
plague (see also Black Death), 23, 48, 215
Platner, Hans, 157
Plauen, Hans von, 155
Plick, Simon, OSB, Abbot of Pegau, 201
Plick, Wolfgang, 203
Polycarp, St., 137
Pömer, Hector, 152
popes, see individual entries
Prague, 155
preaching, lay, 48, 62, 63, 71–72, 91, 94, 177, 199
predestination, 130
priesthood, universal, 62, 73, 95
printers, 121, 201
Prognostica, see almanacs
purgatory, 98

Ratgeb, Jörg, *38*
Ratisbon, see Regensburg
Redwitz, Weigand von, Bishop of Bamberg (1523–56), 150, 152, 153, 155
Reformatio Frederici III, 109
Reformatio Sigismundi, 155
Regensburg, *29*, 198, 200, 205, 217
Reiser, Friedrich, 155
relics, 78, 148, 172
Reutlingen, 26
Rhegius, Urbanus, 118, *119*, 182, 183; influence on pamphleteers, 137
Rodericus Zamorensis, *Speculum Humanae Vitae*, 24, *97, 122*
Rome, 30, 150, 153
Rychssner, Utz, 10, 16, 54; protest activities, 120; theology of, 121f.

Sachs, Hans, 10, 19, 54; theology of, 165f.
sacraments, see individual entries
St. Gall, 83, 88
sanctification, 103
Schappeler, Christoph, 54, 83, 95, 101, *108*, 110, 182
Schedel, Hartmann: *Weltchronik, 51, 113 149, 204*
Scherenberg, Rudolf von, Bishop of Würzburg (1466–95), 52
Scheurl, Christoph, 152, 153

Schilling, Johann, 117, 120, 145
Schmaldkald League, 172
Schmid, Ulrich, 88
schools, see education
Schultheiss, Hans, 86, 88
Schütz, Catherine, 10, 186, 204, 210, 265
n54; theology of, 205f.
Schwarz, Ulrich, 115
Schwenckfeld, Casper, 207, 208
Sebald, St., 151
Sebastian, St., 103
Seehofer, Arsacius, 191f.
shoemakers, 11, 74, *168*, 173, 176
Sigismund, H.R.E. (1433–37), 36;
Reformatio, 155
social history, 1f.
sola scriptura, 2, 76, 158, 159, 165, 175,
183, 194, 201
soldiers, 128–29
Spalatin, George, 62, 191, 200
Speiser, Johann, 115
Spengler, Lazarus, 152
Speratus, Paul, 191
Stadion, Christoph von, Bishop of
Augsburg (1517–43), 85, 114, 118–19
Stauffen, Argula von, 10, 15, 62, 91, 167,
186, *193, 199*, 221, 225; theology of,
193f.; meeting with Martin Luther, 200;
at Nuremberg Diet, 197
Stauffen, Hieronymus, 191
Staupitz, John von, OESA, 152, 191, 223
Stein, Hermann von, 155
Steinheim, 86
Stephen, St., 63–64, 222
Stoss, Andreas, O. Carm., 153
Stoss, Veit, 156
Strasbourg, 90, 107, 121, 127, 155, 186,
204
Stuntz, Bernhard, 118
Swabian League, 33, 80, 86, 88–90, 110,
128
synderesis, 129, 132, 136, 141, 222

Taborites, see Hussites
tailors, *27*, 121
tau, see *synderesis*
Tengler, Ulrich, *Laienspiegel*, 42, *43, 142*
Theologia Deutsch (see also mysticism),
18–19, 220
Theresa of Avila, St., 227
tithes, 86, 97, 98, 138
Törring, Adam von, 197
tradition, church, 101, 135, 164, 169,
175, 194, 202
Treger, Conrad, OESA, 205
Tübingen, 90; pamphlet research project, 7
Tucher, Anton, 155–56

Turks, 64, 76, 125, 164, 202, 225
Twelve Articles, see Peasant Articles

Ulhart, Philip, 121
Ulm, 28, 78, 80, 82, 121; city council, 48
Ulrich, Duke of Württemberg (1498–1519,
1532–50), 127
universal priesthood, see also vocation,
61f., 68–69
Ursulines (OSU), 186

Valdes, Peter, 34
Valladolid, 119
veneration of saints, 45, 101f., 110, 161,
164
Verena, St., *188*
Vincent de Paul, St., 227
Vischer, Georg, 119, 121
Voburg, 195
vocation, 63, 70, 183, 187, 218
Vögeli, Jörg, 8, 54, 109, 167
Voehlin family, 83
Volprecht, Wolfgang, 152–53

Waldensians, 18, 33–35, 52, 56, 110,
114, 117, 127, 155, 158, 179, 217; in
Augsburg, 117f.; in Nuremberg, 155f.,
182
Wanner, Johann, 54
weavers, 11, 25–26, 28, 74, 82, 117, *122*,
123f., *124*, 127
Weiler, Anna, 155
Wellenburg, 118
Weyda, Ursula, 10, 16, 186, 208; theology
of, 202f.
William IV, Duke of Bavaria (1508–50),
191, 195, 196
Wittenberg, 167, 192, 200, 213
Wöhrd, preaching peasant at, 52–53
works-holiness, 61, 133
works of holy mercy, 76, 92, 126, 132,
139, 173–74
Worms, 54; Edict of, see imperial edicts
Württemberg, 17, 226
Würzburg, 10, 52, 54, 198; Bishop of, see
Rudolf von Scherenberg

Zell, Catherine, see Catherine Schütz
Zell, Matthew, 186
Zollern, Frederick von, Bishop of Augsburg
(1486–1505), 115
Zürich, 10, 17, 73, 213
Zwingli, Huldrecht, 17–18, 56, 65f., *66*,
69, 169, 183, 207; attitude toward
laity, 65–70; attitude toward lay
preachers, 71–72; influence of
pamphleteers, 111, 219, 242 n39